ENCYCLOPEDIA OF MYSTERIOUS PLACES

The life and legends of ancient sites around the world

ENCYCLOPEDIA OF MYSTERIOUS PLACES

The life and legends of ancient sites around the world

ROBERT INGPEN & PHILIP WILKINSON

For E. M.W. and in memory of N. L. W.

First published by Dragon's World Ltd 1990

This edition published by Barnes & Noble, Inc.,
by arrangement with Collins & Brown Limited
1999 Barnes & Noble Books

British Library Cataloguing in Publication Data

M 10 9 8 7 6 5 4 3 2

ISBN 0-7607-1614-5

DESIGNER Robert Ingpen
EDITOR Michael Downey
ART DIRECTOR Dave Allen
EDITORIAL DIRECTOR Pippa Rubinstein

Printed in China

CONTENTS

INTRODUCTION

This is a book about the imagination. It is about the imagination of the people of the past as they transformed their environment to provide themselves with shelter and to find their spiritual identity in their temples and shrines. It is about their creative imagination, as they took the materials available to them and used them to produce buildings unique to their settings and times. And it is about the special interactions between peoples' lives, customs and ceremonies, and the buildings they used.

It is also a book designed to stimulate our own imaginations as we think about these places. We have called these sites 'mysterious places' because, for all but the specialist, places that are centuries or even millenia old and that may be thousands of miles away inevitably hold many mysteries. Innumerable questions are raised as we look at the remains and, although archaeologists have solved many of the riddles, others can only be answered tentatively. There are fundamental questions about the very purpose of many ancient buildings: What exactly was Stonehenge *for*? What religion was practised in the great stone temples of Malta? There are questions of the basic motivations of peoples long ago: What drove the Aztecs, and their Central American predecessors, to perform human sacrifices? What made the people of Ellora or Petra carve their temples out of the bare rock, like gigantic sculptures?

There are questions concerning structures and places so shrouded in myth that it is hard to tell whether they existed in the form usually supposed: the labyrinth in the Palace of Minos at Knossos, the Tower of Babel. And there are questions about the ultimate fates of many of the places: What brought the Indus civilization of Mohenjo-daro and Harappa, apparently so successful, to its end? Why did the Assyrians abandon their great city of Khorsabad so soon after building it? Questions like these, which cannot be answered with real certainty, add to the air of mystery that surrounds these places. For every reconstruction we have to use our imagination.

But it is not all mystery. Archaeology, that most exact and exacting discipline, has revealed much about the sites that it explores. In this book we have used information accrued by archaeologists to reconstruct our chosen places. But we have gone further, attempting to fill gaps in knowledge with intelligent speculation about what might have been. So an illustration of the prehistoric settlement at Skara Brae can be quite accurate when it comes to showing the buildings, which have survived remarkably well for over 4,500 years. But about the inhabitants and their costumes we can be less sure. With other sites, such as the theatre at Epidauros, we know much more – thanks to the evidence of texts and vase paintings – about the appearance of the people and what they wore. But we are more ignorant when it comes to the details of the building that have not survived.

We have also tried to recreate the spirit of the places in the book. In visual terms this has usually meant including at least one illustration (generally the first one for each place) that is an imaginative recreation, recalling an evocative myth, a key individual in the place's history, an important symbol, or a crucial event. Such illustrations are meant to supplement the more historically accurate ones that follow, providing the reader with another approach to the culture, atmosphere, and myth surrounding each place.

Early civilizations

Some of the places in this book represent the quite considerable steps made by humankind before the development of the urban culture we call civilization. Such pre-civilized cultures have their own remarkable qualities and can be highly sophisticated. The religious sites at Tarxien and Stonehenge, for example, could not have been built without meticulous planning, rigorous organization, and sheer artistic flair. On a smaller scale, even settlements like Skara Brae and Biskupin could only have been created with the discipline of cooperation and highly developed skills in stoneworking and woodworking respectively. So we should not look down on these early cultures because they are not 'civilized' in some vague modern sense.

Likewise larger towns, such as Catal Hüyük in Turkey and Pueblo Bonito in New Mexico, separated by thousands of miles and thousands of years. Places like these lie on the brink of civilization. They have most of the features we associate with city life, yet their people could not read or write. It is in cultures such as these that we see civilization in the process of emerging. But treating each culture as an individual entity allows us to see the unique qualities of each – for it is these peculiarities, not the place where they stand in the history of civilization, that makes them fascinating.

The places that follow are a tiny sample of the sites that could have been chosen to represent the world's great civilizations. From the early civilizations of Mesopotamia and Egypt, through those of the Aegean, Greece, and Persia, to the empires of the Romans and the Byzantines, one can see clear connections as links of trade and conquest allow the different places to influence one another. These cultures are the heritage of much of western civilization today, and we can be forgiven if we persist in seeing them as central. But there are other areas just as interesting. Most obvious are the cultures that developed in isolation of this central group – the cities of Central America, the Chinese Empire, the Khmer culture of Cambodia. Then there are less well known places that found themselves in the melting pot at one particular point in their history – Petra, the Nabataean city in Jordan, because of its position on trade routes; Mistra, the tiny Byzantine city in the Peloponnese, that briefly became the focus of a whole empire.

Most of these sites are cities or parts of cities. There are many different definitions of what makes a city and therefore of what constitutes civilization. A relatively large number of people living in a relatively small area is clearly a major requirement, as are specialized trades, organized religion, and large construction projects involving specialist builders or architects. For some people, written language is also a requirement. All these things foster interdependent life, the personal safety of the inhabitants, and, for some of the population at least, the possibility of job satisfaction and even social mobility.

But how did cities come about in the first place? There have been many theories. A popular one used to be that the rise of agriculture pushed up the population while at the same time giving a surplus of food. This meant that sections of the population did not need to grow their own food and so would gather together in urban communities to practise the crafts and trade that typify town life. But this ignores the fact that many societies (including those in ancient China and Mexico) could farm long before they had cities. Another ancient theory, grounded in what the Bible tells us and in the fact that writing developed early in Mesopotamia, held that the idea of the city first developed in Mesopotamia and gradually spread outwards across the globe. But recent discoveries such as the town at Catal Hüyük in Turkey have shown that earlier urban communities existed outside Mesopotamia. There were also independent urban cultures in Central America and China.

Clearly, a more complex set of causes lies behind the creation of most cities. Efficient agriculture would be necessary to produce the required food surplus. Access to a valuable raw material (such as

SKARA BRAE
STONEHENGE
DELPHI
EPIDAUROS
MISTRA
MYCENAE
TARXIEN
KN
ALEXA
LEPTIS MAGNA
PUEBLO BONITO
CHICHEN ITZA
TENOCHTITLAN
COPAN
MACHU PICCHU
GREAT
EASTER ISLAND

BISKUPIN
HAGIA SOPHIA
TOPKAPI
BOGHAZKOY
TROY
CATAL HUJUK
RHODES
KHORSABAD
SOS
BABYLON
ORIA
PETRA
UR
PERSEPOLIS
SAQQARA
KARNAK
ABU SIMBEL
MBABWE
GREAT WALL OF CHINA
PEKING
NARA
YOSHINOGARI
MOHENJO-DARO
TAJ MAHAL
ELLORA
ANGKOR

obsidian at Catal Hüyük, or copper at many sites) would enable the craftworkers to produce artefacts, which in turn would give prospective merchants something to trade. The resulting banding together of disparate people would create a need for services – perhaps defensive walls, irrigation or sanitation, public and religious buildings – typical of the city. The need to control the people and provide the services would stimulate the need not simply for a government but for an administrative class, comprised of people who might come from one of the other social strata, the merchants perhaps, or, more commonly, the priests. It is the coming together of a number of factors, as in this highly simplified picture, that is likely to create a city.

Another key factor was power, and this was almost certainly linked not simply with military power, but with the power to distribute goods. In order to trade, or to control supply and demand, a city had to hold sway over a considerable hinterland. It had to be a centre to which people needed to travel to bring their raw materials and buy goods in markets. Or, like the Nabataean city of Petra, it had at least to be a place from which the local trade could be controlled. The importance of the space surrounding cities has been stressed by recent studies of these early civilizations. A pattern of a group consisting of ten or twelve separate cities, each with a surrounding area of about 1500 square kilometres (580 square miles), has emerged in many early civilizations.

Archaeological investigation will continue to throw light on patterns like these and our view will be modified as time goes on. Each generation's view of history is different from that of the generation before – and not just because of the accretion of new evidence. We are all the children of our own civilizations. It was not unnatural for the historians of the early twentieth century, for example, to espouse the diffusionist view – that things were invented in one place and at one time and spread gradually across the globe; and that the appearance of new types or styles of artefact in the archaeological record was usually due to the area being taken over by a new people with different skills. It was a cultural picture not unlike the political situation of the time, when the building of empires to bring 'civilization' to the rest of the world was a respectable activity.

But we now know that many key developments appeared independently in different parts of the world at different times. Writing, for example, was once thought to have started in Mesopotamia and spread from there. But we now know that it was also invented separately in Central America and China. Another example is the development of stone building. The Victorians and, shamefully, some later European writers, found it unthinkable that the indigenous people of Zimbabwe could have built the great stone walls we now know as Great Zimbabwe without direction from some outside 'civilizing' force. But we now accept the evidence of archaeology that these people were stoneworkers and designers of genius in their own right.

Our perceptions of early places are still shaped by our day-to-day preoccupations. The age of the computer has produced studies of Stonehenge as a vast calculating machine and accounts of early civilizations in terms of their efficiency of information processing. Each adds something to our knowledge, but only gives us part of the picture.

Some important concepts

Unfortunately our understanding of some of the concepts involved in studying these ancient places is also shaped – and sometimes blurred – by our present experience. Thus, just as an early city is very different from a modern one, so many words – such as priest, empire, and army – have had different meanings in different times.

For example, we might think of an empire as a tightly-knit political unit, large, but closely administered by the forces of the central controlling power. But for many early peoples an empire was much more a zone of political and economic influence, a geographical area from which the emperor could expect to be paid taxes, and whose people would give the emperor homage and fight for him in times of war. It was perhaps only with the Romans that the modern concept of the empire found its first great example.

Similarly, an 'army' was a much more fluid concept in the ancient world than it is today. A great power might have a small standing army, but would augment this with men from dependent states in times of war. And campaigning might follow a particular season of the year – war has not always raged with the relentlessness of modern conflicts.

The priesthood is another class that has changed its role continuously. Priests in the ancient world were often men of great power. As the people who officiated at the ceremonies that apparently controlled the fertility of the land and the king's good fortune in battle they were central to the success of their culture. So a priest in an early civilization was often much more than a spiritual leader. He could be a high-ranking administrator, an adviser to the king or emperor, or a wealthy landowner.

Networks and relationships

The places covered in this book have been treated as individual entities. In this way we hope we have been able to convey the unique features and atmosphere of each. It is these peculiarities that make us go on thinking about cities like Babylon and Peking, sites like Angkor and Stonehenge, imagining what it was like to live there, marvelling at the skills of their builders, retelling their stories and their myths.

But considering such a broad spectrum of places individually should not make us lose sight of their place in the story of the human race. For no place, especially a city, can exist in splendid isolation. Even cities like Nara, capital of a famously isolated Japan, owed much to influence from China, while Peking – a place we are used to thinking of as cut off from the outside world – received embassies from far and wide. Most cities *relied* on communications for survival. Whether it was the guardians of Machu Picchu looking out from their watchtowers along the Inca roads for travellers from the capital, or the rulers of Knossos or Mohenjo-daro receiving oil and grain from their dependent farms to swell Minoan and Indus Valley wealth, or the people of Great Zimbabwe trading with merchants from the east, or the Persian emperors receiving tribute from their vassal states at Persepolis – all these places were centres of communication lines.

And they continue to communicate with us today, although sometimes the message is difficult to read. But what we can read, through the archaeological record, through legend, and through reconstructions like those in this book, usually has great fascination. From the perspective of the twentieth century, when urban life can often seem uncivilized, it can also be inspiring.

SKARA BRAE
STONEHENGE
BISKUPIN
HAGIA SOPHIA
TOPKAPI
DELPHI
MYCENAE
MISTRA
EPIDAUROS
RHODES
TARXIEN
KNOSSOS

EUROPE

The continent of Europe provides us with some of our most tantalizing glimpses of prehistoric life and some of our best evidence for the development of civilization. Sites like the great prehistoric stone alignments of western Europe represent the earliest large-scale religious monuments. Stonehenge, the most famous of the stone circles, and the temples of Malta, especially Tarxien, stand for these places in this book. But a host of other megalithic monuments, from Avebury near Stonehenge to Carnac in Brittany could easily have been chosen. There is enough material here for a whole book of mysterious places.

If evidence of prehistoric housing is less spectacular, the sites that have been preserved, such as Skara Brae on the island of Orkney and the village of Biskupin in Poland, are remarkable enough on their small scale.

But these prehistoric places, standing at the edges of the continent, also stand at the edges of this part of the book. The central focus is on the Aegean, where several cultures have left remarkable imprints. Of these, the Minoan civilization of Crete and the Mycenaean culture of mainland Greece have left enough evidence of their buildings to allow reconstructions of the sort we have attempted in this book.

The classical Greek civilization that came after them has, of course, been extensively reconstructed too. Here the vast accumulation of evidence from ancient writers and modern archaeologists has made most ancient Greek sites seem inappropriate for a book of mysterious places. Yet they all have their puzzles, few more than the religious complex at Delphi and the theatrical centre at Epidauros. The later history of this part of Europe is represented by Rhodes, whose Colossus is the most enigmatic of the classical Seven Wonders of the World.

This section next looks eastward. First there is the Byzantine Empire – the eastern branch of the Roman Empire which eventually became a considerable power in its own right. It is exemplified by Hagia Sophia – the great church in the capital, Constantinople – and Mistra, the tiny southern Greek city that became an important centre in the Empire's twilight years. Finally, we examine Topkapi, the palace of the Ottoman sultans who replaced the Byzantine emperors at Constantinople.

Places of pilgrimage

There is nothing new with our fascination with sites like these. Many of them had a unique magnetism in their own time. We can only speculate about the numbers who flocked to Stonehenge each year at midsummer. But we can be sure an army of workers was needed to erect the stones in the first place. There is also the possibility that people came there from very far afield. Mycenaean objects have been found in Britain, particularly in the area of Stonehenge. Although they did not necessarily come directly from travellers from the Aegean, the mobility of the Mycenaeans suggests that they may have done.

More conventionally civilized places drew people for other reasons. Knossos seems to have been a combination of a religious site and a redistribution point for the riches of the Aegean. Mycenae was the fortified headquarters of a military power with wide influence. Delphi was a focus for religious pilgrimage with strong political power. Epidauros was the site of a famous festival. Hagia Sophia was a spiritual focus at the centre of Christendom. Topkapi was the hub a very different empire, to which vassals would flock to pay their respects to the sultan.

So if many of Europe's mysterious places are famous, they have long been so, and for good reason. If, as we visit their remains or read about them, we sense that we have been preceded by many and that, in spite of the enigmas, the paths to these places are well trodden, we should not be surprised.

True, there are exceptions – more recent discoveries – like the uncovering of the village of Skara Brae in a storm in 1850. But more typical are the sites that have endured in history, myth, and travellers' tales. And if these tales are sometimes like Chinese whispers, taking us further from, not nearer to, their reality, we should return to the buildings themselves and marvel, like the early travellers, at their stones.

TARXIEN

Megalithic temples on the island of Malta, *circa* 3600–2500 BC

Lying in the Mediterranean Sea, about 80 kilometres (50 miles) south of Sicily, the island of Malta hardly seems far from civilization. But 5,500 years ago it was far enough away from other settlements for its people to lead an isolated life and develop in a unique way. They have left behind a series of imposing stone temples that provide western Europe's earliest evidence of organized, temple-based religion, as well as our first glimpse of conscious architectural planning. But we know tantalizingly little about the people who created these remarkable buildings and about the deities they worshipped in them.

The original colonists of Malta, who arrived, probably from Sicily, in about 5000 BC, were a stone-age people. They found an island that was rich in stone and that gave them enough space to practise the basic agriculture that allowed them to survive. They settled down to grow staple crops such as wheat, barley, and lentils, and to raise cattle, sheep, and goats. But the island did not provide a perfect environment. There was no flint for tool making, so they either had to make do with bone or antler tools, or to import flint from Sicily and other islands of the Mediterranean when they got the opportunity to trade with their neighbours.

In the shadow of a megalithic statue, at which offerings are being made, a Maltese islander grinds corn at a communal quern. When carried out at or near a temple such an activity would have been ceremonial, embodying the hope that it would grant fertility to the soil for another year.

The megalithic temples

The buildings these people left behind have an atmosphere all their own. Apart from a few sites at Otranto in the heel of Italy, they are unique. There are numerous temples scattered across Malta and the nearby island of Gozo. The most spectacular of these monuments are in what are now suburbs of the capital city, Valletta, at Tarxien and Hal Saflieni. Although larger than most other Maltese temples, the one at Tarxien has many features that are typical. It is built of very large stone blocks (known to archaeologists as megaliths); it consists of pairs of semi-circular chambers, each pair connected to the next by a short, narrow passage. The largest pair of chambers is at the front of the temple, nearest the doorway, and the chambers get smaller the further you penetrate inside. Some of the stone blocks are decorated with a striking, foliage-like pattern; the exterior of the temple, however, is quite plain, and the impression given is that it was the interior that was most important to its original users. All these features are common to most of the megalithic monuments in Malta, but the buildings vary in size and complexity.

Although these monuments are in ruins today, it is still possible to work out roughly what they would have looked like when they were being used, during the period 3600–2500 BC. But what exactly were they used for? If they are temples, which gods were worshipped there and what ceremonies were performed?

The beginnings of religion

To answer these questions, we have to go back to the very earliest surviving artificial structures in Malta. These are hardly buildings at all, but chambers cut directly into the rock. Like the later temples, these chambers have an unusual plan, made up of lobe-shaped rooms. Human remains found inside them indicate that they were tombs, and some are no more than simple grave chambers with little room for anything other than the bodies themselves. But as time went on these graves grew bigger and more elaborate than mere burial pits. Archaeologists assume, therefore, that they were beginning to turn into temples and that some sort of ancestor-worship or ceremony involving a cult of the dead was practised there.

If this is the case, what we are looking at in Malta is one of the great steps in human evolution: the development of organized religion. This is especially remarkable since, in Europe at least, there is little conclusive evidence for organized religion before this time. Archaeologists have found older statues that may represent gods, but these might just as well have served some other purpose (ancient idols often look the same as ancient dolls). And even if these early figures were employed in a religious way, they were probably used in the home or in some small local shrine. Again, megalithic tombs found in Europe suggest that religious ceremonies were performed nearby, but we have no actual place of worship to show us how organized this religious observance might have been. So it is not until the buildings in Malta that we see purpose-made religious temples.

We do not know for certain why the

The temples of Tarxien 3000 BC

Part of the temple complex at Tarxien is shown here under construction. The walls, built of large, heavy stones are still visible today. The thatched roofs are conjectural. The plan (bottom left) *shows the different-sized semicircular chambers and narrow interconnecting passageways.*

early Maltese tombs evolved as they did, turning from simple holes in the rock to complex, multi-chambered structures. But what is clear is that the later, above-ground buildings for which Malta is famous are modelled on these earlier structures. What evidence do we have that these buildings are true temples? They are unlikely to be places where people lived – the sort of remains that people leave behind in their homes, from domestic pots and pans to household rubbish, are not present there. There are no burial remains from the time that they were built, so they cannot have been planned as tombs. The fragments of pottery that have been found seem to come from non-functional vessels that could have been offering bowls. Add to this the facts that the statues that have been found (including examples that are far too large to be dolls) resemble cult figures, and that many of the stone slabs look like altars, and it seems very likely that these buildings were temples.

A mysterious deity

It is difficult to say how the temples were used or exactly what deity was worshipped there. Even the statues that have been found are mystifying. It is common to see these, and similar cult figures found elsewhere in Europe, described as 'fat lady' or 'earth mother' figures. Yet many of these statues of large-bodied figures sitting on a stone bench have no sexual features at all. There is one characteristic that is common to many of them, however: they are all so fat that to modern western eyes they can only be termed obese. In many 'primitive' cultures obesity is a symbol of fertility (a well-nourished person indicates plentiful crops), and a fertility god is exactly the sort of deity one would expect a prehistoric agricultural community, dependent for survival on the fecundity of the soil, to worship.

There is other evidence of the deity's link with the land and its products. It is likely that animal sacrifice played an

MEDITERRANEAN SEA
GOZO
MALTA
Valletta
TARXIEN

Remains of obese stone figure from the temple at Hagar Qim

important part in the rites performed in the Maltese temples. It is not always easy to be certain whether ancient people carried out this sort of ritual. The remains of animal bones alone at a site do not provide sufficient evidence, because every meat-eating society will produce animal-bone debris. People may also need bones to make simple tools. But the situation in Malta is different. Fragments of bone and horn seem to have been deliberately hidden in holes in the temple walls, in a way that suggests they have special sacred power or significance.

There is one piece of evidence that points to a different type of use for the temples, again one which signals the importance of agriculture in this community. There is a stone at one of the temples at Kordin that has often puzzled archaeologists. It is a long piece of coralline limestone which contains a row of seven deep depressions along one side. One expert on the prehistory of Malta, David Trump, has suggested that it is a communal quern, used for grinding corn. Although this seems a strange activity to perform in a temple, this is not necessarily surprising in an agricultural community. We should guard against thinking of ancient temples as buildings that were only occupied for short periods for specific acts of worship – an ancient society would get the maximum use out of its buildings. Moreover, bringing corn to be ground under the watchful eye of the deity could in any case be seen as a religious act – it would ensure that good bread would be produced and improve the chances of a good harvest next year.

One can imagine the row of people kneeling at the quern to grind their corn, while others waited their turn in the outer chambers of the temple. From their bones and carvings we know that these early Maltese were short in stature, had rather long heads, that some of them wore their hair straight and that others, probably priests and priestesses, wore it in pigtails or in an arrangement rather like a barrister's wig. Once they had ground a token amount of corn in the temple, they would probably go off to their homes to finish the task, rejoicing that next year's harvest would be rich.

The sleeping lady and her sisters

Not all the statues found in the temples are of the fat-bodied asexual type. Some remarkable female figures have also been found. Two of these, both found at Hal Saflieni, are figures reclining on a low bench of the same type as the one on which the obese figures usually sit. The large reclining figure, usually known as the 'sleeping lady', is naked to the waist and, although her features are rather distorted (she has a rather small head) she is carved much more naturalistically than the fat-bodied cult figures.

Some naked standing female statuettes have also been found. If these figures are goddesses, they provide another mystery – how do these deities fit in with the fat figures? It may be that they represent some form of popular magic or homespun religion that has little or nothing to do with the temples.

The power of the priest

The architecture of the Maltese temples developed as time went on. As the skill of the builders grew (and perhaps as the temple rituals became more elaborate) some of the temples increased steadily in size. The temple at Tarxien is a good example of this. It started as three small temples but gradually these were joined together to form a single large building. The temple at Mnajdra shows a similar process of amalgamation to produce a larger structure. Elsewhere on the island the oldest temples tend to be the smallest and to have the simplest ground plans and fewest rooms. The temples become more elaborate in other ways. The stone of the first buildings was left plain, or decorated with a few sparsely made pit-marks across its surface. Later masons made deeper, denser pit-marks. Then they began to carve the stone with simple patterns of stylized foliage. Finally the foliage becomes more elaborate and the carving finer and more confident.

Perhaps the Maltese extended and improved their temples in this way because they wanted to put all their new-found skill at the disposal of their gods. But there were other reasons. In the ancient world priesthood was power. This is a theme which constantly recurs as we explore the world's mysterious places, from Stonehenge to the temples of the Aztecs. In a less spectacular way it was true in Malta too. As controllers of the richness and fertility of the soil, the priests held the key to health and prosperity on the island. Those with the largest, most beautifully decorated temples had the most potential power and wealth. Some archaeologists have pointed out how the large temples are distributed across the island, suggesting that each was the centre of a 'territory' of influence. It is even possible to see the priests as princes. Although such a direct equation of political power with architectural evidence is open to question, it does remind us how important the priest could have been in this sort of society. Yet we should not fall into the trap of exaggerating their influence. When the temple-based society reached its height around 2800–2500 BC it is thought that the entire population of the island consisted of between one and two thousand people gathered around two or three major temples.

Another way in which priestly power is indicated is in the overall design of the temples. The way in which the inner rooms are smaller, for example, suggests that there was only room there for a few people. This isolation of priests from the rest of the population in a 'sanctuary' or 'holy of holies' marks the priest as someone with special privileges and points to his or her potential power over the rest of the community.

An underground labyrinth

Another structure that shows the power of the priest to commission large projects is the complex of underground chambers known as the Hypogeum of Hal Saflieni. Very different from the temples, it is a labyrinth of passages and chambers on three different levels. Some of the twenty chambers in the rock are natural, some were cut into the soft limestone using picks made of horn or antler. The main group of chambers runs north-south, and there are also many side rooms. In these the excavators of the early twentieth century found thousands of human bones – it has been estimated that between 6,000 and 7,000 people were buried there. The Hypogeum is interesting because it is so extensive. There are other, older rock-cut tombs in Malta, and similar tombs in Sardinia and Portugal, but none as well finished or as complex as the Hypogeum.

The fact that the Hypogeum is larger and more complex than was necessary for a mere tomb suggests that its original users performed quite lengthy ceremonies when burying their dead. The chambers may have had other uses too. Communication between some of the rooms is only possible by means of mysterious holes in the wall. These are sometimes described as 'oracle holes', the idea being that a person would stand in the outer room, pose a question, and then hear some sort of reply from within. This is a possibility, and the resonant acoustics of the Hypogeum would make the priest's reply sound impressive, but it is hardly likely – the idea of an oracle is a later one and there is no real evidence for it in Malta. It is also unlikely that the early builders knew enough about acoustics to produce the effect deliberately – the sound effects were probably a happy accident of the design.

Building the temples

How did an apparently primitive, stone-age people manage to build temples of the complexity of those at Tarxien? How were the structures planned and how were the stones moved into place? The success of any large building operation is likely to be a blend of individual vision and communal effort. We are used to thinking in terms of a single architect who produces the plans, and a large team of workers who put the plans into effect. It may seem difficult to imagine a professional architect existing 5,000 years ago on a prehistoric Mediterranean island. But something very close to this must have been the case, because actual model buildings have survived. In some cases these show details of construction which could not be guessed at from the finished temple. One model, found at Tarxien, shows a temple facade. Although only some fragments have survived, this limestone model can be reconstructed to give a very good idea what the original temple facade would have looked like. Other models, such as one of an unroofed temple chamber found at Hagar Qim, give an insight into ground plans.

Fragment of spiral carving from temple masonry

This leaves the question of how the temples were constructed. Fortunately for the Maltese there was ample stone near at hand – they did not have the transport problems faced by the builders of Stonehenge. But large blocks of limestone still had to be shifted into place. One clue as to how this was achieved may lie in the numerous limestone balls found near the temple at Tarxien. The early twentieth-century archaeologist Sir Themistocles Zammit, who first excavated many of the Maltese temples and whose books brought these sites to international notice, first discovered the stone balls. He thought they had some ritual significance, imagining a sort of priestly game in which the balls were pushed through perforated stone slabs that were also found on the site. What is more likely, however, is that these pieces of stone were used as ball bearings, on which larger stones could be rolled into position.

As time went on the temple builders grew more skilled in handling the large building stones. The first temples were built mainly with rubble masonry, with megalithic outer walls and doorways. Later buildings like the Tarxien temple were almost entirely made of megaliths. One of the great mysteries of how the temples were built concerns the roofing system that was used – none of the temples survives with roof intact. The evidence is that the inner walls were corbelled. In other words, succeeding courses of stones were laid slightly nearer the centre of the room, so that an angled effect was produced, with the walls sloping towards the middle. This was probably done for several courses, so that a narrower roof opening was made than would have been the case with straight walls. This could then be covered with thatch or other perishable materials. The underground complex of Hal Saflieni shows this type of corbelled design still intact, although of course in these rock-cut chambers there was no need for a thatched roof.

A vanishing culture

By the time the final spirals of vegetation had been carved on their temple walls, the people of prehistoric Malta had achieved a culture of some sophistication – in their sculpture and architecture if in nothing else. But that culture was not long-lasting. For in about 2500–2400 BC the temples were abandoned and the people disappeared. Why this happened is unknown. The sort of fertility ceremonies that probably took place in the temples, though, gives us one clue to an answer. Regular good harvests were essential to these peoples' survival. A long drought, or soil exhaustion, followed by famine, would wipe out the majority of a people practising subsistence farming on limited land. To the few who were left the old religion of fertility would have failed: the decline of the people and of their temples would be simultaneous.

We can put together many facts and theories about the people of ancient Malta. We know what they looked like; we know that their main skills were farming and working the local stone. And we can infer that their religion was closely linked to the fertility of the soil. Their ability to plan and build temples is impressive and seems to have been achieved with only a minimum of help from beyond the island. However, we know little else about them. We do not know exactly what their relations with the people of Sicily or mainland Italy were. Indeed we do not know where they came from or where they went after abandoning their temples. Magnificent as their architecture is, they remain an enigma – but one of the most fascinating enigmas that European prehistory has left us to ponder.

SKARA BRAE

Miraculously-preserved stone houses on Orkney, *circa* 3100–2500 BC

The islands of Orkney contain some of the most remarkable prehistoric remains of northern Europe. Tiny isolated stone-built villages such as Skara Brae, miraculously well preserved for their age, give us many answers to our questions about how people lived in the cold northern regions of the earth before the conveniences and comforts of civilization took hold. But Skara Brae also puzzled its discoverers: exactly how old could such a well preserved settlement be? What kind of community lived there and what, if any, was their relationship with the other communities on the islands of Orkney and beyond?

Questions such as these were to tax archaeologists for decades after the village was discovered in 1850, when a storm blew away the protective layers of sand that covered its walls. The storm revealed a compact collection of about half a dozen houses, each between 4.6 and 6.4 metres (15 to 21 feet) across. Their stone walls rose within a mound of earth and debris which no doubt helped to conceal the houses, protected the inhabitants from the harsh winds, and kept in the warmth. Each house was entered through a single doorway, hardly any of the houses had windows, and each was furnished with items made mainly of stone – including shelf units and box beds.

How old were these buildings? V. Gordon Childe, the eminent archaeologist who carried out the first proper excavations at Skara Brae in the late 1920s, put the date at *c.*500 BC. Childe also unwittingly confused the issue by suggesting that Skara Brae was a 'Pictish' village, although it is now accepted that the term 'Picts' was actually that used by the Romans for people living to the north of the Antonine wall. The term was not used until AD 297. But in 1936, Stuart Piggott was able to show that the remains were much earlier than either the Picts or the people who lived about 800 years before. He did this by comparing the style of the pottery discovered with that from other areas. When the site was investigated again in the 1970s, it was possible to obtain radiocarbon dates from animal bones found there. This process gave 3100–2480 BC as the time when the village was occupied. Skara Brae thus gives us unique insights into life in the far north of Europe at this very early period.

Inhabitants of Skara Brae had to protect themselves from bitter cold. We know that earth ramparts helped to make their houses draftproof. Stout skins and thick furs would have been used for their clothing.

A typical house

In the southern part of the village the dwelling that modern archaeologists know as House 7 is the best preserved house at Skara Brae. The evidence it provides allows us to reconstruct a typical dwelling in the village. The typical Skara Brae house was roughly square with rounded corners, and was about 5 metres (16 feet) across. It was reached from one of the covered passageways that connected the houses of the village via a door kept in place with a stone bar. The walls were of stone and were about 2 metres (6 feet) thick; in some houses they may have been 'plastered' with a coat of clay. There was an earthen floor but the area around the doorway was paved with stone slabs. In the centre of the floor was a square hearth surrounded by four upright stone slabs that kept the fire in place.

The fire was the focal point of all the activities that went on in the room. At one side of the house was a raised area where a bowl of whalebone and two cooking pots were found: perhaps this was where the food cooked over the fire was eaten. At other points around the walls were stone box beds. These were not unlike the wooden box beds that were widespread in the Scottish islands until quite recently. They would have been filled with mattresses of heather or straw and covered with furs and skins, so would have been warmer and more comfortable than the stone frameworks that we see today. In addition, the stone frame may have been extended by wooden posts, which could then be covered with skins, to give extra shelter from draughts. This was certainly the pattern with the beds in the much more recent houses in the Hebrides.

But it is easy to over-indulge the temptation to make close comparisons between prehistoric and modern settlements. Some writers, for example, have pointed to the fact that in some of the Skara Brae houses there were smaller beds on the left, larger ones on the right; beads were found in the left-hand beds in two houses. This has been taken as evidence that these beds were reserved for the women, especially since in recent societies in the Scottish islands, women have often traditionally slept in a left-hand bed. But there is little reason to suppose

(Left) *A plan view of the settlement as it is today shows much of the stone furniture still in place. But in 2500* BC *when the last of these houses was constructed, the sea coast was further away from the village.*

(Right) *A reconstructed interior shows the central hearth surrounded by stone beds, 'dressers', and limpet boxes. The island's meagre supply of wood was probably used as a framework for thatched or turf-covered roofs.*

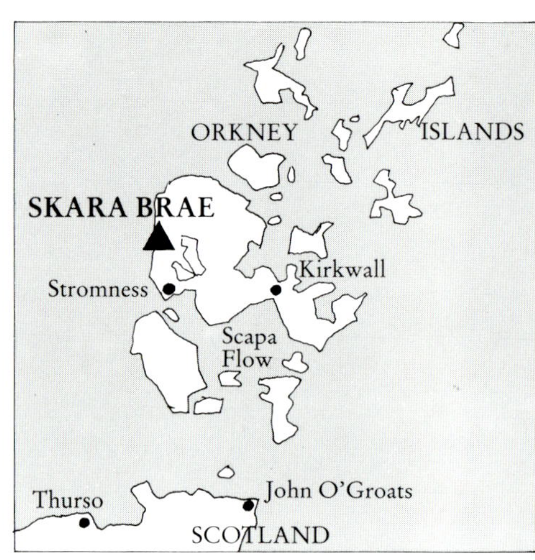

Skara Brae 2500 BC

that such a tradition has continued for 4500 years, or that only women wore beads at Skara Brae, or that women necessarily slept in the smaller beds (a view which tends to assume that the men were the dominant members of this society). The larger beds may simply have been intended to accommodate more than one person.

Other features of the houses included stone shelf-units rather like modern Scottish dressers, alcoves in the walls that would have served as cupboards, and curious stone boxes sunk into the floor. These containers show signs of having been sealed with clay to make them watertight. This has led archaeologists to believe that they were tanks that could be filled with water and used to store limpets for use as bait in fishing. Limpets provided excellent bait – so long as they were softened; this was best achieved by soaking them in fresh water. The limpet boxes would therefore have the double advantage of providing bait that was ready to hand and which was soft enough for immediate use.

Revealing rubbish

So the small community of Skara Brae lived their lives in compact, well designed houses. Each piece of furniture was built in long-lasting stone to fulfil a specific purpose in a way that we can appreciate today – a fact which makes the community come alive in our minds. And yet there are oddities about the village of Skara Brae. Perhaps one of the strangest things is that the dwellings are built inside a mound that is not the simple heap of earth that it seems. Skara Brae is built inside a rubbish heap or 'midden' consisting of dung, bones, peat ash, and other domestic remains.

Midden dwellings were not uncommon in early rural communities. This

in itself does not mean that the people lived in unsanitary squalor, although finds in the beds at Skara Brae do seem to suggest that people sometimes took bones to bed with them and left the gnawed remains amongst the heather and straw of their mattresses. But the rubbish in the midden at Skara Brae belonged to previous generations whose houses have all but disappeared. The later inhabitants simply used the midden to provide the shelter that they needed. They cut channels though the mound to create their passageways and houses, and then brought in stone to build the walls. Thus both houses and passageways were sheltered, preventing inhabitants from walking out-of-doors from one house to another.

As for the people who left the mound of debris in which Skara Brae is built, they seem to have led a similar life to the later occupants of the site. Parts of some houses are visible at the foundation level of the later settlement and seem to have been similar stone structures, with central hearths,

A simple headdress

dressers, and barred doors. The only major difference is that the beds are built into alcoves in the earlier houses.

More mysterious were the layers of waste material found inside the houses themselves when excavations were carried out. At first it seemed that later people had used the dwellings as a dumping ground after the original inhabitants of the village had left; it was as if the village, which had started life as a rubbish heap, had reverted to its original state. But there was something strange about the debris inside the houses. The accumulations of earth, shell, antlers and bones, and sand seemed to have been deliberately arranged in layers, laid down carefully and not thrown in haphazardly as they would be on a conventional rubbish tip.

The most likely explanation is a religious one. Evidence is emerging in other parts of Orkney that when houses were abandoned they were ceremonially filled with remains connected with their original occupants – in some cases, actual human remains. The roof would be removed and these layers would be inserted, filling up the house so that it could not be reoccupied. Such a practice confirms the close identification of the house with the family that lived there. This link also goes some way to explain why people were sometimes buried within the walls of these houses. For example, beneath the wall of House 7, near one of the beds, the bodies of two elderly women were buried. Revered ancestors, they would have represented the closest link between the house and the continuing tradition of occupation by a particular family.

Such ceremonies suggest a more refined culture than might be guessed from the midden around the houses. But the inhabitants would have scarcely noticed the rubbish, enclosed as it would have been by courses of stone and a covering of turf. Another pointer to the sophistication of the Skara Brae people are the small stone chambers off the main rooms of the houses. Several of these were served by a drain running under the settlement, and were probably privies.

People and environment

The world of Skara Brae was a world of earth and stone. In these basic materials lies the first clue to the environment and life on Orkney when the village was built. There was very little wood, and what there was had to be kept for uses that could not be met in any other way. So the door of each house would almost certainly have been wooden and timbers were probably used for the main structure of the house roofs (though there is a possibility that the people could have used whalebones, in a similar way to that in which the early inhabitants of Siberia used the bones of the mammoth).

How did the people of ancient Orkney survive in this bare, treeless landscape? The soil was good enough to produce adequate pasture, and the people seem to have raised sheep and cattle, of which there are many bones in the midden. We can tell from the remains that the Orkney farmers

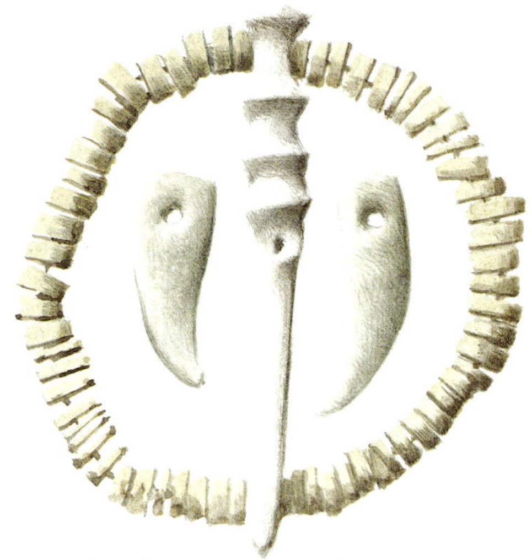

Bone beads, pendants, and a dress pin

gelded their cattle. The bones of the sheep reveal that they did not have to kill off the young animals when winter came: there must have been enough feed to see them through the winter. A few pig bones have been found; their rarity confirms the fact that there were few trees on Orkney at this period, since early farmers left their pigs to forage in the woods. Animals – both wild and domesticated – were another source of skins for clothing and bedding. The people could also supplement their diet by fishing. The village was further from the coast than it is now – sea erosion is rife – but near enough for an easy walk to the sea to catch cod and other fish. Plants were probably also eaten, although we have little evidence apart from some grains and hazelnut shells.

A community in context

One of the most striking things about Skara Brae is the small size of the village. What is more, it is unlikely that Orkney was able to support a very large population at this time. There were other villages like Skara Brae (examples have been found at Barnhouse on Orkney, Rinyo on Rousay, Pool on Sanday, and Noltland on Westray). In addition, some of the houses in the Shetland village of Jarlshof are similar to those at Skara Brae. But there would not have been many such settlements and they would not have been large. The biggest seems to have been the settlement at Noltland, and this, with an area about four times as big as Skara Brae, was no metropolis. Consequently, although chiefdoms were starting to develop on the mainland at this time, the society of Skara Brae was probably a simple, cooperative family group, in which the members had similar or equal status.

We do not know how much contact these people had with the other Orcadian islands or with mainland Scotland. Nothing has been found at Skara Brae that could not have been made there. On the other hand, the designs on the Skara Brae pots are similar to examples found on the mainland so, even if they were made on Orkney, there could have been some influence from mainland designs.

Potters and carvers

So the Skara Brae people could make pots and decorate them with simple decorations. The most popular designs were zigzags, wavy lines, and other basic geometrical patterns. These vessels were functional, but they were not of very high quality.

More impressive were the objects carved in bone. These ranged from awls and scrapers used for dressing animal skins to simple beads, pins and pendants. Larger objects included bone chisels and adzes. Stone tools were also made. It may be that such items were produced at House 8, a freestanding structure on the western edge of the village. House 8 has no limpet boxes or dresser, and no beds, although it does have a central hearth. It may therefore have been a communal workshop. A large number of chips of chert, a stone related to flint, have been found. Chert tools were probably made here, and pieces of chert were probably heated and cooled repeatedly to make them easier to chip and flake. The floor was lined with stones that had broken up with the heat from the fires required to do this. There are traces of other freestanding buildings around the edge of the village, and there may originally have been more workshops or other communal buildings, such as kitchens.

The craft at which the people of Orkney excelled was that of stoneworking. Their masonry has clearly stood up to the test of time. The slabs are neatly laid to make strong walls, corbelled gradually inwards as they rise, so that the span of the roof would have been narrower than the floor area. (This would have been another way of saving timber.) The stone furniture is also worked simply and accurately.

But the most outstanding examples of stone craft found at Skara Brae are quite intricately carved objects such as stone balls with spiral designs and several curious carved objects whose purpose has baffled archaeologists since they were discovered. One is an oval stone with multiple pointed ends. This looks rather like a macehead but is much more ornate than anything that could have been used as a working weapon. Another is a sphere covered with sharp pointed spikes. People who could make such items were clearly accomplished workers. They probably had well developed religious rituals too, since a religious use is the only convincing suggestion for these items that seem not to have any obvious practical use.

Many carved balls have been found in Scotland, on the mainland as well as on the islands. The records of nineteenth-century archaeologists show that some of these were found on burial sites, although these were probably later than the examples at Skara Brae. Nevertheless, such finds point to the importance of these artefacts for their owners, and again suggest some religious or ritual significance. But we know nothing of the rituals in which objects like these were used.

Could they write?

One of the most intriguing suggestions to come from Skara Brae is that some of the carvings represent a written script, perhaps allied to the Scandinavian runes. Some of the stones found at the site do exhibit marks, mostly vertical and diagonal lines in different combinations, that look as if they have been made with care, yet do not look like abstract patterns. When the theory held sway that writing was invented at one time and in one place and gradually spread from Mesopotamia to the rest of the world, it was difficult to imagine a written script being used at a place at once so ancient and so remote. But it is now acknowledged that writing was invented independently in different places and at different times, the suggestion that the Skara Brae people were able to write is perhaps tenable.

One of the mysterious stone objects found on the site

But it is hardly likely that they had a fully developed script; a small population existing by means of subsistence agriculture, with virtually no trade had little need for written language. They would have had no accounting system, no elaborate government or administration, no need to send written messages from village to village. Yet it is just possible that what we see at Skara Brae is the beginning of writing – the making of marks with meanings, but in a limited and specialized way. The marks may have evoked the names of gods or ancestors, for example. Or they may simply have been decorative. If they are inscriptions we will never be able to read them. They are too small in number and too unlike any other writing system – even their relation to runes is dubious. They remain another enigma.

A neolithic Pompeii

Visitors, impressed by Skara Brae's state of preservation, have called it 'a neolithic Pompeii'. Perhaps such descriptions have encouraged speculations about how such a serviceable set of buildings came to be abandoned. No one knows for certain why this happened, but some theories can be set aside. The village shows no signs of a violent end. The idea, once put forward, that a violent sandstorm, of the same sort that revealed the village in the nineteenth century, covered it over and made it uninhabitable is disproved if we accept that the houses were deliberately filled in by their original inhabitants.

There is positive evidence that the houses were squatted in after being partially filled in, and that a subsequent sandstorm completed the filling in and covering. But the squatters probably lived at Skara Brae much later than the people who built the village and their immediate descendants. Their fate remains a mystery.

STONEHENGE

The greatest early British ceremonial site, in regular use from *circa* 3200–1650 BC

One of the most famous prehistoric sites in the world, Stonehenge is also one of the most mysterious. There has been some sort of man-made structure there since *c.*3000 BC, and the sight of its stones silhouetted against the sky on England's Salisbury Plain is familiar the world over. But no one knows exactly how these stones got there, or what they were used for.

The closer we look at Stonehenge, the more baffling it becomes. In addition to the well known circle of large upright stones there is a host of other stones, together with a circular earthwork and a strange ring of filled-in pits. Each of these features seems to beg the question 'What was it for?', adding to the mystery even more.

Another odd thing about Stonehenge is the way it is constructed. The uprights and their lintels are joined together as if they were made of wood by a carpenter. Clearly, the neolithic people of Salisbury Plain would have been more used to working with plentiful local wood than to building with stone, a material that was sparse locally. But why did they turn to stone on this occasion?

Finally, what is the significance of all the astronomical alignments that have been discovered at Stonehenge? Was the monument, as some writers have claimed, really a sophisticated stone-age computer for predicting the dates of eclipses? Or does the astronomy of Stonehenge have a more down-to-earth meaning? The best way to answer these questions is to look at the history of Stonehenge. It was not built in one go but evolved steadily; and each stage in its growth can tell us something about how it was used.

The beginnings

The first Stonehenge was a simple affair. It consisted of a circular ditch and bank with a large round wooden building at the centre. The remains of the earthwork are still visible today, although centuries of erosion since it was constructed between 3200 and 2700 BC have levelled it, so that it is far less imposing than it would originally have been. Current estimates put the size of the bank at about 2 metres (6 feet) high and 6 metres (20 feet) wide; its diameter is about 98 metres (320 feet). The building in the centre is more difficult to describe because it has long disappeared. But surviving post holes suggest that it was as much as 30 metres (100 feet) across; it probably had a thatched roof. Already the alignment of this first Stonehenge is significant: the main entrance faced south. But the principal use of Stonehenge at this time has probably less to do with observing the heavens than burying the dead. The central building is likely to have been a mortuary where bodies were stored before the remains were cremated and buried.

At some point between 2700 and 2200 BC one of the most intriguing features was added to Stonehenge. A series of fifty-six pits were dug in a circle inside the earthwork. They are now named 'Aubrey holes' after the eighteenth-century antiquary John Aubrey, who discovered them. Many of the holes contain cremated human remains, but archaeologists have proved that the holes were dug long before the ashes were buried in them. So the holes were probably not originally intended for this purpose. This has led writers about Stonehenge to look for other explanations about the purpose of the Aubey holes. The result in the 1960s was one of the more fashionable theories about the use of Stonehenge, first put forward by the astronomer Gerald Hawkins. He sees the circle of holes as a stone-age calculator, designed to predict eclipses of the moon. He noticed that the dates of eclipses can be foretold if six stones are placed on six of the Aubrey holes in a certain pattern and are then moved around the circle one hole per year. This is a fascinating theory, and one that has proved attractive in the age of computers.

But did the original builders of Stonehenge really think in this way? If the principle on which it is based was a commonplace of stone-age thought one would expect it to be reproduced in other monuments of the period. The essential feature is the number fifty-six – the system does not work with a different number of holes. But no other neolithic monument has a ring of fifty-six stones or holes. The most obvious of the astronomical alignments at Stonehenge remains the one that is most likely to be significant – the fact that on midsummer day the sun rises roughly above the Heel Stone.

So what were the Aubrey holes used for? The most likely explanation for the holes is that they are offering pits, into which ritual libations were poured. They would then have been sealed with local chalk, which might have been kept white to mark the place where the offering had been made. We know from classical writers that pouring a libation was a recognized way of making an offering to the gods. It has also been found that similar pits at other monuments show signs of having contained liquid – although this might simply have been rainwater. If this theory is true, it suggests that for the people of 2700–2200 BC the gods of the underworld, contactable through the soil, were as important as those of the heavens.

The beaker pottery

The time of the Aubrey holes is also the period when there was a marked change in the type of pottery found in graves and on other archaeological sites in Britain. Many burials from this time have been discovered in which the corpse was accompanied with a distinctive pottery beaker. The appearance of the type now known as 'beaker' pottery was once thought to indicate the coming of a new people to the region. But there does not seem to be any other evidence for an invasion of 'beaker people' – what seems to have happened is a change in the fashion in pottery styles. This may well have some religious significance if the beakers, as is now widely thought, were sacred vessels. A cult that involved both the pouring of libations and the drinking of sacred liquids is not hard to imagine.

The arrival of the stones

Before the beginning of the 'beaker' period, Stonehenge still looked unremarkable – an earthwork, a glorified wooden hut, and a circle of pits. But some time between 2200 and 2000 BC there was a dramatic change: the guardians of Stonehenge started to put up circles of stones on the site. The most mysterious thing about these stones is how far they had to travel to get to Stonehenge. For they are bluestones, originating in the Preseli mountains in South Wales, almost 322 kilometres (200 miles) from Stonehenge. How did neolithic people transport them so far? It is possible to imagine an epic journey in which an army of short, slightly built British people used boats to carry the stones along the Bristol Channel and up the local rivers, with a final stage in which the stones were dragged across land on sleds. The truth may be more prosaic. Glaciation might well have moved the stones most of the way. This would account for one other mystery. There are many bluestones in the Preseli mountains that are of better quality than those used at Stonehenge. If the builders had had a choice, surely they would have made a better selection.

However the stones arrived, the masons of Stonehenge started to arrange them in circles. But they had hardly installed the stones when another, far more grandiose scheme was proposed.

Between 2000 and 1600 BC the great upright stones with which we associate Stonehenge today were brought to the site and erected. These massive stones, which rise to a height of 4 metres (13 feet) and are buried 1.2–1.5 metres (4–5 feet) beneath ground level, are made of sarsen, a type of limestone. They come from Marlborough Downs, about 27 kilometres (17 miles) north of Stonehenge. Although this seems a short distance today, transporting the stones and getting them into position was still an awesome task for a people equipped only with wooden levers and sleds. The terrain between the Downs and Stonehenge includes one steep slope, which they would either have had to climb or travel many extra miles to avoid.

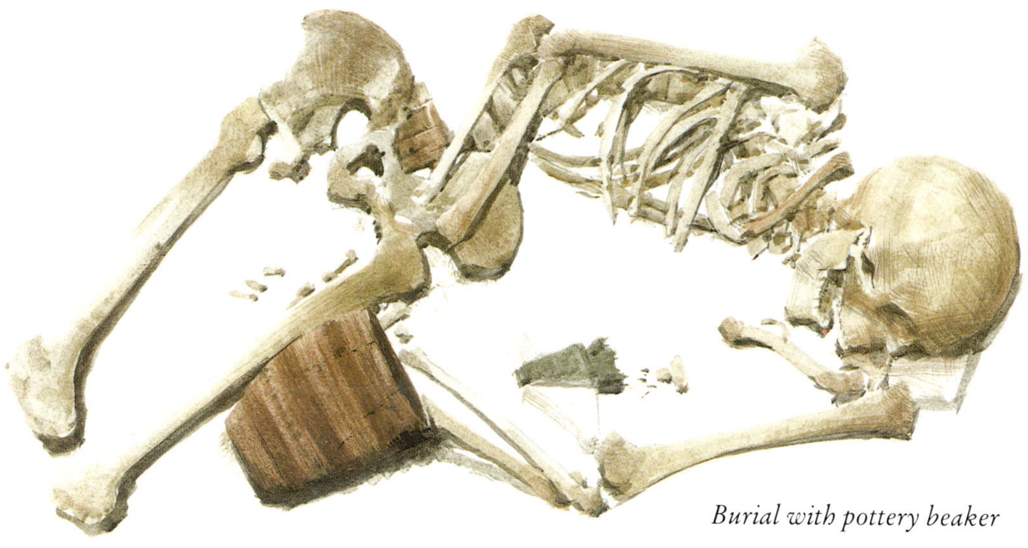

Burial with pottery beaker

Moving the stones was not their only remarkable feat. The sarsens are positioned with amazing accuracy. The site of Stonehenge slopes slightly – there is a variation of about 38 centimetres (15 inches) from west to east, 15 centimetres (6 inches) from north to south. Yet the lintels on top of the sarsens were level. In spite of the fact that they only had basic stone tools, the builders could dress the stone very accurately and must have been able to measure very precisely in order to achieve this.

Another example of their accuracy in stone cutting is the mortise and tenon joints that hold the uprights and their lintels together. It is as if the builders were trained as woodworkers rather than stonemasons. This fits in with other facts we know about the people of Stonehenge. The other monuments that they have left – especially the numerous burial mounds that they made all over this part of England – show little evidence they were used to handling large stones. The mounds are made mainly of earth, with only a few stones used at the entrance. And their other ritual rings and similar monuments were made either of smaller undressed stones or of wooden posts. It is natural, then, that the lintels at Stonehenge should be made as if they had been put together by a team of carpenters: they were.

With the large sarsens in place, and the groups of three even bigger sarsen stones (*trilithons*) arranged in the centre, one further major alteration to the design of Stonehenge was made. The bluestones were moved into the centre, arranged in an ellipse inside the space surrounded by the trilithons.

The Stonehenge that we know today was largely complete at this point, although now only about half the original stones remain. The effect of the site is therefore very different. Stonehenge in 1650 BC would have been a rather dark place, a forest of stones casting shadows across each other. Standing at the centre it would not have been easy to see much more than small sections of the surrounding countryside through the narrow slits between the sarsens. What you could see through these slits is obviously important for Stonehenge's possible role as an 'observatory' of the sun and stars. Narrow as the gaps are, they do not produce an effect that is accurate enough to predict the precise time and position of a sunrise. Where the sun appears on the horizon depends on

Stonehenge, midsummer sunrise 1650 BC

We do not know exactly what ceremonies Stonehenge played host to in its heyday, c.1650 BC. But the effect of the midsummer sunrise aligning with the Heel Stone (top right) *and the centre of the monument must have been awe-inspiring, the raking light making the priests seem larger than life and the great stones larger still. The sunrise would no doubt have heralded the climax of the ritual.*

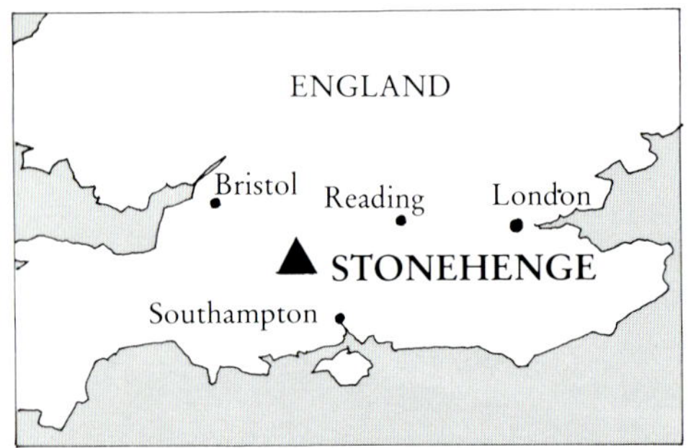

exactly where you stand, even on how you hold your head. But, the fact that famous alignments like the appearance of the sun roughly over the heel stone on midsummer morning do occur, makes Stonehenge a dramatically successful ritual centre. At the climax of the midsummer ceremony, the shaft of light penetrating the shadowy area between the stones would have been an awe-inspiring reminder of the repeating cycles of time and the seasons. For a few moments, Stonehenge would seem to be the centre of the universe.

A source of power

Why did the woodworkers of Stonehenge turn to dressed stone for the final phase of their building? No one knows for certain but a reason may be provided by what was happening in British society at the time. Around 2000 BC things were changing. The barrows of chieftains were getting larger, and their contents – especially the weapons – were bigger and more showy. Clearly the chiefs were becoming more powerful and wanted to show their power. The new enlarged Stonehenge is a symptom of this, although it is more than just an enormous status symbol. Because religion was itself the key to power in this period, Stonehenge was a source of power as well as its symbol. The way in which its fascination endures is an eloquent testimony of this.

KNOSSOS

Centre of the Minoan civilization of Crete, *circa* 2000–1450 BC, and site of the legendary labyrinth

The Aegean island of Crete was the centre of one of the greatest early civilizations. It was a civilization centred around a number of great palaces – at Phaistos, Mallia, Myrtos, Zakro, and, the greatest of all, at Knossos, on the northern edge of the island, on a low hill about 5 kilometres (3 miles) south of the modern city of Herakleion. The palace of Knossos was the centre of a civilization – but which civilization? The writings that the people who lived on Crete between *c.*1900–1400 BC have left behind have so far proved indecipherable, so that we do not even know what these people called themselves. The tradition was that Knossos was the home of the legendary king Minos, and so, searching for a name to put to their discoveries, the early archaeologists settled on the term Minoan, the name that has stuck to the people of Knossos ever since.

Knossos is steeped in legend. It was here, the ancient Greeks believed, that King Minos lived in his vast hillside palace. At the centre of the palace was supposed to be the labyrinth designed for him by the inventor and master craftsman Daedalus, and here Minos kept the Minotaur, a hideous monster, half bull, half man. It was the Minotaur, so the story went, that made Minos the terror of the Greek mainland. For every year he exacted tribute from the Greeks in the form of seven youths and seven girls, who were fed to the beast. When the time came around for the third payment, Theseus volunteered to go with the victims and kill the monster. The story of how he penetrated the labyrinth, killed the Minotaur, and found his way out using the thread given him by Ariadne, is well known. But even after its death, the Minotaur had its grisly revenge on the family of the Greek hero. Theseus had promised his father, Aegeus, that he would replace the black sails of his ship with white ones if he was successful. But intoxicated with success and with his love for Ariadne, Theseus forgot his promise, and it was a black-sailed ship that Aegeus saw approaching the mainland. The hero's father killed himself in despair.

Three Minoan images – the bull, the snake goddess, and the bare-breasted women who adorn the palace walls – are brought together here. The way in which Minoan painters brought together humans and dangerous animals in a similar fashion points to their fascination with both the creative and destructive powers of nature.

Who were the Minoans?

On the face of it, it seems odd that the Greeks should have imposed such a gruesome legend on such a sunny and so obviously civilized place as Knossos. And this is not the only mystery that surrounds the site. We are not even sure who the Minoans (genteel, yet apparently feared by the Greeks) were, where they came from, what religion they followed, or how they governed themselves. They seem to have arrived in Crete in *c.*7000 BC, and probably came from Asia Minor, although this is far from certain.

There are other enigmas. First, they were obviously a powerful people – the richness of their palaces and the scale on which their goods were distributed around the Aegean is evidence enough of this. But Knossos was not fortified to defend their power, and neither were the other palaces on Crete. Second, their paintings, especially the one showing the extraordinary scene of an athlete leaping over a bull's back, offer tantalizing glimpses of mysterious – almost unbelievable – practices. And third, their civilization came to a sudden end when their palaces were destroyed; but how this dramatic demise came about – by natural disaster, invasion, or revolt from within – is still a cause of vigorous debate.

But the Minoans left much that does allow us to form a picture of their culture. The most famous remains are the five palaces scattered around the island of Crete, the largest, most magnificent and most labyrinthine of which is Knossos. The palaces provided the centrepiece of Minoan life – the government, administration, and much of the artistic activity were carried out in them. They were also centres of trade. When he excavated the palace at Knossos, Arthur Evans discovered dozens of huge jars (called *pithoi*), each taller than a man, which were used to store vast quantities of olive oil – as much as 60,000 gallons according to one estimate – an impressive store of wealth.

Trade and society

This trade was an important source of the Minoans' power. An island people, they clearly used their prowess at sea to keep peace in the Aegean and foster the exchange of goods. But what was the nature of Minoan trade? Cretan ships certainly plied the Aegean, trading with nearby islands.

The palace of Minos, Knossos
1500 BC

A vast complex arranged around a central courtyard, the palace at Knossos fulfilled many functions. The royal apartments were in the eastern wing (far right), *the many store rooms were towards the west. Also in the western section, but nearer to the courtyard, were the official chambers and ceremonial rooms where public business was carried out.*

The legend of the labyrinth
Although the labyrinth itself probably existed only as a metaphor for the palace's baffling array of passages and staircases, it has remained a powerful image in myth to this day. There has always seemed to be something magical about mazes – both something sinister in the ease with which one can get lost in them and something fantastic in the skill with which the experts find their way out. As the first labyrinth, the maze of Knossos, with its myth of Ariadne's thread, looms as large in the imagination as the real palace.

Plan of the palace:
Official apartments A
Private apartments B
Workshops C
Entrances 1
Central courtyard 2
Throne room 3
Main sanctuary 4
Stores 5
Grand Staircase 6
Western courtyard 7
Theatre 8

The Minoans also exchanged goods with the people of northern Africa and the eastern Mediterranean. They exported raw materials and pottery, importing luxury materials such as gold and silver from the Aegean islands, alabaster from Egypt, ivory from Syria, and ostrich plumes from northern Africa. Trade also gave the Minoans tin (from Italy or central Europe), which they could mix with local copper to make bronze.

Such an influx of luxurious materials suggests a strong contingent of local craftworkers who could make status items for the inhabitants of the palace at Knossos and the other Cretan palaces. The towns built near the palaces would have housed many such workers. Villas in the countryside often also had adjoining workshops where crafts were practised. And the palaces themselves had their own staffs of artisans. It is possible, though we cannot be certain, that a sort of feudal relationship existed between the palaces and these people, as also between the palaces and the agricultural community. The rulers would take tribute in the form of a certain percentage of their products or produce, and in turn the workers would be free to distribute the rest of the fruits of their labour as they wished. Another possibility, especially with the palace-based workers, is that some form of slavery existed.

It is equally uncertain exactly who lived at Knossos. The quantity of religious and ceremonial imagery, together with the lavish surroundings, led Sir Arthur Evans to the idea that a 'priest-king' was the chief occupant of the palace. Later writers have pointed out that the legend of King Minos comes from the very end of the palaces' history and is interpreted through the writers of Classical Greece much later still. Abandoning the idea of King Minos, some authorities have seen the palaces as primarily ceremonial centres of temples, while others, emphasizing the trade carried out by the Cretans, see them as primarily centres for the redistribution of goods. Clearly, with such strong evidence for both trade and religion, the idea of a duel centre – and with it the idea of a 'dual-purpose' priest-king – is not so fantastic after all.

A practical architecture

The wealth that the people of Knossos accrued from their trade in the Aegean must have been considerable.

Contemporary model of small Minoan house

Their palaces are magnificent feats of construction. Knossos, like the others, is a vast assemblage of private apartments and public halls, store-rooms and bathrooms, corridors and staircases, chaotically grouped around a central courtyard. Unlike the ancient Greeks, the Minoans did not prize external symmetry in their buildings – the wings, halls, and porticoes often look as if they have been added at random, where they were needed rather than in the place that would make a symmetrical shape. But each individual room has its own beauty, and many are decorated with frescoes of surprising elegance.

Among the most stunning parts of the palace are the huge staircases, such as the one leading up to the private apartments of the first floor. This is not just impressive to look at, with its large, accurately cut blocks of stone. It also demonstrates that the Minoans were centuries ahead of their time when it came to sanitary engineering. It incorporates a drainage channel especially designed not to overflow because of the zigzags, corners and basins cut into it to slow down the flow of the water. This would have taken waste water from the apartments above to drain away below. And it is not just the staircases at Knossos that are well drained. The whole palace is testimony to the importance the Minoans placed on cleanliness – even if the baths in the sumptuous bathrooms are not connected to the plumbing system in the way that modern ones are.

The architecture of Knossos is highly practical in several other ways. It is well suited to Crete's climate, with its cool winters and hot summers. Many of the rooms are almost subterranean, cut into the rock of the hillside on which the palace is built. They are delightfully cool in summer and easy to keep warm in the winter months. Colonnaded porches, balconies and loggias also keep off the sun, as well as affording some extra shelter in colder weather.

Another important feature is the structure of the palace. Large mud bricks are the main material used for the walls, but there was also often a wooden framework, and the original columns were made of wood. Such a building would have had a better chance of surviving Crete's earth tremors than a stone structure.

The royal apartments were elegantly decorated. The modern visitor to Knossos can appreciate this from the restorations of Arthur Evans. His attempts to replace missing sections of many Minoan frescoes have been criticized and the results cannot be totally accurate. But they are true to the spirit of the fragments that survive. These frescoes give a likeable picture of the Minoan aristocracy. They portray a people dark-haired and slim, although the women have exaggeratedly full breasts. The people are shown enjoying themselves – especially in activities such as boxing and the mysterious bull-leaping ceremony.

The development of the palace

How did such an enormous palace come to be built? The early, neolithic culture of Crete, with its small rural communities did not immediately transform itself into the elaborate palace-based system that was Minoan civilization. Excavations of the hill on which the palace of Knossos stands reveal that it is an artificial mound made up of the remains of previous settlements. And these were by no means primitive. The most recent – dating from the time immediately before the palace was built – was quite sophisticated, with stone-paved roads connecting quite substantial houses. It was this network that formed the environment for the first palace at Knossos, which started out as a number of connected blocks of buildings alongside, sometime during the period 1900–1700 BC. Towards the end of this period most of these houses were demolished and pits were dug in their place to take debris from the palace. Soon afterwards the pits were covered over with the paved courtyard that was to become the western court of the 'new' palace, which was rebuilt in *c.*1700 BC to a coherent plan.

Although the architects of 1700 BC managed a unified design, with recurrent motifs of the plain, cylindrical, red-painted columns creating visual echoes and re-echoes around the building, they had to accommodate a great diversity of function. There were the ceremonial areas, such as the throne room; the king's residential apartments; the workshops for craftsmen who kept the palace supplied with both everyday tools and luxury goods; and there were the store rooms that alone took up a space over 60 metres (200 feet) in length along the western side of the palace.

There is little wonder that the legend of the labyrinth attached itself to this building. With the network of rooms, corridors, and staircases it would have been easy for a newcomer to get lost. And the idea of power that the palace no doubt came to embody would have seemed all the more overwhelming since the building itself could seem to suck people in. There is little need to imagine a literal maze or labyrinth at Knossos (there is no archaeological evidence for such a construction) because the palace itself fulfilled this role so effectively.

The other large Minoan palaces on Crete – Mallia and Phaistos – show a similar variety of uses, with store rooms, workshops, and residential apartments gathered around a courtyard. Both buildings are smaller in scale, but have enough similarity to suggest that they were used in similar ways and grew up because of similar needs. In order to see how they were used, it is helpful to examine the position of the palaces in the history of Crete's agriculture and in the development of the island's arts and crafts.

Figure of the snake goddess

The rise of the palaces

It is impossible reconstruct accurately the way in which society on Crete developed to a point where the island could support palaces of such size and richness. But one can make educated guesses based on the fruits of excavation and on the ways in which other similar societies have developed. Briefly and simply, there was probably some sort of improvement in agricultural conditions on Crete in the years immediately before the palaces were built. Such an improvement would lead not only to a healthy, increasing population; it would also provide a food surplus. This would in turn stimulate the creation of a number of centres at strategic points around the island where surplus food could be redistributed. Centres like this would need to be well sited; they would need plenty of storage space for oil and corn; and they would quickly become the home of a powerful elite who, by directly controlling the food supply, would have power over the lives of everyone on the island. This is how the Minoan palaces, with their elaborate systems of storerooms, may have evolved.

With power comes status, and status requires status symbols. Not surprisingly, the palaces became centres of craftwork and artistic activity. Workers with particular skills congregated at the palaces, supplying their masters – and the people of the neighbouring area – with superb luxury goods. The results of excavation suggest that some palaces specialized in certain trades. Phaistos seems to have produced large quantities of bronze artefacts; Zakro was known for its ivory; Mallia's goldsmiths produced work that is still admired. The palace of Knossos was large enough to support several trades, but its gemstone workers and seal carvers were outstanding.

The seals of Crete form one of the Minoans' most characteristic and interesting products. The first seals, adapted from the sort of cylinder seals that the people of the middle eastern civilizations used for identification, were made of soft stone such as ivory and steatite. Later makers mastered the difficult art of carving rock crystal, agate, carnelian, and jasper. The images on the seals – of animals, people, and ceremonies like the famous bull-leaping – give us valuable insights into the Cretans' religion, their dress, and their interest in the natural world. They are also exquisitely carved items in their own right.

Of the other crafts of the Minoans, perhaps the most important was bronzeworking. This gave the elite of the palaces luxury items from vases to armour. But its greatest importance was that bronzeworkers made tools for other crafts. Minoan saws, axes, crowbars, and pickaxes were all made of bronze. No doubt the carpentry of Knossos and the other palaces – none of which has, of course, survived – was of high quality as a result of these tools. As time went on, bronze was used more and more decoratively. This tradition of metalworking was so strong on Crete that it continued into the Mycenaean period, when the two civilizations each learned something from each other's craft.

There is no doubt that the Minoan upper classes lived a luxurious life, surrounded by the prestigious artefacts their craftworkers created for them. With their black and white pottery, their elegant stoneware vessels, their gold jewellery and ivory brooches, their utensils of bronze, the occupants of the private apartments at Knossos would have exuded wealth and privilege. The craftsmen themselves would also have been valued highly enough to enjoy a relatively comfortable lifestyle.

Stone ceremonial vessel in the shape of a bull's head

But what of the ordinary Cretans, the people who provided the food surplus from which this wealth originally flowed? Most would have been agricultural workers living in small rural communities. They probably lived in tribal groups, joined by family bonds that had existed before the coming of the palace civilization in the twentieth century BC. And once the redistributive system set up by the palaces was in operation, they would have to give tribute to their overlords in the form of a large share of their produce. They would also have been liable for military service, although the palace society seems to have kept the peace for most of its existence.

Linear B fragment containing a farmer's stock list, and late Minoan pot

An unknown language

When Arthur Evans excavated at Knossos, his most intriguing finds included tablets inscribed with the symbols of several mysterious scripts. It was impossible to translate these inscriptions. The best Evans could do was to sort them out into types. There were three. The first, and most primitive, was a system of hieroglyphs – symbols of the actual objects they represented, together with other symbols that were not so obvious in their meaning. Second were two scripts that seemed more sophisticated. The symbols, though possibly derived from earlier hieroglyphs, were not simple pictures. Evans called these two scripts 'Linear A' and 'Linear B'. From the contexts in which the tablets were discovered, it was possible to give rough dates to the scripts. The hieroglyphs were the earliest, and they all dated from the period of the first palaces, before *c.*1700 BC. Next came Linear A. Examples of this script were dated both to the early palace period, and to the time after the palaces were rebuilt in 1700 BC. This was an important discovery, since it confirmed the archaeologists' suspicions that the palaces were not taken over by an alien power in 1700 BC, but were reconstructed by the people who had lived in them before. Linear B was a later script. Most of the tablets bearing Linear B inscriptions dated from the end of the palace period, when the domination of a foreign power looked much more likely.

During Evans' time, none of the scripts was decipherable. All three remained something of a mystery. But in 1939, Linear B inscriptions were found at Pylos on the Greek mainland. Later, still more were found at Mycenae. The inference was clear: Linear B was the script of the Mycenaeans, and it was they who came to dominate Crete after the chain of disasters that befell the island around the middle of the fifteenth century BC.

It took until 1952 for a convincing attempt to decipher Linear B, by which time several thousand inscriptions in the script had been discovered. Then the British architect Michael Ventris stunned the archaeological world with the announcement that Linear B was in fact a primitive version of Greek. Ventris' conclusions have been generally accepted, to the benefit of our knowledge of the Mycenaeans. But no comparable discovery has been made about Minoan Linear A. There are far fewer inscriptions to work on, and this alone makes it difficult to crack the code. For now, and probably the foreseeable future, the language the Minoans spoke and wrote remains unknown, and the archaeologists have to resort to guesswork based on the context of the finds when trying to interpret the meanings of Cretan texts.

The religion of the Minoans

The palace wall paintings give clues about Minoan religion. The double axe symbol appears frequently – notably in the room which Evans dubbed 'the hall of the double axes' and in small indoor shrine-like rooms. This symbol seems to have had an importance akin to that of the cross in Christianity. Another clue is the prominence of goddesses in Minoan mythology. Cretan statuettes of bare-breasted women holding snakes are well known. The naked breasts make these figures seem like fertility symbols, but all Minoan women – even those picture in quite mundane scenes – are depicted with naked breasts, so we should be wary of reading too much into this.

The female goddess figures are probably derived from the earlier, simpler marble female statuettes that have been found in great numbers all around the Cycladic islands. These were probably idols, used to encourage the protection of a goddess such as the primitive earth mother. Respect for an earth goddess is certainly appropriate to the Minoans, who were fascinated by the natural world. The palaces are full of wall paintings of plants and animals – birds, dolphins, griffins, octopuses, and fish – many of which are connected with the sea. The palaces are also built in places that command spectacular views, something that is not difficult in Crete's hilly country, although the Minoans could have found more sheltered or secluded sites if they had wished.

Work carried out by more recent archaeologists has given us much more information about Minoan religion. In particular, storerooms have been found at Knossos that contained a rich variety of religious objects. As well as the familiar snake goddess figures there were many objects – such as faience models of animals and plants, fruit and flowers, fishes and shells – which confirm the Minoan love of the natural world that we see in the paintings on their palace walls. Stone pouring vessels and storage containers for wine and oil suggest offerings, while deer bones may be evidence for animal sacrifice.

Finds such as these are hardly surprising. They fit with what else we know about the people of Knossos. But another excavation, in 1979, revealed Minoan religion in a rather different light. The finds were in the basement of a building about 350 metres (1,000 feet) from the palace, a building which also contained stored religious objects such as ritual vessels. The bones of four children, many of which showed signs of having been cut many times with a knife, as if to remove the flesh, were hidden there. Part of a sheep's skeleton was also discovered, with knife marks that suggested that its throat had been cut.

From what is left of their bones, the children seem to have been in good health when they met their end, so how did the tragedy of their early deaths come about? There are several possible explanations. This could be the scene of a simple, cold-blooded murder, although the religious objects on the same site make this unlikely. It could be evidence of survival cannibalism during the period of crisis at Knossos towards the end of the Minoan period, but this too is unlikely. Sacrifice is the most likely reason for the children's deaths, perhaps, as archaeologist Peter Warren has suggested, sacrifice in an attempt to avert a major disaster. Such an explanation would account for the fact that no other evidence of human sacrifice has been found at Knossos; it was not a normal part of Minoan religion, but something that the priests could call upon as a last resort.

And this seems to conform with what we know of animal sacrifice in Minoan religion. The evidence of carved seal stones shows that the sacrifice of bulls and goats was well known. The animals' throats would be cut, and the blood collected and offered to the gods by being poured into the ground. If such rituals were common in times of stability and prosperity, perhaps it was a logical step to sacrifice humans during times of difficulty or crisis.

The seal stones of Crete also give some insight into the sort of ceremonies performed in the sanctuaries of Knossos and other Minoan palaces. There would be dances to invoke the presence of the god, ritual obeisances and salutations of the cult figure, and the making of offerings. The latter would include pouring libations and a ceremony involving the offering of a robe to the goddess in which either the cult statue or the priestess were clothed in the proffered garment.

The Cretan bulls

The scenes of bull-leaping in the Knossos frescoes pose some of the most intriguing questions about the Minoans. Are these scenes meant to be taken as literal representations of what happened or are they scenes from a lost mythology? Is it significant that two of the athletes in the most famous fresco are girls? Is the ceremony religious or merely sporting? And where did it take place?

Modern scholars think that the ceremony – in which an athlete somersaults over the horns of a bull – actually did take place and that it was almost certainly religious. As to where it might have happened, there is less agreement. Arthur Evans thought that the bull-leaping was done in the palace courtyards themselves. Other archaeologists have reasonably objected that the courtyards at Knossos and the other palaces are hardly well adapted to such a dangerous pursuit. Recently, evidence of an arena-like structure outside one of the palaces has suggested that Evans may indeed have been wrong.

What kind of religion would have encouraged its followers to perform such dangerous feats with temperamental creatures like bulls? The Minoan fascination with the natural world scarcely seems enough to explain it. But one particular feature of Cretan geography would have made the people respect and even fear nature – the fact that Crete is subject to earthquakes. It is not surprising that the islanders had a cult of an animal that was as violent and unpredictable of the tremors that could lay their houses low. Classical writers lend some support to this theory. Homer said that Poseidon, Greek god of the sea and storms, known to them as 'the earth-shaker', 'delights in bulls'. It may have been a forerunner of Poseidon that the Cretans were trying to appease.

The beginning of the end

The Minoans had good reason to respect the 'earth-shaker'. There is evidence that in about 1700 BC, when they were at the height of their success, an earthquake badly damaged the palaces of Crete. It was probably not the first time that such damage had occurred, but previous attacks were less severe. Even so, the wealth and influence of the Cretans, together with the fact that even a serious earthquake would not have had too great an effect on their sea trade, meant that they could rebuild. And this they did, restoring the palace at Knossos to an even greater glory.

Bull-leaping scene

The real blow came about 250 years later and was far more severe. This time the damage was so great that reconstruction was impossible. The thing that mystified archaeologists for years was that the damage caused was different from the previous disaster, and yet there did not seem to be any evidence of the most obvious outside force of destruction – an invasion.

The vital clue came when geologists started to examine the material through which Arthur Evans had dug to uncover the palace. Knossos had been buried under volcanic ash in about 1450 BC, at about the time of the eruption on the island of Thera, some 110 kilometres (70 miles) away from Crete. The ash thrown high into the air by the volcano and landing far away on Crete would not have been the only problem. The attendant tidal wave would have wrecked the Minoan ships and made the sea treacherous – their sea power would have been destroyed. There would be little chance to reconstruct, little opportunity to trade.

Yet Knossos was not like a Minoan Pompeii, the Roman city where people were killed and petrified as they walked in the streets by the sudden eruption of Vesuvius. It is almost as if the Minoans had had some warning of the coming disaster and had been able to escape in their ships. Some scholars believe that an earthquake preceded the eruption and gave the Minoans time to prepare for an escape. At the beginning of the eruption they could have taken to ship quickly before the effects of the ensuing tidal wave made themselves felt.

But even if they did make a successful escape, they probably suspected their time of prosperity was nearing its end. The coming power in the Aegean, the warlike people of mainland Mycenae, was already in the ascendant. Had they not begun to threaten the Minoans before the eruption of Thera, they would have done so soon after 1450 BC. The time of the peaceful traders, the worshippers of the earth goddess, was over; the domination by a more outwardly masculine warrior society had begun.

MYCENAE

Home of the warrior kings of mainland Greece *circa* 1600–1100 BC, and legendary site of the palace of Agamemnon

The people of mainland Greece during the period *c.*1600–1100 BC have left extensive remains. One of their most important sites was at Mycenae, on a low hill about 19 kilometres (12 miles) from the Gulf of Argolis in southern mainland Greece. It was a large multi-purpose site – part royal palace, part home for the king's subjects, part graveyard. But above all it was a fortified stronghold, with great gates and massive defensive walls following the contours of the hill.

Today, Mycenae seems an isolated, desolate fortress, a place that might have been the home of a small community clinging to the craggy hillside. But it was the centre of something much larger. Mycenaean artefacts have been found in significant numbers in places as far afield as the Cycladic Islands, southern Italy, Sicily, western Asia Minor, Cyprus, and Egypt. For example, Mycenaean vases have been found on sites around the coast of Cyprus; more than sixty sites in the area of Syria and Palestine have yielded goods that were originally imported from mainland Greece in this period; and Mycenaean pottery reached over twenty Egyptian sites, with gold travelling back to Greece in return. This exchange is crucial to the success of the trade. The Mycenaeans were rich and powerful enough to travel all over the Aegean and impose their will on many neighbouring powers. But they lacked valuable raw materials like precious metals: they needed their neighbours as much as their neighbours needed them.

A Mycenaean warrior king seen against the background of one of the royal audience chambers. Some of the details of the reconstruction are based on the palace at Pylos, but the details would have been similar at Mycenae. Above is the beaten-gold face mask of a Mycenaean king, unearthed by Heinrich Schliemann.

Clearly, the Mycenaean people traded far and wide. What is more, some of the remains found nearer their home – on Melos and Rhodes – point to actual Mycenaean settlements. But did these early Greeks, if that is what we can call them, control anything as organized as an empire? What does Mycenae tell us about the origins of classical Greek culture? And what exactly was their relationship with the people of the Minoan civilization, from whom they seem to have learned a great deal? To answer these questions we have to begin with the origins of the Mycenaeans.

Who were the Mycenaeans?

Before the great stone-built complex at Mycenae started to be occupied in *c.*1600 BC, Greece was dominated by a culture known as the Helladic. The people farmed, lived in long stone houses with a porch at one end, could make bronze tools but do not seem to have done so widely, hunted with the bow, and buried their dead in pits or tumuli. It was a simple life compared with the contemporary palace civilization of Crete or with Troy VI. But around 1600 BC there was a change on mainland Greece. Prosperity increased and centres of power – marked by more lavish burials – started to appear at Eleusis, at Lerna, and above all at Mycenae.

Why did this change come about? One important influence was contact with the Cretan palace civilization. The Mycenaeans borrowed the techniques of wall painting, pottery decoration and seal-making from the Minoans. And contact between the two cultures may well have led to new trading contacts around the Aegean for the Mycenaeans. But more than this is needed to explain the change in the life of mainland Greece. In particular, there is one key difference between the two cultures: in contrast to the peaceful Minoans, the people of Mycenae were warriors, and some of the most impressive items buried in their graves were arms and armour. At the same time as learning the ways of a leisured trading life from the Minoans, the Mycenaeans were also developing a tradition of their own, that of the warlike opportunists who would go on raids around the Mediterranean in search of tribute and booty. This combination of traits made the Mycenaeans very successful and very rich.

This is a kind of lifestyle that is familiar to readers of the Homeric epics, the stories of the gods and heroes who were supposed to have been the forerunners of the classical Greeks. But are we justified in calling these Mycenaeans 'Greeks', and is it possible to draw the sort of close parallels that have led writers to talk about Mycenae as if it were the headquarters of Homer's great warrior Agamemnon? One clue to the peoples' Greek identity came when Michael Ventris proposed that the Linear B script so common on tablets found on the Greek mainland and also on Crete was in fact a way of writing

This overhead view of Mycenae shows the royal palace on top of the hill. Below, the scene is dominated by the massive walls, the well-defended lion gate, and the circular graveyard. Houses of high-ranking soldiers and officials can be seen beyond the grave circle.

an early form of Greek. The great majority of scholars agree with Ventris' findings, and the resulting translations have told us a lot about the lives of the Mycenaeans and their neighbours. One set of Linear B tablets, discovered at Pylos, the best preserved Mycenaean palace site, mentions offerings made to the same gods and goddesses as those known in classical Greece. So the people of Mycenae were Greek in their language and in at least one other important element of their culture.

But whether we can equate these people with specific characters in Homer's epics is much more doubtful, tempting as it is to do so. Past archaeologists took this temptation too far. For example, one of the most important structures at Mycenae was a building that became known as the Treasury of Atreus, father of Agamemnon. This is a circular structure in the shape of a domed beehive about 14.5 metres (50 feet) across, approached along a narrow entrance corridor and covered by an earthen mound. In fact, it is not a treasury at all, but a tomb, and the original occupant is unknown. Each of the finely cut stone blocks in the vaulted roof contained a bronze nail, to which was attached a bronze decoration (probably a rosette), and the monumental doorway with its massive 120 tonne lintel would also have been lavishly decorated. The tomb is one of many

The citadel of Mycenae 1500 BC

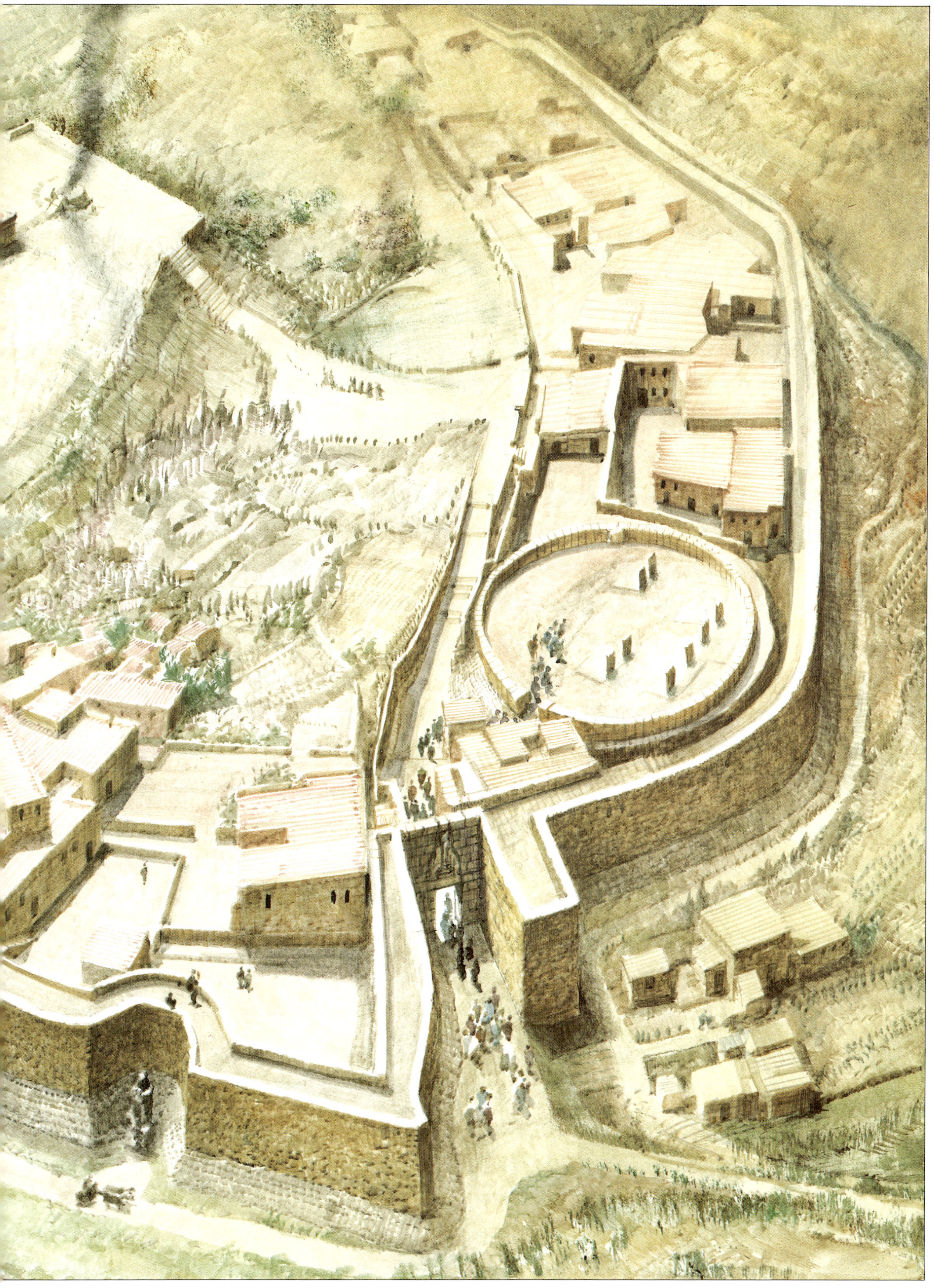

of its type (which are known as *tholoi*), which became fashionable on mainland Greece in the thirteenth century BC and replaced the earlier 'shaft-graves', that were little more than sunken pits. It is a magnificent building, and was clearly the tomb of someone important – presumably one of Mycenae's warrior rulers – but this is the nearest we can get to an identification of the owner.

Sadly, this tomb, like other tholoi, was robbed quite soon after it was constructed, so few objects have been found that tell us more about its occupant. But meticulous sifting of debris in and around the tomb has brought to light a few fragments of gold and other precious metals that hint at the magnificence of the original contents.

Life in the citadel

In spite of these robberies, enough archaeological evidence has been assembled to give us some idea of the way of life of the Mycenaeans. Pottery – jars, flasks and bowls – made on the mainland indicates the influence of the Minoans, especially before the collapse of the palace civilization on Crete. Ivory was exquisitely worked into boxes, plaques and figurines, including a famous royal head wearing a helmet that is itself reinforced with tusks of the wild boar, a beautiful example of the artist's material mirroring the subject matter. Other decorative trades included metal inlaying and wall painting.

The Linear B tablets give more information about trades and professions; the tablets from Pylos tell us most, but the story for Mycenae would have been similar. Among the trades mentioned are bakers, bronze-workers, potters, masons, messengers and heralds, shepherds, carpenters and fullers. The picture that emerges is typical of a large number of people grouping together: there is enough demand for specialized trades to flourish, and an upper class who require luxury goods to make their lives easier and symbolize their status.

Goblet of gold, known as Nestor's Cup

The most magnificent of the status items were the work of the Mycenaean goldsmiths. A gold cup, an offering vessel in the shape of a lion's head, gold tiaras and decorative gold discs that were sewn on to womens' dresses like huge sequins, and the extraordinary beaten-gold face masks found in some of the royal graves are the best examples. The masks in particular are intriguing, since they give us suggestive glimpses of the actual faces of the Mycenaean rulers – the features certainly vary enough to make it likely that these are lifelike portraits; they are certainly not designed to flatter their subjects. While it is fanciful to suppose that we are face to face with Agamemnon, these masks certainly make us feel close to his people.

At Mycenae there was another trade that often flourishes well in early urban communities – that of armourer. Swords, daggers, spears in a range of different weights, and shields have all been found. One royal grave contained three bodies and nearly one hundred swords. And the quality of these weapons was nearly as outstanding as their quantity. Some had chased gold handles decorated with spiral patterns and dragon heads. Others were inlaid – in gold or silver – with scenes of heroism (one famous example shows the climax of a lion hunt as four men face the charging beast).

One unique find from Dendra, not far from Mycenae, was a suit of armour. Made up of plates of bronze designed to be stitched together, the suit would have been uncomfortable to wear and would have restricted the wearer's movement. It may well have been for ceremonial wear, designed to symbolize the impregnability of the wearer's position.

The palace complex

Even if not all of these products were actually made within the walls of Mycenae, the citadel was obviously home for a large number of people, and no doubt more would take shelter there and help to defend it in times of strife. In addition to the palace itself, in the centre of the citadel, there were numerous other houses, including a group along the southwestern edge of the citadel, several nearer the eastern point of the triangular site, and a few by the lion gate, near the northern corner. Some of these, such as the House of the Columns, were clearly quite large stone structures belonging to military leaders and wealthy families. But the presence of a workshop next to the palace suggests that at least some artisans worked here, and probably lived within the walls in more modest houses.

Bronze suit of armour

All of these buildings, for all the influence of the Minoans, were constructed in a much more austere style than the palace of Knossos. The Mycenaeans do not seem to have gone in for the inviting colonnades and staircases that mark the exteriors of Minoan palaces. Their buildings seem to shun the outside world, giving an impression almost as austere as that conjured up by the defensive walls that surround the whole citadel. They were the homes of a people always conscious of the need to defend, the possibility that their military domination might be threatened from without. Another difference was that the courtyard – so important to the Minoans – was much less of a feature in Mycenaean architecture. This is because the Mycenaean palaces were essentially *megarons* – great halls with a portico in front, based on the long houses lived in by the Helladic people who preceded the Mycenaeans on the Greek mainland. There were courtyards, but they were not as large or important as those on Crete.

But in the interior of their palaces,

the Mycenaeans allowed themselves greater luxury and decoration. Rich coffered ceilings were emblazoned with abstract designs, while the walls were adorned with figurative paintings. Fragments of frescoes have been discovered at Mycenae and Tiryns, south of Mycenae, and both display a Minoan influence in their colouring and in the style of the painting of figures. Even so, it is unlikely that the Mycenaeans reached the sophistication of their Cretan neighbours in matters such as sanitation or ventilation; one comes away with the impression that they were a much more spartan people.

The gods of Mycenae

One of the odd things about Mycenae and the other palaces of its period is the lack of temples or religious buildings. Apart from one or two cult rooms, there is very little remaining of the places where the Mycenaeans worshipped. Yet they did have an elaborate pantheon of gods, including those who, according to the Linear B tablets, bore the same names as their later Greek counterparts.

Scant archaeological evidence paints a confusing picture. Mycenaean religion owed much to Minoan Crete: terracotta household snake gods, animal sacrifice, and some of the male and female idols all reveal similarities to remains and practices on Crete. Even the worship of gods named Zeus and Poseidon could be due to Minoan influence. Perhaps the Mycenaeans' religion seems most characteristic in their lavish burial customs; on the death of a warrior, his two horses would be sacrificed.

The Mycenaean network

We do not know the exact nature of the regime of which Mycenae formed the centre. The society, which has been recorded in detail on Linear B tablets, was rigidly hierarchical. There were, in descending order, a king, war leaders, officials, landholders, councilmen, and artisans. Each had their precisely defined roles in Mycenaean society. But the broader picture of government and the state is far less clear. Although it was powerful and wide-ranging, the Mycenaean state was probably not formal enough to be called an empire. More likely, it may have been a loose confederation of small states that were dependent on the central authority.

What remains in less doubt is that Mycenae stood at the hub of a network for the redistribution of goods. Like Knossos, it was surrounded by small communities – towns and villages – that did well producing and collecting raw materials which would be distributed around the network to be turned into manufactured goods before being redistributed. At each point the central power would be involved, regulating the proceedings and taking some of the profit.

The Linear B tablets from Pylos bear witness to the strength and complexity of this economic system. And they make it clear that it was a system – something that was regulated very carefully and closely by the authorities. One group of tablets, for example, contains lists of men's names divided into groups and allocated to different places; these are almost certainly lists of soldiers who were put to the task of guarding various sections of the Greek coast. Linear B tablets also include lists of chariot wheels and armour. Another group of tablets lists further names, probably female slaves. Further groups give amounts of grain and the land on which it grew. Again the lists are tied to particular names, this time the owners or tenants of the land. There is a group of tablets listing amounts of bronze, including accounts showing how much of the metal should be contributed by officials from different areas. To the archive from Pylos can be added yet more records from Mycenae itself, mostly dealing with herbs and spices – coriander, cumin, fennel, sesame, and celery seed. These and many other tablets look like tax assessments, and point to a highly organized administrative system. It is sometimes tempting to think of the Mycenaean military leaders as all might and no subtlety, accruing their wealth by force alone. The Linear B tablets show this to be an incorrect view: accounting and record-keeping were just as important for their success.

The Lion Gate, main entrance to the citadel

The decline of Mycenae

During the second half of the thirteenth century BC the fortunes of this successful people started to change. A series of fires swept across the Mycenaean world in *c.*1250 BC, another about 50 years later, and another some 50 years after that. The first wave destroyed most of the houses outside the citadel at Mycenae; the second took the citadel itself, together with those at Dendra, Tiryns, Krisa, Gla, and Thebes. Further strongholds went in the third wave of destruction.

But the Mycenaean culture did not disappear with these blows to its fabric. In fact, it seems unlikely that external invasion was the cause of the destruction, since Greek culture remained Mycenaean after the palace burnings had taken place. Natural causes do not seem to have been to blame – there is no evidence of any drought that may have caused the fires; the destruction looks deliberate.

The most likely explanation is revolt from within. There were rich pickings to be gained, and the success and splendour of the ruling families might well have caused resentment amongst those who did well out of the system but felt that they could do better still. But whoever stimulated the revolt did not take over the redistributive system – or at least did not keep control of it for long. After a brief flowering around the time of the first wave of fires, Mycenaean culture started to decline. Single-mindedness on the part of the rulers and unity amongst the ranks was obviously vital to hold the system together.

With the resulting reversion to a more rural economy, the arts and crafts fostered in the palaces and citadels disappeared. Linear B ceased to be useful and went out of use; there was no demand for intricate ivories; there were no great palace walls on which to paint frescoes; pottery styles started to show strong variations from region to region, suggesting that the communications network was breaking down too. The sense of purpose that had marked Mycenaean culture had clearly ebbed away.

BISKUPIN

Polish fortified village *circa* 700–400 BC

The fortified settlement at Biskupin, about 230 kilometres (143 miles) west of Warsaw, Poland, gives us a vivid image of the life of one type of community in eastern Europe between the eighth and fifth centuries BC. Although the houses and fortifications were all made of timber, deposits of sand and mud meant that many of the original timbers have been preserved, giving archaeologists a unique body of evidence with which to reconstruct the settlement. The work of excavation and recording went well in the 1930s, but much of the evidence (both the archaeologists' records and some of their actual finds) were destroyed by the Nazis in World War Two. So instead of a near-perfect reconstruction, our picture of life in this agricultural community in central Europe must be drawn tentatively.

The village was built on a peninsula that jutted out into the lake of Biskupin. The ground was marshy peat, meaning that the wooden supports had to be sunk deep below the surface to keep the houses and walls upright. The boggy ground also had to be covered with wooden pavements. The settlement had an area of about 2 hectares (5 acres). During the first phase of occupation, in *c.*720 BC, the village was at its largest. It was surrounded by a wall that was really a wooden box frame 6 metres (20 feet) high and 3 metres (10 feet) wide, filled with earth. On the lake sides, there was also a breakwater about 7 metres (23 feet) wide. A gateway of about 8 metres (26 feet) long gave access to the village from the land. The surviving timbers indicate the presence of towers or a superstructure, but we do not know exactly what this would have looked like.

Rebuilding was often needed at Biskupin. The wooden structure made fires a common hazard, and the fact that the houses adjoined each other meant that the flames could spread quickly. But this was a highly cooperative society, and repairs could be carried out quickly.

Inside, there were just over one hundred houses. Most of these had one large room, though occasionally they were split into two. Their doorways mostly faced south, to let in the light. The floors were wooden, and rested on layers of birch sticks that were placed above the bog itself. There were hearths of stone, covered with a layer of clay to keep the fire away from the timbers and minimize the danger of the houses catching fire.

The houses were arranged in rows, under a single continuous roof. Between these rows of buildings ran a dozen parallel 'roads' paved with logs, giving the grooved appearance known to archaeologists as 'corduroy'. There was also a wooden road running around the village, just inside the wall. The settlement was obviously planned as a whole, in a highly organized way. By 560 BC, Biskupin was slightly smaller: one street had disappeared, the houses were more compact, and there were fewer of them. But the village still kept its basic form.

The people of Biskupin

The population has been estimated at about 700. As all the houses were the same size, the archaeologists have assumed that there was no 'chieftain' or elite class – although there is always the possibility that size of dwelling did not indicate social status for these people, or that there was a controlling chief who lived elsewhere. They must certainly have been well organized to build in such a planned and uniform way – the fact that all the houses in a street are joined together, and that many of them share common dividing walls, shows a high degree of cooperation. They also needed to defend themselves – otherwise they would not have had to pack their houses tightly within a rampart.

The skills of the people were both agricultural and industrial. Of the animal remains found on the site there are many from cattle, pigs, sheep and goats, fewer from hunted creatures such as deer and wild boar. The mud of the lake has also preserved some evidence that they grew crops: as well as a ploughshare, traces of wheat, barley and pulses have been found.

In some houses finds of loom weights and spindles suggest that they were inhabited by specialist clothworkers. Awls found in other buildings point to leather workers. And some of the buildings show evidence of metalworking (at first bronze casting, later ironworking). In view of the heat needed for this work and the wooden construction of the houses, it is not surprising that the village was several times partly destroyed by fire.

There is also evidence of trade. Beads of glass and amber found at Biskupin may have come from the Baltic. Other objects found on the site came from Hungary and Italy. But we should not make that much of long-distance

Seen from above, the rows of houses give an ordered impression, and the village must have been well organized for some 700 people to live so closely together. In winter, the surrounding water and marsh would have frozen over and the snowdrifts would have isolated the settlement. In this depiction, the villagers are rallying to put out the fire that caused the rebuilding shown on page 44.

contacts with southern Europe. The objects may have been traded several times before they came to Biskupin. The village was not the centre of a trading network, but may well have been a port of call for local traders.

An embattled culture

Why did the people of Biskupin need to defend themselves so carefully? Biskupin is not the only fortified village discovered from this period in Poland, though it is by far the best preserved. It seems that these villages belonged to people of what is known as the 'urnfield culture'. Thought to be an ancient Slavonic people, their hold on the area was threatened by the people from Pomerania, who had their origins in the Baltic. Fortification was the obvious answer.

Unfortunately no burials have been discovered at Biskupin. This is not surprising, given the marshy location of the village. We cannot therefore say for sure that they cremated their dead and buried the remains in the characteristic urns that mark this particular rite. There is perhaps a cemetery somewhere on the dry land away

The town of Biskupin 650 BC

from the lake which will show this theory to be correct.

The rising waters

When Biskupin was first built, the water level of the lake was probably much lower than today. In fact it may have been little more than a marsh at some times of the year. But the climate of this part of Poland was gradually changing during the centuries when Biskupin was inhabited. It was getting damper and colder, and the waters would have risen steadily. At first this would have been an advantage, making the place easier to defend. But when the water level got too high it caused problems. There are signs that the houses in the second phase of building were built at a higher level – and constructed quickly and less well than their predecessors. The people were becoming desperate and needed to have dry homes as rapidly as possible.

The makeshift building work was successful for a time. But eventually disaster struck for the people of Biskupin. It came in the form of a flood that made the village uninhabitable. Ironically the force that drove the people away also helped preserve the timbers of their houses. 2,300 years later, the archaeologists could gain from their loss.

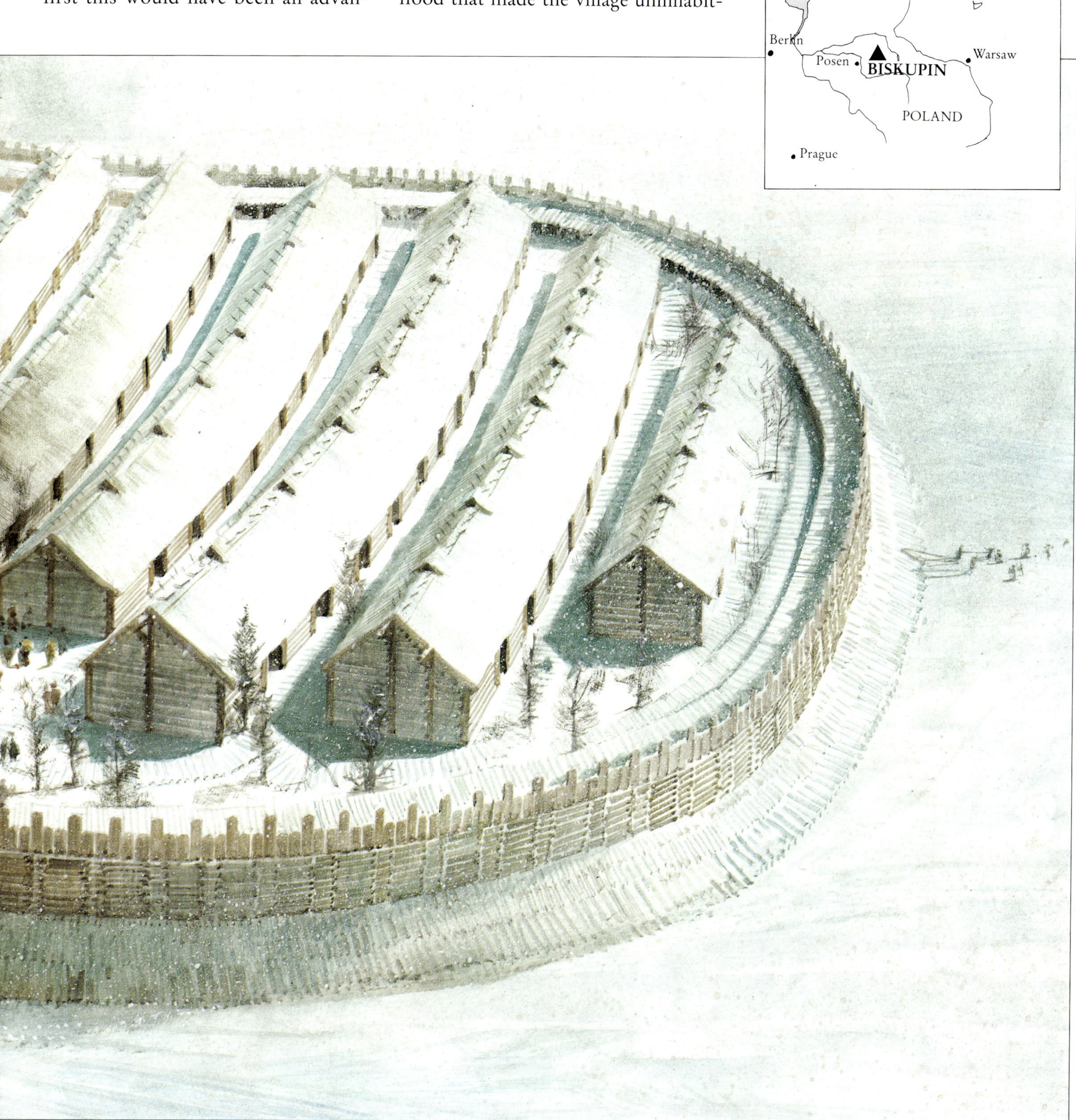

DELPHI

Classical Greek sanctuary of the god Apollo, and 'navel of the world'

Delphi is one of ancient Greece's most sacred sites. North of the Gulf of Corinth, above the valley of the river Plistus, on the cliffs of Mount Parnassus itself, it is a complex of buildings that stood for much in ancient Greek religion. Delphi is one of the most well known sites in the ancient world. Its superb mountain setting, together with the fact that the land around is subject to earthquakes, makes Delphi an obvious sacred site. More than a mere temple, Delphi is a whole sacred complex or sanctuary to the god Apollo, and a place of such magnetism that it has influenced the political as well as the religious history of Greece. We know what buildings stood there and can reconstruct them with a fair degree of accuracy. Some of them, such as the Temple of Apollo, the theatre, and the famous circular building called the *tholos*, are familiar to all who are interested in Greek architecture. But how was this complex used? What was its great significance for the ancient Greeks and why did they feel so drawn to Delphi? And how do the stories of the Delphic oracle, so often mentioned by ancient writers, fit in with the architectural remains?

The home of the oracle

Even today, most people who have heard of Delphi have also heard of the oracle. In ancient times, people came from all over the Greek world to consult the oracle, and to be given advice about the future. The replies were usually couched in some form of riddle; or, if they seemed simple and straightforward, had an uncanny way of backfiring on the recipient. One of the best known examples was the hidden warning given to Croesus. He was told that if he went to war with the Persians he would destroy a great power; little did he suspect that it was his own great power that he would put in jeopardy.

The origins of the oracle go back to the most distant times. Tradition has it that Delphos, the hero of Delphi, taught how to make predictions from entrails. Another local hero, Parnassos, after whom the mountain is named, made predictions from the flight of birds. The drawing of lots or pebbles was another ancient method of divination – the myths speak of a group of women called the Thriai, a word also used for the stones used in divination.

But amongst all these methods of foretelling the future, one in particular stood out at Delphi. Since the site was sacred to Apollo, himself the god of divination, it was natural that the chief voice of the oracle should be his own. He spoke through a female intermediary called the Pythia. In early times she was a young virgin. Later on a woman more advanced in years was chosen, but she still wore the clothes of a young girl to symbolize the fact that, on being selected, she would lead a pure life, leaving behind any family she might have to devote herself entirely to the work of the oracle.

The Pythia worked according to a well established ritual. Before she began, a goat would be brought for sacrifice to Apollo. It would be sprinkled with cold water and, if it shivered, this was taken as a sign that Apollo consented to give voice to his oracle through the Pythia. Meanwhile, the Pythia would cleanse herself by bathing at a sacred spring and would burn a fire of laurel leaves, immersing herself in the purifying smoke. After the sacrifice and the cleansing ritual were complete, the woman would sit behind a screen on Apollo's three-legged throne. It is not known for certain where this took place, but one of the innermost corners of the Temple of Apollo is the most likely location. The questioner, who would sacrifice an animal to Apollo before the proceedings could begin, posed his question to one of Apollo's priests. He then waited in one corner of the temple while the Pythia fell into a trance and started to utter messages from the god in a series of cries. These noises were not comprehensible to the person who asked the question. They had to be interpreted by the priests of Apollo, who wrote down their interpretation in verse and handed it to the questioner – who would then be left to make what he could of the often mysterious message.

Enigmatic though the replies of the oracle were, its fame grew far and wide, and people came to Delphi in large numbers to consult it and to pay homage to Apollo. Those who are supposed to have consulted the Delphic oracle range from Oedipus and Agamemnon to Philip of Macedon and Alexander the Great. As the oracle became more famous, Delphi

The first priestesses of the oracle of Delphi were probably young women, although later in the history of the sanctuary older women took over the role. The figure behind is pouring a libation to the god Apollo.

Past statues and the treasuries of the various Greek city states, the sacred way wound up to the temple of Apollo, which dominated the sanctuary. With its hillside setting, it was a place of great drama.

The sanctuary of Delphi 375 BC

grew into a centre for pilgrimage. While originally the oracle only performed once a year, on the birthday of Apollo, divinations later took place every month in spring, summer, and autumn. By the time ancient Greek civilization reached its peak in the sixth century BC, the sanctuary of Apollo at Delphi was one of the most popular pilgrimage places in Greece. There was a setback in 546 BC when the temple was damaged by fire. But a new temple was built and the fame of Delphi continued unabated.

At the centre of the world

There was another myth which set Delphi aside from other Greek religious sites. This is the story of how Zeus wanted to find the centre of the world. He had two eagles released at the same moment from the western and eastern ends of the earth. They flew towards each other at equal speed and the place where they met was the centre of the world. They met at Delphi. In the fourth century BC,

1. TEMPLE OF APOLLO
2. THEATRE
3. STOA
4. ATHENIAN TREASURY

the famous navel stone (called the *omphalos*) was set up there, flanked by two eagles, to commemorate this fact.

This story points to the unique importance of Delphi for the Greeks. But it obscures another fact. Navel stones had been a feature of religion in the Aegean long before classical times – many have been found, including three at Delphi itself. The presence of an omphalos at Delphi therefore suggests that it is a religious site of the greatest antiquity. No doubt drawn to Delphi because of its ready supply of spring water and the great beauty of the place, the earliest priests practised cults of which we have no knowledge. But their symbol, the circular omphalos stone, was borrowed by the classical Greeks and adapted to their own myths, so that we can glimpse the earlier religion faintly through them.

And at the centre of Greece

What sort of questions did the oracle answer? Those about which we know most were religious and political questions. On religious matters, the oracle's response was usually interpreted conservatively by the priests. The best way to worship might be described by them as 'according to the custom of the city' or 'according to ancestral custom'; above all, it was according to the gods of Mount Olympus (especially Apollo, of course), along with local gods and Dionysus. Dionysus – a god traditionally worshipped in an orgiastic frenzy – seems an odd choice for the conservative priests of Delphi. And yet the frenzy of Dionysus must not have been unlike the whirling trances of the Pythia. In any case, the Delphic priests tamed the wild god's cult so that it did not clash with the gentler cult of Apollo. So in the three winter months when the oracle did not perform, the cult of Apollo gave way to that of Dionysus at Delphi.

Delphi, however, was not only a religious centre. The sanctuary was a centre in another sense. The advice of the oracle was not sought only on personal matters, but also on political ones. Many of the pronouncements of the oracle suggest that Apollo, or at least his priests, showed a well-tuned – if again somewhat conservative – political sense that made them a valued source of information.

This political advice was especially important because at the time when Delphi started to become a popular religious centre Greece was expanding politically. Many of the Greek city states were starting to set up colonies, both to expand their influence and to ease the pressure put on native lands by a rising population. Leaders came to Delphi to consult the oracle about where to colonize.

So it came about that representatives of most of the Greek city states would visit Delphi regularly. The sanctuary became an important meeting-place for people from all over Greece. Many cities set up treasuries at Delphi. These are the buildings, looking rather like small temples, that line the sacred way up the hill to the great Temple of Apollo itself. Here people from the various cities (Athens, Thebes, Corinth, and many other places had treasuries here) could make offerings to the god. The treasuries were magnificent buildings. Although quite small, many were adorned with freestanding sculptures and carved reliefs of great quality. The treasury of the Siphnians (the people of the island of Siphnos, one of the richest Greek islands, with ample reserves of gold), is a good example. It bore friezes showing scenes from the Trojan War, the Judgement of Paris, and the Gigantomachia – the battle of the gods and the giants. The quality of the work has been compared to that of the Parthenon frieze.

Carving from the Siphnian treasury

Indeed the sculpture of Delphi as a whole was of high quality, and much of it has survived. A great deal of the ancient Greek carving we now have comes from Delphi. In addition to the carvings on the treasuries and the Temple of Apollo, there was the great 15 metres (50 feet) statue of Apollo on the temple terrace. This is described by ancient writers as gold (though we do not know whether this description refers to the colour or the actual material). It was paid for by a fine levied on the Phokians as a punishment for using items stored in the treasuries to pay mercenaries. The most famous work of art from Delphi that has survived is the bronze charioteer.

Apollo's sanctuary

The sanctuary itself, the repository of all these riches, lay within a walled enclosure on the hillside. The main entrance was at the bottom of the hill, from where a winding path or sacred way took the pilgrim up past the treasuries of the various Greek city states to the Temple of Apollo itself. The visitor's first impression would have been a lasting one. The great temple with its Doric columns loomed ahead, surrounded by statues. But the entrance to the sanctuary was equally impressive. To the right as one entered was a statue of a bull on a tall pedestal. This was dedicated to Apollo by the Korkyraians in *c.*480 BC. To the left was a large group of human figures dedicated by the Athenians in *c.*460 BC, after their victory over the Persians at the Battle of Marathon. Nearby was the wooden horse of Argos, set up in 414 BC to celebrate an Argive victory over the Spartans. Other statues, dedicated by the Argives, Spartans, and other groups also lined the sacred way near the entrance. Further along the path were niches, designed to hold offerings, and further along still, as the path began to wind back on itself to take the ascent of the hill more gradually, were the treasuries themselves, small well decorated buildings with friezes indicating their patrons' wealth and commitment to the sanctuary.

Having passed the treasuries, the visitor would be face to face with the stone podium upon which Apollo's temple stood. It too was surrounded with statuary, including numerous statues of Apollo, again dedicated to the god by the representatives of the different Greek city states. The temple itself was rebuilt three times. The structure about which we know most is the last temple to be built on the site – the rebuilding of the fourth century BC. Surrounded by fluted Doric columns, it was quite a simple building architecturally. Its beauty came from its fine proportions and the sculpture on its two pediments, the triangular panels above the columns at either end of the temple. The eastern

Sphinx of the Naxians

relief showed the arrival of Apollo at Delphi, accompanied on his chariot by his sister, Artemis, and their mother, Leto. The western pediment portrayed the setting of the sun and the other important god of Delphi, Dionysus. Behind the temple was a stout retaining wall, preventing landslides and protecting the temple from falling rocks from the hill above.

Running the sanctuary

Such riches, and such a complex of treasuries from all over the Greek world, required a formal system of administration. The local people looked after the everyday affairs of the sanctuary, but, as Delphi was a meeting place for people from all over Greece, it was felt that a council with wider-ranging roots was needed to oversee the complex. Thus it was that the council, whose members were referred to as the 'Amphiktyons' or 'dwellers around', became responsible for looking after the sanctuary. Originally this council had nothing to do with Delphi – it had first been set up to administer the Temple of Demeter at Thermopylae. Its membership included men from central Greece who were selected by race rather than according to the city they came from.

The Amphiktyons thus represented another way in which the unity of Greece was expressed at Delphi: the ancient tribes who occupied the area we now call Greece were brought together in their council and could meet and discuss their affairs. Achaians and Dorians, Ionians and Thessalians could join together to shape the destiny of Greece as a whole. In bringing all these racial elements together, the Amphiktyons clearly wielded great power. The result of this for Delphi was that the sanctuary was declared independent of Phokia, the area in which it stood, so that it at last achieved a true autonomy worthy of its importance to the surrounding states.

We have inherited additional evidence of how the sanctuary was run in the shape of fourth century accounts. We also know that the council issued coins and benefited from a good exchange rate against currencies like the drachma during this time

It was also during this century that the resources of the administration were stretched to the full when the temple was rebuilt once more. We learn from surviving inscriptions how each part of the project was put out to tender, and how money had to be raised from the city states. There was also the physical effort of transporting tons of stone up the steep hill on which Delphi stands. The town of Delphi was never large and there would not have been an unlimited supply of labour. Once again Delphi stands testimony to the ability of the Greek states to cooperate and pool their resources.

An athletic attraction

By this time, there was another attraction which probably drew as many people to Delphi as the oracle itself – the Pythian Games. These competitions have a long history – in fact they started as an integral part of the festival that was held in celebration of Apollo. But during the sixth century BC they were reorganized. The Amphiktyons took over responsibility for the games and, in addition to the artistic competitions that had formed the backbone of the games in the past (singing, recitations, drama, and instrumental music), athletic events were incorporated. These ranged from foot races, held in a stadium built above the sanctuary, to chariot races in a hippodrome on the plain below. The games were also held more often and grew in popularity. And they were held long after the time when classical Greek civilization held sway. As late as AD 66, the Roman emperor Nero visited the Pythian Games, when he directed that many of the statues still standing at Delphi should be taken to Rome. The games were second only to the Olympics.

It was the Pythian Games that inspired Delphi's most celebrated piece of sculpture. The Charioteer, a magnificent bronze figure who was originally portrayed with a four-horse chariot, was dedicated by a tyrant of Gela called Polyzalos, victor at the Pythian Games in *c*.478 BC. A young man about 1.8 metres (6 feet) tall, the charioteer holds the reins of the horses in his right hand. He wears a charioteer's robe (clasped tightly under the armpits to stop the cloth fluttering too much when the wearer was moving at speed). Around his head is the victor's wreath.

Delphi in later years

Although its importance was self-evident, Delphi's history did not run smoothly. Even in the sixth century BC, when Delphi's influence and importance were at their height, there was a sacred war between rival local factions. There was more fighting during the conflicts between Athens and Sparta in the 440s, and further fighting in the 350s. The sanctuary of Apollo did not escape unscathed but, as we have seen, rebuilding got efficiently underway after 373 BC.

The fame of the sanctuary continued during the Hellenistic and Roman periods, and offerings continued to be made. One that has survived is a fine stone statue of a philosopher in the style of that of *c*.250 BC, another is a portrait head that may represent Flaminius, a Roman general of the second century BC.

So people still came to Delphi. They consulted the oracle and made their offerings. But the priests of Apollo did not exert their old influence. As political power began to be transferred much more as a result of military conquest, the sanctuary lost its role as a unifying force.

And yet Delphi remained magnificent. Even after Nero's visit when so many statues were sent to Rome, there were still enough to take away the breath of Pausanias, when he wrote his *Guide to Greece* in the second century AD. It was only when the Roman Empire became Christianized, and the emperor Constantine once more plundered the site, that Delphi began to fall into disrepair, and began to seem irrelevant to the affairs of the Roman world. Until then the fame of the site, its setting, the splendour of its buildings, the pronouncements of the oracle, and the competitions of the Pythian Games continued to give the place a magnetism for visitors – a quality which it has retained to this day.

EPIDAUROS

Site of the best preserved Greek theatre, and sanctuary of Asklepios, the god of healing

On the northern side of the Argive peninsula, 30 kilometres (19 miles) away from Corinth and 50 kilometres (31 miles) from Athens, lies Epidauros. This modest town was not one of the major Greek cities, but it was independent and it had a particular attraction that drew people from far and wide – the sanctuary of the god of healing, Asklepios. Today, we look to the town for a different reason – as well as the ruins of the sanctuary, it contains the best preserved theatre of ancient Greece, and so provides a setting in which we can imagine the performance of the plays that we have inherited from the period.

The cult of the healer

Epidauros seems to have begun as a centre of the cult of Meleatas, a local hero who was originally worshipped in his own right, but whose cult was eventually absorbed into that of Apollo. Asklepios was thought to have been the son of Apollo and the mortal Koronis; he was therefore a mortal himself, although, like Herakles, he was a hero who was eventually deified for his deeds on earth. It may be that this is more than a mere fiction. It is not impossible that there was a real man called Asklepios who was a healer, and whose fame led to his being made into a god after his death and to his being linked with the great god Apollo. Or it may be that Asklepios' origins lie purely in the realm of myth. The myths surrounding him are certainly potent.

Asklepios was a deity of the underworld, but he also had important powers of regeneration. His symbol was the serpent, which the Greeks saw as living both above and below ground; they also believed that the serpent had the power to promote the wellbeing of people via its underworld connections and its knowledge of plants, especially medicinal herbs – hence Asklepios' healing abilities. And these were supposed to be considerable. He was reputed to have healed otherwise incurable diseases, and to have raised people from the dead. Often, simply being ritually cleansed and spending a night in the sanctuary at Epidauros was enough to make people well.

The powerful cults of Meleatas, Apollo, and Asklepios had a long history at Epidauros. Meleatas was worshipped from the eighth century BC. The cult of Apollo–Meleatas was still in existence in the fourth century BC. The worship of Asklepios probably started in the fifth century BC. So the cult was functioning long before the people of Epidauros built their magnificent sanctuary to house it.

By the beginning of the fifth century BC quite an elaborate festival had grown up to celebrate the cult. It was carefully timed in late April or early May, just after the festival of Poseidon on the Isthmus of Corinth. This meant that people who attended the earlier festival could easily go to Epidauros without taking up too much extra time or energy. And so it was that, in addition to the steady stream of people who came as individuals to Epidauros to have their illnesses cured and to pay homage to Asklepios, large numbers of people turned up from all over Greece for the annual festival.

We do not know for sure exactly what they did at the festival. There would probably have been ritual cleansings, the sacrifice of animals, and elaborate banquets. But we do know that there were contests, both athletic and artistic. The athletic contests included all-in wrestling, and the artistic contests would have involved singing, dancing, and theatre.

The cult centre

The burgeoning cult required buildings to match its popularity. In the fourth century BC this need was met with a great new temple. Its size shows that this was an important cult – even the famous sanctuary of Zeus at Olympia had no temple at all until the fifth century. It was built largely of local limestone, although the Doric columns were made of stone from Corinth and, like the other buildings at Epidauros, it had terracotta roof tiles. Its triangular pediments were decorated with relief carvings by a local sculptor, Timotheos, but the large statue of the god inside, embellished with gold and ivory, was by the artist Thrasymedes, who came from Paros. The god was seated on a throne, holding a sceptre, with a dog at his feet. At least one serpent would also have been incorporated into the statue.

Amongst the other buildings in the sanctuary were a hostel where visitors

The muse of tragedy would have been a presiding deity of any Greek theatre. Here she is seen with a variety of terracotta masks – from the dignified to the grotesque.

With a seating capacity of about 14,000, the theatre at Epidauros was able to accommodate people who came from far and wide. We do not know for sure what the building behind the stage looked like – there were probably three doors and a strong crane for 'flying' props, and occasionally actors, on to the playing area.

The theatre of Epidauros 300 BC

could be accommodated (the complex was some distance from the town of Epidauros). There was also a building called the *abaton*. This was used in the healing process; after a ritual cleansing the sick would spend the night in the abaton and the god would appear to them in a dream to suggest the appropriate treatment for their ills.

The oddest building in the sanctuary is the circular *thymele*, surrounded by columns and containing a stone maze. Its use is unknown. It may have been a place where sacred snakes were kept; it may mark the burial place of Asklepios; it may have had some ritual purpose, perhaps the place where sacrifices were made to the god.

The construction of these buildings and their upkeep was in the control of a panel of four local citizens and the priest of Asklepios. Some of their inscriptions record the details of the construction projects. From them, for example, we learn that the architect of the temple was called Theodotos. For designing the temple and supervising the building work he was paid 353 drachmas a year during the four or so years of the temple's construction.

The theatre

Just outside the main area of the sanctuary stands the theatre, the most celebrated to have survived from the ancient world. It was likely to have been connected with the sanctuary, but we do not know what plays were performed there. Archaeologists are handicapped as all the play texts that have survived from ancient Greece began life in Athens; but the theatre of Dionysus at Athens is in a poorer state of repair than that of Epidauros. So if we are to try to imagine the performances at Epidauros we have to

take our evidence from Athenian texts as well as Epidaurian stones.

But we can at least begin with the stones. It is not certain who the architect was. The writer Pausanias, in his *Guide to Greece*, refers to Polykleitos, the architect of the thymele. He was working on the site around 360 BC. But the modern scholars von Gerkan and Muller–Wiener, authorities on the theatre, prefer a later date, because of the style of the decorative mouldings and because of the probable influence on the theatre's design of the theatre of Dionysus at Athens. They therefore prefer a time nearer the beginning of the third century BC. Dating the theatre is important because it shows that the cult of Asklepios was already well established when it was built. There would already have been a strong tradition of dramatic art at Epidauros (not to mention the tradition that existed at Athens) to influence the building of the theatre.

The theatre comprised three main parts: the *theatron*, the large fan-shaped tiered area for the audience; the *orchestra*, the flat circular area in front of the theatron where the action took place; and the *skene*, the building behind the orchestra that acted as a backdrop and a place for the actors to prepare for their entrances.

Asklepios, god of healing

When looking at the empty theatre, it is the great scoop of the theatron that dominates the site. With a seating capacity of almost 14,000 it was vast, but its shape ensured good acoustics and uninterrupted sightlines. Radial staircases and a horizontal passage about two thirds of the way up the seating rake meant that the audience could get to and from the wooden seats, built on to the stone tiers, with the greatest of ease. The important members of the audience, such as the priests and officials who judged the dramatic competitions, sat in the front row, in seats with stone backs. Citizens and visitors to the sanctuary could take up the other seats. The great number of seats meant that the population of Epidauros itself would hardly have filled the theatre. Clearly, visitors to the sanctuary of Asklepios made up the majority of the audience and no doubt the theatre would be full during festival times.

At the bottom of the sloping theatron was the orchestra. This word means 'dancing place', recalling the fact that cult dances would have been performed here as well as plays. In fact the circular shape of the orchestra might have derived from ancient dance forms, the ring-dances performed in honour of the gods and the dithyramb (a combination of dance and choric hymn), in which the dramatic form of tragedy is said to have its origins. At the centre of the orchestra there was an altar, pointing to the fact that the performance of dithyrambs and dramas was originally part of an act of worship.

Beyond the orchestra, along the edge of the theatre not occupied by places for spectators, was perhaps the most mysterious part of the building – the skene. This was a long rectangular structure, probably built of wood on stone foundations. It provided a back wall for the stage and a place to store props and stage machinery. It also had a number of doors (probably three) through which the actors could enter. The front of the skene could be painted with a backdrop or, more likely, movable panels of scenery could be propped up in front of it. The more the plays developed, with the addition of more actors and the provision of special effects such as the crane-like flying machine implied by some Athenian sources, the more important the skene must have become. And yet we do not know exactly what this central feature of the theatre looked like.

The view from the stalls

So much for the fabric of the theatre building. What would an actual performance have looked like? To answer this question we have to look at the great dramas produced at the theatre of Dionysus in Athens. To modern eyes, one of the least familiar things about these performances would be that in any particular play two groups of people, the actors and the chorus, would appear on stage and would look and act quite differently from one another.

The chorus, whether dancing or singing, formed an important part of the drama. One red-figure vase in the Antikenmuseum, Basle, gives us an idea of what the members of a tragic chorus looked like in 500–490 BC. They wear short tunics with geometrical motifs and masks that cover their heads (these masks have artificial hair as well as covering the face). The six figures are standing in pairs in a conventional pose of grief at a tomb, with their hands outstretched and their knees slightly bent. There would have been another six men on the other side of the tomb, since the early choruses had twelve members. A musician (playing the *aulos* or double flute) would also be present. This was a very early chorus – later ones no doubt acted, dressed, and looked similar, although by the time of Sophocles and Euripides their number had increased to fifteen.

The actors would have looked rather different, whether in tragedy or comedy. Both types of actor would be heavily disguised. Once he stepped out on to the floor of the orchestra, a Greek actor was not thought of as an individual, so his body was well covered. For a tragic actor this meant first of all a mask. In the early days of the Greek theatre at least, this meant a mask that covered the whole head, like that of the chorus members. The facial part of the mask would be flexible and fit quite tightly – the masks were designed to be used by actors who moved around a lot, so the popular idea of a rigid mask is probably inaccurate. But the other well known features of the tragic mask – the stylized hair, eyebrows, eyes, and gaping mouth – had all evolved by the time the theatre at Epidauros was built.

Some of the other parts of the costume also furthered the tragic actor's disguise. He wore garments with long sleeves and on his feet he wore soft, broad-fitting boots with toes ending in a beak-shaped tip. These boots, called *kothornoi*, covered the legs and feet, reinforcing the disguise yet again, and also imposed a different gait on the actor.

Comic actors wore rather different clothes. At the time of the 'Old Comedy' of Aristophanes (*c*.450–*c*.388 BC) they had costumes that were meant to act like a false skins. Their bellies and bottoms were padded, and male characters bore large artificial penises on the outsides of their costumes. This grotesque tradition relates to the fact that comedy derives from the 'phallus songs' sung at festivals of Dionysus in rural areas. Another feature of Old Comedy – choruses of creatures such as birds, frogs and wasps, no doubt added colour and variety to the costumes to be seen on the comic stage. In the 'New Comedy' of dramatists like Menander (342–292 BC), more conventional costumes were used, with the addition of long sleeves.

The costumes, especially the masks and the bold, stylized costumes of Old Comedy, would have made the actors stand out. And in a theatre as large as the one at Epidauros this was essential. The size of the theatre made the actors look very small from the back rows of seats. The set designers probably also used scenery to give a sympathetic background to the action. Here the front wall of the skene helped. In a tragedy, for example, it could support a backdrop with an architectural painting – and the doors built into the skene could be incorporated into this so that the actors could enter through the backdrop.

This was not all that the audience had to look at. Characters who were immobile for some reason, such as the 'bound' Prometheus, had to be wheeled on to the stage. This was achieved with a device called the *ekkyklema*, which was probably some form of platform on wheels. In addition there may have been some sort of crane for 'flying' characters on to the stage. The theatre at Athens certainly needed such a device to stage several scenes in the tragedies of Euripides, not to mention parodies of such scenes in Aristophanes' comedies. It would be surprising if Epidauros did not have a crane too. The machine consisted of an upright, which was probably sunk some way into the foundations of the skene, and a wooden cross-piece pivoted in the centre. There would have been a counterweight on one end of the beam and the other end would be able to swing out some distance into the space above the orchestra. It was a large, if simple, piece of machinery.

Plays and festivals

What sort of plays would people have seen here? By the time that the theatre at Epidauros was constructed, the Old Comedy of Aristophanes, with its grotesque costumes, satirical plots, parodies, and topical comment, had given way to New Comedy. This sort of writing is known to us from the comedies of Menander, which were produced in Athens between *c*.323 and *c*.263 BC. They feature typical incidents in the lives of well-to-do people, realistically portrayed, in more naturalistic costumes. Tragedy, too, had passed from the ritualistic dramas of Aeschylus to the more naturalistic plays of Euripides. But it was still a drama of large gestures, strong characters, and brilliant language. It was worthy of its imposing setting, as the setting was worthy of the plays.

The audience did not simply come to the theatre to be entertained. The theatre began as a part of religious ritual.

Black figure vase

At Athens, it was part of the festival of Dionysus. At Epidauros it no doubt had its origins in the cult of Dionysus, but would also be an adjunct to the festival of the healer god Asklepios. So theatre was above all a very spiritual experience for the people who attended. One should not imagine that there was anything solemn about this religious experience, especially where a god such as Dionysus was concerned. In particular, an extra thrill was added to Greek theatrical events because they were competitive. At each festival a number of dramatists would apply to an official for permission to compete with a fixed number of plays. If the writer was accepted, the official would appoint someone to act as backer, to finance the productions, providing actors, costumes, and props. To be successful, the backer would need to be both wealthy and sympathetic to the needs of the plays he was backing. The production would then be staged in front of the officials who would award the prize (usually a symbolic prize, such as a laurel wreath) to the playwright whom they thought most successful.

The decline of the sanctuary

With the coming of Christianity, the cult of Asklepios was superseded. Interestingly, the myth of Asklepios has parallels with the story of Christ: his parents were a god and a mortal woman; he was a healer; he brought about miraculous cures and raised people from the dead; he died but was given divine status after his death. Such similarities must have worried the Christians; they may even have led to the deliberate destruction of the cult centre.

As for the theatre, it fell into disuse, but fate was kinder to its stones. The tiered theatron filled up with earth. Whether this was due to a landslide, or whether it happened gradually over many years we do not know. But the covering preserved the tiers of the auditorium on the hillside which were unearthed by nineteenth-century archaeologists, to stand as our best surviving example of an ancient Greek theatre, and to resound to the voices of twentieth century actors recreating the dramas of classical Greece.

RHODES

Home of the Colossus, the most mysterious of the Seven Wonders of the World

Of the Seven Wonders of the World, the Colossus of Rhodes is the most mysterious. We do not know exactly where it stood, quite what it looked like, or how it was built. But, like its six counterparts around the world, such a body of myths and allusions have sprung up about it that it is difficult to disentangle them from what we know of the reality. What is more, the Colossus was the most short-lived of all the Wonders. It lasted a mere half-century before being brought down in an earthquake, which meant that comparatively few ancient writers actually saw it. Fortunately a few people did write down their impressions, so we are able to form some picture of the story of the Colossus and what it looked like.

The community of Rhodes

The island of Rhodes lies in the northern Mediterranean, off what is now southeastern Turkey, and has an area of about 1,110 square kilometres (420 square miles). On being settled by Dorian Greeks it split into three separate city states that were successful enough to start colonies of their own. They were members of the Athenian confederacy and had democratic constitutions. In 407 BC, however, they broke away from Athens and joined together to form a joint Rhodian state with a new capital in the north of the island, also called Rhodes.

The new Rhodian state was successful. The island was well suited to profit from sea trade, being well placed between Egypt, Cyprus, and the Aegean. By the third century BC, Rhodes was the most prosperous of all the Greek states. The city of Rhodes reflected this wealth. It was built to a classical plan featuring a grid of streets. With a population of over 60,000 it showed how successful the state of Rhodes had quickly become.

Another feature of the city that bore out this prosperity were the harbours. The site was well chosen for moorings since the coast is sheltered by several bars that project hundreds of metres into the sea. There were harbours for military ships (as well as for trading vessels) since Rhodes had established itself as a formidable police force against piracy – the Rhodians jealously guarded the trade that gave them their riches.

But the Rhodians did not have it all their own way. They suffered conquest by Mausolus, king of Caria (he came from Halicarnassus and his mausoleum was another of the Seven Wonders). Then they were conquered by the Persians, in whose power they remained until Alexander the Great once more conquered the island in 340 BC. When Alexander died the Rhodians were given their independence, but they kept their close links with Alexandria, supplying the Alexandrians with goods from the east and distributing cargo from Egypt around the Mediterranean. Once more, the island was rich and powerful. Their success seemed assured when they allied with the Alexandrian king Ptolemy and fought victoriously against Antigonus of Macedonia. The victory strengthened their links with Egypt and seemed to make their trade even more secure. But Antigonus decided to put pressure on Rhodes. He asked them to join him in battle against Ptolemy and, when they refused, sent his son Demetrius to besiege the city.

Demetrius, renowned in battle and a specialist in siege warfare, was confident. He had some 40,000 soldiers, numerous workmen, and elaborate siege engines with which to take the city. But the Rhodians resisted with success. They won their freedom and allied with Antigonus against everyone except the Egyptian Ptolemy. This was the triumph that inspired the building of the Colossus of Rhodes.

In honour of Helios

The god that the Rhodians chose to commemorate their victory was Helios, the Greek sun-god. To anyone familiar with Greek mythology this might seem an odd choice – they could have selected one of the more celebrated gods, such as Zeus or

No one knows quite what the Colossus looked like. It might have been an archaic-looking statue like this, or a more classical figure. But whatever its appearance, it would have required extensive scaffolding to support it while it was being built.

Apollo. The sun-god was dismissed by one of Plato's characters as a god of the barbarians, and other Greek writers took a similar view. But Helios, although he was not accorded great sanctuaries like that to Apollo at Delphi, was prominent in Greek popular religion, and he was especially dear to the people of Rhodes.

But for the Rhodians, Helios was the patron god of their three states of Lindos, Ialysos, and Kameiros; indeed these three states are actually named after the three sons of Helios. The cult of Helios was thus an obvious way of uniting the island. It is not surprising, therefore, that the priesthood of Helios was a state appointment, nor that the city of Rhodes organized games in his honour complete with religious processions and sacrifices. Some texts give recommendations for these sacrifices. Goats and kids, cows and calves, were regularly sacrificed to Helios, and there is one odd record of a team of horses being driven into the sea in honour of the god.

What is more, the people from mainland Greece were not so snobbish about these festivals as they might have been. Many of the Greek city states sent representatives to the games at Rhodes, and such an action was a recognition that the city was an important centre recognized throughout the Greek world. So a great statue of Helios was a natural choice for the Rhodians. Standing somewhere near the waterfront it would signal to all comers the importance and unity of the island, the pride of the people in their local god, and the steadfastness with which they withstood the siege of their city.

The mysteries of the Colossus

For all its fame, we know very little about the Colossus of Rhodes. Ancient writers tell us that it was a huge statue of Helios about 33 metres (110 feet) high, and that it took about twelve years to build. They do not say exactly where it stood or quite what it looked like. And we are not helped by the short life of the statue. A mere fifty-six years after it was built it was brought down by an earthquake.

Many of the more recent descriptions of the Colossus are therefore based on little more than the fertile imaginations of their authors. For example, the strong tradition that the legs of the statue bestrode the entrance to the harbour so that ships would have to pass beneath them, simply cannot be true. The bronze-workers of Rhodes, for all their skill, could not have produced such a strong structure. And in any case, the harbour entrance was about 400 metres (1300 feet) across. The figure of Helios is more likely to have had its feet planted firmly together.

Building the Colossus

Fortunately we are on firmer ground when it comes to how the statue was built. One account, by the writer Philo of Byzantium, devotes some space to how the Colossus was put together. It appears to have been done by casting individual sections, which were then bolted together and reinforced with iron struts. The artist began by putting up a solid platform of white marble on which the Colossus was to stand. Then the feet were produced in position, followed by the legs, and so on, up the statue. In other words, if we are to believe Philo's account, each section was actually cast in its final place. This meant that, as each new part was cast and the statue rose higher above the ground, the lower sections would be supported by an ever-increasing mound of earth or mass of scaffolding.

Iron bars and blocks of stone were used to reinforce the Colossus from within, giving the structure the added strength that came from diagonal struts and the extra stability resulting from additional weight, especially in the lower portions. Such a method of working was revolutionary. The man who achieved it, the sculptor Chares of Lindos, must have been an inventor of considerable skill as well as a notable artist. The only comparable structure is the modern Statue of Liberty in New York harbour, although in the case of the American statue the parts were built separately before being fastened in place.

The method of casting in position that Chares is said to have used would have imposed conditions on the shape and appearance of the statue. As well as it being very unlikely that the Colossus bestrode the harbour, its arms were probably not stretched out at right-angles to its body. One arm may have been stretched vertically, and it may well have held a torch to symbolize the light of the sun. The other arm was probably held by the figure's side. The resulting column-like shape would not have been too difficult to cast or to support during the construction process. It would also have been fairly stable when finished – earthquakes permitting.

The site of the statue

None of the ancient writers tell us exactly where the Colossus was. The harbour entrance remains a strong contender, even though its legs could not have spanned the channel. This would have been the natural place for the people of Rhodes to express their pride and identity – just where visitors arriving in their ships would see it. Later on it became traditional to place great statues at harbour mouths – a fashion whose origin can be traced to the Colossus of Rhodes.

The writer Reynold Higgins, author of the most recent account of the Colossus, makes two objections to a harbour site. First, that the Rhodians would not have wasted such a valuable piece of land by leaving its ruins there after it had toppled; second, that according to one ancient writer, many houses were knocked down by the Colossus when it fell. Higgins therefore proposes a site in the Street of the Knights in Rhodes, where the temple of Helios stood in ancient times. This, he argues, would have been a likely spot for the Rhodians to have commemorated their special god. There can be no definitive conclusion about this. The harbour site may well have been regarded as sacred enough for the ruins to have been left on the valuable waterside land. The reference to houses being demolished seems odder, but may be a misunderstanding on the part of the ancient writer since houses were probably laid low in the earthquake. So a harbour site for the Colossus remains a possibility.

The fall

The earthquake came in about 226 BC. Its result was described by the geographer Strabo who tells us that the statue broke at the knees – the head, torso and thighs lay where they fell. Strabo also says that the Rhodians consulted an oracle who forbade them to re-erect the Colossus – another reason for leaving its remains on the waterside. Later, when the influence of the oracle had waned, various people tried to restore it. But the most skilled engineers of Greece and Egypt failed in the attempt. During the Roman period, when Rhodes was part of the empire, the city kept its beauty, although it lost its political influence. The ruins of the Colossus were allowed to remain as testimony to the

The position of the Colossus in the elegant city of Rhodes is as mysterious as its actual appearance. But it could not have 'bestrode' the harbour. Perhaps it stood on one of the jetties, or on its own island, as here.

former greatness of the city.

Perhaps the importance of the Colossus was emphasized by the scholars who congregated on the island in Roman times, since it became something of an academic community. The stoic philosopher Panaetius and the historian, scientist, and philosopher Posidonius (one of the most influential scholars of the ancient world) were the island's two greatest academics. Men such as these would have been as well aware of the significance of the statue as the ordinary inhabitants would have been of its extraordinary size. By AD 672, when Arabic peoples took control of Rhodes, the remains had little or no meaning for the island's leaders or its other inhabitants. They were content to sell off the metal for scrap, leaving the Colossus of Rhodes to legend.

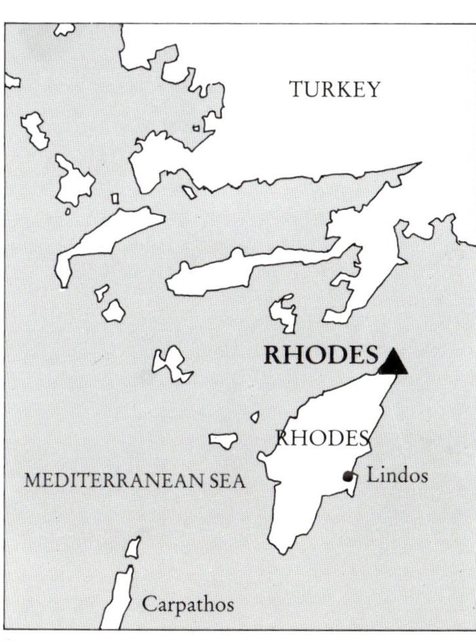

HAGIA SOPHIA

The great church of Emperor Justinian at Constantinople

The city of Byzantium occupied a superb position on the Golden Horn in what is now Turkey, at the junction of Europe and Asia. Surrounded by water on three sides (the Golden Horn, the Sea of Marmara, and the Bosphorus), it was well placed to defend itself. The Romans took control in AD 196, but the city was to come into its own later. In the fourth century AD Rome was under threat from various European peoples – the Goths, the Franks, and the Alemanni. Constantine, who was emperor between AD 307 and 337, saw the potential of Byzantium to become the empire's second capital. This it became in 330 when its name was changed to Constantinople. The name Byzantium was reserved for the group of provinces ruled from the city.

In AD 395 the Roman empire split into two parts. Rome itself continued to be beset by 'barbarians' and fell to the Visigoths in 410. From then on the Byzantine Empire, ruled from Constantinople, took up the heritage of classical civilization.

One of the most illustrious Byzantine emperors was Justinian (AD 527–565). His reign was marked by many achievements, for some of which the credit must be shared with his wife, the empress Theodora, a woman of exceptionally strong character and influence. Justinian was a renowned military leader, defending his frontiers from the Sassanians in the east and from the Goths in Italy and northern Africa. He was also a legal reformer, codifying existing Roman civil law to create an influential body of statutes. But today Justinian is remembered above all for his public buildings, particularly for Hagia Sophia, the great church of the divine wisdom in the centre of Constantinople, a building that struck wonder into the minds of all who saw it, and that was destined to influence Christian and Islamic architecture for centuries to come.

The greatest church of its time, Hagia Sophia typified the coming together of a great individual idea (in this case a vast central space, covered by a magnificent dome) with the various talents of a range of artists and workers (masons, mosaic makers, silversmiths, textile workers) that make a memorable building. But today it takes a leap of the imagination to picture quite what Hagia Sophia would have looked like in Justinian's time. Sure enough, the great dome still stands, the vast space beneath it just as impressive as it was. But the jewels, hangings, and many of the mosaics have disappeared, along with the rituals that originally took place in the church.

The interior of Hagia Sophia was lit mainly from windows high in the balconies and the dome. The light would stream down, reflecting off the mosaics, icons, and decoration in precious metals to create a golden glow. The vast space dwarfed the elaborate religious and imperial processions it was built to contain.

The day of destruction

A church was already on the site at the beginning of Justinian's reign. The emperor Constantine had founded it in AD 360 and, although it had been damaged and repaired, it survived until 15 January 532. This was the day of the notorious Nika riots. The people had assembled in the Hippodrome to support their favourite charioteers. Generally the supporters were divided into two groups, the Blues and the Greens. The two factions had different political colours too, the Blues being more conservative than the more liberal Greens. But on this occasion the two groups found themselves united in opposition to the emperor and in their desire to reduce taxation. So the factions rebelled and swept in mayhem throughout the city, destroying many buildings including the original church of Hagia Sophia.

It was a great test for Justinian who, following a rallying speech from his empress Theodora, was able to quell the riots, bring peace to the city, and carry on his policies very much as he had done. It also gave him the chance to rebuild Hagia Sophia in greater glory than before. Judging by the speed with which the plans were made and the building was constructed, he was probably intending to do this anyway. A great new church would give him the chance to rally the Christian world together around Constantinople as he had managed to rally his own people and suppress the riots.

Building the church

No one had attempted such a large dome before. The calculation of the stresses and strains involved, the placement of the supports, their size and all the curves and angles, required the skill of a mathematician. Justinian had the services of not one mathematician but two, Anthemius of Tralles and Isidorus of Miletus. As

If Justinian's great church gave an ethereal impression from inside, it was nothing if not solid-looking without. Its domes, buttresses, and heavy expanses of masonry give a massive appearance. Even so, the original dome partially gave way and had to be rebuilt to slightly altered specifications. The overall layout, with a central dome surrounded by smaller domes and galleries, had many imitators – both Christian and Islamic.

Hagia Sophia AD 563

well as being master masons both were acknowledged masters of the sciences of geometry and mechanics. In addition to the considerable mechanical problem of supporting the weight of such a structure, they also had to overcome the design problem of moving from the circular dome to a square building.

These problems had to be tackled together. The bulk of the dome's weight was supported on four massive arches, which also defined the square floor space beneath the dome. The triangular spaces between the arches and the base of the dome were filled with masonry which sent the weight down towards the great piers below. These triangles of stonework, called *pendentives*, became the hallmark of buildings that were roofed with domes. To the east and west were smaller, lower, half-domes, and beyond these were yet smaller half-domes. The effect of these smaller domes was rather like buttresses, spreading the weight of the roof further and supporting the structure. Low buttress towers in the church's north and south walls also contributed to this effect.

All these elements were constructed with great speed. Work is thought to have begun in AD 532 and was completed in time for the consecration in 537. This fast progress and the originality of the design has led some

scholars to believe that a rebuilding had been planned before the original church was destroyed. It has also led to much speculation that Justinian himself was closely involved in the planning. The architects would certainly have consulted the emperor over work of such size and originality.

It was a daring plan. Churches in the Roman world had been based on a plan similar to that of a Roman basilica – a long rectangle with the altar at one end. But Justinian's church was to have a centralized plan, much wider and squarer. This was not an entirely new idea. The much smaller church of Saints Sergius and Bacchus in Constantinople had already been built to a similar design. But Hagia Sophia was daring because it was so large, and its central dome was so shallow. This gave a strong outward thrust that meant that it ran the risk of collapse much more than a taller dome. But it probably would have survived if the area had not been prone to earth tremors.

Sadly, in AD 557 an earthquake destroyed part of the dome. Anthemius had died by this time, but Isidorus was still alive to attend to the repair. He made the dome slightly taller – though it is still much shallower than most large domes – and it has survived in this form. Partial rebuildings in the tenth and fourteenth centuries did not involve radical changes in the design, although changes after the Islamic conquest in 1453 have altered the appearance of the church considerably. Minarets were added outside, while the interior furnishings were removed, many mosaics painted over, and large boards containing Islamic texts were put up.

Contemporary reactions

People who saw the church after it had been built could hardly believe their eyes. The historian Procopius, for example, marvelled at the way the dome seemed to have no solid foundation – it seemed to be suspended as if from a golden chain from heaven. He was also impressed by the lighting of the building, the way in which sunlight flooded through the windows to catch the gold of the mosaics and the silver of the screen and altar furnishings – it was as if the most sacred parts of the building were suffused in a divine light. In addition to his admiration of the mystical properties of Hagia Sophia, Procopius was also impressed by the sheer quality of the building's engineering. For all his remarks about golden chains suspended from heaven, he appreciated the elaborately calculated system of supports that actually existed in the building, in particular how each section of the church is supported by the section next to it so that the weight of the dome is transferred gradually to the ground. After the dome had been repaired following the earthquake in AD 557, reactions were similar.

The court official Paulus Silentarius again commented on the dome's apparent lack of support and on the building's mosaics and marbles, beautifully lit by the sun. The awe with which the interior has been greeted ever since has been almost universal. Even Mehmet the Conqueror, invading Constantinople with his janissaries, far from pulling down this great symbol of Byzantine rule and Christianity, stood and stared in silence when he first entered Hagia Sophia.

The decorations

Visitors to Hagia Sophia today, like their predecessors, are impressed by the masterly handling of space in the building. But the church's decorations and fittings – many of which have long vanished – impressed contemporaries even more. Entering the building one would first of all pass through two entrance halls or *narthexes* – tall, narrow rooms running across the width of the building. The first of these was small and plain. But the inner walls of the second were faced with marble panels and roofed with a vault decorated with mosaics featuring geometrical designs, stars and crosses picked out in gold. In Justinian's time this room would have formed a worthy gathering point for imperial processions about to enter the nave. But splendid as it was, it hardly prepared one for the nave itself. Again, the walls and surfaces of the great piers were faced with marble – tall slabs of various colours standing out from a background of lighter marbles. In some places this facing is applied with meticulous attention to detail. Often, a slab of marble was cut in two pieces which were then placed side by side so that their identical grains repeated each other like mirror images. In other places the subtly contrasting colours of the stone were allowed to speak for themselves.

Monogram of Justinian

Higher up, the next decorative achievement at Hagia Sophia was the capitals on top of the columns on either side of the nave. These are carved in an intricate, open-work style which was to become popular in churches throughout the Byzantine empire. It is a style that owes something to the Corinthian capitals of classical architecture, but the carved foliage motifs are repeated so that each capital looks like a veritable vine of leaves, stems and runners. In contrast to Greek and Roman buildings, the carved decoration is often carried up on to the arches themselves, increasing the impression of enthusiasm for the stonecarver's art.

Higher still were the mosaics. Although Hagia Sophia is today famous for its figurative mosaics, these are later in date than the original building. From the evidence that survives, many of the original mosaics, like those in the narthex, would have been abstract or symbolic designs. They were made of tiny sections called *tesserae*. When Hagia Sophia was first built the tesserae were usually small pieces of glass. Colour was added by attaching gold leaf or other coloured substances to the back before the tesserae were fixed in place. This combination of gold and glass gave the mosaics their ability to catch and reflect the light, a quality that explains the otherworldly feel of the building. As Paulus Silentarius put it, the tessarae poured 'golden rays in an abundant stream striking men's eyes with irresistible force'.

None of the early writers on Hagia Sophia specifically mention figural mosaics. This is surprising since many contemporary churches contained them. But even at the centre of the dome, where one might expect to see the figure of Christ, Paulus reports that there was a simple cross.

The fittings

The high altar was the focal point of the church and it was surrounded by canopies and fittings of unparalleled richness. In the nave, in front of the sanctuary, was the ambo. This was a pulpit-like platform, approached by two sets of stairs, surrounded by a circular open screen. Its columns had gilded capitals and supported an architrave that could carry lamps and crosses. There was room enough inside the circular screen for a choir.

Behind the screen was a raised walkway (the *solea*), which led to the chancel screen. This open, three-sided screen had columns, parapets, and architraves that were covered in silver. Lamps above the architrave shone down and reflected on the silver, picking out the various designs on the silver below – the monograms of Justinian and Theodora, images of Christ and the Virgin, angels, prophets, and saints. It must have been a glittering array but, because the parapet of the screen was very low, it did not obscure the altar beyond. Rather, it provided a rich frame for the altar and the ceremonies that took place beside it.

The altar itself, given a further frame by the silver canopy or *ciborium*, was adorned with gold, jewels, and cloths of silk with gold embroidery. Everything around it was designed with a reflective surface to bathe the sanctuary in light.

Pomp and ceremony

The lay congregation was restricted to the nave (they could not go beyond the barriers around the ambo and solea), the aisles, and the galleries. The men probably occupied the nave, the women the other areas, and people were probably arranged by rank in areas defined by the green marble inlays on the floor of the church. The congregation stood throughout the service.

The Byzantines celebrated the Eucharist in a ceremony that went back as far as the second century AD. The service would have begun with the entry of the clergy who would process from the narthex into the nave. At their head would be a deacon carrying the gospel, followed by the clergyman of highest rank – at Hagia Sophia this would often be the patriarch himself. The other clergy would be behind, singing the introit psalm. The procession would walk along the solea to the sanctuary, where the gospel would be placed on the altar and the patriarch would sit on his throne at the centre of the tiered platform called the *synthronon* behind the altar; he would be flanked by the other clergy. Readings from the Bible would then be given from the ambo. For the reading from the gospel, the most important part of the ceremony,

Justinian with members of his court

the book would be brought from the altar before the reading and replaced immediately afterwards. Sometimes a sermon would follow, delivered by the patriarch from his throne, and this would be devoted to explaining points in the texts of the readings.

Next the clergy would come down from the synthronon for the Eucharist itself. This part of the service was begun by the ceremonial bringing of gifts to the altar by a procession of clergy accompanied by the singing of a special chant. The gifts would be consecrated and placed on the altar. The clergy would then take Communion, followed by any others in the congregation who wished to.

This all would have happened very slowly. In a building the size of Hagia Sophia the congregation could be large. Even if few laity were there, there could be many clergymen. In the time of Justinian there were sixty priests at Hagia Sophia, together with one hundred deacons, forty deaconesses, ninety subdeacons, and many other lesser office-holders. If the emperor was also attending the service the ceremony would be even more elaborate. He would accompany the patriarch to the chancel screen and would wait by the screen holding a candle while the patriarch took his position on his throne. Justinian would then leave a gift on the altar before coming out of the chancel to go to his own throne, which was in the south aisle. Justinian would also participate in the gift-giving ceremony and, of course, in the taking of Communion. The empress did not take part in the main service, although she would have attended the church. In the great mosaics in the church at San Vitale, Ravenna, which show the imperial processions, both Justinian and Theodora are shown arriving at the church. But whereas the emperor carries his gift with him the empress hands hers to a member of the accompanying clergy.

A movement towards unity

Measured as a religious building Hagia Sophia was a triumphant success. Its plain exterior contrasts with its ornate interior in a way that suggests the stress on the inner person that the Byzantine Christians found so important. Its vast nave and its lavish furnishings provided a superb setting for their religious ceremonies.

But Hagia Sophia was more than a grand new headquarters for the empire's religious life. Justinian wanted to build a place where empire and church could come together in unity. Just as his legal reforms and his military conquests were designed to pull the empire together, so his great church was probably intended to be another binding agent.

How successful was Justinian in his aims? One aim was to bring together two elements within the church itself, the Monophysite and Orthodox groups. Although Hagia Sophia's influence did inspire a spread of the Orthodox faith, the two groups did not come together. And Justinian's policies (particularly his military campaigns and financial policies) left the exchequer weak. Moreover his military gains in Italy and northern Africa proved short-lived. And yet the culture that produced Hagia Sophia lived on, and even the Islamic conquerors who took over the city were stunned by its design and adopted it as a mosque.

MISTRA

Lost Byzantine capital in southern Greece

If the magnificent city of Constantinople, with its fortifications and palaces and Justinian's great church of Hagia Sophia, was the crowning achievement of the early Byzantine Empire, then the small city of Mistra, on a craggy hill on the Greek mainland, is the enduring memorial of the Empire's declining years. Visually, the site is superb. On a hill in the Taygetus range, about 6 kilometres northwest of Sparta, it is easy to defend, inaccessible from some directions and easy to cut off from the others.

And yet the qualities that make it such a good fortress and so dramatic to look at also make it an unlikely site for a town. The slopes are steep and craggy, and any building work would be a major undertaking with the technology available to medieval masons. At the top of the hill, water was also in short supply. It could not be piped right to the top and the inhabitants had to rely on catching rainwater in large cisterns and carrying the rest of it up the steep streets from the valley below.

From crusaders to emperors

How did a city come to be built in such a location? The story of Mistra begins during the time of the crusades. In AD 1204 the soldiers of the fourth crusade captured Constantinople and the land belonging to the Byzantine emperors was divided up between the men who had led the crusaders to victory. Two of these commanders were Frankish leaders from the Champagne district, William de Villehardouin and his nephew Geoffrey. Their prize was the principality of Morea, roughly equivalent to the Peloponnese, the part of Greece below the isthmus of Corinth. They found that much of the territory was easy to conquer. The local Greek population was unaccustomed to fighting and, together with another Frankish nobleman, William de Champlitte, they were soon able to dominate most of the Peloponnese. In 1210, Geoffrey was powerful enough to take the title of Prince of the Morea.

But the Franks did not rule the whole of Greece. Geoffrey's successor, his son Geoffrey II, was prevented by the local population from subduing the southeastern part of the country, with the fortress of Monemvasia. Geoffrey was content with his small principality, and threw his energies into running it smoothly and keeping the peace. But when he died suddenly in 1246 he was followed by a ruler of very different character, his brother William.

William was much more ambitious and in 1248 expanded his rule into the southeastern area. It was at this time that he came across the hill, not far from his home near Sparta, on which Mistra was to stand. This was another area which, though in Frankish hands, was vulnerable to attack. The Taygetus mountains were the home of a warlike tribe of Slavs, the Milengi, who were continually threatening Geoffrey's palace. The prince needed another stronghold, and quickly recognized the area's potential for fortification and built himself a castle there. A local legend says that it was called Myzethra, which is the name of a type of cheese, because the previous owner of the land was a cheese merchant or cheese maker. But a rival legend, more attractive and just as likely, asserts that the people thought that Mistra's conical hill was the same shape as the local cheese.

William did not rule Mistra for long. In 1259 the Byzantines, under their emperor Michael VIII Palaeologus, fought back. They captured the prince, forced him to give up the castle at Mistra, and installed the Byzantine governor of the Morea there in his stead. In 1262 he arrived with his officials. Mistra henceforward became a Byzantine stronghold. A city, with houses, palaces, churches, monasteries and a cathedral quickly grew up around the castle. The local Greeks realized that they could come here to be ruled once more by people who spoke their own language, and the head of the local Orthodox church, the Metropolitan of Lacedemonia, came to live in the town where he knew he would be safe. Eventually, the place would come to have a special importance in the Empire. Its governors would be elected from the members of the imperial family. In years to come it would be yet more important, becoming a seat of learning and a centre for the development of the arts, especially painting. Finally, it would become the refuge of the emperors themselves.

The monastery of the Pantanassa is glimpsed through an archway on the eastern side of Mistra's mountain. Its architecture is typical of Mistra, with stone walls and tiled roofs. The solid belltower, and the occasional use of pointed arches, betray the influence that came from western Europe with the Frankish crusaders.

A centre for the military

First and foremost, then, Mistra was a fortress. As the Byzantines tried to wrest control of the Morea from the Franks, Mistra became the centre of their operations. The Byzantines could count on strong support. With local soldiers and Turkish mercenaries they had several victories in 1263, but the Frankish capital, Andravida in the west, held out against them. The following year the same thing happened in reverse; the Franks retook several towns, but Mistra itself proved impregnable. A truce was the obvious solution, and the Byzantines took to expanding their rule by more devious, diplomatic means. By marrying Frankish princesses the emperors saw to it that they shared common interests with the Franks, but that they gradually increased their own power. As they did this they did not forget that the castle and town of Mistra were essential to their security. It was to remain their centre in Greece for 200 years.

The importance of Mistra, and the province of the Morea in which it stood, was confirmed when the emperor appointed a new governor in 1349. Emperor John VI Cantacuzenus chose his son Manual to be governor at Mistra. He gave Manual the title of Despot and, because communications with Constantinople were poor, he was left at Mistra to pursue his own policies and to run the province as best he could. Since he was an able diplomat and a good administrator, he succeeded. The office of Despot passed to his brother Matthew on his death, and from Matthew to his son Demetrius.

The end of Demetrius' rule came when a new imperial dynasty, the Palaelogi, took over at Constantinople in 1384. Henceforward, the Despots were selected from the ranks of the new imperial family. They kept closer links between the capital and Mistra, but also gave the Despots more power to extend their rule across the whole of the Morea. The result was that the burgeoning programme of building that started under the Cantacuzeni continued and the cultural life of the city was reinforced.

The Byzantine city

Mistra was dominated by the castle, on top of the hill on the southwestern edge of the city, that was originally built by the Franks. From the castle walls stretched down the hill to meet another wall, cutting off a roughly triangular area that formed the upper city. This was the area that contained the Despots' palace and, since it was the best defended part of Mistra, there were doubtless other nobles' houses within its walls. Below this sector, to the east, was another walled section, the middle city. This contained many of the larger churches, several nobles' mansions, and many smaller houses. Further east down the hill was the third sector of the city, this time unfortified. Here would have been the humbler houses of the poorer citizens.

The population of the whole city was probably around 20,000. Many of them were local Greeks who came for Byzantine protection soon after the first imperial officials arrived in 1262. Most of them lived in the northeastern part of the lower town. Soon more Byzantines would arrive from their base at Monemvasia in southeastern Greece and take up residence in mansions in the middle and upper regions of Mistra.

When the Byzantine governors, and later the Despots, arrived in Mistra, they found a house that had been occupied by the Frankish governors of the city. This proved too small for the Despot Manual Cantacuzenus, and he added several large reception halls, rooms for himself and courtiers upstairs, two towers, and a roof terrace. The Despots of the Palaeologi added further rooms of a more business-like nature – storerooms, offices for ministers, and another large ceremonial room, this time with space under a semicircular apse for a throne. This may not have been an excess of grandeur on the part of the Despots themselves, for the emperor himself visited Mistra twice in the early fifteenth century, and would have required an appropriate setting for receptions and ceremonies.

Apart from the great palace, its attendant workshops and offices, a couple of churches including the Despot's church of St Sophia, and a few houses, there were few buildings amongst the craggy terrain of the upper city. Most of the houses were down in the middle and lower cities. Here, as the amount of space was at a premium, the buildings were packed very close together and the streets were quite narrow. Shops, small houses, and larger, more luxurious dwellings with their own private water cisterns jostled together on the hillside.

Christianity and culture

To modern eyes, the number of churches in Mistra is astounding – there seems to be one around every corner. Built of local stone with distinctive red tiles covering the roofs (and even the many domes), they were striking enough from the outside. But, like the Hagia Sophia before them, they were even more remarkable within. The walls of most are decorated with frescoes, and some of the churches contain wall paintings that are among the best of their type. How did so many churches of such artistic quality come to be built in this outpost of the Empire?

Surprisingly, it all started before the Despots made Mistra crucially important in the Byzantine Empire. The man who turned the city into an architectural treasury was not a close relative of the emperor but a clergyman called Pachomius, a man who held down an influential administrative post in the city and who managed to combine this with a love of church building. His greatest building was produced when he decided to retire to a monastery. Rather than retreat to an existing foundation he built a new abbey, called the Brontochion, and made himself abbot. He adorned it with a new church, dedicated to Our Lady Hodeghetria, a Greek title of the Virgin that means 'she who leads the way'. He also obtained lavish grants of land for the new foundation from the emperor himself, ensuring the monastery's future and enhancing his own power.

With its five tiled domes and bell tower, the Hodeghetria stood out halfway up the hill near the wall that divided the upper and middle cities. Its stone walls were interrupted by three or four narrow courses of brick to give a neat, striped effect unusual among the stone buildings of Mistra. Within there were frescoes, sculptures, and marble panelling of the highest quality. For this work Pachomius was able to call on the best craftsmen – probably people from Constantinople itself. The riches that Pachomius obtained for his monastery and the contact that he had with the emperor as a result clearly paid artistic as well as financial dividends.

Patriarchs, prophets, and saints are all portrayed in the church, together with scenes from the life of Christ from the Nativity to the Resurrection. In many of the scenes, several events are crowded together in a single panel to give an effect rather like a confused medieval strip cartoon. The paintings have a limited palette – reds and greens predominate, with gold for the haloes above the saints' heads – but the colours are applied with bold, expressive brushstrokes. Their style reflects many of the mosaics in the churches of Constantinople, which the artists probably studied when learning their skills in their home city.

The links with Constantinople were also kept up by the Metropolitans of Mistra. Many of these senior clergymen are figures of whom we know very little, but at least one, Nicephorus Moschopoulos, had close ties with the capital. He it was who built the Metropolitan church (the equivalent of a cathedral), another building with outstanding wall paintings. He also encouraged scholars to come to Mistra from the capital, many of whom ended up at Pachomius' monastery.

The emperor Manuel II Palaeologus

Later churches, such as the Church of the Peribleptos and the church of the Pantanassa (AD 1428) also have impressive decorations. We do not know whether the painters used by Pachomius stayed on in Mistra and founded a school, or whether fresh painters arrived from Constantinople to take their place. In view of the amount of work available at Mistra it is probable that Pachomius' painters founded a tradition that continued in the town, taking local pupils who went on to decorate later buildings.

An academic centre

Painters were not the only class to be attracted to Mistra. Church leaders of the calibre of Pachomius and Nicephorus also attracted great scholars. This tradition was encouraged by some of the Despots, notably Manual and Matthew Cantacuzenus. But it was the arrival in Mistra of a philosopher called George Gemistus Plethon in about 1407 that was to transform the intellectual life of the city. Plethon was a follower of the ancient Greek philosopher Plato. As such, he was pleased to move to Greece, particularly as he was welcomed by a Despot, Theodore II, who was himself something of a scholar. Plethon gathered a group of scholars around him at Mistra who not only discussed the most obscure and erudite areas of philosophy, but who tried to apply their ideas to contemporary life and government.

As Steven Runciman, the historian of Mistra, has pointed out, the Byzantines had traditionally seen themselves as the inheritors of the Roman Empire. But this tradition, centred on the by now impoverished city of Constantinople, was dying. It was not unnatural, therefore, that a Platonic philosopher living in Greece should look to ancient Greek culture for his inspiration. Plethon proposed a new pagan Greek state with a national socialist-type organization under a benevolent dictator. Although his proposals were unworkable in practical terms, the Byzantines were nevertheless encouraged to look to Mistra for their salvation as the emperors in Constantinople began to lose their grip on power when the Ottoman enemies began to threaten them.

The end of the Despotate

The Despot Theodore II had a long and troubled reign. He had to deal with a difficult nobility, the possibility of invasion by the Turks, and frontier squabbles. He often had little time for the scholarship of which he was a devoted patron. He was also cheated by death of the final prize; first in line in the imperial succession, he died in 1448, shortly before the emperor. The way was left open for his brother Constantine.

Constantine, far away from the capital and knowing that the Empire was dying on its feet, broke with precedent and was crowned at Mistra. There is no record of what the ceremony was like, but, as Steven Runciman has speculated, it must have been unusual. There was no church in Mistra capable of containing the crowds usually present at an imperial coronation, but many of the officials who would have attended at Constantinople would not have been able to come. So Constantine's crowning was probably a rather makeshift affair, not inappropriate for a declining empire. Nonetheless, it was Mistra's finest hour, to be followed only four years later by the fall of Constantinople and the death of the emperor at the gates of the city.

For the Despots, this was the beginning of the end. It was already clear that they depended on the Sultan for their power. Without Ottoman help they would have been unable to defend the Morea against rebellions by the Albanian element. Now, with Constantinople fallen, the Ottomans could impose their will even more on the people of Byzantine Greece. They enforced the payment of tribute to the Sultan, and when the Despots fell into arrears, military retaliation from the ruthless Ottoman army was the inevitable result. In 1460 the Turks finally conquered Greece and the life of the last, lost Byzantine city was finally ended.

The civilization of Mistra was an extraordinary achievement. It owed something to the traditions of both Greece and Rome; it relied on contact with the capital and yet it was oddly isolated; its site was fit only for a fortress yet it survived its military origins to become something otherworldly. In its two centuries of life this tiny city became the essence of an entire empire.

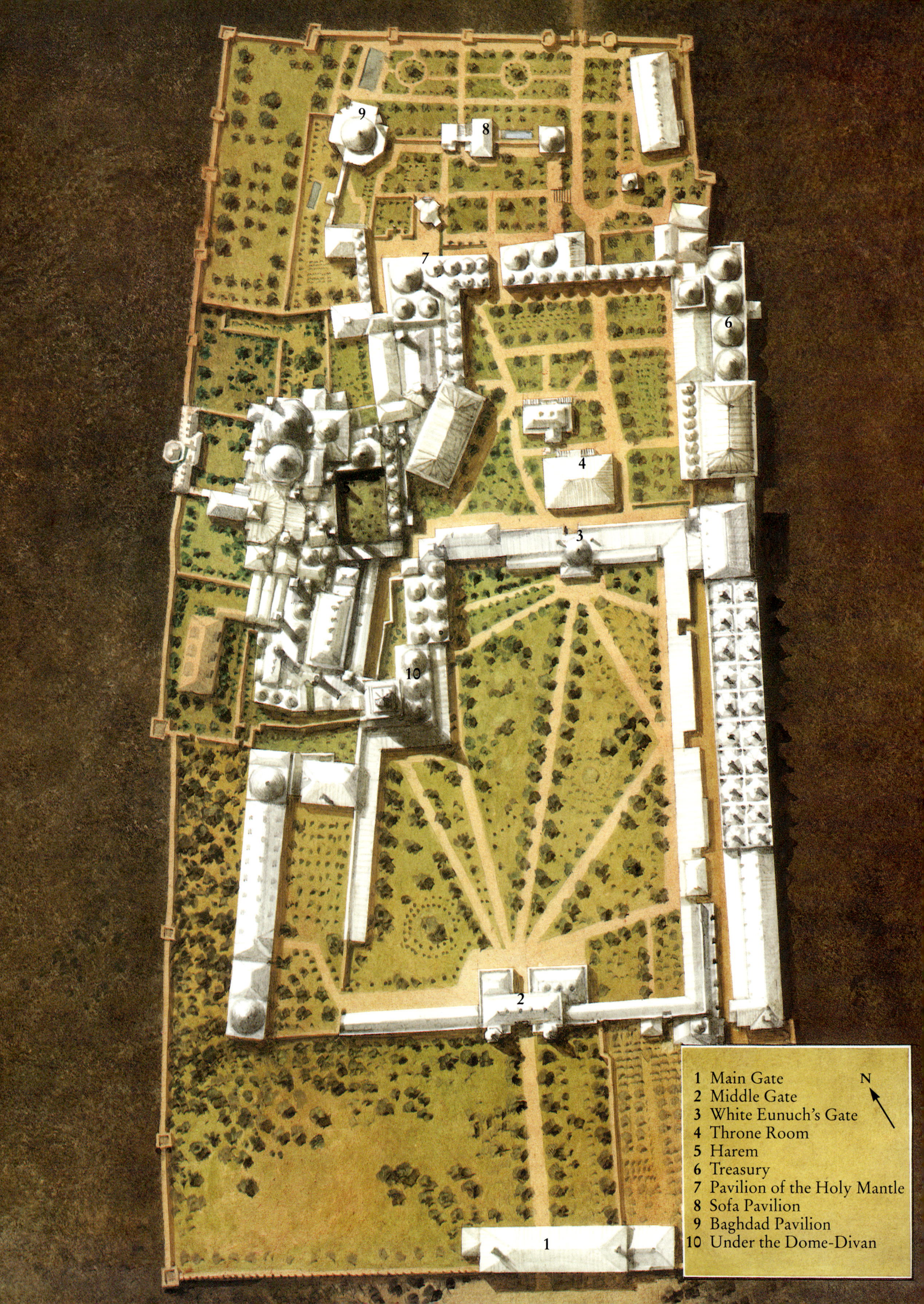

1 Main Gate
2 Middle Gate
3 White Eunuch's Gate
4 Throne Room
5 Harem
6 Treasury
7 Pavilion of the Holy Mantle
8 Sofa Pavilion
9 Baghdad Pavilion
10 Under the Dome-Divan
N

TOPKAPI

Palace of the Ottoman sultans and home of their harem

In the late fourteenth century AD the once-great rulers of the Byzantine Empire had been forced to become the vassals of the Ottoman Turks. In the following century, the Turks gained control over all the lands around the city of Constantinople and it was only a matter of time before they would take the city. The Byzantine emperors, such as Constantine XI Dragases who was crowned at Mistra, tried to rally the Christian west to give them aid. But an alliance between the Greek Byzantines and the people of Rome proved impossible and Constantinople found itself under siege.

In AD 1453 Byzantine control of the city finally came to an end. The new rulers were led by Sultan Mehmet II, known afterwards as 'the conqueror'. He found a city that had passed its former glory. The palaces of the Byzantine emperors were delapidated, and even the massive defensive walls that surrounded the city needed repair.

In the new wall that Mehmet built along the sea coast to supplement the original fortifications there was a watergate guarded by two great cannons. This became known as Topkapi, the cannongate, and when Mehmet started to build his new palace nearby, on the first hill of the city overlooking the sea, it was natural that it should become known as the Topkapi Palace. Topkapi was not Mehmet's only home in the city. He had built a palace for himself on the third hill immediately he took over the city. But in 1465, when Topkapi was ready for him to move in, it became his principal home; the other palace was reserved for the women of the harem of Mehmet's late father.

It was natural that Mehmet should have settled at Topkapi. At the confluence of the three seas that all but surround the city – the Golden Horn, the Bosphorus and the Sea of Marmara – it was an excellent look-out post. It was also near to the centre of the city – the heart of the Byzantine town, with the imperial palace and the church of St Irene, had been here. Justinian's great church of Hagia Sophia was nearby. At Topkapi, the sultan was at the hub of his world.

Topkapi was added to by the sultans who followed Mehmet. The building that we can reconstruct today comes mainly from the sixteenth century. But the palace retained its essential character. It was a place of shady courtyards and lush gardens, of grand chambers and luxurious apartments, of rich furnishings and lavish decoration. It was built mainly of stone, although from time to time wooden buildings were added to it, no doubt in the carved and panelled style still used in the old quarters of the city to this day. Topkapi was never a palace of tall towers or lofty halls. Most of the buildings are low, and the overhanging eaves add to the impression that the palace gives of clinging to the hill on which it is built. This feature, along with the many courtyards and the cool tiled walls, made the place more comfortable. For although there was a sea breeze, the heat could be sweltering.

The people who inhabited Topkapi were as interesting as the building itself. For, in addition to the sultans, the palace was soon to become the home of the harem, scene of dynastic intrigue, the base of the janissaries (the sultan's powerful troops), and of the many ambitious officials who helped in the running of the Ottoman Empire.

The courtyards of the palace

Topkapi was not like the ordered, symmetrical Renaissance palaces that were being built in western Europe. It had to fulfil many functions. Apart from being the imperial residence, its most important function was to house the divan, the governmental body of the empire. There was also a palace school, a mint, a hospital, accommodation for the janissaries, and all the domestic offices that a community of such size required. Perhaps it is not surprising that the design of the palace was somewhat haphazard, with a new courtyard or building being added as the need arose. This produced a low sprawling complex on the hill overlooking the sea.

Some semblance of order was imposed by organizing the palace around a number of courtyards, each of which contained buildings with specific, well-defined functions. The first courtyard was really a vast service area. Open to the public, it took deliveries, and housed storerooms, the arsenal, workshops, the mint, a bakery, and the hospital. It also contained

An aerial view of the palace shows its sprawling layout and its many courtyards. Only a comparatively small area – in and around the harem to the northwest – was occupied by domestic quarters. The rest of the buildings were for the government and the palace staff and guard.

Sultan Mehmet II, the Conqueror, is joined by members of his retinue outside the main gate of the palace. The gate contained many rooms, some of which were occupied by imperial guards who would keep continuous watch over everyone entering and leaving the palace.

Imperial gate, Topkapi Palace AD 1478

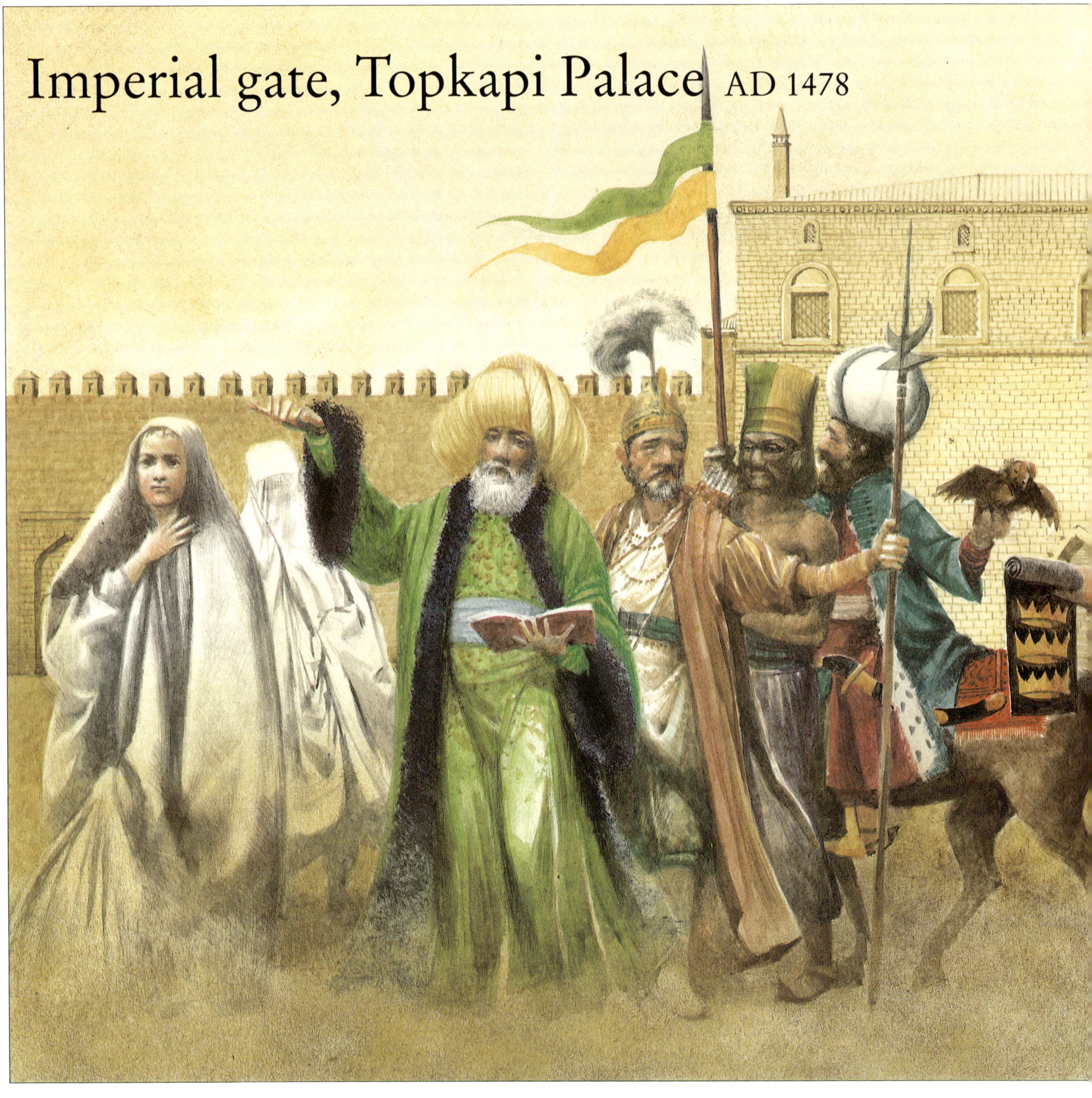

the guards' quarters and the rooms of those servants whose work was in the outer parts of the palace. The first court acquired a rather gruesome reputation as time went on. When the janissaries initiated rebellions to maintain a hold on their declining military power, this was where the trouble usually flared up. But the court also contained a reminder of the power of the sultan. In one corner was the fountain where the executioner cleaned his hands and weapons of the blood of traitors and miscreants.

The second court was where the divan sat. Access to this part of the palace was more restricted, but anyone with business in the divan could enter. The palace kitchens, with their famous domed roofs, ran along one side of this courtyard, so there would also be a busy traffic of servants taking food to various parts of the palace. Each kitchen had a specific purpose. For example, one prepared food for the officials of the divan, another for the women of the harem, another for the sultan himself. A large community like Topkapi needed such lavish catering provision. Records from the seventeenth century tell us the quantity of meat that was consumed every day – two hundred sheep, one hundred lambs, forty calves, two hundred chickens. Such a list reads like an exaggeration until we remember the large force of soldiers, the numerous eunuchs, the court officials, not to mention the servants, who all had to be fed.

In the centre of the court was a garden. It was particularly well known for its fruit trees – almonds, figs, lemons, oranges, and pomegranates. The council of the divan met in

domed chambers looking out on this garden in one corner of the second court. This small, rather unassuming building containing the council chamber, the records office, and the office of the grand vizir was truly the hub of the Ottoman Empire, where laws were passed and justice was done. In a small concealed room the ruler could watch the council's deliberations through a window known as the 'sultan's eye'.

The divan met four times a week, and when it was in session the palace was even fuller than usual. The first and second courts would fill with officials and janissaries, and sometimes there would be as many as 10,000 people present. But on such ceremonial occasions the noise and bustle of the palace were replaced with ordered processions and an unearthly silence, for this vast crowd would not speak unless bidden by the sultan or his high officials.

As befitted the central governing body of the empire, the divan kept close control on finances – the inner treasury was also in the second court of the palace. This was where tribute money from all over the Ottoman Empire was brought to be counted. The officials of the inner treasury would pay the government's expenses every quarter before sending any surplus off to the main imperial treasury. All tax receipts and records of payments were kept at the inner treasury.

In the third court of Topkapi was the throne room. Here the sultan sat to receive visitors from foreign powers and to hear news from his officials of business transacted in the Divan. There was also a range of additional reception rooms for the sultan, although later these were taken over by the treasury. It was from these 'official' rooms, in which the sultan would entertain his guests, that travellers returned with tales of the extraordinary riches of the Ottoman court. Their stories – of rubies the size of eggs, diamonds bigger than hazel nuts – seem too excessive to be true. And yet the sultan's wealth was so vast, and the Ottoman love of display so great, that such stories probably do reflect the reality of life at Topkapi.

Most of the other buildings in this part of Topkapi made up the palace school. This was a unique institution. Most education in Ottoman Turkey was provided in the mosques; naturally, it was a religious education. But in the palace, schoolboys were trained in the purely secular skills that would make them fit for the service of the sultan. Here it was that the most important officers of the Empire would be trained, and it is no exaggeration to say that the palace school was one of the most important influences

Gold-engraved helmet

on the success of the Ottoman Empire. All the pupils would start in one of the introductory classes, but the more talented ones would pass on to more advanced classes that would give instruction in particular subjects relevant to the needs of the sultanate. So budding military commanders would go to the campaign hall, accountants and tax collectors would learn their skills in the treasury hall, and prospective organizers would be trained in logistics in the hall of the commissariat. The most talented young men would be selected for the hall of the privy chamber, the place where the top officials – those closest to the sultan – would be trained.

The harem

When Topkapi was first built, the domestic quarters remained at the old palace and Topkapi was primarily a centre for administration and diplomacy. Sultan Suleyman the Magnificent brought the royal household to Topkapi some time in the early 1540s. But his domestic quarters probably consisted of makeshift wooden buildings at the side of the palace. It was Sultan Murat III (1574–95) who started to build the complex of stone buildings on the left-hand side of the second and third courts known as the *harem.* This not only provided rooms for the women and the eunuchs who guarded them; there were also rooms giving accommodation for the young princes and apartments for the sultan. In other words it was a palace (in the modern sense of a home for a ruler) within the palace.

The harem was large. As it stands today there are over 300 rooms and many of these date from Murat's time. But the rooms are surprisingly small. This is probably because they were essentially private apartments. They were not intended for the receiving of official visitors or for occasions of state, and there was less need to impress. So the scale is much more intimate – even the courtyards are small, some no more than narrow wells designed to let in fresh air but only a little light from the hot sun.

Although the sultan had his apartments in the harem, this part of the palace was in many ways the domain of the women of the royal family. The most important woman in the harem was the Valide Sultan, or queen mother. She was often an influential power behind the throne and, together with her confidant, the chief black eunuch, was often at the centre of palace intrigue. In such a closed community, plots were rife, and remedies often desperate. For example, there was a gruesome tradition that, when a new sultan came to the throne, all potential rivals would be put to death. On one notorious occasion Sultan Mehmet III consigned all his brothers to the executioner when he succeeded to the throne in 1595. His successor Ahmet I abolished this procedure, preferring instead to confine such 'rivals' to house arrest in the harem, in an area that came to be known as 'the cage'. Here they were given all the luxuries they might expect as members of the royal family except for the right to come and go as they pleased. Some writers have speculated that the strain of madness running through the royal family in the seventeenth century came as a result of this confinement.

Indeed it may have been the ambition of a woman that brought the harem to Topkapi in the first place. The woman was Roxelana, second kadin or favourite concubine to Suleyman the Magnificent. After the death of the Sultan Valide and the departure of the first kadin to live with her son, Roxelana rose dramatically to power. She plotted the murder of the Grand Vizir so that she could install one of her own relations, and persuaded Suleyman to have his son murdered so that her own family would be heirs to the throne. Her triumph was complete when she became Suleyman's legal wife. The setting up of the harem at Topkapi was another plank in the platform of her power.

It may have been Roxelana who began the tradition that the harem was guarded by black eunuchs. These people were more than guards. Contemporary sources tell us of their skill in music, their charm and generosity, and their fondness and caring for the children of the harem. They accompanied the sultan's sons until they were removed from the harem at the the age of eleven, and so must have had a considerable formative influence on the characters of the sultans.

The domain of the sultan

Although most of the rooms in the harem are relatively small, the sultan himself was provided with some spacious apartments, next to those of the Valide. The largest of these was the sultan's hall, a domed room designed by Sinan, one of the most celebrated Ottoman architects, in the sixteenth century. It had slender blue-grey marble pillars at either end, and the walls were covered with pale blue ceramic tiles. Here the sultan and his favourite concubines would come to be entertained by musicians. The sultan would

Woman of the harem

sit on his throne under a large gilt canopy and the ladies of the harem would lounge on low sofas placed on either side of the throne.

Near to this hall were the sultan's baths. Bathing was an important part of Ottoman life, reflecting the importance of cleanliness in Islam. Of the many bath suites at Topkapi this was the most magnificent, with marble panelling and basins, inlaid recesses and cupboards, and tiled walls. There were several rooms in the suite, including a dressing room and a massage room as well as the bathing rooms themselves.

One of the finest rooms in the harem was a chamber specially built by Sinan for Sultan Murat III. This room's original decoration still survives, and provides an indication of what the rest of the rooms would have looked like when the harem was built. The most striking features are the ceramic tiles on the walls. Many of these are the traditional blue colour, but there are also red and green designs. The motifs on the tiles are abstract, but recall flowers and leaves (Islam forebad the portrayal of the human figure). There are also tiles bearing immaculately calligraphed quotations from the Koran. Add to this gilt doors, lavish Turkish carpets, elegant hanging wall lamps, and finely carved niches, and one gets an impression of the sophistication of Ottoman interiors at this time. Against this backdrop, the sultan and his household in their rich robes of velvet and brocade, carrying their jewelled weapons, would have cut figures of unparalleled richness.

Life in the harem

The women of the harem were the slaves of the sultan. This did not necessarily mean that they had to do hard physical work. Many held official positions within the harem hierarchy that gave them their own retinue and considerable status. But confined within the palace and denied the company of anyone from outside the harem except for the sultan himself, life for most of the women must have been simply boring.

And yet there were goals that could improve the lot of a woman of the harem if she achieved them. A newly arrived woman would usually be assigned to the retinue of one of the highest ranking harem members. This would give her a chance to learn the way of life in the harem. It might also give her the opportunity to catch the sultan's eye. If he was attracted to her, she would be given her own apartment and servants. If she provided him with a male child she might be made a kadin, joining the small group of women who were closest to the sultan and most powerful within the court. From this point, she would be likely to press the claims of her son to be heir to the throne, a position that would eventually make her Sultan

Sultan Suleyman the Magnificent

Valide, the most powerful woman in the whole empire.

For a woman who did not catch the sultan's eye, life could still hold changes. She might rise within the retinue she originally joined, so that she could eventually join the ranks of the principal women herself, perhaps becoming confidante to the Valide, or holding one of the important offices of the harem, such as Keeper of the Jewels or Mistress of the Wardrobe.

Topkapi in later years

The palace on the hill was to continue as the Sultan's main residence until the nineteenth century. During its working life it underwent many alterations but none of these changed its broad plan, its general character, or the role it played in the life of the empire. But by 1853 Sultan Abdul Meçit I realized that if the palace had not changed radically, life at court had. So he moved to a new palace at Dolmabahçe on the Bosphorus. He left Topkapi to be occupied by the harems of deceased sultans, to become 'a palace of tears'.

TROY
CATAL HUYUK
BOGHAZKOY
KHORSABAD
BABYLON
PETRA
UR
PERSEPOLIS
MOHENJO-DARO
TAJ MAHAL
ELLORA
GREAT WALL OF CHINA
PEKING
YOSHINOGARI
NARA
ANGKOR

ASIA

Viewed from the traditional perspective of the west, the vast landmass of Asia is most notable for the cultures of what European archaeologists used to call the 'near East'. In particular, Mesopotamia, the land between the Tigris and Euphrates rivers, gave us our first civilizations. Cities such as Ur, Uruk, Lagash, and Babylon provide the earliest evidence of activities that we now take for granted – from writing to wheelwrighting.

However, this section of the book does not begin in Mesopotamia but in Anatolia, in a place more remote from western civilization than the great Sumerian cities, yet equally fascinating: Catal Hüyük. This is a place that some have called the first city. It is a prehistoric settlement, one whose people could not read or write, and so for many scholars it does not pass the ultimate test for 'civilization'. And yet its artistic sophistication, its highly developed religion, its exploitation of the local resources, particularly obsidian, and the skill with which its buildings were put together all argue for a culture on the brink of civilization. It is also a place that begs many questions – about its religion and art, and about the large sections of the site that have yet to be excavated.

By contrast, the other sites of western Asia seem familiar. We know of Ur from the Old Testament, of Babylon through the enduring myths of its Tower and its Hanging Gardens, of Troy from Homer and many writers who have followed him. And many aspects of these cultures make us feel close to their peoples. Take the *Epic of Gilgamesh*, the first surviving extended piece of imaginative literature, preserved on Assyrian clay tablets but dating from earlier Mesopotamia. In this text are represented the struggle of the hero against evil, the search for love and friendship, the longing for immortality.

So it is not surprising that we can identify with the civilizations of cities like Ur – or that we are fascinated by the later cultures of the area, such as the Assyrian (represented in this book by the city of Khorsabad) and the Persian (represented by Persepolis).

We do not know when the first people came to Mesopotamia, or who these people were. The earliest inhabitants traced lived by the Tigris and Euphrates in about 4500 BC and tried to irrigate the dry land with canals from the two great rivers. Many of these early people were nomads, although the need to build and maintain the irrigation systems led to the growth of villages. But it was not until the third millennium BC that towns started to appear and writing to develop. Among the first of these cities was Uruk, by the Euphrates. It was in early cities like this that the hallmarks of Sumerian civilization – such as the pictorial writing that was to evolve into the wedge-shaped cuneiform script, and the monumental temples – first developed. This was the heritage of Gilgamesh (who was king of Uruk) and the people of Ur and Babylon. It developed into a rich civilization and a source of agricultural wealth that later rulers – Persian and Assyrian in particular – were to tap into, if not to pillage.

But if we can be forgiven our fascination with Mesopotamia and its near neighbours, we should not ignore the many civilizations that have come and gone in the rest of Asia. The Indian subcontinent alone would furnish enough sites for a book the size of this one: any minimal choice from its riches is bound to be arbitrary and personal. Mohenjo-daro has been selected to embody the civilization of the Indus Valley – another river civilization that was highly successful and sophisticated, but one that was mysterious in its demise. Ellora has been selected for its religious connotations – its caves contain examples representing Hinduism, Buddhism, and Jainisn – and also because its extraordinary rock-cut architecture makes it one of the continent's most atmospheric places. A similar fascination attaches to a much later shrine – the Taj Mahal.

China is another area that offers an embarrassing richness. But perhaps one need not apologize for choosing two of the most famous sites – the Great Wall and the Forbidden City of Peking – to represent this civilization.

Finally, this section contains representatives of some of the smaller, more isolated civilizations. From farther east, Angkor represents the flowering of Khmer culture, and Yoshinogari and Nara offer a glimpse of several centuries of Japanese history. Such is the richness and diversity of the world's largest continent. These are qualities that sent Marco Polo on his travels to China and Edward Lear to Petra. Even today, when one stands at one end of Asia, the other end feels remote. This section of the book tries to bring these places closer without losing a sense of their diversity.

CATAL HUYUK

One of the first urban settlements, an Anatolian town with origins as far back as *circa* 7200 BC

Where was the first city? Fifty years ago, archaeologists would have pointed to Mesopotamia, the land between the Rivers Tigris and Euphrates. Here, it was thought, was the 'cradle of civilization', the area that produced the great cities of Ur and Babylon. This surely was the place where urban life began and from where the idea of the city spread to the rest of Asia and to Europe. In the late 1950s something happened that was to change this perspective. Beneath a mound in southern-central Turkey, on the Konya Plain about 320 kilometres (200 miles) from Ankara, archaeologists uncovered the remains of Catal Hüyük, a town dating back to *c.*7200 BC. This makes it older than any town of similar size so far discovered in Mesopotamia. It also exhibits the key features that we expect in a city – an organized religion, a society in which there were different social classes and specialized labour forces, and a large population (of at least 6,000).

The town was in a fortunate setting. The Konya Plain had been a lake until *c.*16,000 BC. When it dried out it left fertile soil where corn could be grown, and rich pastures that were well watered by the standards of central Anatolia. Yet the area was hardly tamed. Nearby were marshes where lions, gazelles, and wild asses roamed; the Taurus mountains to the south and west were the haunt of leopards and bears. It was dangerous country but a fruitful hunting ground. There were also forests in the mountains, providing a good source of timber: the people had to travel to find most of their raw materials.

The shrine rooms at Catal Hüyük contain some of the most extraordinary interior decoration that has come down to us. Real bulls' horns inserted into plaster heads, and drawings of vultures adorned the walls. Here a burial is taking place under one of the platforms while offerings are made.

The discovery of Catal Hüyük raised more questions than it answered. Was this really the first city? How did it develop so far away from the world's other urban centres? Why did the people build in the extraordinary way they did – houses without doors and rooms with strange decorations consisting of plaster bulls' heads and animal horns? And who were the city's inhabitants and how did they live?

A city without streets

The architecture of Catal Hüyük could hardly be less like that of a modern western city. The houses were made of mud-bricks held together by a strengthening wooden framework. This consisted of vertical posts at the corners joined by horizontals at roof level. The houses had flat roofs which were drained by plaster gutters that directed rain water into the nearest adjoining courtyard. This made them similar to the buildings in many other ancient cities. But they were different in a fundamental way: the buildings adjoin each other so that there are no streets and few open spaces. People walked from one house to another across the roof tops and entered their home from the top – either through a trapdoor in the roof or through a door in the side of a small protruding upper storey. The blocks of houses continue connected for long stretches – you could walk a long way without your feet touching the ground. Not all buildings were of the same height, so short wooden ladders would have connnected the adjoining roofs.

As well as being a public thoroughfare, the space on top of the houses could be used in other ways. Because the roofs were flat, they would be turned into extra living and working areas when the weather was warm. So although the actual buildings were quite small and cramped, many of the activities that would today take place indoors could happen outside.

Although the architecture of the city looks rather haphazard to modern eyes it was in many ways very orderly. Most of the buildings were built of bricks that were made to a standard size. In fact the people of Catal Hüyük probably used a basic system of measurement based on the human hand (about 8 centimetres/3 inches) and foot (about 32 centimetres/12 inches). This gave bricks measuring 1 x 2 x 4 hands. The houses were also built to standard sizes – the majority are about 6 metres (20 feet) long and 4.5 metres (15 feet) wide; rooms, doorways, hearths and ovens were also made to regular sizes.

This unusual form of city planning had one crucial advantage. It was easier to keep out wild animals and human enemies when the entrances to the houses were at roof level. So it gave the inhabitants some of the advantages of fortification without them going to the expense and effort of building big city walls. In one way it was a more effective defence than an outer wall. Once a single wall is broken, the whole city falls. But if an

Catal Hüyük was a city without streets. Access to the houses was from the rooftops, and different roof levels were connected with ladders. This, and the small number of doors and windows, made the place easy to defend. The vultures soaring overhead are a reminder of death; the people probably left the bodies of their dead to be picked clean by the vultures before burying the remains.

attacker broke into one of the outer houses at Catal Hüyük all the occupiers would have to do was to escape on to the roof and take away the ladder. The intruder would find himself trapped in a labyrinth with a bewildering number of walls impeding his progress. Significantly, there is no evidence that Catal Hüyük was ever conquered or 'sacked'.

Inside the houses of Catal Hüyük it must have been pleasantly cool, although the lack of ventilation must also have made them rather airless. Space was also limited, each house being dominated by large raised platforms which, as well as housing the bodies of departed members of the family, were probably used for seating or as workbenches during the day, and as beds at night. The people made up for the deficiencies in their dwellings in several ways. They redecorated with surprising regularity, renewing the plaster on the walls every year. They were also careful about refuse disposal. Courtyards were set aside for this, and wood ash was used to cover over the debris.

The people and their crafts

The inhabitants of Catal Hüyük were illiterate, so we have no written records of their life. Because archaeologists have not yet been able to dig deep enough, we are unsure about their origins. It may be that they came from southern Anatolia, where there are cave paintings (in the caves of Kara'In and Oktzlt'In) that have similar subjects to wall paintings at Catal Hüyük. Another intriguing fact points to this area. Medical experts have noticed when examining human bones from the city that the inhabitants suffered from hyperostosis, a disease that affects the thickness of the skull. This disease is carried by malarial mosquitoes, suggesting that the original settlers came from an area where these insects live. Southern Anatolia is just such a region.

The town of Catal Hüyük
7000 BC

TURKEY
Iconium
CATAL HUYUK
Attalia
Adana
MEDITERRANEAN SEA
CYPRUS

We know something about what the people looked like from their remains. They were fairly tall and quite long-lived for their time. Men could be up to 1.7 metres (5 feet 7 inches) tall and reached an average age of about thirty-four. Women lived to an average of thirty-one and were shorter – about 1.55 metres (5 feet 1 inch) on average. They ate grain (probably in the form of gruel) as well as meat and drank milk from sheep or goats. Farmers outside the city grew emmer and einkorn wheat. Craftworkers inside Catal Hüyük produced pottery and a variety of wooden objects.

There is also fascinating evidence that the textiles of Catal Hüyük were made with great skill. Archaeologists investigating a burial found that the skull had been filled with cloth. A fortunate chain of events had preserved the pattern of the fibres. A fire in *c.*5880 BC had turned the cloth to carbon but the fibres' shape survived in the airless environment. They revealed a cloth with thin, smooth, parallel threads showing that its makers had mastered the arts of both spinning and weaving. The fibres were probably flax, although no seeds have been found at Catal Hüyük to confirm this.

Fertility figure

We can glean more information about textiles from other sources. Imprints made in clay show us the type of weave used in floor mats made from rushes. A diagonal pattern that often occurs in the weave is similar to a motif used in modern Anatolian rugs. Wall paintings in the shrines tell a similar story: kilim-style patterns that can still be seen in homes in the region. The people at Catal Hüyük could dye them too. They could gather local weeds such as woad (which gives a blue dye), madder (red) and weld (yellow). The traces of red that can still be seen in the wall paintings of the city would have originally blended in with a highly coloured decor of matting, clothes, and painted wooden vessels.

The decorative arts must have occupied a further large group of the population. Many of the interior walls of the city were covered with paintings, and these have survived in enough detail for some of the subjects to be reconstructed. Animals such as bulls, stags, and leopards are favourite motifs, but there are also paintings of people (hunters, dancers, and acrobats), as well as flower designs and abstract patterns.

Sources of wealth

Arts and crafts like these must have occupied many people in the city, but, interesting as they are, they would not have provided the citizens of Catal Hüyük with the sort of wealth they needed to sustain a sizeable city. Did they have a unique resource or product that they could exploit and trade?

The answer may lie in the geographical position of the site. To modern eyes the city seems uncomfortably near two volcanoes. But Hasan Dag and Karaca Dag provided a substance that was very valuable in neolithic times – obsidian. This glass-like volcanic rock can be fashioned into sharp knives and polished to make mirrors. Any group of people that had control of a supply of obsidian thus had a doubly useful material at their disposal – they could produce unequalled tools and make luxury objects that could become symbols of status.

A variety of tools, weapons, ornaments and domestic items were produced using obsidian. Many are very finely worked, the knives with carefully chipped sharp edges, the mirrors highly polished. How these craftsmen managed to produce such shining surfaces is not known; neither can it be guessed how they could drill such tiny holes through the centres of their obsidian beads. The workmanship of these objects causes admiration today – when they were first made the obsidian goods of Catal Hüyük must have commanded great respect.

There was one other technology that set Catal Hüyük apart. This part of Anatolia is rich in copper and the local people were quick to exploit it. Before 7000 BC they had discovered that they could hammer raw copper into simple tools and pins. In another thousand years' time they were smelting the ore to make small beads and other items.

Everyday items – a pot, a spindle, flint knives, and a decorated boar's tusk

Although metalworking seems an advanced technique for a people who lived over 8,000 years ago, it was less likely to bring wealth to the Catal Hüyük people than obsidian. The obsidian items they made were finer and more effective than the copper ones: the great age of metalworking in Anatolia was yet to come.

Living with the dead

Catal Hüyük is a city of shrines. Of the 139 buildings that have so far been excavated, forty seem to have been used for religious purposes. It may be that this picture has come about because archaeologists have chanced upon the 'religious quarter' of the city; as investigation goes on and more of the site is dug the proportion of shrines may decrease. But the evidence available at the moment points to a society dominated by religion.

The shrines were decorated with wall paintings and clay friezes in low relief. Many of the subjects were animals. There were deer being pursued by hunters, leopards, and bulls. The most remarkable decorations were the plaster bulls' heads, surmounted by real horns, which were placed on the walls of many of the shrines. The bull is a long-standing symbol of life, virility, and action. Its ancestors can be seen in the earliest cave paintings, including some of those in the caves of southern Anatolia where the Catal Hüyük people may have originated, and it is familiar from the much later palace frescoes of Knossos.

As at Knossos, the bull was not the only god portrayed at Catal Hüyük. Female goddess figurines have been found and female breasts feature in some of the low relief decoration in the shrines. These too would be fertility symbols, totems to ensure the fecundity of the soil and the continuance of the food supply, and symbols of life for the people of Catal Hüyük. There are few male statues in the shrines, and it has been suggested that one of the purposes of the bulls is to represent the male sex.

The figurines are powerful symbols of motherhood. It is not only that they have the exaggerated features common to mother-goddesses in the ancient world. Some of them not only look pregnant, but are actually giving birth. Some stand with hands and legs apart, one is giving birth in a seated position; some are giving birth to bull's or ram's heads, others to human children. The process of birth is obviously important in any society, but few have given it such powerful and enduring imagery.

Obvious symbols of death are also present. The paintings of vultures picking the flesh from human figures are a case in point. The people in the paintings are headless, a device that is probably meant to indicate that they are dead. The birds may be part of an ancient death ritual. Archaeologist James Mellaart, who was the first to excavate Catal Hüyük and remains the foremost authority on the site, believes that the people performed 'sky burials'. The dead would be placed on tall platforms to keep them away from animals such as dogs but within the reach of birds and insects that would gradually strip away the flesh, leaving only the skeleton and dry ligaments. The skeleton was then removed carefully, so that it was kept intact, and buried beneath one of the platforms in the family house.

Studies have shown that there was some variation in the condition of the bodies on burial. Some exhibited fully articulated skeletons with a little fat still attached; others were buried in a much poorer condition with some bones detached or missing completely. There are at least two possible reasons for this. It may be that the skill and care shown by the people who look after the bodies varied, some taking greater pains with the remains than others. Or the differences may throw some light on the burial customs at Catal Hüyük. It is possible that burials only took place once a year, at about the same time as the annual redecoration of the shrines and houses. James Mellaart suggests that people moved to temporary accommodation while the burial rites and replastering were taking place, although we have no way of knowing where they went. However the burials were carried out, the regular decoration of the shrines was obviously important to the people of Catal Hüyük. It was probably accompanied with reconsecration ceremonies that were intended to remind everyone of the continuing renewing pattern of the seasons.

Most of the people of Catal Hüyük were buried beneath the platforms in their own homes. But from what we know about the population of the city it is clear that not everyone was buried at home. There is only one house that has an average of seven burials per generation, the sort of number one would expect from the size of the houses. Most of the remaining individuals were buried in the shrines. They were probably priests and priestesses. Certainly they belonged to a privileged class since many of the shrine graves contained richer grave goods (including copper jewellery and weapons, baskets and wooden vessels) than their counterparts in the houses. Another indication of status is that women were buried beneath the larger platforms in the houses, men beneath the smaller.

An urban economy

The pairing of fertility and death symbols in the shrines is quite natural. It shows a concern with the entire natural cycle – from birth to death – a pattern that was vital for survival. Although this sounds like a rural religion, in which farmers would pray for the continuing of the cycle of growth, decay, and rebirth, it is hardly inappropriate for a city with a dependence on the local farms for its food supply.

Painting showing vultures and headless figures symbolizing death

It also implies a highly organized religion, probably one that would need a large class of priests to sustain, something which is borne out by the number of people who were buried in the shrines themselves. And if there was a large class of priests, there would also need to be other specialist classes, supplying goods to the priests. In the area of the city that has been excavated there is little evidence that anyone worked at weaving, pottery, or woodworking, and yet there are remains of finished objects in abundance. Future digs will probably reveal the area of the city where the artisans lived and worked.

It is also likely that there would be trade with other areas – at least local regions – to obtain materials that could not be found within the narrow confines of the city or its immediate surroundings.

What is the evidence for trade and a truly urban economy at Catal Hüyük? The city itself is in a rather inhospitable area with few natural resources except for reeds and clay. The Taurus mountains, some 80 kilometres to the south, provided a supply of timber; there were also copper and lead in the mountains. Acigel, about 200 kilometres northeast of the city, yielded supplies of obsidian to supplement those from the local volcano of Hasan Dag, for tools, arrowheads, and luxury items such as mirrors. Flints and some pottery came from Syria, while materials for pigments would also have been imported from various places. And Catal Hüyük's own pottery found its way at least as far as Cilicia, 160 kilometres (100 miles) southeast.

The excavators at Catal Hüyük have so far identified fourteen different layers of buildings, each layer built on the foundations of the previous one. What is more, only a fraction of the city has been excavated. Much of the city's story – from its foundation to its end – must remain an enigma.

MOHENJO-DARO

Indus Valley city *circa* 2400–1800 BC, centre of agricultural prosperity

Good soil is vital for civilization. Without the sustenance of an efficient agricultural system nearby no urban culture can survive for long. In many parts of the world the need for good soil has drawn people to areas that are far from ideal in other ways. A well known example were the ancient Egyptians, who put up with a bewildering mixture of drought and flood to benefit from the fertile soil beside the Nile. The people who lived by the banks of the Indus river between 2400 and 1800 BC faced even greater problems. As well as periodic flooding that threatened the very walls of their homes, they had to cope with a swampy terrain that formed the habitat of wild animals and disease-carrying insects.

It must have been worthwhile. The Indus Valley civilization prospered at over seventy sites, most of them near the river or its tributaries, including the great cities of Mohenjo-daro and Harappa. It is clear from excavations at Mohenjo-daro that flooding caused considerable damage to the city on several occasions, and that much rebuilding work was necessary. And yet the inhabitants clung on, maintaining a city of up to 40,000 people in the hostile environment. Their relationship with the land and the river was obviously crucial to them: if we can understand how they benefited from the bounty of the soil and coped with the rising flood waters, we can come close to an understanding of their lives. This relationship may also help us to fathom the great mystery of the Indus civilization: how such a prosperous people declined to poverty and how their cities fell.

Ox-carts would arrive from the fields along the Indus valley to bring grain to the great granary. Some archaeologists have seen this as a form of 'bank'. It certainly contained what amounted to the wealth of an empire.

A town by the river

Of the great Indus cities, Mohenjo-daro provides us with the best evidence of its buildings and the life of its people. Harappa proved a useful source of bricks for the builders of the Lahore to Karachi railway in the nineteenth century, and was badly plundered. Even so, the remains of Mohenjo-daro raise many questions.

Mohenjo-daro was a city in two parts. On the plain itself was the lower city; above it, on an artificial mound to the west, stood the citadel. The lower city consisted of streets of brick-built houses. The remains of the houses are substantial – the walls rise to a height of several feet in many places. They reveal buildings that were plain and utilitarian, but solidly constructed. Most of the larger houses were built around courtyards, with few windows looking out towards the street – this obviously made them more secure; it also helped keep out the hot sun. These houses were big enough to accommodate a sizeable family with several servants – the middle classes of Mohenjo-daro were clearly prosperous.

The bricks used to build these houses were of baked clay, although the builders sometimes used cheaper sun-dried bricks for the inner walls. They were plastered inside, but probably not on the outside. The fact that some of the richer houses have walls built of decorative brickwork (with alternate courses made up of vertically and horizontally laid bricks) suggests that the outer walls were meant to be seen.

The city was not made up simply of large buildings. As well as smaller houses, tiny individual rooms have been found, mostly on street corners and usually with a door leading on to the larger of the two streets. These were probably used by watchmen who guarded the city by night.

They were also well organized. Their city was consciously and carefully planned. The streets were laid out on a grid pattern. A broad main street was crossed by numerous smaller streets; these in turn were bisected by narrow lanes. The fact that the streets had an elaborate and efficient drainage system points to a rich municipality that was prepared to provide services to the citizens. Earthenware pipes and channels directed waste water from the houses into the communal drains, which were built of brick and ran beneath the streets. Any good drainage system requires regular cleaning, and at Mohenjo-daro this was provided for by regularly placed manhole covers that could be opened to give access to the underground channels. Blockages could therefore easily be extracted – and they were: in some places archaeologists have found heaps of debris left near the manhole covers in the street.

The overall impression that we get from these houses is one of prosperity – but not ostentation. The same character emerges from the finds that have been discovered on the site and at

The granary was the hub of the city, and there was plenty of space beside for the arrival of traffic in contrast to the narrower residential streets beyond. Behind the granary is the great bath complex, probably a ceremonial centre, in which some archaeologists have seen the earliest origins of Hinduism. Still further beyond were the courtyards of the college of priests next to which there may have been a large temple.

other Indus Valley towns. For example, many copper and bronze tools and weapons have been unearthed. These are well made, beautifully shaped, but not adorned with the complex engravings that are seen on the status-symbol weapons of some other early peoples. Similarly, archaeologists have found fine jewellery on the site (beads of gold and silver, plus humbler ones of bronze, copper, and steatite; bracelets and rings), but again the design of these objects is restrained. There are hints of richness, such as elegant shapes of carved bone and ivory that were probably pieces of inlay from long-perished wooden furniture. But on the whole it seems that the people of Mohenjo-daro were confident in their position and did not have to assert their wealth or status.

And yet there are sinister reminders that their confidence may have been misplaced. Examining the houses and the way they have been rebuilt several times shows that repeated floods caused much damage. But what is revealing is that the standard of repairs deteriorated as time went on. What is more, houses that had been quite large were sometimes divided up into smaller units – the population was increasing while prosperity was turning downwards. Life in the city's later years must have been hard.

The riches of the fields

Mohenjo-daro's prosperity came from the land. We find the evidence for this in the other half of the city, the citadel area, which overlooks the lower city from the west. It is sited on an artificial mound surmounted by a mud-brick platform. It was defended by a series of towers built of brick reinforced with heavy horizontal timbers. The citadel is the section of the city that has been most extensively excavated, and some tantalizing

WEST PAKISTAN
Lahore
Indus
Delhi
Agra
MOHENJO-DARO
Ganges
Karachi
Ahmadabad
INDIA
ARABIAN
SEA

glimpses of life in the Indus Valley civilization have been revealed.

Probably the most important building was a large granary about 45 metres (150 feet) long and 23 metres (75 feet) wide. This imposing building was placed on a substantial platform of brick and had tall brick walls that sloped inwards slightly, to give the impression of a fortress. Immediately on top of the podium is a brick subfloor criss-crossed with deep channels that allowed air to circulate beneath the grain. This would preserve the grain and prevent fermentation from taking place. Above this would have been a structure of wooden silos in which the grain itself was stored. Along one side a brick loading platform gave space for ox-carts to draw up to collect and deliver grain.

The fact that this was such a massive structure, with walls that made it look more like a fortification than a grain store, may well be significant. For some writers have seen this granary and its counterpart at Harappa as 'banks', where the effective wealth of the Indus civilization was held. While the bank may be a rather modern concept, grain was obviously a valuable resource to the Indus people and would need to be conserved and protected in time of flood: a substantial building was quite appropriate.

As well as the wheeled ox-carts, of which we know because of toy models that have been found at Mohenjo-daro, the Indus people used boats to transport their corn. More than one surviving structure in the city looks like a dock, and we know that the course of the Indus has changed dramatically since Mohenjo-daro was built – the city was originally much closer to the river than it is today. Such a highly developed system of transport points to a people for whom trade was important. This is probably confirmed by the fact that the Indus people used seals, an ideal way of identifying goods quickly and easily. Unfortunately, no convincing translations have been made of the script on the Indus Valley seals. This is because too few characters appear on them to provide sufficient material to crack their code.

But one thing is certain. Indus seals travelled widely. Examples have been found at the city of Ur and around the Persian Gulf, so the trade of the Indus Valley was quite far-ranging. This opens up an intriguing possibility. There are some Sumerian documents that refer to a land called Dilmun. This country held a certain magic for the people of Mesopotamia. Dilmun was located in the east, where the sun rises, and some of the records refer to it as something of a paradise on earth. Ships from Dilmun, brought cargoes of wood to the Mesopotamian city of Lagash in *c.*2450 BC; further cargoes arrived in Babylonia a little later.

Steatite statue of a priest

By *c.*1950 BC tablets from Ur record ships that brought more precious items – metals such as gold and silver; stones like lapis lazuli; ivory and bone artefacts. Although some archaeologists have identified Dilmun with the Persian Gulf island of Bahrain, the mysterious land could be the Indus Valley. Or it may be that the Indus people used Bahrain-Dilmun as a stopping place on their way to Mesopotamia. Whichever was the case, it is likely that the fame of the Indus civilization was widespread.

The great bath

The other building in the citadel that shows us much about the people who built the city is the great bath. This is a large brick building, again plainly but solidly constructed. At its centre is a sunken pool about 12 x 7 x 2.5 metres (39 x 23 x 8 feet). The bottom of the pool was made watertight with the use of kiln-fired bricks, gypsum mortar, and bitumen. Around the large bath were a number of smaller rooms with private baths. Each of these rooms, although only about 3 x 2 metres (9.5 x 6 feet), contained a stone staircase to an upper storey.

It is thought that the purpose of the bath complex was religious rather than hygienic. Ritual cleansing is part of many religions, including modern Hinduism. The theory is therefore that the small baths would be used by priests, who lived in the rooms above. They would bathe in their own small baths before emerging to preside over mass ritual cleansings in the great bath itself.

Who were these priests and what religion did they follow? The most complete and striking portrait found at Mohenjo-daro is probably of a priest. It is a statue in steatite, only about 18 centimetres (7 inches) high but magnificently carved. The head is bearded (but with a shaved upper lip), the nose long, the lips thick, and the eyes narrowed, as if in contemplation. The figure wears a cloak that is patterned with trefoils. This motif occurs on sculptures in Mesopotamia and Egypt as well as in the Indus Valley, and usually appears in religious art. This is the main reason why archaeologists believe that this figure is either a priest or a priest-king.

Alternatively, the statue may be of a god, but the radical difference between this and the statues of gods that have survived makes this less likely. The many narrow-waisted, large-breasted female statuettes that have been found in the Indus cities suggest that the people worshipped a female deity – another example of the fertility goddess in a civilization that got a large proportion of its wealth from agriculture.

On the other hand it may be that the female figures, which are far cruder than their male counterparts, represent a popular or household religion, while male statues were symbols of the official religion of the great bath.

One of the reasons for this uncertainty about Indus Valley religion is that no temple has yet been uncovered at Mohenjo-daro. There is a legend of long standing that beneath the more recent Buddhist monastery built on the eastern side of the citadel the foundations of an Indus-period temple are concealed. There is no real evidence for this, although the tradition of raising a sacred structure on a previously sacred site is a strong one. This, together with the fact that the citadel is a likely location for the city's principal temple, gives the tradition some weight.

The Indus seals

Clues about the religion are provided

by the seals that have been found at Mohenjo-daro and Harappa. These are exquisite objects. Carved on pieces of soft stone, they are usually square, in contrast to the cylindrical seals of the Mesopotamian cities. The most common format is a line of script across the top of the face of the seal, with a relief carving – often of an animal – below. The inscriptions are usually quite short – frequently no more than half a dozen characters – and this shortness is one reason why the script has proved impossible to decipher. The animal carvings are even more intriguing than the unreadable script. In many examples a creature rather like an antelope is shown. The animal appears to have only one horn, and so these seals bear the earliest representations of the unicorn. (It is sometimes thought that the single-horned effect comes from the simple fact that the creature is shown from the side, but seal pictures of bulls, also common on Indus Valley seals, show both horns clearly visible in side views.) The sacred quality of the unicorn is emphasized because it stands in front of a device on a stand that looks like an incense burner.

Short-horned and long-horned bulls, rhinoceroses, tigers, crocodiles, elephants, and other animals all appear on seals from Mohenjo-daro. One of the most popular images is the Brahmani bull. This is the species with the hump, long horns, and heavy dewlap that is held sacred by Hindu people today. Its portrayal on some of the seals is superb – the muscles, horns, and great ripples of flesh beneath the jaw are picked out with strong, decisive modelling.

If the depictions of the Brahmani bull seem to prefigure the beliefs of Hinduism at Mohenjo-daro, another seal image confirms this. This consists of a seated humanoid figure with a horned headdress and three faces. He is sitting with his legs folded in a position that recalls the lotus asana in yoga. Many of these features remind one of the Hindu god Shiva, particularly in his role as Lord of the Beasts – on one seal he is surrounded by images of a rhinoceros, tiger, elephant, and unicorn.

Seal showing bull and Indus script

Although these remarkable seals do not give enough evidence to call the people of Mohenjo-daro early Hindus, their images, in conjunction with the fact that their religion involved ritual cleansing, do suggest that some of the origins of Hinduism can be found in the Indus civilization.

Rising tide, falling city

What brought about the downfall of this once-prosperous civilization, causing the standard of building to deteriorate and the cities eventually to be abandoned? There have been many theories, and it is probable that most of the reasons put forward by historians played some part – the downfall of a whole civilization is rarely a simple process that can be explained away by a single reason. Factors that have been suggested include the collapse of the local irrigation system; the breaking away of provincial territories leading to a decline in the political power of Mohenjo-daro and Harappa; foreign invasion; soil exhaustion as a result of over-cultivation; and malaria.

The most intriguing possible reasons are linked to the key fact about the Indus cities – their relationship with the river. What is especially interesting is that evidence from the soil points not to repeated seasonal flooding of the Indus as the decisive cause of damage, but to a single large flood. Analysis of the silt that built up suggests a process known as 'ponding', the accumulation of mud from a stagnant lake. It is as if someone had built a dam that blocked off the river's natural course to the sea, resulting in a reservoir of water around the city. And in a way this is what happened. The Indus area was subject to movements in the earth's crust. In one of these the land between Mohenjo-daro and the sea rose up, making the river waters run back towards the city. The people found themselves on an island.

At first the streets of the lower city would have been awash. The network of drains would not have been capable of coping with this sort of onslaught – they were not designed to. The only chance was to build upwards from the foundations of the damaged houses, hoping that they would be able to reach a high enough level to keep clear of the waters.

Even if they were successful a change of this sort would have been nothing short of an ecological disaster for the people of Mohenjo-daro. The fields would be inundated and the wealth of the soil destroyed. Trade would still be possible – provided that the people could spare enough time from trying to restore the city and secure a short-term supply of food. Meanwhile diseases – from malnutrition to malaria – would be rife. As we can see from the deteriorating remains of the houses, the city was turning into a slum.

No one knows where the survivors went when the city of Mohenjo-daro was finally abandoned. They may have fled to one of the lesser towns of the Indus area; they could have moved towards the Punjab; perhaps they fled to the foothills of the Himalayas. Wherever they went, by about 1700 BC the city was empty.

For most of its history the Indus civilization was isolated in many ways. It is possible to draw some parallels with Mesopotamia, the other great civilization with which the Indus people are known to have had contact. But the similarities (a well planned city, a literate people who used seals, and so on) are general rather than specific. They are the sort of features that we would expect to see in a civilization of this period. The contrasts are more obvious. The Indus language, although we cannot read it, is obviously very different from Sumerian. The art of Mohenjo-daro and Harappa – the seals, terracottas, and stone sculptures – has a quality of its own.

The lasting impression is of a people with enough self-assurance to remain different and independent. They did not need to copy the art of other countries, they were quite confident in the worth of their own achievements. For the most part their confidence was well placed. But for the disaster of the floods they might have survived to have a greater and longer-lasting influence. But the river on which they depended proved too powerful for them in the end.

UR

Sumerian city *circa* 4000–2000 BC, home of the first great literary culture, site of the ziggurat, and scene of lavish royal burials

Genesis chapter XI sums it up: 'And they had brick for stone, and slime they had for mortar. And they said, "Go to, let us build a city, and a tower, whose top may reach unto heaven; and let us make a name, lest we be scattered abroad upon the face of the whole earth."'

The people whom the Bible records in this way were the ancestors of Abraham, who settled in the area called Sumer or Mesopotamia – the land between the Tigris and Euphrates rivers – between *c.*5300 and 3500 BC. They included the Ubaidians and groups of Semitic nomads from the south-west as well as people from southern Iran. They found a land with fertile soil but with no stone for building, and so, like many middle eastern peoples, they built their homes of bricks. In fact they built more than one city. There were independent city states right across Mesopotamia, but they all had a uniform culture which we know today as Sumerian civilization.

What did the Sumerian cities have in common? First and foremost, a written culture and a common language. This enabled them to communicate everything from legal records and business transactions to myths and legends from one city to another, giving them new opportunities in both administration and the arts. Second, they had a system of trade and commerce that, although it must have put the cities in competition with each other, made the individual states similar in outlook. And third, they shared a religion that produced some of the most remarkable architecture of the period, the great towers or ziggurats, the finest of which was at Ur.

Beyond every bustling street in Ur the tall ziggurat could be seen, reminding everyone of the power of the temple. The clay tablet shown above this scene, with its wedge-shaped cuneiform script, is a symbol of the importance of writing for the Sumerians.

Ur, the city of Abraham's people, was one of the largest towns in Mesopotamia. It was well placed at the centre of an agricultural region on the marshy but fertile land between the two rivers. Ur has a long history, during which two periods in particular stand out as fascinating today. The first, almost 4,000 years before the birth of Christ, was the time of the great royal burials, which tell us so much about the lives and deaths of the early kings and courtiers. The second great epoch in the history of Ur was the Sumerian revival around 2000 BC, when the ziggurat, the most famous building in the city, was constructed.

Looking at a site like Ur today, it is difficult to imagine what it was like in its prime. Although there are substantial remains of the great ziggurat, its outline is reduced to a shadow of the original. There are similar difficulties with the houses, which are even harder to reconstruct to their original glory. But Ur holds deeper mysteries than these. The rich royal tombs that have been excavated yielded jewellery made of gold and lapis lazuli. But the graves also had more sinister contents: the remains of bodies that seem to have been the victims of sacrifice. What is the story of this civilization that was at once literate and brutal, sophisticated and barbaric?

The secrets of the tombs

In 1923 the British archaeologist Leonard Woolley discovered the famous burial ground at Ur. The richness of the grave goods led Woolley to believe that these were royal burials, dating from the period *c.*2800–2600 BC. In total the graves contained about 2,000 bodies, but not all had been members of a royal family – only about sixteen of the bodies were adorned in a way that suggested people of the highest rank. Many of the others seem to have been courtiers – attendants, personal servants, soldiers, musicians. They all carried with them the tools of their trades, but they were not buried with the rich grave goods of a king or queen. This led Woolley to conclude that, just as the Egyptian pharaohs were buried with wooden models of servants to help them on their journey to the afterlife, so the Sumerian kings were accompanied by the corpses of their real servants.

As the excavators gradually penetrated the first of the tombs this impression was confirmed. First they came across a group of five male bodies with nothing to identify them – they had no possessions at all in fact, except for cups and daggers. Next they discovered ten female corpses with impressive jewellery (including ornate headdresses and beads of precious stones), but again with no offerings. Then, remains of a sledge chariot with oxen were discovered, together with further bodies, a large chest, and numerous offerings – tools and weapons; copper, gold and stoneware vessels; and a pair of silver lions' heads, perhaps ornaments from a throne. But amongst all this there was

The ziggurat was a vast platform lined with bricks and entered via a triple staircase. It is one of the earliest of the world's 'temple-mountains' which were centres of both spiritual and worldly power. It was a spiritual centre because of the ceremonies that took place there, a worldly centre because it symbolized the power of the priests to gather together the army of workers needed to create and maintain it.

no single body that could be identified as the beneficiary of these gifts.

The answer to this riddle was found in another chamber beneath the first pit. This contained yet more bodies, identifiable from what they carried or wore as soldiers, grooms with ox-carts, female attendants, and the king himself. Nearby, in a third chamber, lay the queen. Her body was found buried under heaps of beads of carnelian, lapis lazuli, agate, chalcedony, silver, and gold. Amongst these rich offerings was her cylinder seal, from which we know her name was: Puabi.

The ziggurat, Ur 2000 BC

Later excavations revealed other graves with a similar pattern. One, the grave of King Meskalamdug, yielded an even more extraordinary profusion of objects – over fifty copper bowls, numerous other vessels in gold and silver, superb weapons, and a beaten gold helmet engraved to look like a wig. Some of the monarchs' graves contained only a handful of attendants, some had as many as eighty. But in each case the fact that many of the skeletons Woolley found belonged to young people pointed to their sacrificial deaths. This seemed all the more likely since each body was accompanied by a cup, as if they had all taken a draught of poison in the tomb itself.

It is easy to imagine the funeral ritual that would have taken place in the royal graves. First of all the body of the ruler, usually inside a coffin, would be placed in its tomb. Three or four chosen attendants would be entombed with the body and would take their draft of poison. The inner tomb would then be sealed with mud bricks and the wall plastered over. Next the great funeral procession would enter the outer chamber: the women of the court wearing their exquisite gold and silver diadems and headdresses, the musicians playing on harps inlaid with intricate marquetry patterns, the grooms leading ox-carts that perhaps bore further offerings, the lesser servants following behind. They would all have known their fate, and there is no evidence that they did anything other than accept their role in the pre-ordained ritual. With a small guard of soldiers standing at the entrance, all would take their positions and lie down to die. The ritual

complete, servants would enter the tomb, arrange the bodies, kill the oxen, and withdraw. While a funeral feast continued on the surface of the ground, with libations being poured and music played, earth would be thrown into the tomb shaft and the contents of the tomb would vanish from view for 4,500 years.

Some writers who have examined the finds from these graves since Woolley excavated them in the 1920s have concluded that these are are not royal graves but evidence of an elaborate fertility ritual in which death was supposed to lead to a renewal of life. But the richness of the finds and the siting of the cemetery in the heart of the city's sacred area have persuaded most archaeologists to accept Woolley's interpretation. Indeed one would expect an annual burial to accompany a fertility ritual of this sort, but during the 600–year time span of the tombs, there were only sixteen qualifying burials. On the other hand the idea of fertility could have been present in the royal burial ceremony – there is nothing to suggest that the death of a monarch could not be associated with a ritual of renewal before the next king took the throne.

Early king wearing a golden headband

The golden age of Ur

Although Ur had been an important city even before the time of the royal graves, in *c.*2500 BC the city started to grow. We are not quite sure why this happened when it did, but the effects of a good food supply must have pushed the population up, while increasing trade along the rivers meant greater prosperity. Another major influence on the growth of the city was probably the fact that people needed to get together to irrigate the land effectively. The area between the two rivers was prone both to drought and to flooding, and effective irrigation would need the sort of cooperation and organization that would come easiest with a strong city government directing the operations.

The result was that Ur came to the peak of its influence during the years around 2000 BC, under a king called Ur-Nammu. He presided over a period when the whole of Mesopotamia became prosperous. Using a system of about forty civil governors, he divided his kingdom up into districts that could be administered efficiently. For extra control some areas were also put under the command of military garrisons, whose leaders reported directly to the king.

From his cities of Ur and Uruk, Ur-Nammu controlled an area that included not only the land between the lower Tigris and Euphrates, but also the region around Assur (further up the Tigris and later to become one of the capital cities of the Assyrians), and the city of Susa (home of the Elamites, to the east of the Tigris in modern Iran). Naturally this expansion gave Ur-Nammu great wealth, and one way in which he used it was to rebuild his capital cities. In doing so he was keen to make the buildings more permanent than their predecessors. In many buildings, therefore, he replaced the old-fashioned mud-bricks, which often needed repairing after a season of heavy rains, with longer-lasting harder kiln-fired bricks.

The world of the temple

The building on which Ur-Nammu lavished most wealth and effort was the great temple or ziggurat. Even as a ruin, it is a most impressive building. Like many places of worship, from the great 'tower' of Babylon to the temples of Kampuchea, it is based on the image of a mountain and is designed to bring the priest or worshipper nearer to the heavens and therefore nearer to the deity. The ziggurat had a ground plan of 63 x 43 metres (207 x 141 feet) and was about 30 metres (100 feet) high, so by today's standards it was hardly a tall building. Nevertheless it was a remarkable achievement, considering that no brick in the structure is longer than 38 centimetres (15 inches).

The ziggurat originally had three terraces, reached by a triple staircase that obviously had some ceremonial use. The designer made the temple look even more impressive by making the outer walls slope inwards – thereby also giving the ziggurat a more mountain-like appearance. At the top was a sanctuary building in which the most sacred rites of Mesopotamian religion were performed. The whole ziggurat was faced with rectangular kiln-fired bricks. Most of these are stamped with the name of Ur-Nammu, though there are some that bear the names of later rulers – testimony that the temple did need some later repairs.

One of the most surprising things about the ziggurat is that it is solid – the interior is a simple core of mud bricks and only the sanctuary at the top could be entered. During the rainy season moisture would gradually permeate the mud-brick core, and there were drainage holes in the outer covering of baked bricks to allow this water to escape. The ziggurat stands in the sacred precinct of the city, known as the *temenos*, which also contained Ur-Nammu's palace. It was thus set off from the rest of the city and was marked as being the most important building in the greatest city of its time.

What deity was worshipped at the ziggurat? We know from written records that the people of Mesopotamia had many gods – altogether over 2,000 are known. The large number was due partly to the Sumerian custom of taking a personal god – all the citizens would choose a particular god to look after their interests and intercede on their behalf with the more powerful deities. To begin with most of these gods were linked to some aspect of the natural world – in many cases they took animal form. Later they are shown in Sumerian sculptures with human features. Perhaps the most important Sumerian deity was the moon god Nanna, and the many small copper moons found at the ziggurat confirm that he, together with his wife Ningal, were worshipped there.

But the religious aspect of the temple was not its only importance for the Sumerians. It acted as a centre of city life, and employed many people. Obviously a complex of the size of the ziggurat and sacred precinct needed many workers to build and maintain it – artists, builders, and labourers were all required. Scribes and administrators were vital to keep track of the work. And all these people needed to be fed, housed, and clothed, so the temple also employed cooks, bakers, brewers, spinners and weavers. The records of the temple at

Pendant in the shape of a lion-headed eagle

the Mesopotamian city of Lagash show that 1,200 people were employed. At Ur there were probably even more. This army of workers, with the priests and scribes who controlled them, made the temple the most powerful institution in the city.

Writing it all down

To function well, a city needs a bureaucracy. And an efficient bureaucracy needs written records. Some form of accounting procedure, to show who has paid their taxes, who owns what and who is responsible for municipal projects is also essential to city life. Writing is also invaluable for traders, to record deals and keep accounts. Some early cities, like Catal Hüyük, seem to have managed without it. But the Sumerian people relied on writing more than any others before them.

Writing therefore provides the obvious place to look to gain an understanding of Sumerian culture. The records that survive consist of clay tablets, into which the Sumerian scribes pressed a wooden stylus to produce the marks that made up their script. This type of writing is known as *cuneiform* (wedge-shaped) script. When dry, the tablets could be stored – and they have proved a very durable record.

The Sumerians had a thriving class of scribes, who studied hard to perfect the arduous skill of using the 2,000 different signs of the cuneiform script to keep city and temple records. As time went on they took an imaginative leap and started to write down stories and poems – works that had no doubt been handed down orally for many generations before the scribes immortalized them in clay to give us our first written literature. The writings of the Sumerians therefore give us unique insights into both the day-to-day existence and the imaginative lives of the people of cities like Uruk and Ur.

Many of the tablets from this fertile area of the world tell us about the local agriculture. The farmers grew cereal crops, especially barley, which does well locally; they also harvested reeds, as well as raising livestock. Further tablets mention the specialized trades that we would expect from the objects excavated at Ur – bricklayers, carpenters, and metalworkers. Other professionals, such as cooks and physicians, are also mentioned.

The city states of Mesopotamia had one of the most important assets of a flourishing market economy – good communications. The cuneiform script was one aspect of this; transport along the rivers – especially the Euphrates – was another. So it did not matter that they had few natural resources. They could import the raw materials that they needed and sell manufactured goods. They excelled in the crafts of metalworking and inlaying, as we can see from the objects buried in the royal graves.

Recording trade was one of the most common uses to which the people of Ur put their writing. From assorted tablets we learn that semi-precious stones for jewellery, such as lapis lazuli and carnelian, came to Ur from Iran and Afghanistan; the Indus Valley was probably another source of carnelian. Gold came from Anatolia, while silver was imported from Elam and the Taurus mountains. Tin was brought from Afghanistan. The Euphrates provided an excellent route for many goods, particularly the heavier cargoes such as cedar wood, which was floated along the river from Syria, and stone for building.

The tablets of Mesopotamia give an excellent impression of the intellectual life of the people. We can read about their laws, which were quite sophisticated for their time. They converted the traditional morality of 'an eye for an eye' into a system of fines. The law code of Ur-Nammu established a fine of ten silver shekels for cutting off someone's foot, and one silver mina for a broken bone. We can also find out about their literature, which in turn tells us something about their religious beliefs.

The educational tablets are some of the most revealing. They mostly consist of lists of facts and names that were meant to be copied and learned by rote. Of the subjects covered, natural history is one of the most important, with lists of birds, insects, and other animals. There are also lists of rocks and minerals, towns and cities. Some tablets provided examples of different Sumerian grammatical forms; others contained mathematical problems. There were also more literary tablets, containing epics of the local gods and heroes, hymns to gods and kings, and proverbs and fables espousing popular wisdom. Although the main purpose of all this material was to train young scribes-to-be to write cuneiform script, much additional knowledge was imparted by these lists of facts and fables.

One tablet actually gives us an account of a typical school day. It shows that teaching methods were primitive and discipline rough and ready. The schoolboy rushes to school to avoid being caned for lateness. He recites the work he has learned from his tablet, writes out a new tablet, and receives both oral and written assignments. He is beaten for talking, for standing up in class, and for poor copying.

Harp from a royal burial

This was basic but effective education that produced the effective administrative class of a successful urban civilization. It fulfilled the organizational needs of a people whose trade was successful and whose influence was great. And the writing it produced has given today's historians vital insights into the life of the people of ancient Mesopotamia.

BOGHAZKOY

Mountain citadel and capital of the Hittite warriors, *circa* 1700–1200 BC

The Hittites were the most powerful people in Anatolia during the period 1700–1200 BC. But who exactly were they? Their name is familiar from the Old Testament, but the Biblical Hittites were a different people, who came from the area we now know as Syria. Assyrian documents refer to these people as the Hatti, and this name was inherited from the Anatolians whose capital city was at Boghazköy in central Turkey. The Anatolian Hittites were a short, stockily-built, broad-shouldered people. Their characters were as rugged as their appearance and they seem to have been well suited to military life. But compared with the Assyrians, who have a reputation for extreme cruelty towards their captives, the Hittites were humane in victory. And their laws reveal a similar humanity.

Home for the Hittites was a high plateau in central Anatolia. The terrain is rocky and the climate is one of extremes – cold, snowy winters, hot, dry summers, heavy rains in the spring. But the area did have one important advantage: many craggy sites in this otherwise inhospitable country were easy to defend. One such was the city of Hattusas (or Hattusha) near the modern Turkish village of Boghazköy.

It was a Hittite leader called Labarnas who recognized the potential of this site in *c.*1650 BC. He rebuilt the fortress that stood there, giving it solid walls and its first palace, and made it his capital city. And to commemorate this he took a new name, becoming king Hattusilis I. In so doing he founded the dynasty that we now call the Hittite 'Old Kingdom' and became the first of a long line of Hittite kings to base themselves at Boghazköy.

These Hittite soldiers are driving their chariots outside one of the gates of Boghazköy. Speed was of the essence for these warriors as they used their chariots to break up ranks of opposing foot soldiers.

Hattusilis and his successors ruled a large area of Anatolia. Their kingdom was landlocked, which meant that they were surrounded by enemies and were constantly at war with one or other of them. Hittite documents tell us the names of some of these enemies (countries such as Arzawa, Mira, and Hapalla), although we do not know exactly where these places were. But we do know that the Hittites' lack of a coast gave them one advantage – the enemy nations could not unite and mount a concerted sea attack. In this, as in much else, the Hittites turned an apparent problem to their own good.

In the capital

Boghazköy today is a sprawling, enigmatic site; the stones seem to be slipping back towards the ground from which they came, to become part of the natural landscape once more. But if we try to reconstruct the city it can tell us much about Hittite way of life.

The site is a natural fortress. It has a rocky base, and the steep crags to the north and east are all but unscalable. All the inhabitants had to do was to wall off the south and west and they had a secure base. This was done during the Old Kingdom period, and by the time the Hittite empire was established (*c.*1200 BC) the citadel was fortified on all sides. The remains of these later walls survive today. The first thing that strikes one about them is their scale. As well as a long outer wall, enclosing a large area, there is also an inner fortress, again surrounded by walls, that contained the royal palace and other important buildings. Being thick and strong, these walls were remarkable in other ways. They were given extra height by being built up on earthworks, giving the Hittites the ability to fire on their enemies from a great height.

The lower faces of the walls sloped, to provide protection from battering rams and scaling ladders; in addition, missiles such as rocks that were catapulted at the walls could ricochet off at an angle and would do a minimum of damage. Tunnels through the earthworks beneath the walls allowed the defenders to surprise the enemy by attacking from behind their ranks; they also offered a quick escape route if there was a defeat. Further inner walls divided up the city so that it could be defended in sections – another good insurance policy if the attackers scored a partial victory.

One of the results of all this fortification was to separate the king from the rest of his people. A remote king can have an air of god-like mystery, and psychologically as well as physically, the Hittite kings had great power. But they were by no means alone in the citadel. The royal palace was surrounded by a complex of buildings housing all sorts of servants – it was a community in itself. Records show that they king's many servants included pages, doormen, grooms, a chamberlain, a doctor, a

The citadel, Boghazköy 1600 BC

A large mountain site, Boghazköy was an ideal place for a fortress. The Hittites built double walls to supplement the natural defences, and these enclosed a vast area. At the top of the hill the great temple and palace provided a final, and even more heavily defended, refuge for the king and priests.

reciter of prayers, and personal bodyguards. Archaeologial remains reveal the complex needed to feed this large retinue – kitchens, pantries, and a dairy. The king and his immediate family lived in a seraglio-like complex within the walls. But there was also a formal residence (called the 'halentuwa house') where the king and queen presided over royal ceremonies; in addition there was a separate residence for the royal princes.

So the palace was much more than a residence. It was a ceremonial (and therefore also a religious) centre and, since it was able to exert a powerful influence on the supply of and demand for goods, was almost certainly an important economic centre too. By the end of the Hittite period in the thirteenth century BC, the palace was still larger and more complex. There was a series of courtyards, off which led the various royal apartments and an audience hall.

Around the outside of the palace was an even greater community. As far as we can tell, the mixture of good organization and rugged individualism that is typical of the Hittites existed in the outer city as well as in the palace. The streets were well planned and straight, and had a well constructed drainage system. But the houses themselves, built of mud-brick on stone foundations, were irregular in shape and size. The few windows were small, there were flat roofs of

N
0 Yards 500
0 Metres 500
Assyrian Colony
('Karum')
Great
Temple I
Tablets
Citadel (Büyük Kale)
Nisantepe
(inscription)
Southern Citadel
'Yellow Castle'
ion Gate'
'New Castle'
Temple IV
Temple II
'King's
Gate'
Temple V
Temple III
'Sphinx Gate'

dried mud and brushwood resting on wooden beams, and the rooms were far from luxurious. Animals shared the peoples' accommodation, and life for many of the inhabitants must have been cramped and inconvenient.

Hittite society

The people who lived in these different-sized houses came from a number of different social classes. At the bottom were slaves. Then came the farm workers, who went out to the fields to cultivate barley, emmer wheat, fruit, pulses, olives, onions, and flax. They also tended cattle and sheep, as well as keeping bees – early evidence of the production of honey, valued in the ancient world as a food sweetener. Although poor, the farm workers were vital to the Hittites at Boghazköy. At its height, the city surrounding the king's palace contained a population of over 30,000 people and they would have needed a vast food supply.

Next were the artisans. These included potters, carpenters, and cloth workers. The latter spun and wove the flax grown by the farmers into cloth to make garments. From the surviving Hittite sculptures we can see that most men wore knee-length tunics; there were also longer robes probably used on ceremonial occasions. Women had similar garments, with long cloaks for the winter. Soldiers wore a light shirt and a heavy, kilt-like garment. The king had similar garments for battle and robes for ceremonies, and is often singled out by a conical headdress.

There were also blacksmiths at Boghazköy. It used to be thought that the Hittites were the first ironworkers in the world, and that they guarded their methods with great secrecy; but it is now known that this picture is untrue: the idea of iron as a Hittite 'state secret' stems from a misunderstanding of a single document. Nevertheless, iron was important to the Hittites, especially towards the end of the empire period, for making tools, weapons, and probably even armour. The ore was smelted away from the city, near the places where it was taken from the ground. It was then brought to forges at Boghazköy for final working.

Interestingly enough, stone was worked in a similar way by the Hittites. Blocks were cut into the basic shape that was required at the quarry, before being taken to the city sculptor's workshop where the skilled carving was done.

Stele showing Teshub, the weather god

The next group up the social scale were the high officials, nobles, and dignitaries. These people were often related to the king – if not directly, at least by marriage. They included vassals, nobles who held land in return for swearing an oath of allegiance to the king and providing military support in times of war. This feudal system (though nowhere near as sophisticated as the feudal system that developed in Europe 2,000 years later) was an important factor in securing Hittite victories. Conquered states were treated in a similar way. The king would send one of his nobles to govern the state; the noble concerned would obtain income from the land, while the king would get an additional source of troops, plus tribute from the conquered people. The exact arrangements were set out in treaties, and the officials oversaw the agreement and ensured that the terms were carried out. There was also a custom of exchanging gifts between the king and his vassal states, which helped to cement links between the conqueror and his new subjects.

At the top of the social structure were the king and queen. The queen was more powerful than a mere consort. She had an important place in ceremony and government and, if the king died first, she ruled on in her own right. It may be that there is an influence here of the earliest prehistoric societies in Anatolia, which were probably matriarchal. It may also be that the continuing rule of the queen was an important influence for stability in what was often an unstable and strife-torn region of the globe.

The rule of law

Amongst the thousands of tablets unearthed at Boghazköy during excavations in the nineteenth century were a number that included Hittite laws. There is always something slightly mysterious about ancient law codes as we can rarely be sure how effective they were. For example, we know that some of the early Mesopotamian laws were flouted so consistently that they can only represent either the pious hopes of the king or an attempt by some early public relations officer to make the state seem more law-abiding than it really was.

But the Hittite laws are rather different. For a start, many of them are based on actual judgments – like modern 'case law' – so they appear to be a record of what actually happened. In addition, many of them are obviously practical – they have to do with the actual value of goods sold in the marketplace, rather than with crime and punishment.

So what sort of a picture do these laws give us? Prices of goods were controlled rigidly. A unit of value called the silver shekel was used so that, for example, a tub of oil was valued at two shekels, two cheeses were worth one shekel, and a woollen garment was worth twenty shekels. But the shekel was not necessarily used as a form of currency – barter still prevailed, but the shekel provided a guide as to what could be exchanged for what. The labourer's rates of hire were regulated in a similar way so that the king and his officials could keep a tight grip on the economic life of the country even at the lowest level.

Criminal laws were surprisingly humane. The death penalty was reserved only for some cases of murder, for rape, and for treason. Penalties for other crimes were based on the principle of compensation – if you stole from your neighbour, you had to restore goods to the equivalent value; if you burned down a house, you had to rebuild it. We do not have any records of court proceedings to show if all the judgments were based fairly and squarely on these laws. But the records we do have – of inquiries into the crimes of higher officials – show that the Hittites were prepared to question witnesses carefully and persistently in a genuine attempt to find the truth.

Struggles for supremacy

While keeping justice at home, the Hittites were continually trying to keep their position as the supreme power in Anatolia. The very first of the Old Kingdom rulers, Hattusilis I, was engaged in a war with the people of Arzawa, probably an area of either western or southwestern Anatolia. The reason why Hattusilis wanted control over this area was probably its valuable supplies of tin. Other enemies were the Hurrians, who spread to southeastern Anatolia from Mesopotamia, and the people of Aleppo, from the north. By the end of his reign Hattusilis had defeated all except Aleppo, but his grandson Mursilis, who followed him as king, managed to overcome them and conquer the northern part of Syria in *c.*1595 BC. Spurred on by this success the Hittites went on to conquer one of the greatest powers of the time – Babylon. But Babylon was not a lasting Hittite possession – the need to suppress enemies nearer home soon led Mursilis to abandon control of the great city.

This is the pattern of Hittite history during the Old Kingdom and the Empire (*c.*1450–1180 BC) – campaign after campaign to take tribute from the surrounding peoples, keep the trade routes from the Euphrates open, and defend the central Anatolian homeland, with the occasional tussle with one of the other great powers of the region.

To achieve their victories the Hittites needed a large and well organized army. Their 'feudal' system of rule meant that they could draw on a large number of fighting men, and the army consisted of up to 30,000 soldiers on occasion. There was a systematic 'decimal' structure of command (corps of one hundred men, divided into units of ten), with the king in overall command of the entire army. Discipline was strict and effective.

A large range of weapons, both slashing and stabbing swords, have been found together with axes and bows. But their greatest weapon of all was the chariot, which was used in a particular way. Rather than employing them in the Egyptian manner, as portable platforms from which to fire arrows, the Hittites drove them directly through the lines of enemy foot-soldiers, causing terror and mayhem wherever they went. The skill of the Hittite charioteers undoubtedly scored them many victories.

The most famous victory of the Hittite chariots was over the Egyptians at Qadesh in *c.*1286 BC. This was a sorry time for Boghazköy. The Hittite king, Muwatallis, was forced to move the capital because Boghazköy had been ransacked by the warring Gasga people of the northeast. Scarcely had Muwatallis repulsed this invasion than he had to meet the Egyptians under Ramesses II as they advanced towards the Hittite lands through northern Syria.

The king's gate, entrance to the city

The battle that ensued at the important strategic city of Qadesh is one of the earliest that has been recorded in detail. The accounts that have survived are all Egyptian, but they do not underestimate the skill of the Hittites. The key factors in the outcome of the battle were a clever counter-intelligence ploy by the Hittites, who supplied Ramesses with incorrect information about the position of their troops, and the Hittites' skilful and decisive use of their chariots.

The Battle of Qadesh was a great victory for the Hittites, but it was not a final one. Soon afterwards (probably in 1285 BC) Muwatallis died, to be succeeded briefly by his son and then by his brother Hattusilis III. Hattusilis realised that it would be wrong to risk further attacks from the Egyptians and that the best way to hold them off was to form an alliance. Egypt was as eager as he for a peace treaty, since both nations were threatened by the Assyrians, whose power was rising in the east. So the daughter of Hattusilis, it was arranged, would marry Ramesses, and the Egyptians would recognize Hittite rule in northern Syria.

The Assyrians, however, were starting to make moves that were to lead to the decline of the Hittite empire. They took a vital area of territory around the upper Euphrates river, known as Isuwa. This area contained copper mines which provided the Hittites with one of their best sources of metal ore. Although the next Hittite king, Tudhaliyas IV (*c.*1250–1220 BC) succeeded in invading Cyprus, which gave him an alternative source of copper, the Assyrians, together with the other enemies surrounding the Hittite lands, were waiting.

Then natural disaster struck. Harvests started to fail and the Hittites had to buy their grain from Egypt. This meant that they depended even more on keeping trade routes open, making them even more vulnerable to attack. In the end the blow came not from the Assyrians but from waves of people migrating from the northwest. These people moved down the Aegean coast, taking Cyprus and the Hittite's prized source of copper. Then they attacked Syria, removing a crucial source of revenue from tribute, on which the Hittites also depended. Once the Hittite power base was weakened in this way, the Gasga people of the north seized the opportunity and invaded such parts of the Hittite territory that remained in Hittite hands. They had no use for the Hittite capital and there were few riches there to plunder by this time. So sometime in the 1180s BC they burned it to the ground.

TROY

Anatolian city, *circa* 2500–1400 BC, whose story of the Trojan War has lived on through the times of classical Greece to today

There are some places whose fascination is perennial, whose story has fascinated people so much that it has been told in many countries, in many languages, for many centuries. Such a place is Troy, the city in Asia Minor that formed the backdrop for Homer's *Iliad*, with its story of the abduction of Helen by Paris, which led to the ten-year war that eventually destroyed the city. Homer's Troy is on a hill in the middle of a windswept plain. It has solid walls, fine towers, and broad streets. At the top of the hill stands the palace of King Priam, with its throne room and marble-lined chambers. Homer's Troy is a major city and military stronghold.

Yet we cannot take the descriptions we read in the *Iliad* as precise accounts of a real city. The events of the Trojan War were already distant history by the time the *Iliad* was written down. What is more, Homer's poem existed as a collection of stories, handed down orally and embellished as time went by, before Homer committed his own version to posterity. By the time Athenian civilization was at its peak in the fifth century BC, the characters of Homer's epic had already acquired some of the mythic status that they have today.

Nevertheless, the Greeks thought of the Trojan War as a historical fact. The Greek historian Thucydides, who wrote around 400 BC, gave an account of the war and its background, yet he admits that his main sources are the writings of the poets and the testimony of 'tradition'. The fact that writer like Thucydides lived about 850 years after the events they were describing forces one to acknowledge that 'tradition' may have distorted the facts in the ensuing period.

But garbled as these accounts may have been, the pull of the ancient city was strong. Even in ancient times, the attraction of the site was powerful. According to tradition, the city of Troy had stood on a mound in western Anatolia called Hisarlik. It was here that colonists of *c.*700 BC founded a settlement they called Ilion, the classical name for Troy, and here that the Greeks, Persians, and Romans came to soak up the atmosphere of the famed city. But to what extent can we equate the ruins at Hisarlik with the stones of Homer's Troy?

The secrets of the mound

Hisarlik was an earth mound that was first excavated by Heinrich Schliemann in 1870. Schliemann was an archaeologist with a mission. He had decided that he was going to discover the site of Homer's Troy. The geography of Hisarlik, together with the fact that the wind still blows strongly there (giving relevance to Homer's frequent use of the phrase 'windy Troy') directed him to the site.

It is one of those places that modern archaeologists wish had not been excavated as early as it was. Schliemann was not a scientific archaeologist. He dug trenches straight into the middle of the mound, destroying evidence which should have been carefully sifted through. He also removed finds from the site without documenting them properly, so we do not always know what came from where. And yet, as we try to understand what evidence is left, it is difficult not to admire Schliemann, and the passion that made him carry on digging, hoping to find parallels between the Troy of the *Iliad* and the stones of Hisarlik.

The layers of time

One of the surprising things about the city is how small it is. It measures only about 137 x 182 metres (450 x 600 feet), an area that would have given enough space for little more than 1,000 people in a few dozen houses. But for all its small size, Troy was a town with a long history – a history that is sketchily mapped out for us in the succeeding layers of building work that fill the mound. As Schliemann and his more systematic successors dug through the soil, they discovered nine distinct layers that could be dated approximately and that showed distinct differences, together with numerous sub-layers from intermediate periods.

Sorting out these layers and dating them has proved almost as daunting a task as deciding which, if any, can be identified with Homer's Troy. Modern archaeologists number the sequence of different historical 'Troys' with Roman numerals, starting with the oldest, Troy I and ending with the

One of the most famous stories connected with Troy was that of the wooden horse concealing Greek soldiers, which the enemies of the city persuaded the Trojans to accept as a gift. Once night had fallen the Greeks got out of the horse and unbarred the gates so that their army could enter the city. No one knows whether this story of ingenious sabotage is actually true, but it has lived on in the writings of Homer.

The Troy of the Greek imagination would have contained classical pillared temples within its strong outer walls. The buildings of the real, early Troy would have been less ornate and more purposeful, perhaps more like those of Mycenae.

most recent, Troy IX. Between these two extremes, the two settlements that have been identified as most interesting are Troy II and Troy VI.

Troy in the early Bronze Age

Troy II was a city of the early Bronze Age. Its date is controversial, some scholars dating it 2500–2200 BC, others opting for the period 2200–1400 BC. It was already a walled city, with brick and stone ramparts defining a city about 90 metres (300 feet) across. These walls were punctuated at points with square and rectangular towers and this fact, together with the compact size of the settlement, make it more like a citadel than a city. Within the walls were several buildings, including one house noticeably bigger than the others. This was probably the dwelling place of the ruler.

But the most sensational finds from Troy II were the rich gold, silver, and bronze items that Schliemann unearthed from this level. The story of how Schliemann himself discovered this 'treasure' is one of the great adventures of archaeology. He dug it out and removed it secretly from the site with the help of his wife Sophie, for fear the locals would discover what they had found and start to plunder the site for themselves, and he worked feverishly to recover the objects in spite of the risk of a heavy stone wall falling on him. And the objects themselves were as sensational as the story of their recovery. There were cups, salvers, and other vessels; copper lanceheads; and jewels in rich variety, including gold diadems, one of which was made up of over 16,000 individual pieces of gold.

For Schliemann, these finds immediately became 'the treasure of Priam', king of Troy. He saw them as solid evidence that the site was indeed Homer's Troy. Whether this was the case or not, they were certainly stunning – and they seemed to suggest that the tiny city was part of an extensive trading network, with links spreading out to Crete, Cyprus, mainland

Greece, Assyria, and other parts of Anatolia. The importance of Troy seemed indisputable.

But later writers have doubted many of Schliemann's claims. It seems likely that he did not discover the whole treasure in one go, but saved the finds up until he had a substantial hoard that would make news. Another doubt was that all the finds came from the same level of the city – Schliemann's chaotic excavation methods could easily have meant that he found some of the objects in different historical layers. The sad thing is that the finds vanished in Berlin during World War Two, making it impossible to assess the evidence properly.

Even before this loss, the unanswered questions were obvious enough. Schliemann, although he wanted to believe he had found Homer's Troy, was not convinced. His first published excavation reports admit that he has not been able to solve all the problems of the site, and ask other scholars to address themselves to it. But archaeology had to wait until after the death of the great pioneer for a systematic examination of the site. When this happened, attention was taken away from Troy II and focused on later levels.

Troy VI

In searching for an alternative level to identify with Homer's Troy, archaeologists were looking for a period in which the city had been suddenly destroyed. Troy VI was such a level, meeting its end in 1300 or 1250 BC, making it a late Bronze Age settlement. It was also the longest-lived settlement on the site, and had a similar culture to the layer that immediately followed it. So plenty of evidence was available to show what Troy VI looked like, and to suggest the way of life of the Trojans of this period.

Troy VI was bigger than the earlier settlements, its walls being about 200 x 120 metres (650 x 390 feet). But this was still a relatively small area – it hardly sounds like the spacious city with broad streets described by Homer. But archaic Greek standards of spaciousness were hardly the same as our own; while the walled area at Mycenae was much larger, other Greek cities were much nearer Troy's size. What is more, we have no way of knowing what buildings surrounded the city walls. There may well have been a substantial settlement of wood-built houses, the inhabitants of which

Warriors locked in battle

would retreat to the citadel in times of war, although they would spend most of their lives outside the walls.

No evidence for such a settlement remains, but we can reconstruct most of the parts of the city that were built in stone. Traces of the walls remain on the west, south, and east of the city (the northern walls were destroyed by Schliemann). They were substantial, and were constructed of well-dressed, closely fitting blocks of limestone. Their structure – with a sloping lower level topped with a vertical stone superstructure – is unlike any of the other known fortifications of the ancient Aegean world. Another unusual feature of the defences is their deep foundations. One of the bastions has footings that go down over 7 metres (23 feet) below the ground level of Troy VI, and archaeologists think they probably supported a watchtower over 20 metres (65 feet) high, from which all the comings and goings to the east of the city could be observed.

The walls of Troy VI contained about twenty-five substantial houses built on terraces that rose towards the centre of the citadel. The best surviving of these homes is the so-called Pillar House, near the southern gate. It is rectangular in plan and has five rooms, a vestibule, a large main hall about 15 metres (50 feet) in length, and three smaller rooms. It takes its name from the two square pillars that supported the roof of the hall. The Pillar House is probably typical of the houses at Troy VI in being based on a large main hall, though there are variations in the plans – some houses have fewer rooms, one is L-shaped. But all were generously proportioned and well built. Their owners were probably members of the Trojan aristocracy.

On the uppermost terrace, towards the western edge of the citadel, was probably the royal palace. Virtually no evidence survives of any building on this site, because later inhabitants of the site built over it and obliterated all but a few fragments of stonework. But all the roads in the citadel seem to lead to this point, and it would be the natural place for the ruler to have his home. It would probably have been based on the megaron style, with a large central hall, and would no doubt have been surrounded by service buildings – stores, workshops, and domestic accommodation.

If there was a large royal palace at the centre of the group of houses lived in by aristocrats, how rich was Troy VI and what was its sphere of influence? The size of the stone houses and the remaining space within the walls has led archaeologists to estimate the population inside the city itself as little more than the 1,000 people who lived at Troy II. But there might well have been a large number of other people – perhaps as many as 5,000 – living outside the walls.

And the influence of the city might well have stretched much further than the plain on which Troy stood. Traces of pottery from Mycenae have been found, together with some local wares that imitate the style of Mycenaean pots. A number of other goods, many of them quite luxurious items, seem to have come from Mycenae: they include a gaming board, silver pins, and beads of ivory and carnelian. War or no war, the two communities had been in contact for some time.

And these were not the only foreign contacts that have been discovered. Pottery and stoneware from Cyprus and cylinder seals that may be from the Hittite lands have been found at Troy, while similarities in pottery styles with settlements on Lesbos to the south and Gallipolli to the north suggest that the city's influence stretched in these directions too.

What Troy sent to these areas in return is less certain. There is a tradition that the city was famous for its horse breeding, a fact that is bolstered by the discovery of many horse bones on the site. Another possibility is textiles – Troy has yielded many spindle whorls, the circular stone weights that aided the spinning of yarn in antiquity. Fishing was probably another source of wealth. At the time of Troy VI a deep bay brought the coastline much nearer the western walls of the city than it is today. And finally, and more tangibly, the typical grey pots of Troy have been found as far afield as Cyprus, Palestine, and Syria.

The fall of Troy VI

The exact circumstances of the decline and fall of the city are quite difficult to grasp. For some archaeologists, the end was the result of one of the local earthquakes. Such an earthquake probably happened towards the end of the Troy VI period. But it does not seem to have destroyed the city completely. There is evidence of cracks in the surviving portions of the walls, but these do not look as if they would have been beyond repair. And one would have expected the Trojans, who were after all a prosperous people with a solid record of fortification-building behind them, to have carried out the necessary restoration.

But something prevented the Trojans making the sort of repairs one would expect. Troy VIIa, on the next archaeological layer, was a far poorer city than its immediate predecessor. The large houses seem to have been divided up into smaller units, and the atmosphere seems to have changed from a prosperous stronghold into a desperate shanty town.

Why this decline? Carl Blegen, one of the foremost archaeologists to have worked on the site, claimed that this was evidence of a city under siege and that in Troy VIIa we could see the effects of withstanding the attack of the Greek armies on the beleaguered city. And yet there is little clear-cut evidence of military activity during the period of Troy VIIa, which is, in any case, rather late to be the Homeric city.

Looking again at Troy VI, it can be seen that the earthquake may not have been the only destructive force at work. First of all, there is evidence of damage by fire; this may have been the result of enemy action, or it may have been the result of the earthquake bringing down roof timbers on to the hearths of Troy. Second, much more weaponry has been discovered from Troy VI, and much of it – including arrowheads, lanceheads and a knife – is Mycenaean in character. Third, the way the upper sections of the city walls were brought down looks more like the determined work of human attackers than the cracks and shifts one would expect from an earthquake.

Could it be that the forces that destroyed Troy VI were both natural and man-made? Such a theory would certainly help to explain the character of the later city, Troy VIIa. After the warrior aristocracy was slaughtered and the city ransacked by the Greeks, the survivors from the outer city might well have colonized what was left of the citadel and made what home they could amongst the ruins. In many ways this is the theory that best suits the evidence, but it begs at least one major question: would not the Greek ships have been destroyed by the tidal wave caused by the earthquake? Perhaps the bay adjacent to Troy offered them some protection.

Another possible explanation to this problem involves questioning the whole idea of a ten-year siege. It is difficult to imagine the population of Troy (the 1,000 who lived in the citadel, let alone the extra inhabitants outside the walls who would have rushed inside for protection) having enough space to house themselves and their supplies for such a long period. Perhaps it is nearer the truth to imagine the Greeks, like many ancient warriors, campaigning during one season of the year, and the earthquake happening outside the fighting season.

Trojan coin

Indeed it is possible to go even further than this, and suggest that all of the so-called 'earthquake damage' to Troy VI was in reality caused by the Greeks. Homeric tradition certainly alleges that the Greeks destroyed the city once they had fought their way inside. And writer Michael Wood has suggested that the Greeks, like the Assyrians, used horse-shaped battering rams to push down the walls – hence the legend of the wooden horse. Such a theory is doubtful. First, the walls of Troy VI were so solid, and their foundations so deep, that even the strongest battering ram would have done minimal damage. Second, Homer and the oral storytellers who preceded him would have known the difference between a battering ram and a subterfuge involving a wooden statue of a horse. And unusual as the story is, how much more likely that the Greeks would have tricked the horse-loving Trojans with an equestrian statue than worn themselves out trying to batter down such apparently impregnable walls?

It is easy, when dealing with a subject with as much mythic power as the Trojan War, to fall victim to speculation. Perhaps, when further sites in Anatolia are excavated, more evidence, maybe even written records, will be unearthed that throw more light on the history of this city and the conflict that surrounded it. Until then, we are liable to use our imagination. For Schliemann, Troy was a world of nineteenth century opulence; for Carl Belgen in the 1930s and 1940s, it was an embattled victim of prehistoric blitzkrieg. If today, in an age of ecological awareness, it seems to have perished from a combination of natural disaster and folly, we should not be surprised.

KHORSABAD

Capital of the Assyrians under their king Sargon II, 721–705 BC, mysteriously abandoned at the end of his reign

In the rolling hills between the upper Tigris and Euphrates lived the Assyrians. A Semitic people, they broke away from the rest of the Sumerian civilization after the collapse of the third dynasty of Ur in *c.*2000 BC. From their base at Assur, in what is now northern Iraq, they built further city states, such as Nineveh and Arbela. They were one of several peoples to benefit from the suitability of the Mesopotamian soil for farming, and the regular rains of the upper Tigris region made the area especially good for growing crops like barley and sesame, and for raising cattle, sheep, and goats. These early Assyrians also benefited from a trade in copper with the people of Anatolia, and set up a trading colony there.

From these modest beginnings was to grow one of the greatest, most feared empires of the ancient world. The Assyrians would develop a mighty army, an effective system of governing a large area of territory, an unrivalled reputation for cruelty to their enemies, and a unique style of art at which we still marvel. They were also to become great city builders, turning Nineveh, Assur, Nimrud, and Khorsabad into great bastions, symbols of their power.

Of these sites Khorsabad harbours the greatest mystery. It was a completely new capital city that took many years and many thousands of workers to build. It seemed to herald a new beginning for Assyrian civilization. And yet it perished with Sargon, the king who commissioned it. To understand how this state of affairs could come about, we need first to look at how Assyrian power developed before Sargon came to the throne in 721 BC.

Carrying a bunch of poppy seed-heads, this Assyrian soothsayer is pointing the way to the new capital. Sargon may well have taken the advice of such a sage in choosing the site for Khorsabad. In the background are the carved reliefs that formed such a part of Assyrian palace decoration.

The growth of an empire

It was not until after the fall of the Hittites in *c.*1200 BC that the Assyrians started to establish anything like an empire. Even when they did so they had to contend with regular wars with the other great power of the region, Babylon. The most successful kings of this middle period in Assyrian history (*c.*1363–1000 BC) got by with a policy of joining the Babylonians rather than trying to beat them. For example, the founder of the empire, King Ashur-uballit I (*c.* 1363–1328 BC) made a marriage alliance with Babylon to save himself from pointless wars with the city. A later ruler, Tiglath-pileser I (1114-1076 BC), took up the Babylonian system of weights and measures, to foster trade with his neighbours.

Tiglath-pileser was one of the most successful of the Assyrian kings. He developed the use of the chariot in warfare to strengthen his empire and set the pattern for the victories of future sovereigns. His reign also coincided with the development of ironworking in Assyria, providing a powerful technology for the production of tools and weapons.

The following centuries saw something of a decline after this king's exploits, but his namesake Tiglath-pileser III (744–727 BC) staged a true revival. He took over Syria, toppling the Urartians from power in the region. He dealt a crushing blow to the Chaldaeans, who were trying to capture Babylon; this gave him control of Babylon too. And, what was just as important for his successors, he held on to these new territories, using his army to exert Assyrian power while his civil service levied taxes from the conquered lands.

When Sargon II came to the throne in 721 BC he inherited a large well run empire. By taking the name of an early, and almost legendary, king of Babylon, he asserted his power and influence from the very beginning. In fact, since he was probably a usurper to the throne, the name gave him a credibility and prestige that he might otherwise have lacked. But he was soon to prove his worth. After the death of Tiglath-pileser the occupied peoples started to campaign against Assyria. Sargon quickly suppressed them, scoring important victories once more in Syria and Babylonia. He also won additional territory by fighting the Phrygian leader Midas in Anatolia. Sargon was living up to his name.

Sargon was prominent in civil reforms as well as in military victories. According to contemporary documents (which may, it is true, be biased in his favour), he rebuilt villages that had fallen into disrepair; he opened canals and saw to their maintenance; and he founded a library and acted as the patron of scholars. His reign was also a time of great achievements in

Assyrian architecture was built to impress. The main courtyards had imposing gateways with twin towers, the temple had a tall, colourful ziggurat, and the palace was raised on a plinth and approached by stairs for an even more dramatic effect. This whole palace was only a small part of the original city complex – its position on the northwestern wall is shown in the plan.

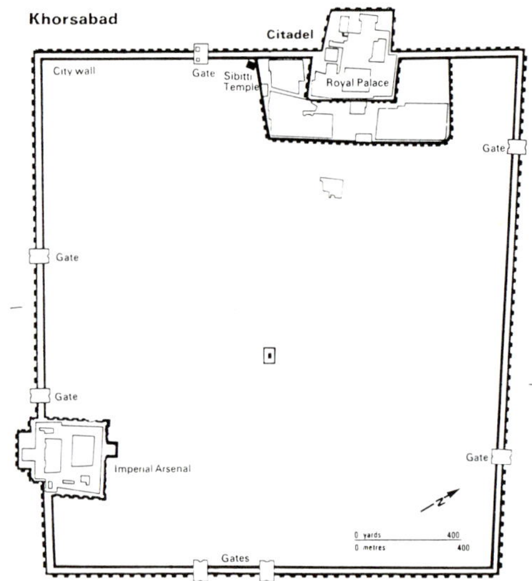

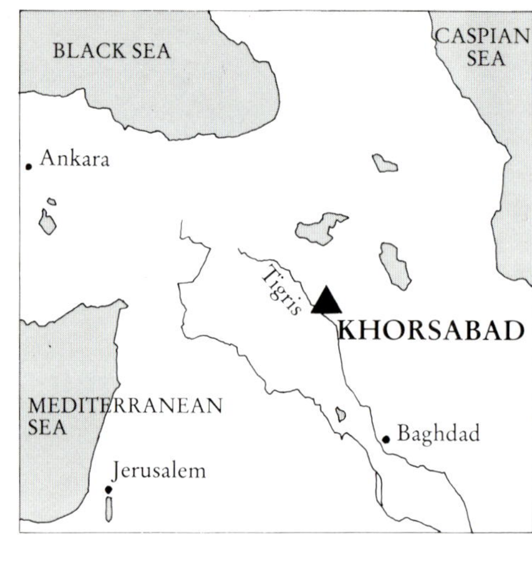

The palace of Sargon, Khorsabad

705 BC

the arts and crafts. Sargon's sculptors produced unparalleled wall reliefs to decorate his palaces. His craftsmen excelled in the making of glassware and in metalworking. It was a successful reign.

Yet there was a strange restlessness about the king. As if travelling about the middle east on campaign was not enough, Sargon continually moved the site of his capital city when at home. He began at Assur, where he repaired the walls and decorated the temple precinct using glazed bricks in a style like that of Babylon. Next he moved to Kalhu, where he reconstructed the royal palace. But this was destined to become the home of the crown prince as Sargon moved once more, this time to Nineveh, where he restored the temple.

It may be that Sargon was acting rather astutely in moving from one city to another in this way. By basing himself in turn in different places and endowing them with lavish building projects he was demonstrating his commitment to these cities and ensuring himself of their allegiance. But in spite of the building activity, these cities, already established and embellished with noble buildings before Sargon came on the scene, did not give the king what he wanted – a personal monument, a city he could truly call his own. So he decided to build one. At the site we know today as Khorsabad, Sargon built the town that the Assyrians called Dur Sharrukin, the City of Sargon.

The king's new city

When you start building from scratch, you have the advantage of being able to choose your site very carefully.

Khorsabad has clay soil, ideal for brick making. The soil is also fertile, and although agriculture was hardly Sargon's top priority, this meant that trees grew successfully in the area. Contemporary reliefs show palms, figs, oranges, and olives, all of which would have afforded welcome shade as well as fruit. Another advantage of Sargon's chosen site was that it was near an alabaster quarry, providing a source of stone for relief carving.

Once the site was chosen, work began quickly. Sargon chose his architect, an official named Tab-shar Ashur, and both the city and the royal palace within it were planned. The city was on a large scale. Four walls enclosed an area that was roughly square in shape and covered an area of 300 hectares (740 acres). All but one of the walls had two gates, giving a total of seven gates in all. It was probably a liking of symmetry and pattern making that made Tab-shar Ashur arrange the gates in this way – from the point of view of traffic, several of the gates are superfluous. For example, vehicles coming out of the gates on the southeast side would have to join to the road to Nineveh, which also passed one of the gates in the southwest wall. But such practical considerations did not concern the king. The important thing was that the city looked impressive and well defended from the outside.

Inside the city the visitor would be engulfed in a maze of streets, most of which were quite narrow. It is this outer section of the city that we know least about. Most of the houses would have been of basic mud-brick construction. They would have been planned around central courtyards and there would have been few windows on the outer, street-facing walls. But unlike the courtyard houses of Ur, they were probably only single-storey buildings. The bricks of these houses have long since disappeared, although archaeologists have unearthed stones that reveal that the streets were well paved.

Home for Sargon

With the royal palace everything is much clearer. The remains are more extensive – both the foundations and carved reliefs from the walls have survived. In addition, letters to and from the royal architect have been discovered that fill in some of the details of construction. From these records we learn that stone and wood (including cedar from Lebanon and other woods from Armenia) had to be imported. Indeed, there is even a surviving letter complaining that ships to transport these materials were not being built quickly enough, and that the construction of the royal palace was being held up.

Winged beasts and a figure subduing a lion from the palace walls

Imports or no, it is not surprising that the building of the palace went slowly. By ancient standards it is huge. The royal apartments alone stand on a base about 300 metres (3228 feet) square. In front of this area is an even larger zone devoted to the more utilitarian parts of the palace complex. There was a domestic area, containing kitchens, a bakery, numerous storerooms and the palace stables. The stores contained all the paraphernalia needed to keep a large royal palace running smoothly – tools, pots and pans, food and drink. The stables were a large and obviously important part of the palace. Documents chronicle the arrival of fresh horses from all over the empire – a good supply of horses was always at the ready. The horse was central to Assyrian warfare and the charioteers wanted the best the Empire could provide.

Between the main complexes of domestic or service buildings was a broad ramp. This led up to a triple entrance guarded by carved reliefs of demons and genii, and this entrance in turn gave access to the palace's largest courtyard, about 28 metres (300 feet) square. Three sides of this great courtyard led to the three key areas of the palace. To your left as you entered was the temple area, which contained several small temples and a great seven-tiered ziggurat. To the right were more service rooms. And straight ahead were the king's residential quarters. Beyond these were the most important rooms of all, the state chambers, including the throne room, 46 metres (150 feet) long.

A state visit

A visiting dignitary would not approach the throne room through the private apartments. The public route was across another vast courtyard behind the service area on the right-hand side of the palace. This approach would provide adequate preparation for the extraordinary sight of this room. Immediately on entering one would see the whole of one long side of the room, with carved reliefs of winged, human-headed bulls arranged symmetrically on either side of the throne to lead one's eye towards the king in the centre. Flanking the king, these images gave no room for doubt about the power of the king. Even today they are impressive – in ancient times they would have been terrifying.

To an ancient Mesopotamian it would not only have been the mythical beasts guarding the throne that would have inspired terror. There are also reliefs show a man holding and subduing a lion. On one level, these reliefs are saying 'This king is so powerful he can overcome the king of the beasts.' On another level, it is thought that these carvings represent Gilgamesh, the legendary Mesopotamian hero, a giant of enormous strength and valour. By making this comparison, Sargon was telling his subjects that it was pointless to oppose him. Other reliefs in the palace forced this point home, with depictions of defeated enemies being put to death and cities being destroyed by Sargon's forces.

Integrated both with the palace architecture and the ceremonies that went on in the palace, the Assyrian reliefs provided a perfect backdrop – whether for petitioning by the king's subjects, the ritual giving of gifts to vassals, or the punishment of traitors. Yet in many ways the art of Khorsabad and the other Assyrian cities is a limited one. The carvings are in shallow relief and the style makes no provision for perspective; all the figures are seen from the side; the poses are stylized; images are repeated; the subject matter is limited. In spite of this, the reliefs make some of the most absorbing art ever created. In a few centimetres of depth and many metres of length a whole world is brought to life, the world of an empire glorious in battle and overwhelming in power. They show charging chariots and marching armies, soldiers fighting, burning, and putting the enemy to death. Fleeing enemies are mercilessly persued; cities are taken; the Assyrians are victorious everywhere. When not fighting, the Assyrians are shown at their favourite pastime – hunting wild bulls, elephants, and lions. So the carvings illustrate the valour of their subjects even when they were at leisure. They represent propaganda raised to the level of high art.

Before this time there was nothing to compare with the Assyrian reliefs. They seem to come from nowhere, with no outside artistic influences, only the inner impulse of the Assyrian need for power and conquest.

The reality of war

The palace reliefs remind us that the Assyrians were famous military campaigners. As the carvings reveal, they were effective in this because they had an all-round military skill that enabled them to tackle most wartime situations and win. On the battlefield they used a combination of foot-soldiers, cavalry, and charioteers. In Sargon's time the techniques of the foot-soldiers were improved, and Sargon was the first king to use bowmen to their full potential. He also developed the chariot – his chariots were better than those of his predecessors because they were larger (a driver, an archer, and one or two shield bearers could be accommodated with ease), and because they were taller, providing better protection for their occupants. The army was also well equipped for siege warfare, and the reliefs show several battering rams, usually protected by elaborate wheeled canopies. In spite of this protection, however, sieges could be costly in terms of men, time, and equipment, so the Assyrians preferred the conventional battlefield whenever possible.

Sargon's other military strength was that he realised the importance of having a professional standing army available at all times. With a campaign virtually every year this was crucial to his success. As well as regular soldiers this force gave Sargon a personal unit to act as his bodyguard; there were also specialist squadrons of crack troops that could be brought into play quickly in difficult situations – the cavalry squadrons were particularly famous in this role. And if this was not enough, more men could be conscripted to provide a force that numbered several hundred thousand.

With such a large army it was essential that it was well organized, and this the king managed to achieve by following Assyrian tradition and putting himself at the head with a well structured chain of command beneath him. The reliefs give a vivid picture of the army on the march. First would come the standard bearers, with their winged-bull standards, followed by the king with his elite bodyguards. Then there would be a cavalry unit, flanked by infantry on either side, ready to move quickly into battle order if needed. The main army would follow, and finally there would be wagons with supplies of food, together with equipment such as ladders and battering rams that would be needed if a siege was planned. The whole would have made an awesome spectacle.

An image of cruelty

The depictions of violence found in some of the reliefs, the Assyrians' habit of stringing up their victims on poles outside the city to frighten their enemies, and their relentless annual campaigning evoke the image of a bloodthirsty people whose main interest was to subdue as much of the middle east as possible, with the maximum cruelty. Bolstered by popular poetry ('The Assyrian came down like a wolf on the fold') and Biblical accounts, this image dies hard. But how true is it?

The Assyrians were not quite as bloodthirsty as they seem. They used tactics of terror, it is true, but by making an example of the occasional unfortunate traitor they avoided much further bloodshed. And they were not normally cruel to conquered people. So long as the taxes were paid and the local Assyrian governor was obeyed, it was not worth their while interfering. It seems that the violence of the reliefs and the gruesome demonstrations on the city walls were largely terror tactics designed to discourage rebellion rather than accounts of regular happenings in Assyria.

And a well organized system of civil servants ensured that, on the whole, things did run smoothly. The system was headed by a network of about thirty provincial governors, each of whom was directly responsible to the king. Beneath each of these was a team of officials, and they were backed up by a military garrison who could enforce law and order. From the evidence that survives, it seems that communications between the palace and the provinces were good. Regular messengers travelled across the Empire and about 2,000 letters between the capital and the provinces have been discovered.

Continuous imports of food and raw materials from the fringes of the Empire to the big cities in the Assyrian heartland also kept communications open. But there was a drawback for the provinces here. Although there was little direct physical cruelty, the economy of the agricultural regions became depressed as the wealthy cities took more and more food from them.

The other weakness in the Assyrian governmental system was the tendency of the kings to use the royal family as a source of high officials. This could lead to strife at home, especially when the king was away on campaign and his concubines plotted against each other to secure preferment for their children. The stronger the king, the less likely this was to be a problem.

Sargon was strong enough, but he finally paid the penalty courted by every warrior king – death on the battlefield. To any people, but especially to the superstitious Assyrians, this was an ill omen. It led to Sargon's son Sennacherib shunning his father's memory and turning his back on the capital city he had so carefully created, going instead to Nineveh. A taboo had been placed on the great city and the Assyrians never returned.

BABYLON

Mesopotamian city rich in stories and legends, of the Hanging Gardens, the Tower of Babel, and the captivity of the Jews

Babylon has lived longer in the human imagination than any other city in the world. Even today the stories of the Tower of Babel and the Babylonian captivity of the Jews under King Nebuchadrezzar have a haunting power. Although the events these stories describe were separated by many centuries they convey a consistent image of the city – a place of great riches and magnificent buildings, but at the same time a city of luxury and decadence, doomed to perish in a terrible apocalypse. As such, Babylon has become the symbol of all doomed and decadent civilizations.

It is thanks to the Bible that this image of Babylon has prevailed. The first picture of Babylon that has come down to us in this way is in the very first book of the Bible, the Book of Genesis. This tells how Noah's descendants, at the time when all the people on earth spoke the same language, started to build a great tower that was designed to reach all the way to heaven. God, seeing the determination of the presumptuous people to build this tower, realised that the only way to prevent them would be to stop them understanding each other. So he unleashed the 'babble after Babel', the confusion of different languages, and scattered the people over the earth.

The second great story that the Bible offers us of Babylon is in the later books of the Old Testament that deal with the conquest of Jerusalem and the exile of the Jews. These accounts have given us a host of enduring scenes – from the exiles weeping by the waters of Babylon, to the adventures of the prophet Daniel in the lions' den. This is also the period of the Hanging Gardens, one of the classical Seven Wonders of the World.

So to search for the Babylon of the imagination among the ruins that are left today, we have to look at two periods – the development of the early city in the eighteenth century BC and the great revival that took place in the so-called Neo-Babylonian phase, about 1200 years later. In spite of this time difference there are striking parallels between the old Babylon and the new. Some of these parallels are the result of the local conditions. Both drew wealth from the fertile lands along the Euphrates river; both also used the river for transport and trade. Both built in a similar style of architecture, using mud-bricks because of the lack of stone and wood locally.

Another parallel exists because of the nature of the Hebrew stories that we have inherited about Babylon. The Book of Genesis took shape while the Jews were captives in the 'new' Babylon. So although their writers, talking about the Tower of Babel, were describing events that happened over 1000 years before, they were reminded every day of the Babylon in which they were forced to live. So their idea of the great tower had as much to do with the temple built by their gaoler Nebuchadrezzar as with the structure that preceded it.

We do not know what the Tower of Babel looked like – it may have been a solid ziggurat, like that at Ur, or a taller tower as shown here. Priests and nobles look down from it as slaves carry baskets of fruit from the Hanging Gardens.

The beginnings of Babylon

But what do we know about the first Babylon, apart from the fact that it had a tower that inspired the myth of Babel? Was it as chaotic and strife-torn a place as the story of the 'confusion of tongues' seems to imply?

After its glorious third dynasty the city of Ur lost its domination of the territory between the Tigris and Euphrates rivers. In the period that followed, there was indeed strife, as several cities vied for power in Mesopotamia – Mari, Larsa and, above all, Babylon. The city became most successful under the sixth king of its first dynasty, a ruler called Hammurapi (1792–1750 BC).

The first great leader in Babylonian history, Hammurapi brought his people together under a strong central administration. But he was too good a leader to think that mere administrative reforms would bind the population together. He also centralized and organized Babylonian religion to give his priests greater power and his people spiritual unity; he laid down a new system of holding and granting territory in return for important public services such as the building and maintenance of canals; and he put together one of the most famous sets of laws of the ancient world.

Hammurapi's law code has come down to us engraved on a huge stele or slab of basalt. At the top of the stone is a relief showing the king with Shameth, the Babylonian sun-god and god of justice. Beneath the relief are listed Hammurapi's 282 laws. The king and his officials probably did not write all these laws themselves: it is likely that many are regulations that

The Hanging Gardens of Babylon

The Hanging Gardens were an oasis in a dry and dusty city. Their exact form remains a mystery, but there would certainly have been terraces with palms and fruit trees. Arches would have given shade, a water supply would have been essential, and a cascade may have added to the cool impression.

already existed. But the important thing was that he had them written out in a consistent style and in a way that was meant to be noticed. As the text says at one point, future kings should 'give heed to the words that I have inscribed upon my stele'.

What do these words tell us about life in ancient Babylon? It seems that there were three main classes of men. The majority were free men, born free, and practising a range of jobs – from farmers, merchants, and artisans to priests and administrators; such people were allowed to own property, could attend the governmental assembly and were protected by the normal Babylonian laws. Next came a class of men who were socially inferior to the free men, although their exact status is not clear from the surviving Babylonian texts; these people were probably not property owners and were not allowed to attend the assembly; they were granted the protection of the palace because they were not covered directly by the legal code. Finally there were the slaves. Women are also mentioned in the laws. They had important but limited rights. For example, women could take part in business life, but could not initiate divorce proceedings.

The laws themselves cover a wide range of issues. Criminal laws make provisions for theft, assault, and murder. Laws of property deal with debt, wages, and the possession of slaves. There are laws covering marriage, divorce, and inheritance, and other regulations covering the way business should be transacted. Although they covered quite a range, these statutes were rather primitively framed – the principle of *lex talionis* (an eye for an eye and a tooth for a tooth) prevailed throughout. And yet some of them strike an oddly modern tone. For example, a doctor could be punished for causing a patient ill-health. However, the punishment was not specified in terms of modern medical compensation: if a doctor caused the loss of a patent's eye he could expect to lose his own.

Baghdad
IRAQ
BABYLON
Tigris
Euphrates
Syrian Desert
Basra
PERSIAN GULF

Unfortunately there is not very much archaeological evidence of what Hammurapi's Babylon was like, so it is difficult to fill out the picture by looking at the ruins. We can guess that the city would be similar to ancient Ur. There would be two-storey mud-brick houses built around courtyards; these would probably have doors made of reeds hung on wooden frames, otherwise little timber would be used in the construction of these houses. The temples would probably have been similar in shape to the great ziggurats of Ur and later Babylon, but built on a smaller scale.

After the reign of Hammurapi Babylon remained an important city, but it diminished in its prosperity and Hammurapi's successors lost much of the territory the great king had gained. The city suffered a severe blow in 1595 BC when the Hittites under their king Mursilis I, sacked the city and plundered the temples and palaces. There followed a period of mixed fortunes for Babylon. Times of relative prosperity alternated with clashes with powerful neighbours – particularly Elam and Assyria. There was even a time when Babylon ceased to be the capital of Babylonia for a while. The city enjoyed something of an upturn under King Nebuchadrezzar I (1125–1104 BC). He was successful in defending Babylon against the Assyrians and Elamites.

The 'new' Babylon

It was Nabopolassar (625–605 BC) who re-established Babylon as the principal power in Mesopotamia. To do this he had to sort out disputing factions within the city itself, as well as carrying on a war with Assyria. The records from this period are incomplete and difficult to interpret, but it seems that Nabopolassar's reign was interrupted on at least one occasion when an Assyrian ruler took over in Babylon. Although he was quick to regain control in the capital, Nabopolassar's influence was limited until he came to an agreement with the Medes.

Emblem of the goddess Ishtar

The Medes were a federation of Indo-European peoples who lived in Elam, an area of western Iran. They too were at war with Assyria, and had succeeded in capturing the important Assyrian cities of Nineveh and Nimrud. With cunning opportunism, Nabopolassar and his army marched to Assur, the Assyrian capital. He hoped to get there and sack the city quickly while the people were weakened by the Median onslaught. But the Medes got there first. By the time Nabopolassar arrived they had captured Assur and were in control of the surrounding area. Nabopolassar could see that there was no point in fighting the Medes for the weakened city, so he made a treaty with Cyaxeres, the Median king, in 614 BC and two years later their combined forces finally overthrew the Assyrians at Nineveh. Although the Assyrian kingdom continued to exist for several years after this defeat, the power of this once-great empire was now minimal – the Babylonians were left to occupy centre stage in the area.

Nabopolassar's son Nebuchadrezzar built on the foundations of empire laid down by his father. He is most famous from the accounts of the war against Jerusalem in the Old Testament, during which he laid siege to the city, took rich tribute and made off with many prisoners.

But the infamous captor of the Jews deserves to be remembered in other ways. For one thing, he increased the prosperity of his kingdom by fostering foreign trade. The fertile soils of the banks of the Euphrates provided the Babylonians with a surplus of crops such as wheat, dates, and wool. Commodities such as these brought much wealth to the city. Babylon used the same system of weights and measures across its whole empire and this no doubt helped the success of the empire's trading ventures. Another source of prosperity was the sophisticated banking and money-lending network that developed in Babylon. Lending money for financial gain was looked on as wrong by most peoples in the middle east at this time, but in Babylon it was quite acceptable. So people came to the city from far and wide to borrow money. In fact by the sixteenth century BC there were great banking families in the city who lived like princes on the interest they accrued from their borrowers.

But Nebuchadrezzar's greatest legacy was his rebuilding of his capital city. If you visit the site of Babylon today, the ruins you see date mainly from the city's great period of revival under Nabopolassar and Nebuchadrezzar. These monarchs were among the greatest builders of the ancient world. They carried on the Mesopotamian tradition of Ur, constructing a large fortified city with magnificent royal palaces and a sacred area with a towering ziggurat. But at Babylon the scale was larger and there is much more of a sense that the buildings are meant to impress.

This effect would have started as one approached the ancient city, with the very walls and gates. First there was a large outer enclosure surrounded by a high wall. This was to provide a refuge for people from the surrounding areas in times of war or other crises. Within this were the city walls proper. Even these were double walls, and there were towers on the outer walls at regular intervals. Herodotus, the Greek historian to whom we owe much of our information about the appearance of ancient Babylon, said that the walls were so wide that two chariots, each drawn by four horses, could pass along them together.

Nine different gates pierced these walls. All were tall, heavily fortified structures, the most famous and elaborate being the great Ishtar Gate, named for the Mesopotamian goddess of war. By the time of Nebuchadrezzar this gate was beautifully decorated with glazed tiles bearing images of bulls, dragons, and lions (the latter being Ishtar's sacred beasts).

Beyond the gate was a processional path, bordered by walls that were decorated with tiles bearing a lion design. It led past the temple of Ninna and the royal palace to the religious centre of the city, the precinct containing the temple of Marduk and the great ziggurat or Tower of Babel itself. The processional way was over 900 metres (3000 feet) long and was up to 20 metres (66 feet) wide. It was paved with slabs of limestone sealed together with bitumen, and the fact that stone rather than the usual brick was used indicates the importance of the route. Inscriptions on the slabs, dedicating

The multiple walls of the city, and one of the towered gateways

the processional way to the god Marduk, press this point home.

We know from the archaeological evidence that the royal palace had a plan based on courtyards and contained five main groups of buildings: the precinct of the palace officials; the quarters of the royal guard; the ceremonial centre or throne room; the king's private rooms; and the women's quarters.

But the most mysterious of the royal buildings was outside the palace itself, to the northeast. Here there are the remains of a vaulted building about 43 x 30 metres (140 x 100 feet), which is probably the site of the famous Hanging Gardens.

How did the Gardens come to be built? When Nabopolassar made his treaty with the Median king Cyaxeres, the treaty was sealed, as was common in the ancient world, with a royal wedding. Nabopolassar's son Nebuchadrezzar was married to Amitiya, the daughter of the king of the Medes. According to tradition, however, the prince's marriage was more than a political alliance. It was a gesture of love, so the story goes, that moved Nebuchadrezzar to build the hanging gardens when he became king. They were meant to remind his bride of the green yet mountainous homeland she had left behind.

Whether or not this story is true, the gardens have lived on in the popular imagination, although we know little about their actual construction. Writers who saw the gardens long after they were built described a terraced arrangement, rising in gradually diminishing storeys, like a Mesopotamian ziggurat. The outer walls were very thick (7.5 metres/25 feet was one estimate) and, since trees were planted in the gardens, each terrace would have had to accommodate a generous depth of soil. The overall effect would have been like a green pyramid. As well as palms, cypresses and other middle eastern species of tree, smaller trailing plants were set along the edges of the outer terrace walls, spilling over to cover much of the brickwork. A complicated series of pipes brought water from the river to the gardens, and the resulting lush earthly paradise would have been a welcome refuge from the Babylonian sun, offering green shade, the scents of exotic flowers, and a quiet retreat from the bustle of the city.

The other building of Babylon that has acquired almost mythic status is the ziggurat, popularly known as the Tower of Babel. We know much more about the actual appearance of this building than we do about the hanging gardens, and there are two accounts of the tower, one archaeological, the other mythical, which it is possible to give.

An archaeologist will tell you that, by the time of Nabopolassar, Babylon's original stepped tower had become a ruin. Nabopolassar, when he saw that he had re-established Babylon as the most influential power in Mesopotamia, decided to rebuild the tower in honour of Marduk, the chief god of the city. The structure that the king had built was huge. Today only the base of the central core of brick remains, but this is enough to show that the tower's base had sides measuring about 91 metres (300 feet) square.

It is impossible to reconstruct the temple accurately, but, in line with other Mesopotamian temples built before and afterwards, it would have had a tapering design, with a number of terraces, the upper smaller than the lower. Access to the top would have been by ramps or stairs built on to the outer walls, but again we do not know their exact arrangement.

The fall of Babylon

Nebuchadrezzar died in 562 BC. He was followed by several short-lived monarchs about whom we know very little, until, in 555 BC Nabonidus came to the throne. He was in many ways Babylon's most mysterious ruler. We do not know how he came to be king of Babylonia. In fact he did not come from Babylon at all, but from Harran, in northwest Mesopotamia. The other odd thing about Nabonidus is that he spent years away from his capital, which he left in charge of his son, Belshazzar, who ruled as regent. The reason for this was probably that Nabonidus worshipped the moon-god Sin. The priests of Marduk in Babylon resisted his attempts to propagate the cult of Sin in Babylon, so he was forced to worship at Harran, where Sin was the local god. Consequently Belshazzar was left in charge of the capital, where he acquired a reputation for decadence that eventually contributed to the city's downfall.

The inflation caused by Babylon's by now well developed money-lending system sapped the economy. During the 550s BC prices rose by fifty per cent; in the following fifteen years, the increase was 200 per cent. Nabonidus may have hoped to foster trade by going to Harran in an attempt to improve the economic health of his realm. If so, he tried in vain. In any case, a still more forceful threat was about to hit Babylon.

Nabonidus returned to Babylon when the Persians, under Cyrus the Great, threatened to invade. But by 539 they were simply too strong for Nabonidus. They joined their military might with an effective propaganda campaign, so that on their arrival in the capital they were greeted as liberators, freeing the people from the tyranny of an absentee king. Babylon lived on under Cyrus, but its great days of independence and influence were already over when he arrived.

PERSEPOLIS

Isolated palace and ceremonial centre of the Persian emperors, *circa* 520–330 BC

In the sixth century BC an empire grew up in the middle east that was larger than any that had existed before and unprecedented in the speed of its growth. The great Persian kings of the Achaemenid dynasty struck out from their base in what is now Iran to conquer territories as diverse as Lydia and the Ionian islands, Babylon, Egypt, and even parts of northern India.

They achieved this growth in the space of a few decades, during which time they also evolved a unique culture. Nowhere is this clearer than at Persepolis, the royal palace built by the Persian king Darius. It is a model of Persian architecture – neither Greek, nor Egyptian, nor Assyrian, nor Median, but containing elements of all. How did the Persians come to build in this strange hybrid style? And what did they do in this strange place, 300 miles from the original capital at Susa in an area remote from the lives of most native Persians, so remote indeed, and so little mentioned in the writings of outsiders that some authorities have thought it to be a secret hideout of the Persian kings? The answers to these questions are closely bound up with the history of the empire itself, and the story of the Persian takeover of the middle east.

The beginnings of a dynasty

The rulers of Persia traced back their ancestry to an early king called Haxamanish or Achaemenes, and this is why they came to be known as the Achaemenids. From the start they were something of a hybrid dynasty. Their earliest kings were Medes, from the mountainous region of western Iran. They were a tough people from a tough country, surrounded as it was by the warlike Assyrians and belligerent tribes such as the Scythians. As the Medes expanded their territory beyond their native Media they became closely associated with their southern neighbours the Persians, so much so that it is as Persians that we know the Achaemenids today.

The first member of the dynasty to come to prominence was called Cyaxares. He was the Median king who made an alliance with the Babylonians, marrying his granddaughter to Nebuchadrezzar and attacking the Assyrian capital of Nineveh in 612 BC. This assault proved a spectacular success for Cyaxares. Using a combination of foot-soldiers armed with spears and bows, and bowmen riding on horseback, he forced the Assyrians back into their city. Finally his troops overran Nineveh itself, plundering, raping, and taking prisoners. The great Assyrian city was wrecked, and the foundations were laid for further Persian conquests.

Cyaxares was succeeded by Cyrus, known as 'The Great' (559–529 BC). Already by this time the link between the Medes and the Persians was well forged. Cyrus was known as the emperor 'of the Medes and the Persians'. Like his predecessor, Cyrus has also already figured in the story of another 'mysterious place' already described in this book. He it was who took Babylon in 539 BC, when he was greeted by the people as liberator and rightful king. Indeed Cyrus' treatment of the Babylonians says something about his style as a leader – and about the way in which the Persian Empire as a whole functioned.

Cyrus was diplomatic. He went to the Babylonian New Year festival, and took part in the ceremony by grasping the hand of the statue of the Babylonian god Marduk. This confirmed that he was the rightful ruler of the city and no doubt endeared him to the Babylonians. In addition, he made an official proclamation so that it was clear to everyone in the city that he was king – a proclamation that he had translated into simple rhyming verse so that even the least educated of his Babylonian subjects would be able to remember and recite it.

Yet Cyrus allowed the errant Babylonian king Nabonidus, whose throne he had taken over, to live on, and when Nabonidus died in 538 BC, Cyrus led the official mourning. As well as the king, most of the Babylonian officials stayed on too, and they kept their jobs. Cyrus was content to install a Persian administrator, but otherwise the city continued to function as it had in its heyday. But not quite as it had done. Cyrus made one important change. He allowed the Jewish exiles – 40,000 of them – to return home to Jerusalem in 537 BC.

The deeds of Cyrus show two essential Persian traits. He cared about people enough to let them live their lives as nearly as possible as they wanted. But his caring approach had a vital ulterior motive. Cyrus knew that a contented people is easy to rule; a relaxed people will pay their taxes and

Images of the Persian kings brood from capitals and doorways at Persepolis. Here, in a brief moment of quiet in the busy palace, a noble has paused beneath one of the sculptures.

The great audience hall, or apadana, and the hall of one hundred columns dominate the palace. The generous space between them could be used by the great assemblies of visiting kings and nobles who came to give gifts and tribute to the emperor, while the emperor himself could relax in the gardens along the northern edge of the complex. Here the inner gatehouse is being refurbished, ready for a royal visit.

The palace, Persepolis 400 BC

respect the authority of the king. By giving concessions to the Jews and the people of Babylon, Cyrus won two important bases in Mesopotamia and Palestine. This was a pattern that was to continue as the Persian Empire grew and prospered, a pattern that would influence Persian life at many levels – from law to agriculture, administration to architecture.

Cyrus achieved a great deal in his thirty-year reign. His son and successor Cambyses ruled in a similar way, although he was not so spectacularly successful. His main achievement was the conquest of Egypt in 525 BC. This was the climax of a quick and efficient campaign, at the end of which Libya and two Greek north African cities, Cyrene and Barca, also surrendered to the Persians. Cambyses wanted to continue farther into Africa, sailing up the Nile to take Ethiopia. But he was finally forced to turn back, probably because his army was not adequately provided with food and supplies for the difficult journey.

Cambyses spent three years in Egypt, and was only called back in 522 BC when he heard that a usurper was attempting to take over in Persia. On the way the rightful king met his death, leaving the way for his cousin Darius to remove the usurper and take over himself.

The builder of Persepolis

We do not know exactly how Darius came to the Persian throne in the confusion surrounding the death of Cambyses. But we do know that he was an effective ruler who took his empire to new heights of achievement. It was during his reign that areas of northern India were added to the empire. He took on board administrative reforms that improved an already smoothly running imperial machine. He streamlined communications, initiating the greatest road-building operation the world had known. And he built

Tehran
IRAN
Baghdad
Isfahan
Basra
PERSEPOLIS
Shiraz
PERSIAN GULF
Bahrain

Persepolis, the most majestic monument to Persian art.

From his predecessor Cyrus, Darius inherited a strong governmental system. The whole far-flung empire was divided into provinces called *satrapies*, each under the command of a governor, or *satrap*, who was responsible to the king. Darius saw that this system worked well when the king was strong. But he wanted to limit the power of the satraps so that they did not start to assume the power of kings in their own right.

Under Darius, therefore, all twenty or so satraps were native Persians rather than men from the areas they governed. Each was partnered by an army commander who was also directly responsible to the king, so that Darius rather than the satrap controlled the armed forces. Other officials in the provinces who reported straight to the king were the tax collectors – giving Darius financial control – and secretaries known as the 'king's ears' and 'king's eyes', who were often Darius' relatives and provided vital intelligence information.

A great communicator

Darius would have been powerless to control this supporting network of officials if he had not also improved communications within his large empire. He did this by building a 1677-mile road all the way across the empire from the administrative capital at Susa just north of the Persian Gulf to Sardis, immediately inland from the Aegean. This linked Lydia, Phrygia, Babylonia and Assyria with the capital, and made many other regions much easier to get to than they were before. A series of 111 post stations kept horses ready for the royal messengers who travelled along the road and numerous inns provided food for travellers.

The royal road meant that all the empire's officials could communicate with Susa with relative ease. It also enabled Darius to keep an eye on other movements within the empire – private citizens as well as the royal messengers could use the road, but guards scrutinized them carefully and could report any suspicious movements straight to the king.

Darius was fortunate in his communications in another way. By his time the cumbersome clay tablets which the ancient Sumerians had used for writing had been partially replaced by scrolls written on papyrus or hide. So documents were more portable and the officials could take full advantage of the royal road.

Cuneiform record tablet

The road had one more vital implication for the Persian Empire. Snaking across the middle east from the gulf to the Mediterranean, it brought together a diversity of peoples. It made possible the great multi-national gatherings and ceremonies for which the Persian kings were famous, and it meant that artists and workers from all the corners of the empire could assemble to exercise their talents on the royal palaces of the Persian kings. It allowed the kings to understand their subjects better and thus govern them better; and it opened up Persian art to the greatest possible diversity of influences. From the point of view of Persepolis, the road was crucial both to the appearance of the capital and to what took place there.

The isolated palace

Yet Persepolis was a long way from the royal road – almost 480 kilometres (300 miles) southeast of Susa, in fact. The site was even some distance from a convenient water supply. But its position did have some obvious advantages. Its southerly location near the mountains meant that its climate was pleasantly cool during spring, the time of the year when it was usually occupied. Indeed the very isolation of Persepolis could be turned to an advantage – a remote king can give himself an air of mystical power, and no doubt this was a benefit which Darius, otherwise at the centre of a vast web of communications, could appreciate.

Having chosen his unlikely site, which contemporary inscriptions tell us was unoccupied before his time, Darius commenced building in about 520 BC. The work was to take at least sixty years, going on through the reigns of Darius' successors Xerxes and Artaxerxes. As well as a host of domestic quarters and the vast public rooms for which Persepolis is famous, they were to build an immense treasury that was to contain wealth form all over the empire. The great terrace on which the whole complex stood, the palace, the treasury, and most of the audience hall with its thirty-six supporting columns were completed during Darius' reign. Xerxes (486–465 BC) finished the audience hall, built more domestic quarters including the harem, and began the vast throne hall or 'hall of a hundred columns'. Artaxerxes (465–425 BC) finished the throne hall.

As this long time span suggests, it was an awesome task. The terrace, 460 x 275 metres (1,500 x 900 feet), on which the palace was to stand had to be hewn from the solid rock. Then the stones for the actual building had to be cut. Some of these weighed twenty tonnes, and even the capitals were so heavy that they had to be winched into position on top of their columns with chains and pulleys. The whole operation was well planned in advance.

Workers came from all over the empire to contribute to the building. Some of the best craftsmen were probably from Greece. Even in the reign of Cyrus, buildings at his city Pasargadae show evidence that the toothed chisel – a Greek implement – was used for stonecutting. Certainly the folds in some of the drapery on the carvings at Persepolis suggests a Greek hand. And there is yet more poignant evidence. When investigating the relief carvings at Persepolis, archaeologists discovered a graffito drawn in the style of a Greek vase of *c*.500 BC. This had been applied to the stonework beneath its final layer of paint, an eloquent indication that Greek workers were present.

So the mixture of styles that blend together to make Achaemenid architecture is hardly surprising. Some of the portals are guarded by stone bulls that remind us of the Assyrians' cities at Nineveh and Khorsabad. The stone lintels are often Egyptian in appearance. The sculpture of drapery often looks Greek. And the layout of the huge halls of columns is reminiscent of earlier Median architecture, although much more elaborate.

But the artists of the Persian Empire did not lift directly from their sources.

They could not, because the Persian kings wanted to achieve a different effect with their palace. For example, the carvings have a different quality from classical Greek sculpture, because they are designed to form a backdrop to the ceremonies that went on in the palace. So the carvings at Persepolis are flat: they must not eclipse the magnificence of the real processions that were to take place in front of them.

At Persepolis today only the foundations remain of most of the palace buildings. The most immediate impression is of hundreds of column bases – the original rooms must have contained a forest of columns, which supported the roof timbers of cedar from Lebanon. The greatest concentrations of columns are in the huge audience chambers – that of Darius, at the western side of the palace, and that of Xerxes on the east. The smaller rooms of the royal palace and harem in the southwestern corner of the complex, and of the treasury in the southeastern sector are built in a similar way.

The columns were not only functional. Their capitals provided the sculptors of Persepolis with some of their best opportunities for decorative work. The most magnificent were at the top of the 20 metres (65 feet) columns of the throne room and audience hall. To maintain the correct proportions on such tall pillars, the capitals had to be about 1.5 metres (5 feet) high. They were often in the form of animal heads – the bull was a frequent motif – and there were usually two heads facing outwards. Eagle-headed griffins and roaring lions are other animals that were depicted in this way, and human-headed bulls, reminiscent of Assyrian art, have also been found. They are all animals of immense power carved with great vigour – worthy symbols of the might of the Persian kings who sat on their thrones beneath them.

Lavish interior decoration would have complemented the buildings of the palace. Much gold was used, with hangings of gold lace and engraved gold plates covering the wooden doors. Tiles were hung on many of the walls, their glazes of blue, pink, and yellow and their animal motifs being reminiscent of the decorations on the walls of Babylon. In addition, most of the walls, together with the carved pillars and capitals, were brightly painted.

Top security

Apart from the audience halls, the most important building at Persepolis was the royal treasury. Placing the treasury at Persepolis was another way of capitalizing on the site's isolation. Away from potential plunderers, the great wealth of the kings was as safe here as it could be. And since much of the wealth came from tribute brought by subject peoples at the new year festivals held at Persepolis, it did not have to be transported far to the treasury. In keeping with the methodical nature of Persian rule, all the offerings of tribute were recorded, and the treasury accounts offices yielded over 30,000 tablets of treasury records.

Full of precious jewellery, crystal and glass, cups and bowls, gold-plated furniture, weapons, and carpets, the treasury was the royal storehouse. And its hundred rooms also accommodated resident workers who used the precious metals and stones brought to Persepolis from all over the empire to make yet more luxurious artefacts.

What was it for?

Apart from being the site of the treasury, a fully fledged palace in the middle of nowhere, specially constructed with all the resources of a vast empire, must have had some other special purpose. It was not the administrative centre – this role was performed by Susa, a city nearer the heartland of the empire and at one end of Darius' royal road. Neither was Persepolis the place where the Persian kings were crowned – this ceremony took place at Pasagardae, Cyrus' residence to the northeast of Persepolis, which was probably also a centre for Persian religion. Persepolis played a different, though no less important part, in imperial ceremony. It was the site of the rituals performed every March to celebrate the vernal equinox and the coming of the new year.

For a short period – perhaps only a few days – each year, Persepolis would buzz with activity. The town near the palace was neither big enough nor luxurious enough to accommodate the visiting dignitaries, so it would be augmented with a great assembly of tents brought by the visitors and pitched beneath the terrace on which the palace stood. Colourful pennants and the diverse costumes of the many peoples of the empire would brighten the dusty terrain. The palace itself would also be brightened – royal servants would finish giving the apartments their annual coat of paint just before the 'invasion' began.

As well as the king, his immediate family and his court, high-ranking representatives would be sent from each of the satrapies. They would salute the coming of the new year and pay tribute to the king. And the tribute that they paid was some of the most exotic ever to be assembled in one place.

The king, already sitting on a throne mounted on a substantial wooden platform, would first of all be carried to the audience hall by servants. There he would await the arrival of the lengthy procession. The limited light in the hall would catch his golden robes, crown, and throne as he waited for his subjects to enter.

The great procession

The first people to come into view gave an impression of formality. Marching guardsmen, the royal grooms with their best horses, and two empty chariots headed the procession. The chariots were for the king and for the god Ahuramazda, reminding everyone straight away of the religious nature of the ceremony.

Next would come a rather more

Relief showing Artaxerxes I on his throne

relaxed group of people. The principal courtiers, sure now of their security for at least another year, would walk rather casually, talking quietly among themselves, perhaps sharing a joke about something that had happened at court, or commenting about the conditions in the strange makeshift town outside the palace precinct.

But from a modern point of view the most interesting group were the next, the representatives from the twenty or so satrapies. Dressed in whatever costume was customary in their area, and burdened down with gifts for their king, they would make an extraordinary sight. And they would be far less confident than the courtiers. For many, it would be their first visit to Persepolis. And there would be nagging anxieties about their gifts – would they prove acceptable? Would they be upstaged by a delegate from another area? Would the king take them to task about the way they were running their region or paying their taxes?

In the circumstances, it is not surprising that they tried to outdo each other in the lavishness of their gifts. Fortunately we know a great deal about the sort of things they brought because of the carvings on the eastern staircase of the audience hall. All brought valuable jewellery, garments and other items of personal adornment. But most tried to bring along some speciality of their region that the others would not be able to supply. The Medes, long known for their horsemanship, brought the best horses they could find for the imperial stables. Other delegates would also contribute horses, but many tried for something more exotic. The Bactrians, as well as the people from Parsa and Arachosia, brought two-humped Bactrian camels, while Arabians brought single-humped dromedaries.

Still more outlandish would be okapis, as well as gifts of elephant tusks, from African provinces such as Ethiopia, antelopes from Libya, and giraffes from Abyssinia. Ionians would bring bees, whose honey was prized as one of the few food sweeteners in the ancient world, in elaborate hives. Delegates who could not manage exotic animals as gifts would try to compensate in other ways – they might bring wagon loads of rich cloth or elaborately decorated weapons by the score. And peoples known for their breeding of domestic animals would come with prize bulls or rams.

Carved finial

The overall impression was one of bright colours, loud noise, and not a little smell. With such a diverse procession, one can immediately appreciate why the Persians built their staircases with easy-rising steps: everything from an Indian wild ass to a wagon-load of armour could – and did – ascend with ease. It is also clear why the audience hall needed to be so large, since not only the delegates, but also their wagons and animals, had to be accommodated. So the great audience hall, which today, open as it is to the sun, seems light and airy, would be dark and almost claustrophobic in atmosphere. Not only would the thirty-six columns (each 2 metres/7 feet in diameter) fill up much of the space, but the rest would be filled with hundreds of people and dozens of braying, neighing, roaring animals.

With so much noise and activity, it is difficult to imagine such a scene having much dignity. But the king would be isolated against one wall of the hall and, gradually, each group of delegates would present themselves to the king and hand over their gifts in relative peace. Later, the king would be still more isolated from the mass of satraps and their representatives. A great banquet would be held where everyone would be entertained, but the king would dine apart with a few select courtiers, secreted behind a screen so that he could see everyone, but not be seen by them.

Why did Darius go to such lengths to celebrate the new year in this way at Persepolis? First of all, and most obviously, it was an effective way of increasing his wealth by exacting tribute from his subjects. But he could have done this anyway through his reliable administrative system of satraps, generals, tax collectors and 'king's ears'. More importantly, the new year ceremony brought the whole empire together. It enabled the king to hear for himself what was going on in the far corners of his territory. Although the king remained a remote figure on his throne or behind his screen, it gave the peoples of the empire a chance to get a little closer to him. And it would enable him to remind them that, in spite of the fact that he was taking valuable gifts from them, he was doing this within an accepted moral code.

The lessons of religion

The Persian religion was Zoroastrianism, a cult that set great store by moral codes. The early Persians had worshipped a number of different gods, all of whom were nature spirits. Their worship involved animal sacrifices, which were performed in order to appease the capricious deities. The magi who presided over this early religion also drank the intoxicating juice of the haoma plant.

The religion of Zoroastrianism contrasted with this in several ways. First and foremost, it was a religion of one supreme god, called Ahuramazda or 'wise lord'. His prophet Zoroaster founded the new religion after he had a vision in which he saw Ahuramazda and was told the key precepts of his new faith. The basic principles were that Ahuramazda was the force for good in the world; he was in continual struggle with the evil spirit Ahriman; people could assist him in his struggle by behaving well; Ahuramazda would eventually win the struggle and those who had helped him would be rewarded with everlasting life.

Many of these tenets do not sound unusual today, because of the influence of Christianity, but in the Persia of the late seventh century BC they were little short of revolutionary. At first Zoroaster had minimal success in preaching his creed until he finally travelled to eastern Iran, where he managed to convert the local king, Vishtaspa. This was the turning point. When Cyrus brought Vishtaspa's realm under the control of the Persian Empire the influence of Zoroastrianism spread and Zoroaster went to court, where he was more influential still.

Zoroastrianism would have had a special appeal for the Persian kings. It was not simply the fact that it valued truth above falsehood. It was also significant for them because its god acted according to a strict system rather than according to whim as the earlier nature spirits had seemed to do. In other words Ahuramazda treated people in the way the ideal Persian monarch treated them: according to just laws.

The new religion, at least in the form adopted in the empire, appealed also to the kings' sense of the diplomatic. We have seen that the Persians liked to leave their subject peoples to live as nearly as possible as they wanted to. In a similar way, Zoroastrianism was not imposed rigidly from above. The magi who administered it were left to incorporate elements of the old-fashioned religion of nature spirits if they so desired

It is impossible from the surviving documents to give a complete picture of this religion. Persian tradition held that a full account was written by Zoroaster on 12,000 hides, which were destroyed by Alexander the Great when he took over the country. This is unlikely, but whatever the prophet did or did not write, the earliest accounts that have survived date from almost 1,000 years after Zoroaster lived. What is clear from the facts that we do know is that Zoroastrianism was highly influential on later beliefs. It shares obvious elements with Christianity and also influenced Buddhism. But for the Persians, it was another essential influence on the smooth running of their imperial machine.

The decline of the Achaemenids

Cyrus and Darius presided over an empire that was on the whole stable and well run. But there were problems. There was another rising power in the Mediterranean, one that would dare to challenge the supremacy of Persian power – the Greeks. At the beginning of Darius' reign the Greek city states were under Persian control. But around about 499 BC a series of revolts began which were to lead to wars that were eventually to sap the power of the empire. The first of the Greek cities to stand up against Darius were Eretria, Athens, and Sparta. The latter two cities came together in an alliance to challenge Darius and in 490 BC the king dispatched an army to deal with the rebellion.

At first they met with little resistance. Eretria fell easily and the Persian ships lay in the bay of Marathon while the army got ready to march toward Athens. It was at this point that the Athenians surprised the Persians. Instead of waiting for the enemy to come to them, they seized the initiative, marching on the Persians and forcing them back into their ships. The Athenians then headed quickly back to their city, ready to repulse a further Persian onslaught the following day. The Persians, their numbers depleted, had no choice but to retreat back to their own undisputed territory.

The Battle of Marathon was hardly in itself a crushing blow to the Persians. They lost only a small area on the edge of their empire. Yet it was significant. A seemingly invincible power had been defeated.

In four years a graver blow fell. Darius, the king who had preserved stability for over thirty years, died. His son Xerxes took over and was immediately faced with rebellions in Egypt, followed by a revolt in Babylonia. In fact the roots of these rebellions lay back in his father's reign. Increases in taxation and high interest rates had placed an increasingly heavy economic burden on the provinces. While Darius reigned, most of the discontent could be put down. But with a new king, discontent erupted.

Nevertheless, Xerxes and Persepolis soldiered on, through a series of wars with the Greeks. Although as a result Xerxes finally lost all his power in Europe, the Persians still held the majority of the Middle East when he died in 465 BC. It was the economic factors that were to erode the power of the Achaemenids. Revolts at home and abroad caused a succession of kings to meet violent deaths, and none of the later kings ruled with the strength or longevity of Darius. The final blow did not come until 330 BC when the Macedonians, expanding their power across the civilized world, conquered Persepolis, and the last Achaemenid king, Darius III, was murdered.

Libyan tribute-bearer

The achievement of the original Darius survived until this time. He had won and held together the largest empire in the world to date. He administered it with the greatest skill. He got to know his diverse domain, commissioning the most extensive survey carried out in the ancient world, even more impressive than the Domesday Book of William I of England, some 1500 years later. He presided over important local achievements in Persian art and communications, and over developments that stay with us today, like the introduction of the domestic chicken from India and the middle east to Europe. And his empire came together at Persepolis, for a few decades the meeting point of an entire world.

After being overun by the Macedonians, Persepolis was an irrelevance. With no more great processions and ceremonies of gift giving little use remained for a palace that was still on the edge of the world as far as the ruling powers were concerned. The magnificence of Persepolis, occasionally mentioned in literature and evoked with pomp and ceremony, became little more than a memory. Even the carvings portraying the processions, and the tablets recording the successes of Cyrus and Darius disappeared beneath the encroaching sand.

PETRA

Hidden city of the Nabataeans, famed for its 'rose-red', rock-cut temples

If ever there was a site appropriate for inclusion in a book of 'mysterious places' then Petra, the rock-cut city in the Jordanian desert, is surely the place. Hewn from the solid rock by an obscure people, hidden amongst crags and hills, lost to western eyes for hundreds of years, rediscovered in the nineteenth century and romanticized as the 'rose-red city half as old as Time', Petra seems to typify the outsider's view of the mysterious Arab world. And yet its architecture – an exotic mix of Persian, Assyrian, Greek, and Roman elements – is distinctly classical in appearance, offering an eloquent reminder that the people of Petra's heyday were living in the shadow of the Roman Empire. Who were these people? Why did they choose to live in such a remote spot and to build in such an unlikely way? And how did they survive independently of the great power of Rome that surrounded them?

The inhabitants of Petra were the Nabataeans, a people who started out as a nomadic tribe in northern Arabia and seem to have moved northwards to the area of south Jordan known as Edom in the early sixth century BC. There they probably integrated peacefully with the native Edomite people, who had suffered in earlier centuries from attacks by the Assyrians, Babylonians, and Chaldeans and were probably glad to welcome settlers prepared to live side by side with them without raping and pillaging their way through the countryside.

The scene in front of the Khasneh would have been one of bustling activity – with travellers from all over western Asia meeting to exchange goods and news.

By the fourth century BC the Nabataeans were well established in the land of Edom and had become less nomadic. They had begun to build their capital at Petra, and were supporting themselves by trading with the peoples of Arabia, by exporting bitumen to Egypt, and by raising livestock. In addition they were gaining increasing revenue from the source that was to remain the key to their success and the prosperity of their city. Petra, in spite of its apparent inaccessibility today, was near some of the ancient world's most important trade routes. Control this trade, and you would be rich and powerful – this the Nabataeans managed to do.

One key route came up the rift valley that connects the Gulf of Aqaba with the Dead Sea. Caravans would would travel along the eastern coast of the Dead Sea down a path connecting Damascus in the north (from which there was also a road to the Mediterranean) with Aqaba (and therefore Arabia) in the south. It was a difficult route along the side of the valley, and stopping places with supplies of fresh water were vital. Petra, midway between the Gulf and the Dead Sea, was a good stopping place and an ideal point from which to control trade.

There was also an east–west route passing through Petra, connecting the civilizations of Mesopotamia and Egypt. Later, this east–west axis extended even further in either direction, to become part of the silk and spice road that stretched from China, through India, across the middle east to the Mediterranean, where ships could carry the products of the far east to Greece and Rome. There was a route to the sea at Gaza, northwest of Petra. So Petra was at a crossroads. If you could control it you had prosperity, the pick of the ancient world's supplies of every imaginable commodity, and power.

There were different ways of taking advantage of the trade. The crudest, and perhaps that employed by the earliest Nabataean settlers, was to act as glorified bandits, taking what you needed and letting through enough not to discourage the caravans entirely. A more regulated approach would involve levying taxes as the trade passed through Nabataean territory. But the people of Petra went a little further than this. They lived in difficult country and they came to know it like no one else. So they took physical control of the trade, joining the caravans and shepherding them through the narrow paths and rocky defiles that surrounded their city.

This policy was so successful that the Nabataeans became acknowledged masters of quite an extensive territory. Unfortunately there is very little written evidence about them. The historian Diodorus Siculus portrays them in the fourth century BC as still a largely nomadic people, yet we know from other sources that trade was already passing through Petra by this time and it is unlikely that they did not exploit it. They had certainly settled down in the following century, when many Nabataean villages are recorded. In another one hundred years we begin to hear of Nabataean kings, as well as piracy by Nabataean ships off Gaza – clearly no trade could escape their clutches, not even that carried by ships exploiting the newly discovered monsoon winds.

But it is not until *c*.168 BC that we begin to hear about the Nabataeans in enough detail to know the names of their kings or the true extent of their kingdom. At their height, they ruled towns as far apart as Damascus and Gaza, and large areas of land in between. The arrival of the Romans, who had provinces in Syria and, after AD 6, in Judaea, curtailed their political power. But it probably helped them in other ways, providing the stability that allowed trade to flourish. This stability also enabled the Nabataeans to create some of the most remarkable buildings in their city.

Arriving at Petra

The usual traveller's approach to Petra is through a narrow rocky defile known as the *Siq*. It is one of the most famous routes into any city, and yet, impressive as it is, dark and dramatic as are the looming rocks, eerie as are the echoes of the traveller's steps, none of this prepares the visitor for the sight at the end – the Khasneh, one of the city's most perfect rock-cut facades, and the most famous building in Petra. Its frontage, cut deep into the rock, fills a niche about 30 metres (100 feet) wide and 40 metres (130 feet) tall. It is remarkable for its excellent state of preservation, its elegant classicism and its unusual style (its Corinthian capitals with the curled acanthus leaves are a rare feature in Nabataean art).

In fact the Khasneh's unusual style has suggested to some scholars that workers from outside the local area were responsible for the building. Whoever conceived it, it is certainly a triumph of design. The lower row of columns, six rather than the usual four in number, give the facade greater width than normal. The upper columns mirror this, but, to prevent too heavy a weight seeming to press down on the lower row, they are not connected by a single lintel or triangular pediment as is normal in a classical building. Instead, the pediment is 'broken' in the middle to accommodate the master touch – the circular central feature with its crowning urn.

The Khasneh is also intriguing because of the different stories that surround it. The recent Bedouin people of the area were convinced that the urn contained hidden treasure, and would fire their rifles at the urn in an attempt to break the stone and release the gold from its centuries-old prison. The fact that the name 'Khasneh' means treasury is an indication either of the partial truth of this story or of the endurance of the myth.

But the Khasneh, like the majority of the rock-cut buildings that have survived at Petra, was probably a tomb rather than a treasury. Within, the structure is certainly tomb-like. The main room is a nearly perfect cube, completely plain; a small chamber behind it may have contained the remains of the original inhabitant. Rooms on either side could have been used by priests preparing for the rituals of burial or worship. It may have been the tomb of King Aretas III (86–62 BC). He it was who extended the Nabataean domains to Damascus and Syria, and he was known to have been interested in the style of art fostered by the Hellenistic world. With its Corinthian capitals, human statues, and complex interplay of shapes, the Khasneh is certainly reminiscent of this style.

The city of the dead

Petra is full of tombs. Few are as magnificent as the Khasneh, and they vary in architectural style, reflecting the influences of the different cultures with which the Nabataeans came into contact as a result of their trade. But in spite of the differences in style the tombs of Petra have a unity of appearance which comes from the fact that they are all hewn from the rock of the hillsides around the city. The colours of this rock are like no others. John William Burgon, in his poem 'Petra', was inaccurate when he called it a 'rose-red city'. A more precise account of the colours – and a no less memorable one at that – was given by Edward Lear's chef Giorgio: 'chocolate, ham, curry powder and salmon'. The variations in the colours and shades of the rock are amongst the most attractive sights to be found in the natural world.

The tombs have fascinating man-made variations, too. They develop from monuments with such minimal decoration that they seem little more than holes in the rock to full-blown classical designs like the Khasneh. Iain Browning, the scholar who has written the best modern book about Petra, has classified the tombs according to the designs of their facades. He traces the development from basic 'rectilinear' tombs, which have simple decoration and often do not truly have a 'facade' at all, through types showing an Assyrian influence, with a multiple-step decoration that recalls the buildings of Mesopotamia. There follows the introduction of corniced and double-corniced tombs, which often have classical-style doorways, prefiguring the later tombs.

Next come the full-blown Nabataean classical tombs like the Khasneh, no doubt influenced by King Aretas III's love of all things Greek. All these buildings are on a large scale compared with the earlier tombs, and although they vary greatly in quality, they all show a striving to create dramatic effect and an impression of magnificence. Pediments, pilasters, blind windows and niches, cornices, capitals and urns – the whole vocabulary of Hellenistic architecture is here, mixed into bizarre combinations and emerging from the multicoloured rock like a half-remembered dream of the glory that was Greece.

Quite how these tombs were used is difficult to tell. It is thought that at least part of Nabataean religion involved the worship of kings who were deified after their death. We know for sure that one king, Obodas, was regarded in this way. The magnificence of their tombs suggests that other kings were too.

But otherwise we know frustratingly little about Nabataean religion. Apart from the kings, two gods have been identified. The first, Dusares, was probably inherited from the original inhabitants of Edom when the Nabataeans arrived. He is thought to be a god of the upper classes. The other deity, the goddess Al Uzza, may have been brought to the region by the Nabataeans and worshipped by the whole population.

It is appropriate that Dusares, the principal god of Petra (the city of stone) was himself symbolized by stone – he was represented not as a statue but as a block of stone. Such blocks of stone, still visible at Petra, were thought of as the dwelling places of Dusares; they were also used as altars. Obelisks, which are incorporated into some of the tombs of Petra, were probably also regarded as symbols of Dusares. In fact the connection between the god and stone was not unique – the god of the Hebrews was also spoken of as a rock. This much we know, but the mute stones tell us little more about the religion of the Nabataeans.

The city of the living

Such a profusion of tombs, together with the unworldly silence that can pervade Petra today, gives the impression of a city of the dead, a place of ritual and retreat. But the city would originally have contained many more freestanding buildings than now survive, and these would have been the domain of the living. In its heyday, Petra would be buzzing with activity. It would have been a place full of noisy, smelly caravans and bustling merchants, crowded streets and thriving markets. And Petra would have been a cosmopolitan city, full of visitors from every staging post on the trade routes, some of whom would no doubt stay on.

By the time of Aretas III, the city would have been like a Roman town, with a sacred area or *temenos* containing a large central temple at one end of a square bounded by colonnades. Nearby would be a busy market, beyond that the citizens' houses (some people were rich enough to have stone ones) and further away still the great multicoloured cliffs, with their tombs that we see today.

The great temple at the end of the temenos, the Kasr el Bint, is one of the few freestanding buildings that survives. Fronted by a large four-columned portico and a marble open-air altar, it is the biggest of the surviving freestanding buildings in the city. It dates from the reign of King Obdoas II (30–9 BC) and became the centre of an area that was developed by the Nabataeans and later by the Romans when they finally took over the city in AD 106.

The Nabataeans provided a fitting gateway to the temenos area, another substantial structure, which was rebuilt towards the end of the first century AD. The Romans added a colonnaded street to the city centre, which was well paved with stone and led up to the great gateway and newly built temples. Excavations have shown that there were Nabataean tracks here before the Romans came, so it is likely that the Romans took over this and many other aspects of the city plan from the Nabataeans. On the southern side of the colonnaded street were three markets. These too had probably been on the site for many years before the Romans came – especially the lower and middle markets, although the upper market, with its grandiose pillared entrance, looks more like a Roman creation.

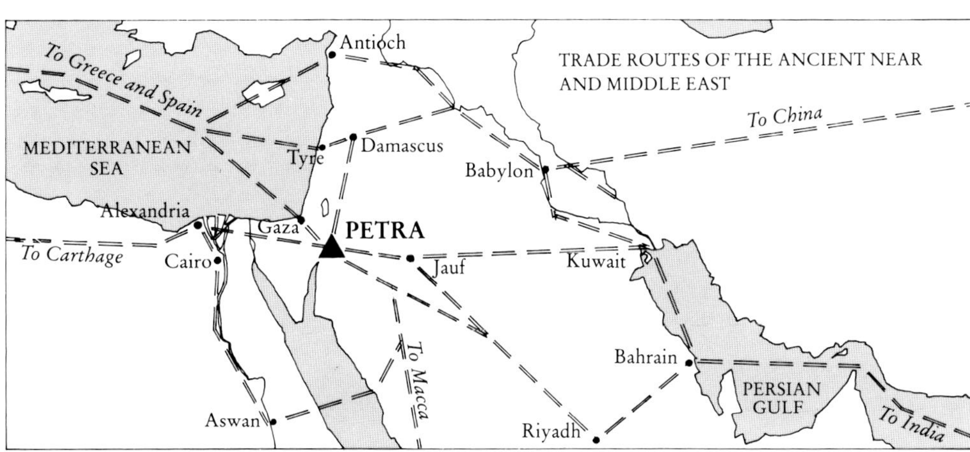

Map showing the many trade routes passing through or near Petra

The other achievements that the Nabataeans made before the arrival of the Romans are less immediately obvious to the visitor, but important nevertheless. The Nabataeans were excellent potters. Recently, some of their kilns have been discovered in Petra, some of them full of pots or vessels waiting to be fired. The wares have designs unlike any others, using natural motifs like leaves and branches in delicate colours. The effect is modern, and the unusually thin earthenware adds to this impression.

The other original contribution of Petra was in the field of engineering. Water was the most valuable commodity in the desert of Edom – the city's survival as a stopping-place, not to mention the literal survival of its 20,000 residents, depended on a good water supply. But the rains were far from regular. There could be many dry months followed by downpours that could turn narrow pathways like the *Siq* into treacherous rivers.

The solution to this problem was Al Birka ('the pool'), a reservoir with a capacity of over 2,500 cubic metres (88,275 cubic feet). From here, a rock-cut water channel sent the rain- and spring-water across an aqueduct and down to the city, where there was another reservoir from which supplies of water could be drawn. This was the main network for the distribution of water, although other pipes have been discovered taking water directly from the springs to the city. It was an impressive achievement, and a vital one for the success of Petra.

The coming of the Romans

The Romans had long had their sights set on Petra and the territory of the Nabataeans. Before the time of Emperor Trajan in AD 106 they had acquired enough land in the area to create the province of Judaea in the area around Petra. The city was close to being surrounded by Roman territory. What was more, the trade routes were changing. More traders were using the sea to transport goods from the Arab lands to Egypt and back again. And favoured land routes were moving northwards, to take advantage of a road connecting Dura, on the Euphrates, with Damascus and Tyre via the city of Palmyra. King Rabbel II (AD 70–106) moved the Nabataean capital from Petra to the city of Bostra in Syria, to try and attract trade. But the final blow to Nabataean independence came when Rabbel died and left the way open for the Romans. Trajan's Syrian general moved in and the Romans quickly established the new province of Arabia, of which Petra became a part.

As one can see from the remains of the colonnaded street, Petra flourished under the Romans. The peace and stability they brought provided better trading opportunities, and improved irrigation meant that the land around Petra was more viable for agriculture. As well as new buildings in the city centre, Petra boasted a new theatre (the Nabataean king Aretas IV had probably built a smaller one on the same site) and enjoyed the benefits of Roman civilization until the Sassanian invasions in the third century AD. Petra eventually became part of the Byzantine Empire, but never enjoyed again the stability it had had under the Nabataeans and the Romans. It lost its pre-eminence as a trading post, and fell from the consciousness of people beyond the immediate area and was ultimately visited only by the occasional adventurous traveller.

GREAT WALL OF CHINA

The world's longest defensive wall, begun in *circa* 214 BC and extended and maintained for centuries afterwards

The world's largest structure and the only man-made object visible from the Moon is the great defensive wall that stretches from the Yellow Sea to the north of Peking across 2,400 kilometres (1,500 miles) of Chinese countryside. Today most of the wall is still about 9 metres (30 feet) high and 4.5 metres (15 feet) broad at the top. So although it was extensively rebuilt in the fifteenth and sixteenth centuries AD, it is still an eloquent testimony of the vision, skill, and persistence of its original builders, the first Chinese emperor, Qin Shih-huang-ti, and his armies of labourers in the period immediately after 214 BC.

The Great Wall of China has been surrounded by legend ever since it was built. Its twisting, undulating course across mountains, through deserts, over valleys and ravines was supposed to resemble the body of a dragon. There was thought to be something magical about the wall's planning. Stories circulated that the first emperor was a magician who rode across China one night on a horse that could fly through the sky; as he went he mapped out the course of the wall. Another story describes a magical whip that the emperor used to carve a way through the mountains and alter the course of the Yellow River to accommodate the wall. Giants were supposed to have helped in moving the stone necessary for construction work. And so on.

The armour of this foot soldier is based on that of the famous terracotta warriors unearthed in the tomb of the First Emperor at Mount Li. Such soldiers would have been seen around the wall in its early years. Rural workers going about their daily chores would also have been seen near the wall.

The question the Great Wall poses is a conceptual one. What was the pressing need that drove the Chinese to make such an unprecedented effort? What was the mighty enemy that they were trying to exclude, or was there a deeper urge that drove them on to complete their task?

The enemy without

Part of the answer comes from outside the Chinese Empire. The Great Wall was built to protect the Chinese territory from attack by the nomadic tribes of the north. The Chinese referred to these people as the Hsiung Nu, and their descendants may have been the fearsome Huns who invaded parts of the Roman Empire in the fifth century AD.

They were a fearsome enemy, and like the marauding Mongols under their leader Genghis Khan who followed them in later years, they would not have been stopped by a mere wall, even a very solid one. In any case, there is some doubt as to the exact form the original wall took. Some excavations have suggested that it consisted mainly of banks of earth, and little early stonework has been discovered.

This confusion about the construction of the early wall is probably because the building method varied in different areas. In the east, where stone was plentiful, a rubble core was covered by a very solid outer skin of dressed stone, and topped by a roadway, also of brick or stone. This was reportedly so wide that five horses could walk abreast along the top of the wall. But in the west there was little stone available to the early wall builders, and transporting large amounts of stone would have been impossible in the difficult terrain. So a mixture of the local yellowish-grey earth and water was used. It was packed between two wooden barriers and left to dry hard. When the barriers were removed a serviceable wall was left, although it is difficult to believe that it would have been a significant threat to a determined invader.

However the wall was built, it had to be adequately garrisoned along its entire length, and this is where the Great Wall's thousands of watchtowers came in. Their extra height, combined with the mountainous setting of much of the wall, meant that the emperor's soldiers could be permanently on the watch for prospective invaders. We are not sure of the exact appearance of the towers that contained these soldiers. They were likely to have been less elaborate than the fine stone towers that survive today.

The united nation

The years leading up to the building of the Great Wall had been troubled ones for China. There had been many wars as the different dynastic families vied for supremacy. In the end the Qin were the victorious family. Their victory meant first of all gaining supremacy in a series of wars with the other dynasties, the Qi, Yan, Zhao, Han, and Wei. In 221 BC the Qin toppled the then leading dynasty, the Qi. In doing this they established for the

The Great Wall of China AD 50

The wall and its watchtowers followed the succession of hilltops across the northern boundaries of China. Here a skirmish is in progress as northern nomads try to take part of the wall and reinforcements rush in from the Chinese side. The archers in the regular guardtowers provided ample protection for each section of the wall, and ensured that would-be invaders could be repulsed.

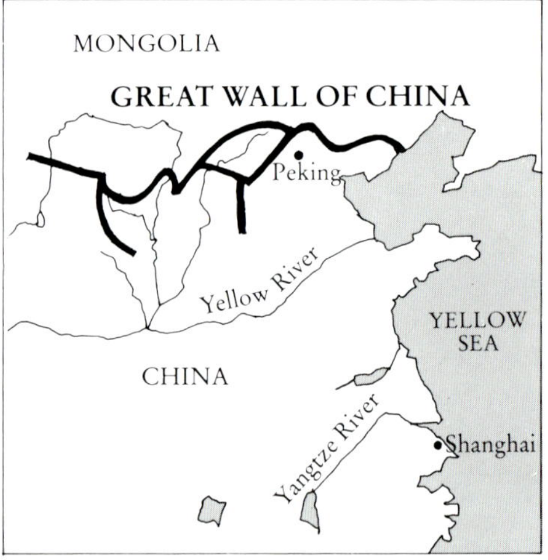

first time a single ruler over the whole of China. The Qin prince who led his family to victory was called Cheng. But to confirm his new position he changed his name to Qin Shih-huang-ti, which means 'the first Qin emperor'. This new unity was of very great significance for China and the wall was one of its most powerful symbols. It represented as nothing else could the unity of the Chinese Empire, a unity that had been hard-won during years of war.

Essential administrative and economic reforms had to be carried out to make the united empire work as a coherent whole under its new leader. Much of the work was the sort of standardization of approach that is needed if a large and disparate empire is to function as a unit. For example, weights, measures, and coinage were made to conform to a uniform system; carts were designed to the same width (so that they carried standard amounts of produce and did not have to be unloaded to have their contents weighed at borders); the same type of characters were used for writing throughout China.

Another reform was the setting up of an effective bureaucratic system and a network of local administrative districts, each with its own garrison. And an improved system of roads was

quickly built to help the empire run more smoothly. The Qin rulers also saw the great truth that has to be grasped by any leader in China – that the key to the country's success lies in the rural agricultural areas. So the Qin encouraged new irrigation schemes that improved soil conditions and provided good harvests – not to mention excellent imperial revenues from the tax on grain that they imposed.

A further set of Qin reforms was intended to weaken political opposition inside China. One story recounts that the first emperor made everyone outside the imperial army bring their weapons to his palace at Hsienyang. Here the arms were melted down and made into huge metal sculptures that adorned the emperor's home. Whether it is true or not, this story indicates the sort of power the emperor needed to exercise.

He did not simply need to deprive enemies of their weapons. The first emperor also went in for social engineering, moving opposing families away from areas where they could rely on support. The emperor had an astute political adviser called Li Ssu who observed that earlier dynasties had been weakened due to the power their leaders gave to their relatives. This led to warring factions and instability within China. One contemporary account tells of 120,000 families being relocated in a single year. Although this may be an exaggeration, it indicates once more that the emperor was prepared to be ruthless to hang on to his power.

But he was not always successful. Frequent levies of troops had to be made to defend the borders of China, and this sometimes led to a shortage of labour to till the soil. Forced labour on the wall itself caused a similar problem. The attendant food shortages lead to unrest in some areas of rural China, undoing the good work of the irrigation schemes and affecting tax revenues. One consequence of this was that some people moved northwards, beyond the emperor's territory. Here they could raise livestock and trade with the nomads, strengthening the economy of the emperor's enemies. Clearly, the people had to be kept at their work in the fields if rural stability and imperial revenues were not to deteriorate.

In the face of developments like these, the Wall was as important for keeping the emperor's subjects inside China as it was for keeping the nomads out. But it also had a symbolic importance for the Chinese people it surrounded. The Great Wall represented the unity of the new Chinese Empire, its civilization and its efficient administration. As a symbol of the empire it reminded the Chinese of the emperor's reforms and his firm rule. It helped to give a diverse people the identity they needed.

One other important factor in the building of the wall was the character of the emperor himself. His personality was a strange mixture – he was both a brilliant administrator and an obsessive paranoiac, preoccupied with his own death. His frantic building projects – a vast palace, homes for other members of his family, his tomb at Mount Li, and the Great Wall itself – suggest a deep-seated desire to leave a legacy in stone, to define his place in history as a supreme Chinese leader. In this light, the wall is above all a boundary: 'These are the limits of my empire,' it says, 'the largest the world has ever known.'

Building the wall

For the Chinese, a wall was the obvious solution to their problems. They were used to walls and wall building. Every Chinese city had a wall – in fact the word for city, *ch'eng*, also means wall. And the Qin rulers were used to wall building too. As early as 300 BC they had begun an extensive wall in the north of their kingdom to keep out the nomads. Victories over the Han and Zhao gave them further stretches of wall. All together the first emperor probably inherited about 2,000 kilometres (1,300 miles) of wall, to which he had to add 800 kilometres (500 miles) to make a complete defensive system.

When the first emperor conceived the Great Wall, these earlier fortifications were to form an important part of it. For the Great Wall, though largely the idea of the first emperor, was not planned as a single unit. It was a joining together of various existing walls with extensive new stretches.

The emperor's general Meng T'ien saw that the great undertaking was carried out systematically. Much of the wall crosses mountains or desert land and little food was grown locally. So before work could begin thirty-four supply bases were set up near the projected route. A network of tracks was also established so that workers, and their stores and materials, could

The First Emperor

be transported to the site. Even so, bandits were the scourge of the early builders, purloining many of their supplies before they arrived.

Next, watchtowers were constructed at intervals about two arrow-shots apart. The entire course of the wall could thus be adequately defended. These towers were also big enough to house the garrisons: they were about 12 metres (40 feet) high, 12 x 12 metres (40 x 40 feet) at the base, and tapered to about 9 x 9 metres (30 x 30 feet) at the top. They were also intended to contain sufficient supplies to withstand a lengthy siege, although bandits on the supply routes did not always allow this. Finally, when the towers were complete, the wall itself was built, filling up the gaps.

Getting the Great Wall built quickly was important enough to the first emperor to make some sacrifices seem worthwhile. And sacrifices there certainly were. Folk songs that survive from the period are testimony to how much people hated the hard work that construction entailed. But the fact that the workers' often resented their efforts makes it likely that some of the stories surrounding the wall are untrue, born of the imagination of discontent. The overseers were said to be so cruel that anyone who made a mistake would be killed and their bones unceremoniously dumped among the wall's foundations.

This version of the workers' fate may be fanciful, but the wall undoubtedly took its toll. Its location alone must have made it exhausting to work on, for it follows the line of greatest resistance through the Chinese countryside, hugging the sides of steep mountains before plunging down into valleys. It is easy for the modern tourist to forget that what makes the wall so spectacular in the mountainous areas through which it passes would also have made the lot of the labourers unbearable at times.

Work was also difficult in the desert sections. Here the wind would carry drifts of sand that threatened to fill in the foundation trenches before construction even got underway. So they had to build small walls to windward to protect the site from becoming covered by sand.

Life on the wall

There is a book on military training dating from the Ming dynasty (AD 1368–1644) that gives us some idea of the sort of conditions that soldiers on the wall had to bear. Although the account is much later than the original building of the wall, it is unlikely that conditions had changed very much until the Ming emperors restored the wall. Before this, the book describes the extremes of weather that had to be endured, from beating sunshine to bitter frost. Shelter on the wall was very basic, stores took a long time to arrive, and there was little space to store supplies once they had been delivered. It would have been a difficult life, and there is no doubt that the many Chinese poems lamenting the lot of relatives serving on the wall were amply justified.

The emperor's warriors

Qin Shih-huang-ti died in 210 BC. His reign had seen great achievements, and the emperor's life was crowned with the most spectacular memorial unearthed in recent times – the mausoleum containing the terracotta army of thousands of model soldiers that has made the first emperor as famous in modern times as he was in his own.

The emperor's model army is illuminating in the context of the Great Wall. It shows us clearly how the different ranks and divisions of the army were dressed. We see, for example, that the armour worn by most of the soldiers covers only the upper parts of their bodies. This confirms what we learn of Qin tactics from ancient writings – that the Qin liked to take the offensive and strike quickly. So their armour was deliberately lightweight, designed to allow rapid movement. Even on the wall this would be useful. One can imagine the sentinels, especially on the mountain stretches of the wall, spotting the enemy when still quite distant. They could then alert the troops who would rush out and take the initiative before the strength of the wall itself could be put to the test.

Yet their armour, although minimal, was quite sophisticated. Seven different designs of chain mail coat have been found in the burial pits at Mount Li. And some of the soldiers did have heavier armour – appropriate if close fighting became necessary.

Two massive projects involving thousands of workers, producing monuments of an unprecedented scale – it seemed a glorious beginning to the new Qin dynasty. But the first emperor was not to know that the glory was to be short-lived. He left behind a capable elder son, Prince Fu-su, who promised to be a worthy successor. But Fu-su's place was usurped by his younger brother Hu-hai, a weak puppet of palace politicians. The second emperor's lack of interest in matters of state led to a series of uprisings beginning in 208 BC, which brought about the end of the Qin dynasty in the following year.

The Great Wall in later years

The Great Wall did not die with the short-lived Qin dynasty. Later emperors, in particular those of the Han and Ming dynasties, extended the wall, strengthening its fortifications and adding other features that made it a more effective line of defence. We know that much construction work was carried out during the Han period (206 BC–AD 20). The garrisons of the Han emperors patrolled a wall about 10,000 kilometres (6,200 miles) long, which stretched from Dunhuang in Gansu province to the Xinjiang region in the west. During the following dynasties, little new building was done, but the wall continued to be used.

It is still referred to in literature, and contemporary sources often give us glimpses of the way life on the wall was organized. For example, one text from the T'ang dynasty (AD 618–906) stipulates how soldiers should signal using the beacon fires that were lit at regular intervals near the wall. These fires were placed in such a way that three could be seen from any one point. They were lit on circular platforms at strategic points – preferably on high ground if there was any in the neighbourhood. A group of nine men were to look after each fire, keeping watch for enemy movements, transmitting signals immediately, tending the fire, and keeping a tally of any messages that were sent. The number of smoke columns represented the number of any troops who had be sighted. Thus up to 500 invaders were signalled by one column of smoke; larger numbers were indicated by additional columns, up to a maximum of four columns for an army of around 10,000. The chain of beacons would allow signals like this to be sent quickly and reinforcements to be sent in from further along the wall.

Tripod water pitcher

Still later, during the Ming dynasty (AD 1368–1644), the wall was still in use. The book Ming Shi, a history of the dynasty, reports that 3,000 watchtowers were built during the reign of the emperor Mu Zong. His general, Tan Lun, surveyed the wall and had the plans for the towers drawn up. When they were completed, 9,000 soldiers were stationed on the wall, with a consequent improvement in border security.

Indeed by the Ming period the wall was less a simple fortification and more a military complex, with the fortified cities, garrison towns, castles, watchtowers and smaller towers all connected by a well-built and well-maintained wall.

YOSHINOGARI

Spectacular Japanese moated settlement of the Yayoi era, with large royal burial

One of the most exciting recent excavations in Japan has been the work done at Yoshinogari, a large site on the southwestern Japanese island of Kyushu, between the modern towns of Saga and Kurume. The site of an extensive settlement hemmed in by a moat, fortified with wooden fences and ditches, and guarded by watchtowers, it has caught the imagination of the people of modern Japan and, when fully explored, will tell them much that is new about their past.

What were the origins of Yoshinogari and how does it fit into what we know already about Japan's early history? And how does it relate to the myths and legends that surround the history of this country? To go some way towards finding out we must look first of all at the history of Japan during the centuries that in western history are remembered for the Roman Empire and the life of Christ.

The Yayoi period

The period 300 BC–AD 300 is known in Japan as the time of the Yayoi culture. It is an important period in Japanese history because it was then that the rural economy – based on the wet growing of rice in paddy fields – developed. This economy was to continue until quite recent times, so the Yayoi period set the trend for the development of Japan, at least in the rural areas, that was to last about 1,500 years. It is not surprising, then, that the Yayoi era has long held a special place in Japanese history.

It used to be thought that the developments it saw were so radical that the new skills of agriculture must have been brought to Japan by invaders from outside. Historians used to see a clean break between the Yayoi period and the Jomon period that preceded it. But as the evidence has been studied more thoroughly, it has become clear that the change was much more gradual. It is unlikely that there were invaders: the chances are that the people of the Yayoi era learned the skills of rice cultivation gradually, over an extended period of time. Nevertheless, if there were no invaders, there were certainly wars, and these played an important part in the history of the times, not least in the story of Yoshinogari.

Some of our knowledge about the Yayoi period is provided by a book called the *Wei Chih*, or record of Wei, which was completed in AD 297. This date tells us that its description of Japanese society relates to the late Yayoi period and the fact that it was composed in a factual tradition of history writing suggests that it is on the whole an accurate and truthful account.

The *Wei Chih* describes a people who once lived in about one hundred separate communities, although the author says that at the time of writing thirty communities kept in touch with him. They lived in a warm region with a mild climate, where they grew a variety of crops: as well as the ubiquitous rice, there were grains, hemp, vegetables, and mulberry trees for the keeping of silkworms. The people are described as law-abiding and decorous in their habits, and blessed with long lives – sometimes as long as one hundred years. They buried their dead beneath sand mounds and observed a ten-day period of mourning. The end of every funeral was marked by a ritual bath of purification for all the participants.

One of the communities or small states described in the *Wei Chih* is the country of Yamatai. This state, having had a male ruler for some time, fell upon a period of some seventy or eighty years of warfare. At the end of this time, the people decided to choose a female ruler, Himiko, who bewitched the people with magic and sorcery. She lived in a palace surrounded by towers and fortifications, attended by one thousand women and a single man. He was not her husband – Himiko never married – but was a sort of intermediary, helping the queen to communicate with the outside world.

Himiko was a successful ruler who won the respect not only of her own people but of the inhabitants of many of the other Japanese states. When she died a great burial mound was raised, more than 100 paces in diameter, and she was given a ceremonial funeral with many mourners. After her death a king was placed on the throne, but he was unable to keep order so once more the people of Yamatai chose a woman to rule them, a relative of Himiko called Iyo. Once more, order was restored.

Who were the people of Yamatai? The tantalizing answer is that no one knows for certain. Several sites from

As well as the wet rice agriculture of the paddy fields, conventional dry farming was practised in Yayoi Japan. Here the fields near the outer moat are being ploughed.

Yoshinogari AD 300

The moated settlement went through various stages of building. This reconstruction shows it during the late Yayoi period. Houses, grain stores, watchtowers, and large residences can all be seen.

the Yayoi period have been put forward, but none seemed important enough for a state of the prominence of Yamatai until the discovery and excavation of Yoshinogari.

Yoshinogari is distinctive for several reasons: its moated settlement is the largest so far discovered; the selection of artefacts found there has been of high quality; and the settlement is remarkably rich in burial remains, including a royal burial mound of unusual size.

The moated settlements

Before the discovery of Yoshinogari, the known moated settlements of Yayoi-period Japan were relatively small. Amongst the larger ones, Otsuka had a moat 200 metres (650 feet) long; that at Karako Kagi was about twice as long as that at Otsuka. By contrast, the moat at Yoshinogari was about 900 metres (3,000 feet) long. How did these defences come about in the first place, and why might it have been that Yoshinogari's moat was so much longer?

The middle of the Yayoi period was a time of tension. There was fighting between the different states and particularly between the people of the outlying villages with those of the larger settlements. So the places with the available resources set about defending themselves with moats, wooden pallisades, and watchtowers. In the later Yayoi period there was more stability as a class system started to develop. The rich upper classes

took over the moated stockades where they could be safe and enjoy their riches; for the rest it was an unenviable life of toil in the rice fields outside. So Yoshinogari was almost certainly a place of privilege, whether or not it was the headquarters of Himiko. What else can the site tell us about life during the Yayoi period?

Yayoi life

Fortunately Yoshinogari has yielded numerous finds that tell us much about the culture of the people who lived within its walls. One of the most obvious things is the importance of rice growing for the people. Many burnished stone knives in a flat crescent shape have been unearthed. These curved stones have two holes which took a loop of string. The string was wound around the fingers and the curved edge was used to cut the rice. These are similar to knives excavated from other Yayoi sites and their use continued in southeast Asia until fairly recent times. Amongst utilitarian objects, pots were also common. Typically, these were bulbous-bodied and narrow-necked containers characteristic of Yayoi work. Most show a careful attention to detail in their manufacture, with a smooth surface being achieved before an abstract design was applied.

There were also more exotic items. These people were highly-skilled bronzeworkers. The items that have been discovered include some objects of unknown purpose, such as a curious bronze disc with eddy-shaped arms. A stone mould for making such an item has also survived. It may have been a decorative item – it is difficult to imagine a practical use for it. Also highly decorative were the bronze mirrors. These could be small enough to fit in the palm of a hand, but were exquisitely worked with abstract, hatched, or zigzag patterns. They reveal a people who valued beauty even in small items, and who probably looked upon such artefacts as marks of particular status. But it is copper mirrors that those who want to identify Yoshinogari with Himiko's home would like to find. One source reports that the queen was given one hundred copper mirrors. If these are ever discovered, the identification of the two sites will be more likely.

The graves

But the human remains are among the most impressive at Yoshinogari. They

Model building showing double roof

are impressive in their number: there are over several thousand funerary urn graves, 350 cave graves, and more than ten stone box-type graves. These statistics alone make the site the most remarkable burial site in Japan. The condition of the human bones found in the graves is even more surprising. Some of the skeletons have no heads, some have other wounds, others have arrows lodged amongst their bones.

We do not know for sure which war brought about these injuries or who the enemy of the Yoshinogari people was. Perhaps some of the outlying communities that were governed from the settlement challenged their rulers' power; or perhaps the soldiers of a neighbouring state attacked the settlement; or perhaps a power struggle started within the fortification itself. Whichever was the case, the skeletons of those who were killed are an eloquent testimony to the severity of the fighting.

At the northern end of the settlement there is a mound tomb that stands out from the rest. The tomb was constructed using alternate layers of red and black earth, a process known as *rammad*. It is the oldest mound tomb known in Japan and is rectangular in shape, measuring 24 metres (79 feet) long and 15 metres (50 feet) wide and sits on top of a still larger octagonal platform. Clearly, the person who was buried here was someone of great power. It is one of the main indications that we are looking at more than a glorified village in Yoshinogari – rather, it is a community that had considerable influence beyond its own walls.

The buildings of Yoshinogari

The people of Yoshinogari lived in typical houses of the middle to late Yayoi period. They were oval or squarish structures, with a floor area measuring about 6 metres (20 feet) across. The main materials of the buildings were wood and thatch. Rather than having separate walls and roofs, the houses probably had a sloping thatched covering that came down right to the ground. In the middle of the floor was a clay pit for a fire and equidistant from this were four sturdy posts that supported the thatch. A raised bench went around the edge of the living area. This was usually simply an earthen construction held together by roughly cut planks along either edge. It acted as a shelf for storage. There was probably very little other furniture. The earth bench had an additional purpose. Because the thatched covering of the houses came down to meet the ground just beyond the bench, the bench acted as a barrier to any water that might seep into the house under the thatch.

Houses were one important type of building at Yoshinogari, but there were others. In an agricultural community where a class system had also developed it was important to be able to store the crops so that the upper classes could control the distribution of food. So there were storage buildings, where rice and grain could be kept. These were rather taller than the houses and were raised on wooden posts to keep the contents away from pests.

Another prominent type of building was the watchtower. In a settlement as large and important as Yoshinogari, it was vital to have good defences. This did not only mean solid fortifications – if enemies could be sighted long before they arrived at the walls, the appropriate defences could be prepared. So tall towers supported on long wooden pillars and covered with typical pitched roofs were built at key points. Such towers also allowed those inside the settlement to keep an eye on the people of the surrounding communities, whom they probably ruled, and on whom they depended for their food supply.

Finally there would be large houses for the ruling class, probably within inner defences – an inner moat or wall

– for additional security. These would be large, more elaborate versions of the smaller buildings of the settlement, and would probably have had taller interiors and a more conventional 'wall and roof' method of construction. The substantial size of the royal tomb at the northern end of Yoshinogari suggests that the royal residence would also have been of considerable size.

Yayoi agriculture

Rice was the principal crop and it was grown in paddy fields on ground that was slightly lower than that of the settlement itself. The fields were divided by earthen embankments which acted both as barriers to control the flow of water and as paths for people on their way to their work in the fields. Judging by other sites, there would also have been ditches or canals which would have been used for irrigation and drainage. Transport around the paddy fields might well have been by small dug-out canoe, a method that is still used in rural areas today. The workers in the wet fields would have worn wooden clogs – many have been found on Yayoi sites – to help to protect their feet from the mud. Again, such clogs are still used in the paddy fields today.

In addition to wet rice farming, dry agriculture was also practised. Among the crops grown were millet, gourds, and melons. There may also have been gardens near the smaller houses where crops such as these, together with other commonly eaten vegetables, would have been grown.

Religious beliefs

What were the beliefs of these people? The Yayoi period seems to have been one of transformation in religion as well as in agriculture. This is not surprising. The change from the uncertain life of hunting and gathering to the more predictable – though still sometimes difficult – life of agriculture meant that the people's perspective changed quite dramatically. The idea took root that, although the forces of nature were strong, humans could strive to influence them for their own benefit. Consequently the Yayoi era saw a fashion for the arts of spell-casting and the prediction of the future. The period also saw an increase in the number and importance of the nature divinities – gods of the trees, rice fields, and rivers that prefigured the later Shinto religion.

Burial customs changed as the religious perspective altered. Burials with urns became common, especially on the island of Kyushu where Yoshinogari is situated. The development of the craft of ceramics in the Yayoi period was such that for the first time potters in Japan could make vessels large enough to contain an entire human corpse. Wooden coffins were also used. At some sites, the same urn or grave contains several skeletons, suggesting that the burial ceremony was in two parts, before and after the flesh had decayed away from the body or had been removed.

The dead were often buried with grave goods, which could be bronze weapons or bronze mirrors. This custom reflects an influence from China; indeed many of the mirrors discovered have a Chinese design. The jars were buried vertically or at a slight angle in the cemeteries. Although these urn burials are usually modest compared to the great royal tombs like the one at Yoshinogari, they indicate that their owners had a certain status. They are always found in prosperous areas and the existence of so many at Yoshinogari implies the existence of a large and prominent middle class.

The enigma of Yoshinogari

For the moment, Yoshinogari poses as many questions as it answers. We do not know exactly how powerful its people were or how far their influence stretched. And we certainly do not know whether the settlement was the home of Himiko or of some other ruler whose story was reflected in that of the great queen. But the excavation of this site, so large and yielding so much material, is a major breakthrough in Japanese archaeology. In a culture where the digging up of the remains of ancestors is looked upon with mixed feelings to say the least, the archaeologists have pursued their task with courage and skill. What they have excavated has already told us much about a period of Japanese history for which evidence is thin on the ground – after all, the wooden buildings and other artefacts of wood have perished and there is very little written evidence about the period, apart from the *Wei Chih*. The excavation of the site brings some of the excitement that digs at Knossos and Troy once did to people in Europe. Like those places, it will surely keep many of its mysteries even as our knowledge of it grows.

Clay figurine from burial chamber

ELLORA

Superbly carved temples of the eighth century AD, hewn into the rock of an Indian cliff

Among the mountains of Hyderabad in northern India lies Ellora, one of the most remarkable of Asia's sacred sites. It is a place of great natural beauty, an area of mountains, fast-running streams and plunging waterfalls, and this must have made it an obvious choice for a place of worship.

And it remained a place of worship for about 500 years, with temples and shrines of different faiths being built as India went through a period of religious change. All together there are now thirty-four temples at Ellora. They are not conventional, freestanding buildings, but have been cut into the cliff face and carved out of the living rock. There are many rock-cut buildings in the world, some of which, at Petra in Jordan and Abu Simbel in Egypt, are described elsewhere in this book. But the temples at Ellora are different. Whereas those at Petra and Abu Simbel are interesting primarily for their facades, many of the temples at Ellora have magnificent, intricately carved interiors. And while the great monuments of Petra and Abu Simbel were cut into the rock from the cliff face inwards, the most outstanding temples at Ellora were made by excavating from the cliff top downwards, a technique that produced a very different visual effect.

To modern western eyes it is perhaps difficult to understand why the people of India wanted to create their temples and shrines in this way during the years AD 600–1100. But there are several reasons why they might have had the initial idea and stuck with it through a period of change. First there were practical reasons for cutting the sanctuaries out of the rock rather than making freestanding buildings. The temple-builders worked by digging trenches downwards from the cliff top into the rock. By doing this, they isolated a massive block of stone which they could carve into the gateways, passages, rooms, and shrines of a full-scale temple. This seems a rather involved procedure, but the labour it entailed could have been no greater – indeed was probably less – than that of quarrying the stone and transporting it across difficult terrain to some other site.

Second, there were artistic reasons for working in this way. As one can see from their method, the creators of the temples were more like sculptors, making gigantic stone-carvings, than builders or architects. The religious sensibility of India has long expressed itself most eloquently in sculpture. Third, and most important, were the religious reasons. Of the thirty-four temples, twelve were made by Buddhists, seventeen by Hindus, and five by followers of Jainism. In each of these religions there are certain features that would have made this type of cave temple in the sort of setting Ellora provides particularly appealing.

The Buddhist monks were the first to choose Ellora, although earlier religions may well have had sanctuaries there too. They began to construct shrines at Ellora in *c.*AD 600 and continued to use the site for over 200 years. A mountain setting would certainly have appealed to them – the Buddhist's path to enlightenment was often portrayed as a mountain, the gradual climbing of which leads one nearer and nearer to nirvana. The isolated setting of Ellora would also have appealed to the early Buddhists, seeking peace to meditate, renounce the life of pleasure, and seek the Truth.

For the Hindus, Ellora and its cliffs would have been attractive for different reasons. The Hindu religion, teeming with different deities, is one that acknowledges the richness and fertility of the natural world. A place of such great beauty, and a temple that is actually part of the living rock, would therefore be a Hindu ideal. In addition, the site at Ellora is crescent shaped, an appropriate setting for temples dedicated to the great Hindu deity Shiva, who was a moon god.

Like the Buddhists, the Hindus also have the idea of the temple-mountain. But rather than representing the route to enlightenment, the Hindu temple-mountain gives the faithful a way of finding their place in the scheme of things. A Hindu temple-mountain will therefore be lavishly decorated with carvings showing the Hindu myths, and illustrating animals to indicate the richness of nature. Not surprisingly, the Hindu temples are the most spectacular ones at Ellora.

Caves are also rich in meaning for the Hindus. Since the earliest times, hermits had sheltered in the quiet darkness of caves, perceiving in the depth of the rock a parallel to the depth of their spiritual quest. It was only one step from this spiritual quest to a more organized and premeditated

A combination of plan and overhead view, this depiction of the Kailasa temple at Ellora shows how the structure was carved out of the rock of the cliff.

one of excavating an artificial cave in which to build a temple. From this point of view the darkness of the Ellora sanctuaries, which frustrates the modern flashlight-carrying traveller, was a positive advantage. The physical shelter that they provided from the hot sun was paralleled by a sense of spiritual refuge, especially in the dark and cool inner sanctum of the temple.

For the adherents of Jainism, the other religion represented at Ellora, the site also held a fascination. Jainism combines some of the traits of Buddhism and Hinduism, and brings together both austerity and luxury. It is hardly surprising that Jain temples should have been constructed here, in a place isolated enough to feel austere, but with excellent stone for intricate and opulent carvings.

The Kailasanatha

The most spectacular of the temples at Ellora is the Hindu shrine known as the Kailasanatha. This temple was created in AD 765 by King Krishna I. Krishna was a member of the Rashtrakuta dynasty, who had defeated the kings of the dynasty of Chalukya. The latter were from southern India, and Krishna was successful in pushing them back after they had expanded their territory in the north. In thanksgiving he sponsored the construction of this temple, the largest at Ellora and the most intricate in both its overall plan and its detailed sculptural decoration. He dedicated the temple to Shiva, and its name refers to the god's mountain home, Kailasa, 'the abode of pleasure'. The name actually means 'lord of Kailasa', so the temple is named for Shiva himself.

The builders of the Kailasanatha used their customary method, digging trenches from above to isolate a block of stone from which to carve the temple. They split the rock by driving tree trunks into the trenches and then pouring in water. The wood then expanded, forcing the stone to part. A large quantity of rock had to be removed before the carvers could get to work on the temple proper. When they did start to carve, they had only chisels that were about 2.5 centimetres (1 inch) wide. Even so, they worked on a much larger scale than they had before. Their original trench was dug to form a rectangle 85 x 49 metres (280 x 160 feet) and penetrating to a depth of 30 metres (100 feet). This provided enough stone for the designers to run riot with their architectural scheme. The interior has gateways, porches, halls, galleries, staircases, and shrines. It is surrounded on three sides by a great rock-cut colonnaded gallery that acts as a viewing platform for the sculptures on the outer wall of the temple proper. There are also two side chapels, themselves large enough to be temples in their own right.

Tranquil figure from the temple facade

Entering the Kailasanatha is a breathtaking experience – and one that has been carefully controlled by the original designer. The visitor first passes through an imposing gatetower before entering the Nandi pavilion. This is the shrine of Nandi, the sacred bull that was the 'vehicle' of the god Shiva. On either side of the pavilion, stretching up from the floor below, are two immense pillars, each 15 metres (49 feet) high and surmounted by a trident, another symbol of Shiva. Next to each pillar was a sacred stone elephant, each approximately life-size.

Having passed these features, arresting as they are, one walks over a rock-cut bridge to the terrace, steps, and entrance to the mandapa, or main hall of the temple. This is an imposing room, about 16 metres (53 feet) square, with a flat roof supported by sixteen columns. This was the hall for worshippers which leads in turn to the inner sanctuary, a dark shrine containing the *yoni-linga*, a phallic sculpture representing Shiva's creative energy. The priest was the only person allowed to enter this ultimate holy-of-holies, and the atmosphere inside is suitably mysterious and intense, a feeling, as the writer Alistair Shearer has put it 'of a subterranean and awesome darkness, as if you were entering the very bowels of the earth'.

But the glory of the Kailasanatha is its sculptural decoration. This starts at the entrance and covers much of the inside and outside of the temple. As well as the large stone elephants on either side of the main entrance, more elephants are cut into the base of the temple itself, so that they seem to be supporting the structure on their backs. On many of the walls are carved relief panels illustrating scenes from the Hindu epic the *Ramayana*.

The *Ramayana* was composed some time between 300 BC and AD 300. Briefly and simply, it is the story of the king Rama and his beautiful queen, Sita. Sita is abducted by the demon Ravana, who carries her away to his fortress on the island of Lanka. The story tells how she is finally rescued by Rama, with the helping of the monkey Hanuman. The religious importance of the story is that Rama is seen as the incarnation of the god Vishnu. So although the Kailasanatha is dedicated to Shiva, its original creators did not exclude other gods from appearing on its walls –admittedly in human form.

Acts of worship

How was Shiva worshipped at the Kailasanatha? Hinduism does not require the participation of a 'congregation' in the western sense – the priest is the representative of the people in religious ceremonies and can in theory worship alone. In practice, however, a number of devotees would normally also be present, although they would not be allowed into the inner shrine. This explains the division of temples like the Kailasanatha into a large hall or *mandap*a and an inner sanctum that would be the preserve of the god and the ritually-cleansed priest.

The ceremony would begin with a careful opening of the doors to the shrine, after which the priest would chant and recite mantras in front of the statue, in order to encourage the god to inhabit his temporary home in the shrine and to draw his power towards the temple. The next stage would be to adorn the image, bathing it, annointing it with oils and sandalwood paste, and burning camphor to purify the air. Next, offerings would be made to the god. These could consist of incense, flowers, holy water and food. The latter would range from fruit, milk and ghee (clarified butter) to cooked rice dishes. As in ancient Egyptian religion, where the god was also thought to dwell in the temple and was offered food as part of the ceremony, the food would later be taken away for distribution amongst those present. Finally the shrine doors would be closed, allowing the god to sleep until the next ceremony.

This type of worship took place four times every day, at dawn, noon, sunset, and midnight. In addition, the priest could undertake extra offerings at the request of an individual. Further activities taking place in the 'public' part of the temple included special festivals, at which there might be recitals of traditional stories, song, dance, and processions in which a portable version of the god's image would be carried around the temple. So although the Hindu temples at Ellora may seem quiet today, we can imagine them echoing to the sound of priestly chanting – and sometimes to yet more exuberant noises from the mouths of the local congregation.

As befits a shrine of the god Shiva, the temple contains many relief panels showing episodes from the god's life. A number of these can be seen from the courtyard that surrounds the temple, particularly from the colonnaded walk. Here we see Shiva in a number of scenes with his consort Parvati. They can be found playing dice together, for example. We see Shiva playing a type of sitar called a *vina*; since in Hindu mythology the universe was said to have been created by sound, Shiva is being portrayed in this panel as a creator. On another relief Shiva is getting married to Parvati in a ceremony that is presided over by Brahma, the god of creation. Elsewhere he is shown dancing.

Another group of reliefs shows scenes from the life of the god Vishnu. Still further panels portray episodes from the Hindu epics – the *Mahabharata* and the *Ramayana*. All in all, the temple is a feast of carving, as full as any western cathedral of visual versions of sacred stories, intended for the enlightenment of those who could not read and the delight of those who could.

The Buddhist sanctuaries

For the Kailasanatha alone, Ellora would be a site of major historical importance. The other thirty-three temples, though not as outstanding as their great neighbour, are nevertheless fascinating too. The simplest are Buddhist shrines – plain caverns with cells for meditation around the walls; they have no pillars or ornate sculptures.

The Buddhists also produced monasteries which provided somewhere for the monks to live and eat as well as to study and meditate. These were rather more complex than the small shrines, although still relatively plain in their style. There would be a central communal hall with stone platforms to act as tables and pillars to support the roof. Cells around the edge would be for the monks to study and sleep. There would be a shrine at one end of the monastery; this would contain a statue of the Buddha and would have wooden doors so that it could be closed when worship was not in progress.

Not all the Buddhist monasteries are completely plain and austere. Some (such as the monastery known as Cave 10 in the usual numbering system) are large three-storey structures with balconies containing the monks' cells. The local name for Cave 10 is 'the carpenter's cave' because it is carved in a style that suggests a wooden building. There are stone 'rafters', which are purely decorative, and other details that recall earlier wooden buildings. Some commentators have seen in this style of architecture a nostalgia for an earlier period, when the Buddhists of India lived simple, rural lives, with few of the pressures of the world impinging on their meditation. It could be added that coming to an area like Ellora in the first place may well have been something of an escape from the cares of the world.

Looking across at the colonnade surrounding the Kailasa

The Jain temples

King Amoghavarsha (AD 815–877) was the most famous king of the Rashtrakuta dynasty. He converted to Jainism and gave welcome support to this sect, resulting in several new temples at Ellora. Jainism is a curious mixture of asceticism and luxury, and it is the luxury that emerges from Jain architecture. The temples at Ellora are no exceptions, being virtuoso examples of stonecarving.

Although they produced nothing at Ellora to equal the Kailasanatha, one of their temples, known as the Indra Sabha, is a small gem. Like the Kailasanatha, the Indra Sabha temple has a central rock-cut shrine surrounded by an independent gallery. It is decorated with ornate pillars, stunningly carved porticos, and reliefs showing the god Indra. There is also an enormous lotus flower – symbol of enlightenment – carved in the ceiling.

Enduring memorials

The artificial caves of Ellora were originally begun as alternatives to shrines of less permanent materials such as wood and bamboo. But their creators found in their unusual form a way of expressing their beliefs that was uncannily appropriate – and resoundingly successful. It is not really surprising, then, that the site continued in use for so long, or that it was colonized by the devotees of three very different religions.

Ellora's position – on major trade routes between Ajanta (itself a renowned site with its own caves) and Ujjain, and between Pathan and Broach – helped the site's enduring success. Where traders went, so did pilgrims and wandering monks, with the result that Ellora was not 'lost' like many of the places in this book. Its fame has lasted, although this has not detracted from its enduring mystery or its unique atmosphere.

NARA

Japanese imperial capital and headquarters of Buddhism in Japan AD 710

During the sixth and seventh centuries AD, two developments occurred in Japan that were to have lasting effects on the history of the country. First of all, in the sixth century, Buddhism started to become fashionable, spreading from China via the Korean peninsula. Second, during the following century, a strong imperial government was set up in the city of Asuka, from where Japan was ruled as a whole, turning from a united nation rather than a group of independent peoples.

The change in government began in AD 645, when an event called the Taika Reformation took place in Japan. A royal prince, Naka-no-Oe and a courtier, Nakatomi-no-Kamatari, seized power from the dominant family, the Soga. It was their aim to take away as much power as possible from the various aristocratic families in Japan, who had ruled almost as kings in their own regions. They were helped in this by the fact that Nakatomi was an expert on Chinese systems of government. His training had taught him two important ways of keeping power. First of all, a decree was issued taking away the lands of the regional lords and giving them, and the peasants who worked on them, to the new emperor. To ensure this edict was carried out a census and survey of lands was commissioned.

Although the inhabitants of the famous monasteries at Nara lived a fairly Spartan life, the imperial family and court that endowed the monasteries lived in luxury. This painting of a man and woman of the court is based on a mural contemporary with the temples.

The second decision was to build a new capital city where the emperor would have his home. No longer would the site of the capital change with each new monarch. There would be a permanent seat of government, and the administration of all the provinces would be carried out from there. At first, the new emperor, who took the name Tenchi when he took over the imperial crown, thought of building his capital in the Asuka district, where he already had a palace. But there was not enough clear ground on this site for a full-blown, Chinese-style city, with space for the administrative buildings, temples, and other buildings that were required. So Tenchi's successors chose Nara, about fifteen miles northwest of the original site, and in AD 710 the new, purpose-built imperial city was founded.

The new city

Nara was magnificent. Laid out on a grid plan, and incorporating palaces, administrative buildings, markets, granaries, Buddhist monasteries, and pagodas, it was a capital worthy of a powerful emperor. In several ways it also set the tone for Japanese architecture for many years. With their overhanging roofs supported on stout painted pillars of wood, their brackets joining together pillars and roofs intricately carved, and their cool stone floors, the buildings of Nara have a style that has come to be thought of as typically Japanese.

The decree to construct the new capital came from the empress Gemmei, who ordered that the city should be properly built so that nothing would need to be added later. Indeed she wanted a city that would be so perfect in its proportions that it would not be possible to make further additions without spoiling the design. So the city was meticulously planned. Its grid system was subdivided, so that each main city sector was divided into blocks. This method of subdivision not only looked effective; it also provided a convenient way of apportioning property in the city. Residential land was allocated to noble families block by block, the most powerful family being given four city blocks. So as well as being a place of beauty and elegant proportions, the new capital was to symbolize the careful organization of the state under the emperor. And in both respects, as in so much in Japanese architecture, it owed a great deal to the culture of Japan's powerful neighbour, China.

The debt to China

In accepting the influence of China the empress and her architects knew what they were doing. Contacts with the great power had been built up over the past century. Indeed this had started even before Nakatomi-no-Kamatari had encouraged Chinese contacts after the Taika Reformation. In AD 607 a Japanese imperial envoy had been granted an audience with the Chinese emperor Yangdi; he returned to Japan with two Chinese envoys, signalling the beginning of a period of regular communications between the two countries. Monks, scholars and officials from Japan visited China during the reign of Empress Suiko (AD 593–628) and the tenets of Buddhism and Confucianism began to spread to Japan. These were enshrined in a code

The large courtyard was used for ceremonial processions. It also housed the pagoda and the main hall. A covered gallery around the courtyard could be used for walking and talking. The monastery is the world's oldest wooden building.

composed on the order of Empress Suiko's Prince Regent, Shotoku, showing how important the Japanese felt this influence to be.

The Chinese influence made its presence felt in many other ways, for example in medicine, astrology, technology, and the arts. It seemed that the Japanese were keen to exploit every aspect of Chinese civilization that was more advanced than their own. Often the Chinese concept fitted Japan very snugly. Nowhere is this clearer than in Japanese architecture. For example, the idea of the pagoda,

The Horyuji monastery, Nara AD 710

one of the most well known features of Japanese temples was imported from China during this period. A pagoda is a tower, usually with five storeys though there can be many more, each of which is graced with a generously overhanging roof. The bottom floor contains Buddhist images or shrines; the upper floors provide galleries in which one can meditate – or simply admire the view. In other words the pagoda was similar in purpose to the great Buddhist monuments in stone, which could house images of the Buddha, represent the world mountain Mount Meru, and use different physical levels to symbolize degrees of enlightenment.

But the pagoda's useful gift to Japan was its structure. Japan is a country beset by frequent earthquakes. The pagoda, built around a single tall wooden post, is able to withstand many tremors and thus offered Japanese architects a way of creating tall buildings that would survive these movements.

The pagoda was not the only evidence of the Chinese Buddhist influence on the culture of Nara. In fact the influence was far broader than mere building design. One crucial example of this is the teachings of a Chinese monk who came to Japan in the middle of the eighth century AD. This man's Chinese name was Chien-chen, although he was known to the Japanese as Ganjin. A renowned Buddhist master, he had been invited to Nara in AD 741 to guide the training of the monks in the new monasteries that were being built there. After many setbacks and a difficult journey, Ganjin arrived at Nara in AD 753.

Famous as the monk was, the people

of Nara were probably unprepared for the impact Ganjin's arrival was to have on them. He was expected to train the monks, helping them to stand by the strict rules of their order. This he did, but his teaching also spread to the imperial court and the emperor himself. In fact the emperor's family gave Ganjin one of their palaces, which was reconstructed to provide a new monastery, including a lecture hall for the master. This monastery, known as the Toshodai-ji or T'ang Monastery, is one of the many that made Nara into a living monument of the Buddhist faith in the eighth century AD.

In view of this powerful influence, it is not surprising that the Japanese went to Chang'an, the Chinese capital city, to find a model for their own capital. Although Nara was not quite as large as Chang'an (at that time one of the biggest cities in the world), it could certainly compete in terms of the beauty of its monuments, as the surviving temple buildings show.

The Horyu-ji monastery

The oldest surviving temple in the prefecture of Nara is the Horyu-ji monastery, which is in fact about 18 kilometres (11 miles) southeast of the city and was built before work was started on Nara itself. But it is important not only because of its age but also because it can be seen as a model for the buildings that followed and because it is an example of the Chinese influence at work from the very start.

The monastery is entered through a tall gateway of two storeys, each with typical overhanging roofs. Having walked through the entrance gateway, visitors find themselves inside a large galleried courtyard, at the middle of which are the two main buildings of the complex, the pagoda and the main hall, or Kondo, another impressive two-storey structure. Beyond the courtyard are numerous ancillary buildings housing accommodation for monks, students and visitors, and a library.

Apart from the great beauty of the Horyu-ji complex, with its sweeping roofs, intricately carved brackets, and ancient wall paintings, one feature stands out above all – the entire monastery is built of wood. This makes it one of the oldest substantial wooden structures in the world. Although wood is thought of in the west as a perishable material, in Japan, the monastery's wooden structure has helped its longevity. A building of wood is more likely to survive an earthquake than one of brick or stone.

Asura, one of the supernatural guardians of Japanese Buddhism

The temples of Nara

With the influence of Ganjin and Buddhism, the dominant religious power in Japan, it was almost inevitable that the new capital would be well provided with Buddhist monasteries, many of them even more magnificent that the Horyu-ji. Many of the monasteries would have been built as a matter of course, to foster the religious life of the capital. Nevertheless, semi-legendary stories have persisted about some of them. For example, the most magnificent of all the temples, the Todai-ji, was founded by the emperor Shomu (AD 724–749).

It was said that an epidemic of smallpox that hit Japan in AD 735 took the lives of several of the emperor's relatives. So the emperor ordered the creation of a vast statue of the Buddha, either to appease the gods or as thanksgiving when the outbreak subsided, and the great monastery of Todai-ji was built to house the statue. There is probably a measure of truth in this story. Many of the Buddhist scriptures list rewards for those who found monasteries or invested in their rebuilding. Monarchs are particular beneficiaries of this goodwill, being offered a prosperous realm and a stable succession for their heirs if they give generously to a monastic foundation. An emperor might well have felt that further plagues might be prevented if he created the largest, most spectacular monastery in his kingdom.

Whether or not this is true, the great Buddha, albeit heavily restored, still stands 16 metres (52 feet) tall in the temple built around it. The statue represents the Vairocana Buddha, the source of all things in the cosmos according to the Buddhist theology of the time. The statue was surrounded by other images of the Buddhist faith – two lacquer Bodhisattvas, each about 10 metres (33 feet) high, and four clay figures of the four Guardian Kings, one at each corner of the hall. These two were imposing in size – each was about 13 metres (43 feet) tall. These images dominate the hall for which they were built.

Another of the halls of the Todai-ji, known as the Sangatsu-do, contains many other statues that represent figures from the world of Japanese Buddhism. Most are Indian deities who are guardians in Japanese Buddhist theology. Amongst them are a huge image of Fukukensaku Kannon, who wears a glittering crown made of silver inset with pearls, quartz, agate, and other gems; Gakko, a character derived from an Indian moon-god, in a serene pose of prayer or contemplation; Nikko, the sun-god, in a similar attitude; and, in contrast, a brightly coloured image of Shukongo-jin, a guardian who carries a thunderbolt and looks ready to let it loose.

As well as a large hall to house the Buddha, the temple boasts two pagodas, each of ten storeys. The splendour of the complex was appropriate. It formed the climax of a concerted effort by the emperors to get Buddhism accepted as the state religion of Japan. First, in AD 685, Emperor Temmu decreed that every family should have a Buddhist altar where memorial services could be held. In AD 741 Emperor Shomu issued a further decree. Each province was to have its own chief branch temple, and there would be a national temple that would act as an administrative centre for the whole country. It was the destiny of the Todai-ji to fulfil this role.

The large central hall (often called the Golden Hall) of the Todai-ji was bigger than any of its counterparts in Nara, measuring about 85 x 50 metres (280 x 164 feet) inside. But it was similar in construction to the other Golden Halls – a series of red-painted wooden columns supporting an overhanging roof. In addition, the two pagodas follow the same pattern as usual in Japanese architecture, but are taller than most pagodas, having ten storeys rather than the more usual five.

The temple's large size caused problems. First of all, it was extremely expensive to build, meaning extra taxation and increasing discontent amongst the workforce on which both emperors and priests relied. Second, the very fact that they were consuming such a large amount of the national income made the priests more powerful than they originally were. Many priests entered government and this led to the possibility – and the reality – of corruption. So here, in the very creation of Nara's greatest monument, were the origins of the state of affairs that was eventually to lead to the decline of the Nara culture and the removal of the capital away from Nara altogether.

The Japanese builders were to learn from the problems created by the construction of the Todai-ji. When the temple was rebuilt in the eleventh century AD, a simpler form of construction was used, standardizing the sizes of materials and making the structural engineering simpler. It was vital to avoid the expense, discontent, and corruption that surrounded the creation of the first building on the site.

Life in imperial Nara

Tradition has taught us that before the arrival of the Americans in the nineteenth century, Japan was a nation that closed its doors to the world. Although this is basically true, foreign influence and foreign products did enter Japan during the early imperial period. The Chinese influence on the architecture of Nara and on its Buddhism is obvious. But this was not all that China provided. Medicinal plants were imported from China's ancient tradition of herbal medicine. And China was not the only civilization to bequeath the Japanese a cultural legacy. For example, glassware from Iran and textiles from central Asia found their way to Nara during the eighth century AD. The Iranian influence on objects made at Nara can also be seen in some of the designs on furniture inlays.

But although the wealth of the emperors was not limited to items manufactured at home, the dominant note amongst the products used at court was Japanese. Superb textiles (especially silks and brocades) and luxurious pieces of inlaid furniture are the most remarkable objects that have survived. Some of the finest objects were placed in a warehouse behind the main hall of the Todai-ji monastery by the Empress Komyo, who left them there for the good of her husband's soul. Pots, textiles, and other examples of the craftwork of Nara were placed in this treasury. There were inlaid musical instruments, lacquered vessels, items of precious metals such as silver incense-burners decorated with a pierced filigree design. Again, much in the appearance of these objects shows a Chinese influence, particularly the two- and three-coloured glazes on some of the pottery.

There are also objects made of materials from southern Asia – tortoiseshell, ivory, and mother of pearl. These objects may have been made in Nara with imported materials. The overall impression is of a life of great luxury – for the court, at least. The boasts of some of the Nara emperors that their court was as sophisticated and well-appointed at that of the Chinese emperor were obviously well founded.

We learn something about the life of the court from the chronicles commissioned by the emperors and empresses and written during the period when Nara was newly built. Another source is the vast poetry anthology of the period, called the *Man'yoshu*. This contains about 4,500 poems, many of them written by members of the imperial family. They give the impression of a leisured life, in which there is plenty of time to contemplate nature and in which the main cause for sadness is the passing of the seasons, the coming of old age, or the loss of love.

But there are also poems in the anthology written by poorer people – laments of frontier guards compelled to spend time away from home, and accounts by monks of their lives of poverty. Many of the poems show a love of the Japanese landscape and the native eye for a telling detail – although Nara was a large city, the countryside was never far away. On the whole they show little Chinese influence, and it is almost as if the energy of Japanese culture, diverted away from architecture and many of the other arts, found its rightful place in these poems. They are as vital a product of the culture of Nara as are the Homeric epics, in a different way, of the culture of Mycenae.

The great wealth and leisure of the emperors was provided by a large and subservient peasantry. Most of these lived outside the city and worked the land or tended silkworms to produce the raw material for the clothes of the aristocracy. These people also paid the taxes that the emperor levied in order to finance the building of the capital. They paid dearly and got little in return except for a greater stability than had been the case when the country was ruled by different regional families.

On the route to civilization

Nara was the vital step on the road to the development of a truly Japanese civilization. It gave the Japanese a capital, a cultural centre, and religious roots. And it has bequeathed to the modern Japanese a clear sense of their early history – both in its magnificent buildings and artefacts and in the literature that was produced in and around the court.

But Nara's time as capital city was short-lived, and its downfall came as a result of the city's mixture of religious and secular power. It was the Buddhist monks who eventually became too powerful for the emperor. In *c.*AD 794 the peasants revolted against imperial taxation by leaving their fields. The monks took control of the land and thereby increased their power still further. They were turning into a force that the emperor, Kanmu, found it difficult to resist. He responded by moving the capital away from Nara to Kyoto. The era of Nara's ascendancy was over.

ANGKOR

City and temples of the Khmers, lords of Cambodia, *circa* AD 900–1150

Among the civilizations of the world, the Khmer Empire of Cambodia is one of the least well known. It has not left us a great literature or religious system as India has; it does not seem to have had the administrative and philosophical sophistication of ancient China. And yet the Khmers left a unique stamp on the landscape of Cambodia in the shape of stone temples that are among the world's most beautiful buildings. Of the many temples they built, Angkor Wat, the enormous complex near the imperial capital, is one of the best preserved and perhaps the most perfect examples of Khmer architecture.

But who were the Khmers? Modern politics have ensured that we are familiar with their name, but this has only tended to obscure their origins and the story of the religion that inspired their extraordinary buildings. To trace the beginnings of civilization in Cambodia we have to look back to the first century AD, well over 1,000 years before the building of Angkor Wat itself.

Funan and Chenla

The earliest Cambodian kingdom of which we have written records is the kingdom of Funan. Funan's origins are shrouded in myth. Chinese legends tell of an Indian adventurer called Kaundinya who sailed eastwards to Cambodia and met a native princess who was half-human, half-serpent – the equivalent of a water spirit in Indian mythology. Kaundinya married this princess and together they ruled an area comprising Cambodia, southern Vietnam and southern Thailand. This story is obviously a legend, but it points to an important element in later Khmer culture – the fact that there were close relations between India, China, and Cambodia from the very beginning.

The sculptures at Angkor Wat and the other temples of Angkor depict the Khmer kings to whom they are dedicated in attitudes of repose. But they also show the livelier side of Khmer life, and elegant dancers are a recurring motif.

Funan was a successful kingdom. It dominated its corner of the world until *c.*550 AD. The people learned the skills of metalworking and carving ivory and coral. The success of the kingdom was undoubtedly linked to continuing trade with India. When Buddhism began to spread, this trade was even more important, because Buddhism effectively fostered trade by doing away with the rigid Hindu caste system and allowing the upper classes to enter commerce. One other development in Funan was important for the future. Although their homes were made of wood and perished long ago, the people of Funan began to build brick temples in the Indian style, and some traces of these remain. The illustrious history of Cambodian religious architecture had begun.

At the time of Funan, the Khmer people lived to the north of Cambodia in a territory called Chenla and were vassals of the Funanese kings. At some point in the mid-sixth century AD there was a dispute about who was the rightful heir to the throne of Funan and a Khmer king took power. From then on, the state was known as the kingdom of Chenla.

The early Khmer kings were strong and effective absolute monarchs. According to contemporary chronicles they were helped in their rule by a capable aristocracy, and they governed a people who were lively and industrious. The effect of this efficient administration was a closely knit, centralized kingdom which would eventually become large and powerful enough to become a true empire. The fruits of the peoples' industry that survive today are a few dozen temples, small in scale but decorated with stone carvings.

The empire of the god-kings

At the end of the eighth century AD there was a crisis in the kingdom of Chenla. A weak young king occupied the throne and the future of the Khmer monarchy was in doubt. There is a contemporary story that the king made a rash remark that he wanted the head of the king of Java brought to him on a plate. This remark was reported to the Javanese, who sent an army to Cambodia to capture the Khmer king and pay back the insult by sending his head to Chenla. The new king of Chenla was obliged to stay in Java as a hostage until he accepted the suzerainty of Java. But eventually the new king, Jayavarman II, was allowed back to Cambodia, probably in *c.*AD 790.

Jayavarman learned the lesson of history and ruled with force. He was also fortunate in his health, reigning for sixty years. Although he moved the site of his capital city several times, it was he who first selected the area around Angkor, he who instigated the large building projects for which the

The towering conical roofs and spreading terraces of Angkor Wat lie inside a moat that isolated them from the surrounding buildings and countryside. This emphasizes the way in which Khmer temples are set apart from the rest of life, providing vast, quiet places for contemplation and for veneration of the dead kings they commemorate.

Khmers are famous (although few of his own buildings survive), and he who put the unique stamp on Khmer religion. It was also Jayavarman who was the first true Khmer emperor – from his time the country was known not as Chenla, but as Kambuja.

In Java the kings held a semi-divine status, and Jayavarman may have been influenced by that fact when he established king-worship in Kambuja. But Jayavarman's religion was if anything more extreme than that of Java in its adulation of the king. The ruler was known by various titles, including

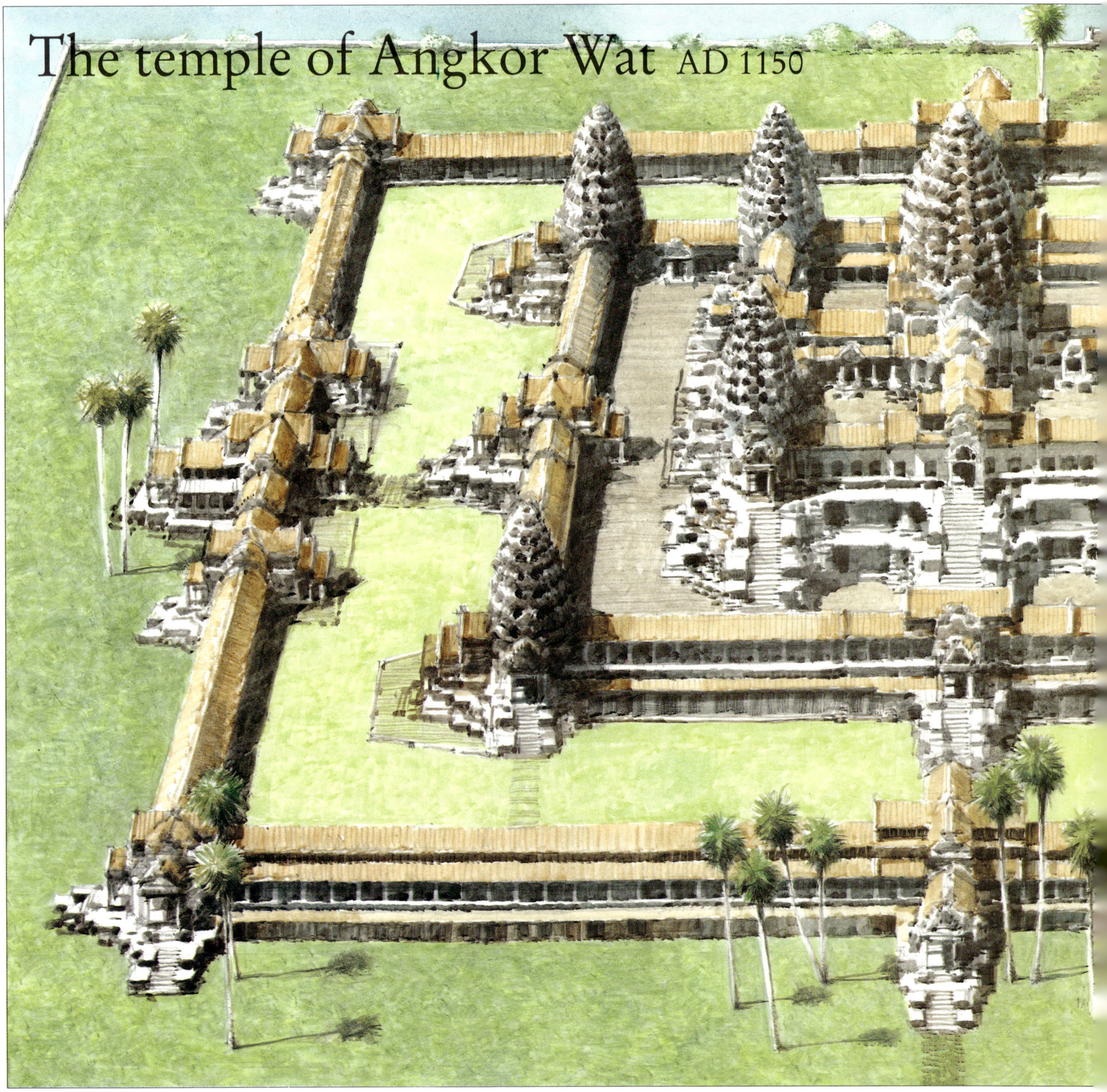

The temple of Angkor Wat AD 1150

'The lord of the universe, who is king' and 'devaraja' or 'god-king'. He was worshipped as a heaven-sent life force, symbolized by a phallic statue called a *lingam*. Each new Khmer king built a temple in which his lingam was housed, and these shrines of king-worship are the monuments for which Khmer civilization is famous.

Although this form of religion seems bizarre today, it would have seemed fitting to the Khmers. It was clearly influenced strongly by Java. There was also an Indian influence: the god Shiva had long been worshipped in the form of a lingam. And the fact that Jayavarman himself came to Kambuja as something of a saviour figure, rescuing the country from the excesses of a weak ruler, would have made his semi-divine status seem credible.

The Khmers also took on board some of the mountain symbolism of other religions. To begin with, they chose mountain sites for their religious buildings. Their later shrines, built on the plains, have tall, tapering towers that mark them as true 'temple-mountains', recalling other mountain-shaped religious buildings such as the Buddhist shrine at Borobudur in Java.

The builders of Angkor

Few of the Khmer kings reigned as long as Jayavarman. But some of his successors left their stamp on the empire of Kambuja. Indravarman I (AD 877–889), for example, undertook ambitious irrigation schemes that led to better rice harvests and an increase in the urban populations of the area. He also built the impressive temples of Preah Ko and the Bakong. His successor Yasovarman I (AD 889–900)

built the first real city at Angkor. It used to be thought, largely because of the extravagant inscriptions left behind by Yasovarman's propaganda writers, that Yasovarman built the great monuments of Angkor, such as Angkor Wat itself, that survive today. It is now accepted that his achievements were of a lesser nature, and that the inscriptions are sheer bombast.

Angkor's golden age did not come until the eleventh and twelfth centuries AD. It was King Suryavarman I (AD 1001–1050) who built the palace and the grand plaza at Angkor, and the temple known as the Baphuon. His namesake Suryavarman II (AD 1113–*c*.1150) was responsible for the crowning glory of Khmer architecture, Angkor Wat. We know little about Suryavarman II, but his architects were the most talented the Khmers had known.

A monument to a king

No one knows who those architects were. In common with Khmer practise, the names of the designers of Angkor Wat were not recorded. But anonymous as they were, they created a magnificent temple for their king. It is enormous. It stands on an area of land 800 metres (half a mile) square with a moat that is 200 metres (650 feet) across. Within the temple precinct, as well as various ancillary buildings, the temple rises like a tall pyramid on three superimposed terraces. The fact that it is entered via an approach road about twice as long as the total width of the facade forces one to look at the temple from the exact angle the designers intended for quite some time. It is a building of great drama, and the architects must have been aware of this.

In fact it is the summit of Khmer art. Its earliest ancestors, created over 1,000 years before, were the little temples of the kingdom of Funan, with their single towers of brick. Nearer to Angkor Wat in both time and spirit were the temples of Chenla, which looked like a group of Funan temples assembled together. Still later, the architects of Kambuja raised the towers on terraces, to make them still more mountain-like in appearance. And then, as time went on, and the kingdom of Kambuja grew more powerful, the temples got larger until Angkor Wat itself was created.

Angkor Wat is planned as a series of concentric rectangles, each one taking us nearer the central mountainous pyramid with its shrine. After crossing the great moat, the visitor enters a monumental entrance portal. After passing through this, one finds oneself in an enormous gallery decorated with carved reliefs showing stories from the legend of Vishnu and the land of Yama, the Lord of Death. Beyond this is a staircase, leading through a square structure with four small courtyards, to another staircase, and onwards to a large colonnaded courtyard with a smaller pyramidal tower at each corner. The great pyramid is at the centre of this courtyard.

Reflected in the water of the ornamental pools nearby, these tall towers make an imposing sight. The fact that there are five towers is in itself significant. Mount Meru, at the centre of the universe for both Hindus and Buddhists, was supposed to have had five summits. It is likely that the builders of Angkor Wat conceived this central area as the monument's temple-mountain. This reminds us of the strangely hybrid nature of Khmer religion. It has both Hindu and Buddhist elements (the two religions co-existed for some time in the kingdom of Funan), together with a liberal dose of king-worship.

The towers themselves have a strange design unique to the Khmers. Each stands on a square base, but, as they rise in their nine levels of stonework, they become star-shaped in plan and taper towards the top. Each layer of masonry has many protruding ornaments which, however, do not interfere with the overall design that emphasizes the towers' soaring, mountainous shape.

The sense of architectural space conveyed by this succession of galleries, staircases, courtyards and towers is breathtaking. The sculptural details adorning the walls are of an equally high standard. Amongst the teeming figures the graceful forms of the *devatas* (divinities) and the *apsaras* (nymphs) are particularly noticeable. Many walls also contain superb carvings of plants and leaves, dragons and other mythical creatures.

More absorbing still, because they tell gripping stories, are the reliefs around the gallery on the first level of the temple. These carvings are done in very shallow relief, yet the sculptors managed to achieve an impressive degree of subtlety in their work. In the shallowness of their relief they are not unlike Assyrian wall decorations, but are completely different in subject matter. Instead of the triumphs of the Assyrian kings, they portray episodes from Indian mythology, especially from the great Indian mythological texts, the *Mahabarata* and the *Ramayana*, but are not there simply to tell diverting stories. The most dynamic examples are about 2.5 metres (8 feet) high and stretch right around the gallery of the temple's vast outer terrace. The episodes chosen for depiction here have direct relevance to the career of Suryavarman II.

A few examples of the scenes will show how these parallels work. One episode is called the Churning of the Sea of Milk. This shows the god

One of many Khmer carvings showing the lives of mariners and fishermen

Vishnu, together with the demons (or *asuras*) and deities (or *devas*) pulling back and forth on the long serpent Vasuki. As they do this, they churn up the sea, which is shown teeming with fish and other life forms. Stirring up the waters in this way allows Vishnu to extract from the sea such good things as the ambrosia of immortality and the jewels of good government, implying that Suryavarman himself is immortal and is blessed with the gift of ruling his people well.

Another area of reliefs shows Vishnu's struggle against the asuras. The climax of this section of carvings is the famous Battle of Lanka, in which Rama defeats Ravana, and good triumphs over evil. This is clearly meant to parallel Suryavarman's conquests over his evil enemies. In a third area, the reliefs show that the only final victor is death, but that the king will be deified. The mythological parallel is this time the Battle of Kurukshetra, at which nearly everyone died and there were no real winners or losers. The figure of a supreme judge heading off to the kingdom of the afterworld symbolizes Suryavarman's fate as a deity.

As if to make the point bluntly obvious, another pair of panels shows the Hindu heaven and hell, with a panel depicting a procession of Suryavarman's court in between. In this context, Hell seems to be the place where the king's enemies end up, an eloquent demonstration of the link between Khmer religion and political power. But not all the carvings are intended to make this sort of religious or political point. The building is alive with carvings of many sorts. There are vast numbers of devatas and asparas in groups and pairs; there are single holy men, meditating or praying in the quieter corners of the building; there is a veritable zoo of animals – lions, serpents, and monkeys (the latter no doubt part of the army of Rama).

Temple and tomb

The writers who first saw the close similarities between the life of the king and the lives of the Hindu gods in the carvings at Angkor suggested that such commemorative reliefs would most likely appear on a tomb. But they are equally appropriate on a temple dedicated to a god-king. The most obvious answer to this riddle is that Angkor Wat was both – a temple during the king's lifetime, his tomb when he was dead.

This agrees with what we now know about Khmer religion at the time when Angkor Wat was built – that temples often became tombs and that the distinction between the two functions was a false one. In any case, the two uses were not as different as might at first seem to be the case. For the Khmers, a temple was not a thronging place of worship like a medieval cathedral. A temple was first and foremost the symbolic home of the god-king. It would be used by priests for certain rituals, and no doubt it would also become a centre for pilgrimage. But it was not a place of worship in the conventional sense. How appropriate then, that his symbolic home should become the god's literal home when he had died – the two functions were in fact united.

The Khmer achievement

Angkor Wat is a masterpiece. In the planning of its spaces, the variety of its decoration, and above all in the way its shapes take advantage of bright local light, it has no equal in Cambodia. Yet it is a strange mixture of the simple and the sophisticated. For example, the Khmer builders only had knowledge of the most basic form of vaulting – corbelling, in which overlapping concentric rings of masonry gradually converge to meet at the middle of the ceiling. This simple technique was used to build the towers at Angkor Wat, but the Khmers took it to its most highly developed level – iron dowels join the masonry which is otherwise held together by weight and gravity alone, no mortar being used at all.

Another example of this strange mixture of the primitive and the advanced is the fact that the temple has little in the way of foundations. But the basic above-ground structure is so stable that it has remained standing, such is the balance of the design.

In political as well as artistic terms, the reign of Suryavarman was the high point of the Khmer civilization. There was one further flowering in later years under the rule of Jayavarman VII (1181–*c.*1220). Like his illustrious forebear, he too was an enthusiastic builder, remaking the capital at Angkor Thom, and creating another great temple, the Bayon, which rivals Angkor Wat in size and beauty.

The achievements of Jayavarman VII went further than these building projects. He was an ambitious military campaigner, and he fought to extend the boundaries of the Khmer Empire to take in Burma, southern Malaya and Vietnam. Indeed so many cities and temples did Jayavarman build, such an army of slaves did he need to complete the work, and so obsessive was his military campaigning, that he ignored the more vital work of keeping the empire unified. It is not surprising that Kambuja was exhausted

Detail of one of the causeway statues

after such frenetic activity. The administration was simply not capable of handling the extensive new territories, and provinces began to be lost almost as soon as they had been won.

The result was a steady collapse after his reign, with wealthy provinces breaking free from the Khmers, leading to a loss of revenue and labour. The end came for the Khmers in the fifteenth century. The Thais captured Angkor itself in 1437 and by the end of the following century the whole of Kambuja was ruled by the Thais. They set their seal on the fate of the old Khmer capital by destroying the reservoirs and irrigation canals that had made life in Angkor bearable.

As the Khmer kings lost their power, the fashion for king worship declined, the more contemplative way of Buddhism became the norm, and the day of the temple-mountains of the Khmers was at an end.

PEKING

The 'Forbidden City' of the Chinese emperors rebuilt during the Ming dynasty *circa* AD 1403, and embellished by the following generations

Peking has not always been China's principal city. Indeed, the site of the capital has moved several times during the country's long history. During China's first great civilization, the bronze age, the capital was at Anyang, north of the Huan River and south-west of Peking. Later, during the Han and Tang dynasties, the main city was Chang'an, the modern town of Sian on the Wei River. Later still it was at Nanking, still further south on the Changjiang River.

Even when, during the Yuan period (1260–1368 AD), the emperor moved the capital to Peking, it was not destined to remain there. In 1368 Hung Wu, the coming leader in China, overthrew the Yuan, destroyed the imperial city, founded the Ming dynasty and moved the capital back to Nanking. The decision was no doubt partly political. Peking, or Ta-tu as it was then known, was closely linked with the Yuan rulers. Hung Wu wanted a Ming capital. In any case Peking is dangerously far north, near the territory of the barbarian people who were forever threatening the country's northern defences. The story of how Peking was re-established as the capital, and how it acquired an imperial palace so vast that it was like a city within a city, is one of the most fascinating stories in Chinese history.

The Ming emperor Yong Le sits and contemplates the plan of his new imperial city. The main audience halls, palaces, gates, and walls were built at this time. Future emperors populated the courtyards with offices, storehouses, and residential buildings.

The dream of Yong Le

The third emperor of the Ming dynasty was Yong Le. As Prince of Yen before he ascended the imperial throne, he had been a brave military campaigner, suppressing rebellions and invasions in the north. In doing this he had come to respect the peoples of the north, in the way that a military campaigner respects the skill and determination of a worthy opponent. Perhaps it is not surprising, then, that when Yong Le became emperor he should confirm his affinity with the north by choosing Peking, only about 64 kilometres (40 miles) from the Great Wall, as his imperial city.

The story of how he came to choose Peking, and how he planned his new imperial capital and palace, is, like many of the major events in Chinese history, shrouded in legend. One story says that a mysterious astrologer appeared when Yong Le was made emperor and handed Yong Le a sealed package in which were the plans of the new imperial city. Another version of the story involves the Buddhist monk who was Yong Le's teacher. This man, who had been Yong Le's tutor when the emperor was a boy, and continued as a trusted adviser, had a dream in which the plans of the city were revealed to him.

Whether or not there was a revelation of this type, the imperial city that Yong Le created has a dream-like air. Its succession of different buildings with their bewildering variety of titles and functions recalls some of the other surviving palaces that also formed the hub of a great empire – Topkapi, for example. But it is larger, richer, and more mysterious than any of its rivals.

There are good reasons why it should be. The China of the Ming period was a vast country with a highly developed culture. The role of the emperor was as complex as the country he ruled. He needed audience halls for receiving delegations large and small, local and overseas. He needed a place for ritual purification and temples for Buddhism, Toaism, and Lamaism. And he also required large domestic quarters – for his family, which included numerous wives; schoolrooms for the children; and a place for ancestral rites. As well as all this, the administrative accommodation that was built, together with the gardens, gates, and processional ways, turned the palace into a metropolis, a community that was closed to the outside world yet highly populous – hence the apparently contradictory name, the Forbidden City.

In fact, Peking consisted of several cities, each the preserve of a different element of the population. To the south was the outer city, later called the Chinese City, which contained the famous temples of Heaven and Agriculture, together with many residential buildings. In the middle of its long northern wall was an enormous gate, called Qian Men, which led to the three concentric rectangles of the inner City. The outermost area (often called the Tartar City) contained a mixture of buildings – from temples to granaries, palaces of the princes to elephant stables. At its centre was the Imperial City, and at the heart of this area, surrounded by a broad moat and its own walls, was the Forbidden City

MONGOLIA
PEKING
CHINA
Yellow River
YELLOW SEA
Seoul
Yangtze
Shanghai

itself, with its audience halls and ceremonial buildings. From the great Qian Men gate to the centre of the Forbidden City ran the Imperial Way, the emperor's processional route to the heart of his sanctuary.

A glance at any plan of Peking during the Ming period will show that it was arranged very formally. Most of the streets run north–south or east–west; all the major buildings of the Forbidden City itself are constructed along the same north–south axis. The reason for this is that the exact alignment of buildings has

The Meridian Gate, Peking AD 1450

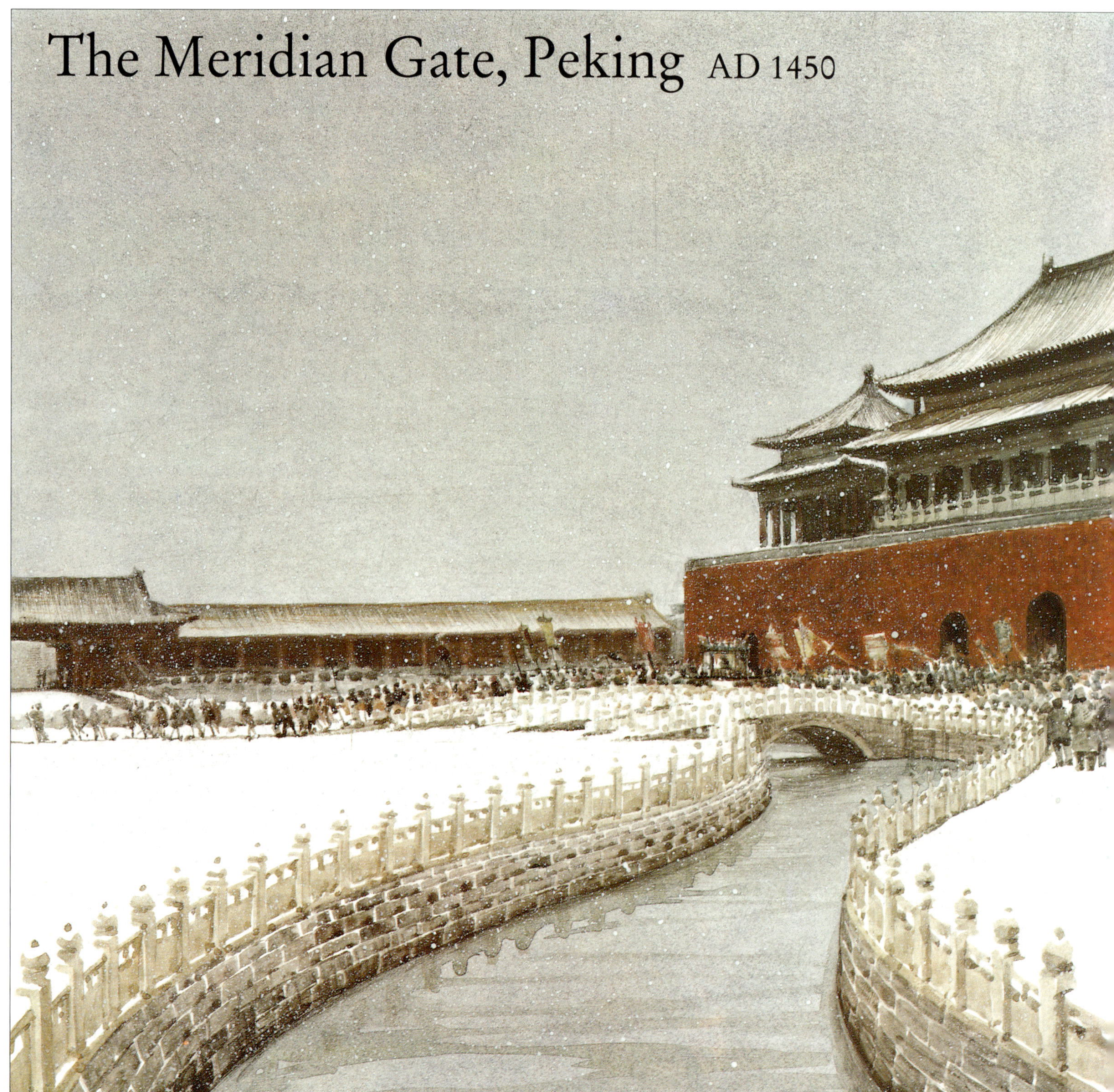

Snow falls over the great Wu Men, or Meridian Gate, but the bustle of crowds entering and leaving the outer parts of the city continues unabated. In the foreground is the River of Golden Water, with its marble bridges.

always been vitally important for Chinese architects. The mysterious art of *feng shui*, the correct planning, alignment and interior design of buildings to give the most auspicious arrangement, is still practised today. Instructions as to alignment were a key part of the plans given to Yong Le by the mysterious astrologer or Buddhist monk who helped him plan the city.

Feng shui means wind–water, and it is an attempt to harmonize buildings with the natural forces that are already in existence in the natural environment. Building according to the doctrines of feng shui, therefore, was supposed not only to produce those palaces that would confer health and good fortune on their residents; it would also have the effect of creating structures that were in harmony with their surroundings. One would expect not only large halls designed to be impressive and to purposefully assert the power of the emperor, but also scenic elegant squares, relaxing gardens, and jewel-like watercourses. Such features are indeed to be found within the imperial city of the Ming rulers.

Building the city

Yong Le began rebuilding the city in AD 1404. He employed three architects, Hsu Tai, Yuan An, and Feng Chiao, all of whom already had excellent reputations. The style they chose was based on the traditional Chinese methods of building, with timber frameworks, complex arrangements of beams to support the roofs, and lavishly carved brackets, cornices, balustrades, and other details.

Most of the buildings in the Forbidden City are quite low – single- or double-storey, in fact. So from a

distance, the halls and palaces seem to cling to the ground. There are few tall buildings, partly because wooden structures did not easily lend themselves to the creation of towers, partly because Chinese tradition insisted that high buildings would disturb the spirits that dwelled in the air.

The decorative style was also traditional. Common Chinese motifs – from flowers to butterflies, bamboo to tortoises – dominated the carvings on the halls. And of course the most famous of Chinese symbols were also prominent – the dragon, symbol of the emperor himself, and the phoenix, representing the empress and her family. These mythical beasts appear everywhere in the Forbidden City, but the finest examples are carved into the marble of the Dragon Pavement, the pathway leading through the centre of the city that was meant for the spirits alone. Not even the emperor was allowed to tread on the pavement – he was carried over it on a palanquin by servants who walked on either side of the sacred stones.

One of the tallest buildings in the city is the great main gate, Qian Men. It forms a worthy prelude to the outer area of the Forbidden City, with massive walls of brick and stone, windowless for the lower half of their great height, a roof of green tiles, and a large central portal that was reserved for the use of the emperor alone. The large doors – made of wood but reinforced with iron studs – would be closed every night at sunset, barring passage to all, and separating the inner and outer cities.

But the outer gate was only the first of a series of gates along the central north–south axis that gave access to the central halls and palaces. To reach the Forbidden City proper, the visitor would have had to pass through the Qian Men, the T'ien An Men, or gate of heavenly peace, the Wu Men, or meridian gate, the Tai He Men, or gate of supreme harmony, and the Qian Qing Men, gate of heavenly purity.

One can imagine the chaotic atmosphere as one passed through the outer gates and got nearer the imperial palaces themselves. The scene around the Qian Men and in the large square in front of the T'ien An Men would be chaotic. The diverse peoples of a large empire would converge on Peking. There might be groups of Mongols from the north in shabby but serviceable sheepskin coats and boots, contrasting with elegant nobles on richly caparisoned horses.

Imperial dragon, based on images on the Dragon Pavement

Noisier and more obtrusive than any of the people would be the herds of animals being driven through the gate – the food supply for a large city arriving from the countryside. And trying to force their way through the herds of pigs and flocks of sheep would be the wheeled traffic, from compact passenger carts to large freight wagons. As all this traffic pushed its way out of the narrow passages through the outer gate, the square in front of the T'ien An Men would fill almost to bursting point, making a mockery of the idea of a 'Gate of Heavenly Peace'. It was no idle assertion of power that made the emperors choose to reserve one path through the outer for themselves alone. Had they not done this, they would have had to take their chance in the undignified hullabaloo.

Passing through the succeeding gates and getting nearer to the centre of the city, one would notice this traffic gradually thinning out so that, by the time one arrived at the Wu Men, the entrance to the Forbidden City proper, many of the more unruly elements would have disappeared and the scene would be dominated by courtiers, officials, and visiting dignitaries from foreign lands. The area in front of the gate was one of the principal ceremonial areas of the city.

Among the most astonishing ceremonies were the ritual exits of the emperor from the Forbidden City. The imperial procession could be vast. One account by a Portuguese traveller tells of twenty-four drummers with large, decorated instruments; the same number of trumpeters; 100 halberdiers and 100 mace bearers; 400 attendants carrying torches; many more lancers, fan bearers and court chamberlains. Eunuchs, nobles, officials, and other dignitaries would follow the emperor.

On other occasions the processional way outside the gate would be lined with elephants. There must have been at least forty-eight of these beasts, since the palatial elephant stables in the outer city contained that many individual stalls. The elephants would stand in two ranks, with their trunks twined together until the signal was given that the emperor was about to emerge from the gate. Then they would part, making a path for the emperor to pass. The monarch himself might travel on a chariot drawn by an elephant, or on an enormous sedan chair borne by 120 servants.

The emperor enthroned

The three great halls of the palace are in the Forbidden City's largest courtyard. They stand on three terraces of gleaming white marble. Each terrace is surrounded by a white marble balustrade beautifully carved with dragons and other mythical beasts. The first hall, the Tai He Dian, or Hall of Supreme Harmony, provided the setting for the biggest state occasions, particularly the celebrations of New Year and the emperor's birthday. Other important state occasions, such as the publication of the list of successful candidates in imperial examinations, and the appointment of generals prior to a new military campaign, were marked by a ceremony in the Tai He Dian.

The architecture was meant to complement these rituals – the effect is therefore rich, but restrained. The hall stands at the top of the three marble terraces and is reached from the courtyard by three stairways. The central stair has at its centre a ramp, over which the emperor's chair could be carried. An extension of the dragon pavement, this ramp is also carved with dragon motifs and was used in the same way – no human foot touched it and it was intended for the emperor and the spirits alone. Anyone else attending a ceremony at the Tai He Dian would climb one of the flanking stairs.

At the top of the ramp the emperor would pass between two of the columns supporting the roof; the six central columns are gilded and carved with dragons, while the others are painted red. This red colour was one element in a design that was intended to reflect Chinese theories of harmony. Thus each of the five colours (as specified by the Chinese philosophers) was involved in the design of the building: the white terrace, the dark, almost black, paving of the courtyard, the red pillars, the yellow roof, and the blue of the sky above.

The Zhong He Dian, or Hall of Perfect Harmony, is a smaller square building on the same terrace, behind the Tai He Dian. It was here that the emperor came to prepare himself before entering the Tai He Dian itself. As befits its purpose, it is a rich but simply furnished building, with a central throne. Sedan chairs were also kept here, to transport the emperor to another part of the Forbidden City if the need arose.

The final hall on the white terrace is the Bao He Dian, or Hall of the Preservation of Harmony. This was an audience chamber in which the emperor received rulers and dignitaries from dependent countries, who would present their tribute and hope to receive the imperial blessing. Scholars and other notables might also be presented to the emperor here. It was fitting that kings and scholars should share the same audience hall, since scholarship was highly regarded by the Chinese. It was from the ranks of the scholars, as well as from the military, that the governors and administrators of the Chinese Empire were selected. So the rigorous training and examinations that scholars had to undergo were of great importance to the emperor. The familiar image of the wandering Chinese Buddhist scholar, detached from the cares of the world, is only half the story of the scholars of China. The other half would be pressing for their audience at the Bao He Dian, and hoping for a prestigious imperial appointment.

The emperor at home

Beyond the three halls was a smaller courtyard containing the three imperial palaces. These are arranged on the same north–south axis as the audience halls. The first, the Qian Qing Gong, or Palace of Heavenly Purity, was the residence of several Ming emperors, although it was later used as an audience chamber. The second, Jiao Tai Dian, or Hall of Union, started life as the throne room of the empress and later became a storage place for imperial valuables such as the seals of past emperors. The third, the Kun Ning Gong, or Palace of Earthly Tranquillity, was the residence of the empress. The Ming concern with imperial symbolism is as obvious in these palaces as it is in the three great halls. Bronze tortoises and cranes stand in front of it, symbolizing the emperor's immortality. A grain measure and a sundial were also placed in front of the palace to symbolize imperial judgment and rectitude.

The decorative style of the palaces was similar to that of the audience halls. Although the Qian Qing Gong has been severely damaged by fire several times during its history, it was always restored to the glory of the surrounding buildings – lavish carvings of dragons, elaborate inlaid decoration, and rich calligraphy once more being the order of the day. Included in the furnishings was a large throne smothered in similar decorations.

The other large palace in this courtyard, the empress' palace or Kun Ning Gong, is unusual in that it is divided into two chambers of unequal size. The reason for this is that it was also used as the site of imperial weddings. Not only would the wedding ceremony itself take place here, but the royal couple would spend their first night in the palace, in the small private chamber provided. So the Kun Ning Gong provides a rare glimpse of intimacy amongst the ritual palaces and audience halls of this central area of the Forbidden City.

Intimate spaces

Beyond the palaces lies one further precinct, the imperial garden or Yu Hua Yuan. If the broad courtyards of the rest of the city evoke great processions and public ceremonies, the imperial gardens have a more intimate, human atmosphere. Among the exotic plants the garden contained, trees were a speciality. There were white pine trees with silver-grey bark, magnolias, and catalpa trees with their pink blossoms. Other attractions were provided by the paths, paved with stones set in elaborate patterns, fountains, pavilions, and natural stones set on pedestals.

Beautiful to the eye as they were, these gardens catered for some of the other senses, too. Bronze incense burners wafted a heavy scent around the precinct. The metallic tinkle of wind bells interrupted the silence. The gardens must have provided a welcome refuge for the leisured men and women of the court when the day's round of official duties and rituals was over. Stories of the women decking the bare magnolia trees with artificial blossom during the winter reveal how much they valued the garden and its adornment. Such tales also confirm that for the Chinese a garden is a supremely artificial creation. These gardeners had no illusions about creating a faithful imitation of a natural paradise like some of their counterparts in the west.

Life beyond the palace

In a short space one can only hint at the glories of some of the central buildings of the Forbidden City. To do so is to ignore the assemblage of service areas that give the place much of its character. For the throng of citizens pushing through the main gate these peripheral buildings – the kitchens, storehouses, treasuries, administrative offices, libraries, and schoolrooms – would have been as important as the great halls and palaces.

For the emperor Yong Le, it might be the residential areas to the east of the ceremonial palaces that would mean the most. Here he would have the privacy to reflect on a lifetime's work – not only the building of the city, but also campaigns abroad, including naval expeditions as far as the west coast of India, the Persian Gulf, and the east coast of Africa. These adventures were impressive. But Yong Le's monument, changed as it has been by centuries of rebuilding, by revolution and unrest, is the Forbidden City, his spiritual and literal home and the centre of his empire.

TAJ MAHAL

A Mughal emperor's mausoleum for his beloved wife

It is one of the most famous buildings in the world. Reproduced countless times in books, in travel brochures, and on packaging, the Taj Mahal has become an international symbol of perfection and purity of design. It is also surrounded by many stories – some true, others probably mythical – concerning the circumstances and methods of its building. In some ways we are so familiar with the Taj Mahal that it is hardly a 'mysterious place' at all. And yet we take it so much for granted that we forget to ask the obvious questions. How did a building of such beauty come to be built at Agra and why did it take the exact form that it did? What were the characters of the man who commissioned the building and the woman who inspired it and are all the stories about them really true?

The Taj Mahal is a mausoleum, built by the Indian emperor Shah Jehan, who lived from AD 1592–1666 and reigned between the years 1628–1658, for his favourite wife, Mumtaz Mahal. Shah Jehan belonged to the Mughal dynasty, and was therefore a descendant of the ruthless Mongol conqueror Genghis Khan, who had been the scourge of Asia during the thirteenth century. By all accounts, he inherited some of the ruthlessness of his infamous ancestor. He is said to have murdered most of his immediate family in order to get to the throne in 1628. As emperor, he was said to be equally merciless with his enemies, both in war (for he was a great military campaigner) and in love (for he guarded the women of his harem jealously, and severely punished any courtier who tried to have an affair with one of them).

The Taj Mahal facade is so familiar that the woman who inspired this architectural masterpiece is often forgotten. Here the image of Mumtaz Mahal can be seen above the domes and minarets built in her memory.

Mumtaz Mahal

But Shah Jehan's love for one of his wives went deeper than his regard for the other women of the harem. Mumtaz Mahal was his chosen consort. She bore him thirteen children and became his constant companion. More than this she obviously had a keen intelligence, and acted as a key political adviser to Shah Jehan. Indeed it has been said that Mumtaz Mahal became the true ruler of the Mughal Empire after her marriage with Shah Jehan. This is probably an exaggeration, but the emperor was not the only person she captivated. She won the love of her people in ways that are familiar from the activities of members of royal families today. She undertook many acts of charity, becoming famous for giving alms to beggars and food to the poor and needy. And the evidence is that this was more than casual charity to the poor who presented themselves outside the palace walls each morning. She actually had lists drawn up of widows and orphans and saw that they were well provided for. Mumtaz Mahal was probably a civilizing influence on the Mughal court.

But we would be wrong to suppose that the Mughal idea of a civilized court was the same as our own. There was still much barbarity, and, the Mughal state being an Islamic one, little mercy was shown to those who followed other faiths. In particular, a group of Portuguese Christians who had settled in Bengal were brutally tortured – and it is thought that the torture was carried out at the behest of Mumtaz Mahal herself.

If stories like this make Mumtaz Mahal seem ruthless, they have to be set in the context of the times. The Mughal emperor had to fight to stay on the throne. Shah Jehan himself had had most of his surviving relatives put to the sword in order to become emperor in the first place. And once he was crowned, when his supporters had been rewarded with lavish gifts, and all possible pretenders had been killed, he was not safe for long. His very sons, especially the notorious Aurangzeb, tried to wrest the throne from him. A Mughal emperor's position was never safe, and the massacres and tortures that took place reflect this insecurity.

A man of action

Shah Jehan worked hard to keep his place on the throne and there is no doubt that Mumtaz Mahal gave him invaluable assistance. The Mughals ruled a large empire via an extensive bureaucracy with its own protocols and ways of governing. Shah Jehan was at the centre of this network. He was closely involved with the business of his empire, sending envoys to the provinces regularly, dictating endless letters, and hearing the petitions of citizens from all over the empire.

There was a close-knit team consisting of the emperor, his sons, and the most trusted advisers, who transacted the confidential affairs of the empire, planning military campaigns and deciding the fate of provincial territories. This group would meet every morning and make decisions made today by presidents and their close advisers, prime ministers and their cabinets. The emperor was always at the centre of the discussions, and it was likely that the next emperor would come from the ranks of the advisers, for this was the best environment to learn the methods of Mughal government.

Shah Jehan participated willingly in these gatherings until the most shattering event of his life: the death of Mumtaz Mahal in 1631 while giving birth to their fourteenth child. They were on campaign. The man of action was suppressing a rebellion in the Deccan and, typically, Mumtaz Mahal had wanted to accompany him. At first all was well. The baby, a girl, was healthy; her mother was reported to be doing well. But suddenly a message came to Shah Jehan that his wife was ill. There was nothing that the large team of doctors who were travelling with the royal party could do, and the emperor was soon embarking on a period of mourning which was to continue for two years.

Shah Jehan's second love

Fortunately for posterity, the emperor found a way of expressing his grief which has lasted until today. He had always had a passion for building: it had been one more way in which he could show his power and fulfil his need for action. Before the death of Mumtaz he had already extended the Red Fort at Agra, rebuilding the main audience halls and replacing with gleaming white marble much of the sandstone that gave the fort its name. He also constructed the Red Fort and a large mosque at Delhi. Another of his great white buildings at Agra was the Pearl mosque – completely white except for some yellow stone used in the floor and a black inscription. Even without the Taj Mahal, Shah Jehan's reign would have represented a highpoint in the architecture of India.

Jewellers of the crown

The name of the mausoleum that was Shah Jehan's greatest architectural triumph means 'the crown of the region'. No one knows who was the master architect responsible for the building, but the records tell us that a huge team of craftsmen worked on its construction. The imperial architect Ustad Ahmad Lahwari was certainly employed on the Taj Mahal; a Persian designer called Mulla Murshid was also probably responsible for some of the work. There are many stories of designers from all over the world – from exiled Italian architects to wandering Turks – who are reputed to have been involved. Most of these characters are likely to be legendary, but we do know the names of craftsmen from overseas who worked on the Taj Mahal – a Venetian jeweller called Veroneo and the French goldsmith Austin of Bordeaux.

So many were the workers needed to complete the project that a town, called Mumtazabad, grew up on the site to house them all. The builders, mosaic-makers, inlayers, calligraphers, sculptors, and artisans who inhabited the temporary town made it a centre of artistic activity between 1632 and 1643 when the mausoleum was being built. Travellers spoke of a team of twenty thousand artisans, a herd of a thousand elephants to transport the marble, and bands of merchants arriving from places as diverse as Baghdad, Tibet, and Russia with precious stones for use in the decoration of the walls. The scale of the operations, and the fact that the project represented one man's tribute to the woman he loved, meant that the Taj Mahal was famous before it was even finished.

The jewel in its setting

The fame of the finished mausoleum spread even further. And one can quickly see why. Even the approach is memorable. Set within a wooded park, the white dome of the mausoleum can be glimpsed before the visitor reaches the precinct of the Taj Mahal itself. A long arcade (originally the main shopping street of Mumtazabad) leads to a courtyard in front of the main gate. This gate is large, heavily inlaid, and originally had a solid silver door. It had several different purposes. Most simply, it was a security measure, protecting the treasures of the mausoleum and the rich metals and stones inlaid in its walls. Secondly, it tells visitors that they are about to enter the precinct of the Taj Mahal. And third, it acts as a division between the worldly outer area, with its hustle, bustle and noise, and the inner zone, sacred and silent.

To emerge from the dark entrance gate and see the Taj Mahal silhouetted against the sky and reflected in the watercourse in front of it is to enter what seems like a paradise on earth. This was exactly the intention of Shah Jehan, who set the mausoleum in a garden because in Islamic art, as in many other traditions, the garden is the prime symbol of the paradise we enjoyed before the fall. Magnificent as the garden is today, in Shah Jehan's time it would have been even more colourful, with the ponds full of fish, peacocks and other exotic birds strutting about the paths and white-robed officials guarding the flower beds and frightening away any birds of prey that might appear with skilful use of their peashooters!

Although the garden would have been quiet, it would not have been empty. Nobles often came here and had picnics on the lawns, sometimes the emperor and court would come to pay their respects. So what seems today the austere symmetry of the garden – with its four square lawns each equally divided into sixteen to give a total of sixty-four square flower beds – would have been broken by people and given a human dimension that it sometimes seems to lack today.

Signs and symbols

It is worth dwelling on the symbolic meanings of some of the features of the building and its garden, for these would not have been lost on the people who originally came to marvel and to pay their respects to Mumtaz Mahal. The first feature of the garden that strikes the eye as one enters is the water that reflects the dome of the Taj. This sums up two of the most important ideas enshrined in the building: water symbolizes purity and initiation, reminding us that this is a holy place and a memorial to one who deserves veneration.

But more than this, paradise was thought to be a mirror-image of this world, and showing a reflection of the dome is an eloquent reminder of this. The Taj Mahal's crowning by a dome reinforces this image, since the dome in Islamic art is said to represent heaven. The symmetrical design of the garden extends this theme of heavenly perfection. The number four, which is crucially important in the garden's design (four lawns, four groups of sixteen flower beds, 400 flowers in each bed) is another Islamic symbol of completeness and perfection. Finally, the whiteness of the building, which also suggests purity, refers to the Islamic image of white pearl, the

Ruthless ruler and gentle lover: this portrait sums up the two faces of Shah Jahan.

substance from which the world was created. The Taj Mahal is truly the image of heaven and earth.

The exterior

In many buildings the most striking feature is the arrangement of the interior spaces. The Taj Mahal works rather differently. Inside, it consists of the central tomb and the chambers and doorways that lead to it. Beautiful as this is, it seems that more effort was expended on the design of the exterior, which works rather like a piece of abstract sculpture. The design encourages one to walk around it, the short sides of the octagon drawing one round to the next long side, so that one can view the building from every possible angle.

From whatever angle one is looking at the building, the eye is drawn to the central dome. Because it is raised slightly above the roof line of the main building, because it is set off with smaller domes, and because the niches on the walls lead the eye upwards, the eye is continually drawn towards it and the mind is continually asked to contemplate the idea of heaven that it represents.

The shrine within

Whichever of the doors to the central mausoleum we enter, we pass beneath texts from the Koran written in elaborate calligraphy. These quotations come from the chapter recited on a Muslim's deathbed. The Taj Mahal bears many inscriptions from the Koran – many more indeed than on any other of Shah Jehan's buildings, and a fitting indication that he regarded this as his holiest and most important creation.

At the centre of the building are the tombs themselves. They were originally surrounded by a rich silver screen inlaid with precious stones. The emperor laid his wife's body to rest in the crypt below the floor, but an empty sarcophagus was placed in the centre of the mausoleum to mark the place beneath which she rests. Again, the casket is covered with inscriptions in elegant calligraphy.

Shah Jehan intended to build a black mausoleum next to the Taj Mahal for his own body. But he never began this project, and after his death, his usurping son the emperor Aurangzeb buried his father next to Mumtaz Mahal, placing another sarcophagus slightly to one side of the queen's. Few visitors have regretted that the beauty of the white mausoleum has been allowed to dominate the Agra skyline alone and that Shah Jehan was laid to rest so near his beloved.

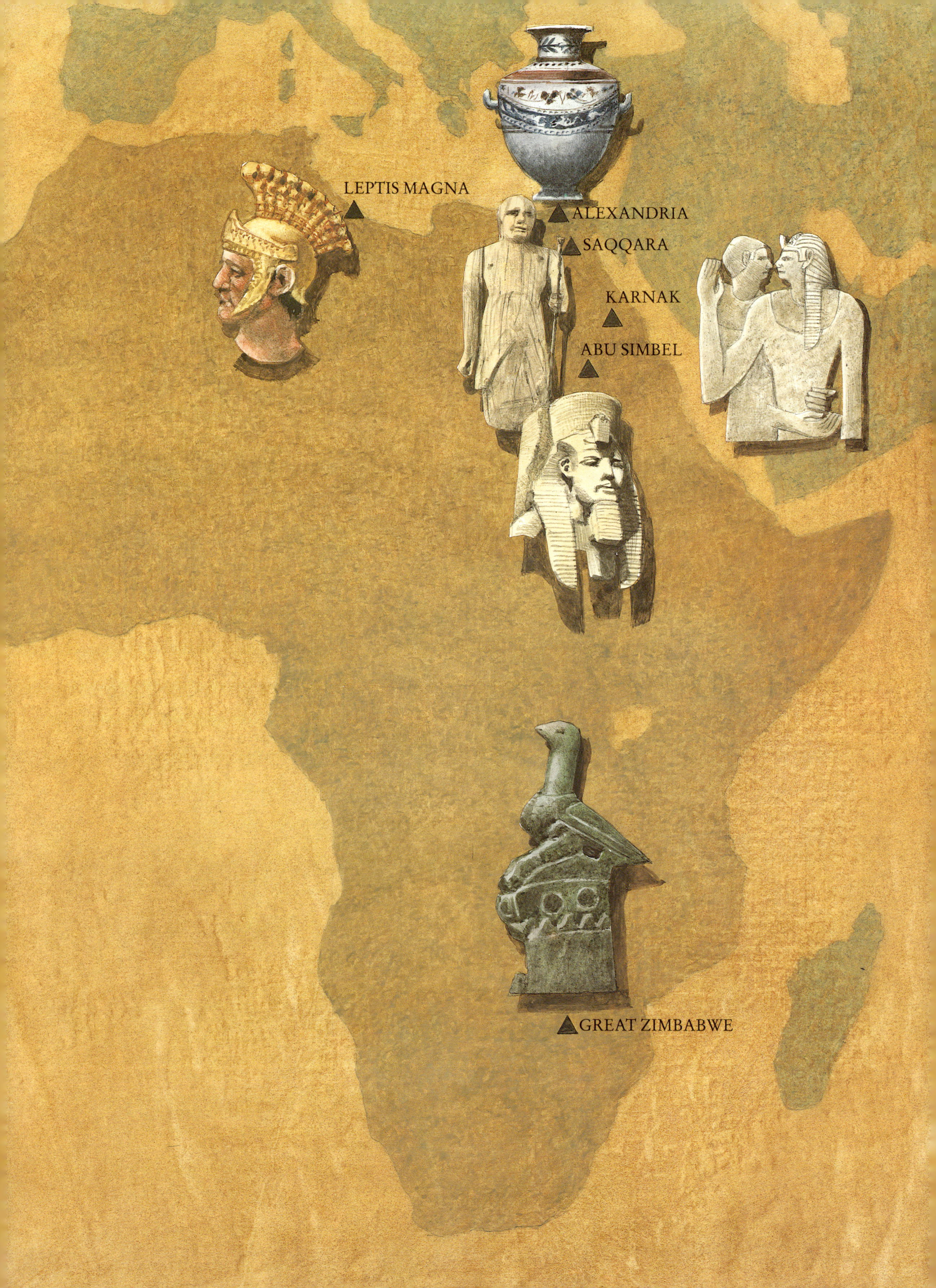
LEPTIS MAGNA
ALEXANDRIA
SAQQARA
KARNAK
ABU SIMBEL
GREAT ZIMBABWE

AFRICA

Africa is where the story of humankind begins. In the Olduvai Gorge in East Africa have been discovered the fossilized bones of the earliest hominids, beings closely related to the species, *Homo sapiens*, to which we belong. It was in Africa, archaeologists accept, perhaps in the Olduvai Gorge itself, that our ancestors first started to walk on two legs and to manufacture tools. This process took an inordinately long time – it may have taken a million years from the first two-legged step to the first tools. Another million years separate these early toolmakers from the first of the world's civilizations.

That Africa has had its own civilizations is something that archaeologists from Europe were at first reluctant to admit. Sites such as Great Zimbabwe in the country after which it is named and Ife in Nigeria were alleged to be the product of 'civilizing' invaders from outside. That we now know different is the result of the work both of African archaeologists and more reasonable Europeans whose work has gone some way to compensate for the shortcomings of their predecessors. But so wrong were the original European writers that many African historians believe that their subject should be theirs alone. In this book we have compromised, including one site because of its importance, its enduring fascination, and its relevance in illustrating this problem of history.

It is also enlightening to most non-specialists who have been brought up outside Africa. It shows, in the most graphic way, the technological capabilities of the original inhabitants. But secondly, and more importantly than this, it signals what would originally have surrounded it. You do not build a substantial stone enclosure in the middle of nowhere. Great Zimbabwe would have been surrounded by dwellings and other buildings of more perishable materials, and would have been at the centre of a network of trade and commerce, agriculture and craftsmanship. As such, it teaches us to look beyond the stones.

Specialist and non-specialist alike feel more secure when they turn to the longest-lasting of the civilizations to have flourished on this continent – ancient Egypt. Because it lasted so long, with apparently so little change in its organization, art, beliefs, and daily life; because it is so well documented; and because it is so familiar, we feel we are on safer ground. So we are, but this familiarity should not breed contempt of the Egyptian culture and achievement. The buildings of ancient Egypt are amongst the most magnificent in the world, and still have their enigmas and mysteries.

The first Egyptian site in this book, Saqqara, represents the Old Kingdom. This is the succession of dynasties that lasted from *c.*2686 to 2182 BC. It was the age of the pyramids, and the Step Pyramid at Saqqara is the earliest. The other two Egyptian sites in this book come from the New Kingdom (*c.*1567–1085 BC). The similarities between the two kingdoms – and the intervening Middle Kingdom – are remarkable. But the sites have been chosen for their individuality. The massive temple complex at Karnak, remarkable for its size alone, and the temple at Abu Simbel, tell us much about Egyptian religion. But they are also works of architectural and sculptural genius.

Another Egyptian place, Alexandria, illustrates the culture that followed the indigenous Egyptian. Alexander's city belonged to the Hellenistic culture that spread across the Mediterranean from Greece. A classical city *par excellence*, Alexandria had a famous library that exemplified a coming together of classical learning, and a lighthouse that exemplified the technology of the times – and the importance of the city for trade.

The other African site in this section exemplifies the effect of another of the great ancient empires on the continent. Leptis Magna was a Roman city of some renown, particularly during the reign of the emperor Septimus Severus, who came from Leptis Magna. It was built in response to the riches that the empire thought it could extract from Africa – the country farther west became the granary of the empire. The Romans also saw its potential as a port. But in spite of the support the town received from its citizens and from Severus, it remained too far east for agricultural importance and did not have enough of a hinterland to succeed as a port. It remained a fine example of Roman city architecture on the road to nowhere. But its architectural interest and its relationship with its most famous son are typical of the dynamic interplay between people and places that is the hallmark of the places in this book. This process is enough to engage us in its story.

SAQQARA

The world's first monumental stone building *circa* 2680 BC

The pyramids of Egypt are among the most familiar buildings of the ancient world. The largest and most famous stand by the Nile at Giza, but in many ways the strangest is the less well known step pyramid at Saqqara, slightly further south near the ancient capital of Memphis. One of the earliest stone buildings to have survived, it contains the tomb of Zoser, one of the first pharaohs, a king of the third dynasty, who lived in the first half of the twenty-seventh century BC. It was designed by Imhotep, a scribe and architect so revered by the ancient Egyptians that he was given the status of a god.

But Zoser's monument was not designed in the familiar pyramidal shape. It is built in a series of six steps, looking rather like a cross between an Egyptian pyramid and a Sumerian ziggurat.

From tomb to pyramid

It was fashionable in ancient Egypt for members of the aristocracy to be buried in underground tombs called *mastabas*. These would be marked by a modest structure on the surface, but the tomb itself, including all the lavish grave goods that the Egyptians buried with their dead to help them in the next world, would be beneath ground level. It seems that such a tomb was originally planned for Zoser. There was to be nothing above ground except a rectangular platform with sloping sides; beneath would be a network of passages and burial chambers.

But as with many building projects, plans for Zoser's tomb changed. For some reason, Imhotep had the idea of adding a low 'lean-to' extension, also with sloping sides, around the base of the mastaba platform. This produced the effect of two stepped platforms, and would have given the tomb a more monumental appearance. After this, various other detailed changes in the design were made, until it was decided to raise the structure higher: if one could have two platforms, why not four, getting progressively smaller as they went up. The original mastaba was buried under a large stone pyramid with four steps, and the concept that was to dominate royal burials in Egypt for the entire Old Kingdom was born.

Even then, Zoser and his architect did not rest content. The final result was a pyramid with six steps, in turn submerging the four-layer pyramid beneath tons of stone. By the time it was finished, its total height was about 60 metres (200 feet). At its base it measured 125 x 109 metres (411 x 358 feet). It was the largest stone structure that had been built to date – in fact the whole mortuary complex was the first such group of buildings to be constructed of stone.

Not surprisingly, the Egyptians admired the pyramid of Zoser. Graffiti have been found written by Egyptians who visited the site about 1,000 years after Zoser's time. The earliest visitors would have seen a pyramid quite different from the one visible today. Instead of the uneven surfaces of roughly dressed stone, they would have seen smooth, white limestone from nearby Tura that would have made the pyramid stand out starkly from the surrounding countryside. It would have seemed so large and so unlike any other building that its construction would have appeared impossible without the assistance of the gods.

Anyone who was privileged to see inside the mortuary complex would have found still greater marvels. The wall decoration alone was extraordinary – richly glazed blue tiles on some walls, finely carved reliefs on others. Then there were the many statues of the king, and of all the gods of upper and lower Egypt. Behind the enormous plug of granite that sealed off Zoser's tomb would be grave goods without equal. Tens of thousands of pots (in every conceivable type of stoneware from pure white alabaster to variegated stones) have survived. But they offer only a hint of the riches later tomb robbers must have removed – from the smallest jewels to the coffin of the king himself, no doubt opulently decorated within a sarcophagus of stone.

The mortuary complex

Modern visitors to Saqqara see the step pyramid in glorious isolation. But in ancient times it was surrounded by a group of buildings unique in Egyptian architecture and no less remarkable than the pyramid itself. A large perimeter wall about 10 metres (33 feet) high and 1.6 kilometres (almost a mile) in circumference surrounded the site. Carved in the stone were fourteen gates, thirteen of which were false gates, carved with

The figure of Imhotep, master architect of the step pyramid as Saqqara, overlooks this ancient Egyptian building site where blocks of stone are being levered into place.

This view of the step pyramid shows its complex of funerary buildings. The courtyard towards the front of the complex is the area associated with the royal jubilee ceremony. The rectangular buildings to the right are the chapels of the princesses.

imitation double doors. Only one door gave access to the pyramid and the surrounding buildings. From the one true gate a colonnade of pillars led to the courtyard in front of the pyramid. These pillars were also false in that they were partially attached to the wall behind and did not actually support anything. Around Zoser's monument were chapels, courtyards, and the funerary temple of the king. Like the doors and pillars, many of the structures within the walls are false: some of the buildings actually consist of a brick core faced with an elaborate stone facade, but with no interior at all.

Why this almost perverse method of construction? It probably owes something to the Egyptian concept of the afterlife. The ancient Egyptians took to the grave everything conceivable that they might need in the next world – from food to furniture, pots to jewellery. If they could not take the real thing, they were buried with a model of the real thing – museums are full of wooden models of servants carrying out every task imaginable: fishing, baking bread, herding and slaughte-

ring their cattle. It is hardly surprising that Zoser should choose to be buried within a model temple complex.

So the bizarre false buildings of Saqqara do not need interiors because they are intended to be inhabited by the spirits of the deceased. By 'representing' true buildings (in a similar way to how Egyptian hieroglyphic writing represents objects by picturing them) they provide 'ideal' buildings for the spirits.

Two of everything

One of the riddles of Saqqara is the fact that many of the buildings are in pairs. There are pairs of chapels, two buildings with courtyards, even two tombs. This is less puzzling when we bear in mind the symbolic role of the buildings. Much of the pharaohs' power came from the fact that they were kings of Upper and Lower Egypt: the double crown that they wear on papyri and wall paintings is a constant reminder of this. We know from papyri that the Egyptian kings carried out elaborate coronation rituals, as well as ceremonies to confirm their dual kingship. The buildings in which these ceremonies took place have not survived. They were probably light wooden structures specially built for the occasion. The rituals that took place around them therefore probably had a twofold nature, with elements repeated for each of the 'two kingdoms', and repeated elements within the architecture would blend perfectly in such dual ceremonies. The buildings in the mortuary complex at Saqqara are likely to be imitations of the ceremonial structures, built not for one occasion but for posterity.

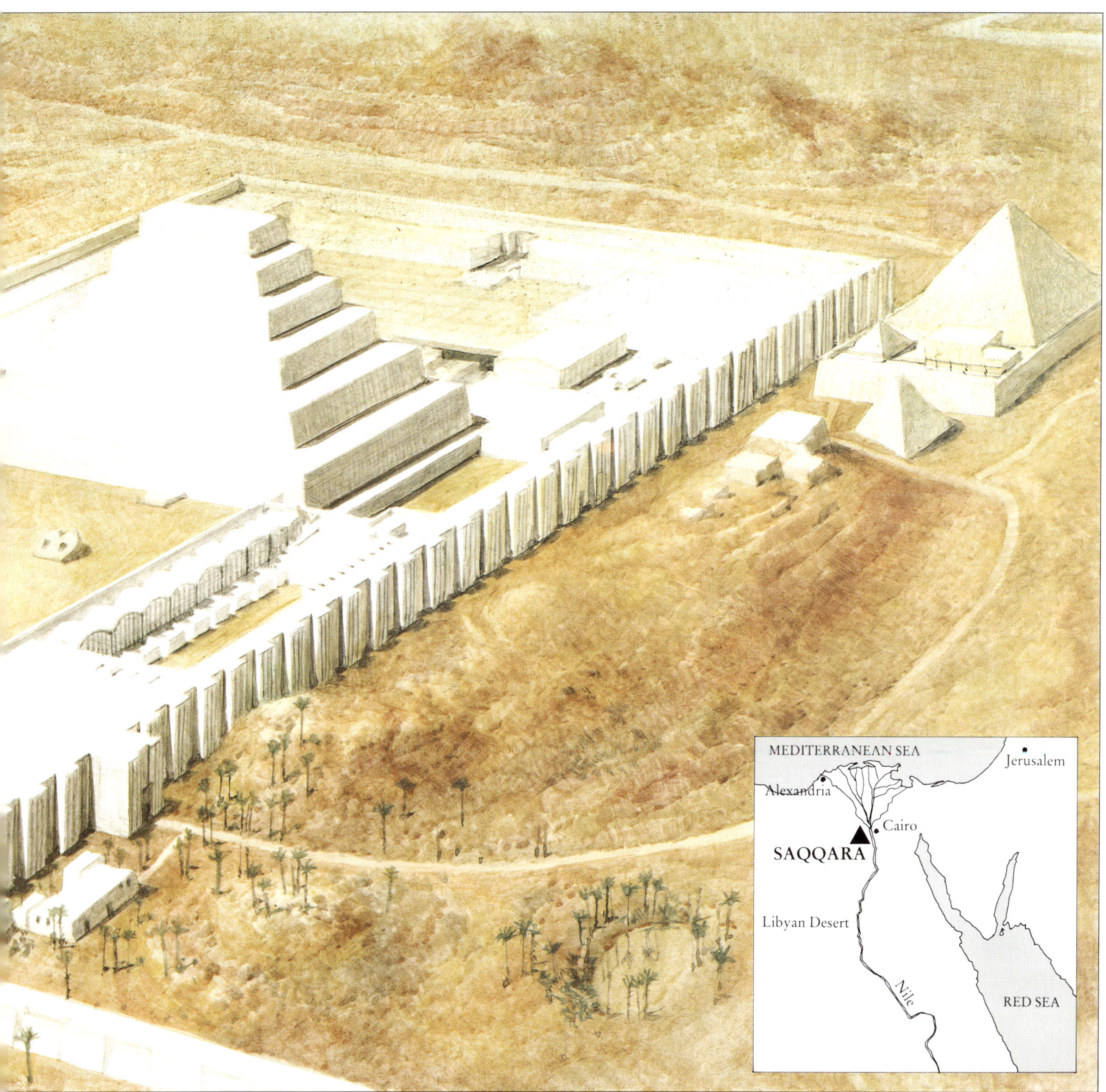

The royal jubilee

One ceremony that worked in this dual way was the royal jubilee, which would be celebrated after the king had been on the throne for a number of years. The jubilee involved some strange rituals, including one, depicted on a wall relief at Saqqara, in which the king ran around the complex carrying his flail. No one knows for certain the significance of this performance, but one purpose of the jubilee was to renew the life of the king and confirm his physical abilities and strength. Running around in this way perhaps showed that the king was athletic and strong enough to have his rule confirmed.

The jubilee ceremony also incorporated a reconstruction of the coronation, in which the king would be crowned twice, once for Upper Egypt and once for Lower Egypt. He would first present himself before one of the chapels where the gods of the districts (or *nomes*) of Upper Egypt would be assembled. After having his kingship confirmed by the gods he would be crowned with the white crown of Upper Egypt, before processing to another chapel to undergo a similar ritual involving the red crown of the Lower kingdom.

Tomb model of river boat

The last rites

The funeral ceremonies of the king were among the most elaborate of any early civilization. The Egyptian custom of embalming and mummification is well known. Zoser's body would have had to undergo a lengthy preparation process before it was entombed. First the parts of the body that decay most quickly – the intestines, liver, and lungs – would be removed. They would be preserved separately from the rest of the body. Next the body was coated with natron crystals to preserve it and then bound with bandages.

It soon became the custom to decorate the mummy with a representation of the person's face together with elaborate designs. Another development was to fill the body cavities so that the corpse kept its shape; a variety of substances, from wood shavings to linen, were used for this. Artificial eyes replaced the corpse's own, plates covered the priests' incisions, and amulets were hidden amongst the mummy's bandages.

Once the body was wrapped and the wrappings decorated, there were still many ceremonies that had to be performed. Amongst the most important was the ritual 'opening of the mouth', in which the deceased was given back the use of his or her senses. Then there would be the entombing of the grave goods and the installation of statues in the tomb. The sculptures were important because the spirit of the deceased could inhabit a statue and in this guise would be able to eat food that was provided in offerings – another ceremony, and one which was performed regularly.

These customs do not explain the presence of two tombs at Saqqara. It is clear that Zoser himself was buried in the larger one, and there are other tombs that were occupied by members of the royal family – some of which are still piled high with the pots that the king's relatives hoped to take to the next world. But the 'spare' royal tomb is something of a mystery. It is very small – at just over 1.5 metres (5 feet) square it would not comfortably accommodate an adult human body – and this has led some authorities to suggest that it may have been the burial place of the king's entrails. Another suggestion is that it had some ritual purpose connected with the jubilee celebrations. Of course, we cannot be certain, and the empty tomb at Saqqara remains one of the many enigmas of ancient Egyptian architecture.

Running the Old Kingdom

One of the most long-lived and successful of all the ancient civilizations, Egypt succeeded because it managed to control the difficult environment of the Nile Valley and because it developed an effective administration system to keep the kingdom running smoothly. The cities and sacred sites of ancient Egypt are distributed along the banks of the Nile in the area that was affected by flooding and thus made fertile. But the floods were so violent that an effective irrigation system had to be built to contain the waters – and efficient administration was once more needed to organise a large project of this sort.

The administrators were members of one of the most powerful classes of Egyptian society – the scribes. Look at ancient Egyptian paintings and you will see scribes everywhere – especially whenever the riches of the fields – the grain harvest, the cattle, even flocks of geese – needed to be counted and the correct tax assessed. One of the most successful scribes was Imhotep, the man who was responsible for the building of the step pyramid itself.

Imhotep, Zoser's vizier or chief minister, was no doubt famous in his time, but his fame spread after his death, and the Egyptians revered his memory as a scribe, astronomer, writer, physician, and architect. His fame as a healer continued into the Greek period, and the ancient Greeks equated Imhotep with their own god of healing Asklepios. So well known was Imhotep that it came as no surprise to archaeologists when they uncovered an inscription at Saqqara that put his name on an equal footing with that of the king.

Even so, we do not know what Imhotep's exact role was in creating the step pyramid. It is common to talk of him as the architect, but we should not assume that this term has always described the same job. Today, we look upon the designer as the central person in the creation of a great building. Ancient peoples, aware of the vast labour force needed to build something as massive as a pyramid, probably accorded more importance to the person who coordinated the whole operation – the project manager or administrator. As a successful scribe and Zoser's vizier, Imhotep might well have fulfilled this crucial role.

Linked as it was with the two greatest men in the kingdom, the step pyramid was more than an impressive building, more than simply the king's tomb. It was a symbol of power, of the strength of the king and his administrators, and of the unity of the two kingdoms of Upper and Lower Egypt. So effective was it that there was no wonder that future Egyptian kings would confirm their position in this life and the next with pyramids.

Although it is an outstanding achievement, the pyramid of Zoser has several features that mark it as an early stone building, aspects that, while they can hardly be called design flaws, would have been treated differently by the more experienced architects of the later pharaohs. Imhotep's workers did not have the techniques to handle the large blocks of stone used by later pyramid builders, so the blocks at Saqqara were comparatively small. Another feature that suggests the early designer's lack of confidence is the pillars, which at Saqqara were attached to the walls along one edge: the Egyptians had not yet mastered the art of building the strong free-standing columns that were to be such a feature of later buildings, such as the great hypostyle hall at Karnak.

Life around the pyramid

It is not only the step pyramid that makes Saqqara one of the world's most remarkable places. The mastabas of Saqqara, those tombs from which the pyramid evolved in the first place, also have a fascination. This is not because of their architectural qualities, but because the carved reliefs they contain give us our most vivid pictures of Egyptian life in the Old Kingdom, allowing us to imagine the sort of life that would have been lived in the shadow of Zoser's monument.

These images show that the pattern of the Egyptian agricultural culture, which was to sustain the kingdom for 3,000 years, was already well established. Some of the most vivid reliefs are in the tomb of the city governor, Mereruka, dating from *c.*2360 BC. They show the corn being harvested, bundled into sheaves, stacked, and threshed. Transport for the harvest is provided by donkeys with panniers (there was no wheeled transport in the Old Kingdom). Other workers are processing flax, the fibres of which will be made into linen, the seeds into oil. Still others are carrying some of the produce away to make offerings to the gods.

The wall decorations in the mastabas also remind us of the sophistication of Egyptian life. For example, there are scenes showing dancers, a family sitting around listening to music, and portrayals of doctors at work healing the sick. Other tomb walls show teams of men building large, complex ships, and other groups assembled in the law courts. Altogether, the tomb reliefs at Saqqara show a rich, complex society.

Saqqara gives us a vivid picture of the delicate balance that allowed the Egyptian Old Kingdom to survive for so long. On the one hand the pharaohs and their priests and scribes, who took a proportion of the crops as taxes in order to pay for the elaborate tomb and temple complexes that survive on the banks of the Nile today. On the other hand, the legions of workers, creating wealth for their social superiors, but glad to do this because the pharaoh and his administrators organized the irrigation system that made the land workable and profitable for them in the first place. It was a superbly effective system – so much so that the Egyptians did not need to build elaborate fortifications to keep their citizens in as many of the Mesopotamian rulers had to do.

Jackal-headed god, Anubis

But the step pyramid is more than a symbol of the pharaoh's power over the people. Some of the Egyptian texts that have come down to us refer to a staircase to heaven being laid out for the king, so that he may ascend to heaven. Perhaps it is not too fanciful to see the step pyramid as the ultimate staircase, the very means by which the king could make the journey for which the rest of the buildings in the mortuary complex have prepared him. The step pyramid shows that characteristic blend of symbolic power and practicality that marks so many of the remains that have survived from ancient Egypt.

The kings who followed Zoser on the thrones of Upper and Lower Egypt seem to have taken up this symbolism and to have wanted to be buried beneath step pyramids. The builders who worked for Zoser's successor Sekhem-khet showed that they had learned from the experience of building the earlier king's step pyramid – Sekhem-khet's pyramid was constructed with much larger stones and was on a more ambitious scale. But Sekhem-khet's reign only lasted for six years, and his pyramid was not completed.

By the time of the fourth dynasty (*c.*2615–2500 BC), the kings had adapted the stepped design to create the true pyramid. In this, they were no doubt influenced by the cult of the sun-god Re, the pyramid's sloping sides representing the spreading rays of the sun. But although the symbolism is different, the later kings' architects had recognized in the step pyramid a powerful shape – one that was to become synonymous with kingship for most of the Old Kingdom, and one which still fires the imaginations of all who look at it today.

KARNAK

Site of some of ancient Egypt's most remarkable temples

Some 600 kilometres (372 miles) south of Cairo lies Karnak, one of the most fascinating of the ancient Egyptian sites. A complex of temples, with perimeter walls, processional avenues of sphinxes, and large ceremonial halls, it is justly famous. Its obelisks, carved pillars, reliefs, and stelae make a lasting impression on every visitor. Yet this very richness, representing some 2,000 years of continuous use and rebuilding, makes the significance of Karnak difficult to grasp. The place is obviously one of the most important temple sites in Egypt, but why was it such a sacred site and how did the temples come to be built here? What was the nature of the religion that inspired them, and which of the many Egyptian gods was worshipped here? What ceremonies took place in the great avenues and halls? And what do the rebuildings and restorations tell us about how this great complex was used over the years?

The New Kingdom of Thebes

In 1786 BC the period of Egyptian history known as the Middle Kingdom came to an end. An 'intermediate period' followed, in which different areas of the country were ruled by different kings. At this time only one kingdom remained intact – Thebes. It was the Thebans who repulsed Asian invaders known as the Hyksos people from northern Egypt; and it was they who eventually reunited Egypt in *c.*1550 BC, to found what came to be called the New Kingdom, with its capital at Thebes.

The Theban kings were successful in building something of an empire. Always men of action, they carried out many military campaigns and, as well as pulling together Egypt, annexed city states in Syria, Lebanon, Israel, and Jordan. Such an extensive kingdom required effective government and the New Kingdom relied more than ever on an efficient administration by well-chosen officials to hold it together. The New Kingdom pharaohs were on the whole careful to select their advisers from people who had proved their capability by rising through the ranks, rather than appointing royal relatives as had often been done in the past. And as the majority of the officials were drawn from the ranks of the priests and scribes it is not surprising that religious building benefitted from the power of these influential people, and that Karnak, adjacent to the royal capital at Thebes, should become the site of rich temples.

In fact Karnak had been a sacred site before the founding of the New Kingdom. Its name in ancient Egyptian was Ipet-isut, meaning either 'the most select of places' or 'the place where tribute was brought', and archaeologists have found that there were temples on the site in the reign of the twelfth-dynasty king Senwosret I (1971–1926 BC). But it was in the New Kingdom, when the worship of the god Amun grew to its height, that Karnak became the religious centre of Egypt.

With its massive columns covered in Hieroglyphs and paintings, and its colossal statues, the main impression given by the religious complex at Karnak is of sheer size

The king of the gods

Amun had long been one of the most important of the vast array of Egyptian gods. Like many of the gods of Egypt, he started life as a local deity, linked to one of the districts of Middle Egypt. But he was already a national god by the time he became associated with Thebes. Back in the time of Senwosret I he had been given the title 'King of the Gods'. It is quite natural that a sun-god should become pre-eminent in a country where the sun is an obvious fact of daily life and where agriculture is vital for survival. In fact the Egyptians had several sun-gods. One was Khepre, a scarab beetle. This creature was often seen rolling a ball of dung along the ground and the Egyptians imagined a similar heavenly beetle propelling the sun across the sky. Another sun-god was Harakhte, whose diurnal course was represented by a boat sailing across the heavens.

Amun was yet another sun deity, more powerful, but also more mysterious than the others. He is pictured in several forms – as a ram, a man with a ram's head, or a man wearing a crown carrying a sceptre and an *ankh*, the Egyptian symbol of life. In the latter form Amun is already close to the pharaoh, who was also crowned, and often carried the sceptre and the ankh. And this association with royalty, protecting the pharaoh, standing over him on military campaigns and fostering his interests at home, is one reason why it was Amun who gained supremacy as the principal sun-god.

It was during the early period of the New Kingdom that his worship was taken up in a major way by the

By Ramesses II's time, the temple has grown to massive proportions. The Hypostyle Hall (top left) *has been built in front of the earlier courtyards, and the pylons were adorned with flags. But the vast complex was quiet – few were allowed inside except for members of the priesthood. The plan at the foot of this page shows the later extent of the complex, when the Great Court and first pylon had been built in front of the Hypostyle Hall.*

pharaohs, and that his role as a manifestation of the sun-god was emphasized. In a similar way, his temple at Karnak has a lengthy history, but the complex reached its peak in the New Kingdom, particularly during the reign of King Ramesses II (1290–1224 BC). One of the longest-reigning of Egyptian monarchs, it was Ramesses II who fought the Hittites and who commemorated his long reign with numerous building projects and monumental statues.

Amun enjoyed a lengthy supremacy, but there were interruptions in his reign. The most famous was during the rule of Akhenaten, the 'heretic pharaoh' (1353–1335 BC). It was he who banished all the many gods of the Egyptian pantheon in favour of a single sun-god. But he did not choose Amun, who represented the rising sun, but Aten, the god of the fully-risen sun. The result was a revolution in the religious life of the country, with the temples of Amun desecrated and images of Amun defaced. Thebes was further affected because the new king moved his capital city to Tel el Amarna, instantly making the neighbourhood of Karnak less influential.

But the supremacy of Aten was short-lived. When the heretic pharaoh died, his place was taken by the boy-king Tutankhamun. Famous in our time for his tomb, Tutankhamun was known during his own reign for beginning the renovation of the old temples, and the restoration of the old gods, including Amun.

The home of the god

The temple of Amun at Karnak, which Ramesses II extended, consisted of series of courtyards, each one entered through a gateway, usually called by Egyptologists a 'pylon'. The courtyards contain the ceremonial halls that were the great glory of the temple. Their most impressive feature

1220 BC

was that the roof was held up by many large columns, and this multiplicity of columns has given the halls their usual name, 'hypostyle halls', from the Greek 'stylos', pillar.

Today, the temple is entered through the first pylon, a structure built after the pharaohs, during the Ptolomaic period. To imagine the temple as it was during Ramesses' time we have to ignore the first pylon and the great courtyard behind it. During the reign of Ramesses, one would have entered through the second pylon. This tall structure, with tapering walls that sloped slightly away towards the back of the temple, would have made an imposing sight. But it would hardly have prepared one for the room that it led to – the Great Hypostyle Hall. One of the largest single chambers ever built, the hall covers an area of almost 5,000 square metres (about 54,000 square feet); the whole of the cathedral of Notre Dame, Paris, could comfortably be accommodated within its walls. The roof was held up by 134 stone columns, arranged in sixteen rows. These include two central rows of six columns each that are more massive than all the others.

Such an awesome structure was not built in a day. The Great Hypostyle Hall was begun during the reign of Ramesses I (1307–1306 BC). After his brief reign his son Seti I (1306–1290 BC) took over the project, but even his reign did not give enough time to finish the hall, and it was completed by Ramesses II, who took most of the credit for the work.

The task of transporting the stone and erecting the pillars was only one aspect of creating the building. All the pillars – indeed most of the stone surfaces – are superbly decorated with relief carvings which would originally have been painted. The reliefs within the hall show religious subjects, especially the adoration of the god Amun. The carvings on the outside walls depict subjects from real life, such as the military campaigns of Ramesses. The carvings even give us the Egyptian text of the king's treaty with the Hittites after the Battle of Qadesh. The less well known battles of Ramesses' father Seti I, including campaigns in Lebanon, Palestine, and Syria, are also shown, and we are reminded that the scenes are depicted on a temple wall, because the spoils and prisoners of war are shown being presented to Amun.

With its forest of columns, most of which are not only very tall but also as wide as the spaces between them, the Great Hypostyle Hall makes an extraordinary sight. With its roofs and walls intact it would have created a very different impression, still awesome, but much darker and more claustrophobic. Some light would have been admitted through the windows above the two central rows of columns. But so close and so many are the pillars, that it would have been impossible to get a true impression of how large the hall itself actually was. The coloured carvings on the surfaces of the columns and the stones would have loomed out of the half-light.

Statue unearthed near the 7th Pylon

Beyond the Hypostyle Hall

To emerge through the Hypostyle Hall and walk to the rear of the temple is to take a journey further back in time. The back wall of the Hypostyle Hall itself is made up of the third pylon of the temple, originally the front entrance in the time of Amenhotep III (1391–1353 BC). This building itself contains the ruins of past temples on the site, and archaeologists are busy extracting stone blocks from the pylon to reconstruct these earlier buildings.

Further back still are three more pylons, leading to progressively older parts of the temple, until we come to the buildings erected in the time of Tuthmosis III (1479–1425 BC). Tuthmosis was another pharaoh who was a successful military commander. His campaigns spread Egyptian power to Libya and Nubia, as well as to Asia Minor. In doing this, Tuthmosis was not creating an empire in the modern sense, with a close-knit governmental system. What he was doing was making other peoples dependent on Egypt, so that he would be able to exact payments of tribute and thereby increase his wealth.

This method of legalized extortion was important for Karnak, as the priests of the temple would have been among the chief beneficiaries of the resulting wealth. One of the buildings of Tuthmosis at Karnak is a Hall of Records. This contained much more than papyri chronicling the life and times of the pharaoh. It would also have been full of booty from Africa and Asia Minor – precious metals such as gold and silver, substances such as ivory, ebony, and lapis lazuli, and luxurious items made from these materials.

The final building in the series built for Tuthmosis III is his festival temple, which is at the easternmost end of the complex. A bizarre design, with pillars that taper towards the bottom rather than the top, it is unique in Egyptian architecture. It has been suggested that the pharaoh deliberately chose this layout because the resulting tent-like structure reminded him of his quarters when on campaign. Whether this is true is unknown. But the effect was eccentric enough for Ramesses II not to want to repeat it when he reverted to the more conventionally-shaped columns in his Great Hypostyle Hall.

The temple rituals

Extensive as the ruins of Karnak are, it is difficult to imagine their exact appearance at the time of Ramesses II. Many details have perished completely. For example, the tall niches in the front walls of the pylons probably contained flagpoles, but we have little idea what the flags that flew there would have been like. It is possible to imagine some of the rituals that took place, and to recreate something of the religious life of Egypt at this time.

For the ancient Egyptians, organized religion was mainly the concern of the priests and kings. Ordinary people might well be religious, but their religion would be directed towards household gods and popular deities rather than the gods of the temples. In fact the temple precincts were closed to the general public and only priests (and the king, who was also the high priest) were permitted to enter.

The rituals that took place in the temples at Karnak had to do with making offerings to the god. It was thought that the god would be sympathetic to the affairs of Egypt if offerings were made every day. The basic ritual involved, as portrayed on the relief carvings on the temple walls, was quite simple. First the priest would undergo a purification ceremony by bathing in holy water. Next he would walk through the temple to the shrine at the back that contained the statue of the god. The doors of the shrine would be opened, and the priest would anoint the statue and dress it in its regalia. Then a meal would be laid before the statue and the priest would withdraw, walking backwards and sweeping the ground as he went to clear away any footprints that might be left on the floor.

The fact that the statues never accepted the food that was offered to them did not deter the priests. Their lack of acceptance was merely an indication that they were content – the important thing was that the offering had been made. When it was clear that the gods did not require the food, it was carefully removed and offered to the more accepting priests in part payment for their duties.

Not all the ceremonies were carried out in priestly privacy. There was one temple at Karnak, the temple of Amun, Hearer-of-Prayers, where people could go to supplicate to the god and say their prayers to him. The god was supposed to respond to questions by leaning towards the supplicant or by choosing between alternatives. Another example of this type of public access came during the reign of Tuthmosis III (1479–1425 BC), when the king had his own statue set up next to that of Amun in an area of the precinct open to the public. Thus people were encouraged to pray to the god-king as well as the king of the gods, and the semi-divine status of the pharaoh was demonstrated.

Priestly power

Perhaps still more remarkable than the rituals at Karnak was the size of the retinue that surrounded Amun at Karnak itself and elsewhere in Egypt. According to a papyrus from the reign of Ramesses III (1194–1163 BC) there were over 80,000 servants and slaves in the service of the god. The cult possessed over 5,000 statues, and 46 building yards were involved in creating and restoring property belonging to the cult.

Perhaps this is all less surprising when the size of the temple estates is considered. The temple owned almost 283,000 hectares (700,000 acres) of land and over 421,000 cattle. The estates included properties all over Egypt, from the Nile Delta in the north to Nubia in the south. As well as the cattle there were other animals, some of which were sacred to the gods worshipped by the Egyptians. Amun's sacred animals were the ram and the goose. Sphinxes with rams' heads are still to be seen on the site; flocks of sacred geese were kept near the temple.

All this land, livestock, and staff is a clear indication of the power of the priests and temples during the New Kingdom. When the king and priests worked together, as in the time of Tuthmosis III, the result was to make Egypt more powerful. But when the balance was turned in favour of the priests, Egypt's position could become unstable. This is what happened in *c.*1080 BC when Hrihor, High Priest of Amun, claimed kingly status and tried to turn Egypt into an ecclesiastical state. Hrihor is shown in a relief at the temple of Khonsu, to the south of the main temple complex at Karnak, making sacrifices to the gods. He is standing in the position normally occupied by the pharaoh.

Partly as a result of Hrihor's takeover and Egypt's failing grip on wealth-giving provinces like Nubia, there was a succession of invasions. The Libyans, the Kushites, and the Assyrians ruled in Egypt in turn. Although there was a brief recovery during the twenty-sixth dynasty, during which Egyptian nobles turned the kingdom round economically, this was the beginning of the end of Egyptian independence.

In spite of this, many of the invaders respected the temple complex at Karnak. The Kushites even did some building of their own. And the sheer quantity of stone at Karnak meant that, however much was removed in later years for building work elsewhere, a substantial quantity would still be left to help us reconstruct Amun's sanctuary today.

King Amenophis III making an offering to his deified image

ABU SIMBEL

Temple built by King Ramesses II, cut into the rock of the cliff face near the Nile in Nubia

For the ancient Egyptians, Nubia, the area above the first cataract of the Nile river, was one of the most sought-after prizes. It was an area rich in precious natural resources, particularly gold, but was inhabited, at least above the second cataract, by a warlike people who were keen to hold on to what was theirs.

So the Egyptians had to fight for Nubia, and they would wrest control of the territory from the natives in one battle, only to lose it again in another. Several Egyptian paintings record Nubians bringing tribute to their Egyptian masters – and large, heavy rings of gold figure prominently in these paintings. Nubia was a territory of great value for the Egyptians, and they acknowledged this by building two of their greatest monuments in Nubia – the two temples commissioned by Ramesses II, some 80 kilometres (50 miles) north of the second cataract of the Nile, at Abu Simbel. Although much of Nubia is arid, with little fertile land even on the banks of the river in many places, at Abu Simbel there was a greater area of land suitable for agriculture, which was probably able to support quite a substantial population. It was an appropriate place for a centre of worship – and for a monument that would serve as an indication of the strength of Egyptian power in the area.

The four colossal statues that make up the facade of the great temple at Abu Simbel represent King Ramesses II, the temple's founder. Cut into the bare rock, they made the building much more open to the world than most Egyptian temples, which tended to be hidden away in elaborate precincts. They ensured that Ramesses' presence was always in the mind of the passing Nubians on the edge of his kingdom.

The legacy of Ramesses

It was the pharaoh Ramesses II who left his mark most indelibly on Nubia. As his work at Karnak and elsewhere showed, he was one of ancient Egypt's greatest builders. He was also a famous soldier and, as well as his famous battles against the Hittites he campaigned in Nubia. His work there was probably built on foundations laid by his father, Seti I . Seti, in turn, inherited a viable administration in Nubia from King Horemheb and from his immediate predecessor Ramesses I. Even so, Seti had to quell rebellions in Nubia, and Ramesses II had to continue the fight for Egyptian supremacy there. And he achieved a great deal, turning has father's schemes of conquest and administration to resounding success.

Nowhere is this clearer than in his exploitation of Nubia's gold mines. Under Seti I the mines had not been able to reach their full output because of a water shortage. Seti's staff had tried to remedy this problem by digging wells, but none of their attempts yielded water. And so, according to an inscription found at Kuban, not far from the mines, people who came to extract the gold continued to die of thirst on the way. It had always been like this, said the officials, reminding Ramesses that even his father's well has failed to produce any water. The pharaoh responded by commanding that they try Seti's well again, boring deeper to see if water lay lower down in the rock. Sure enough, a mere twelve cubits below the level reached by Seti, water was found. The way lay open for the full exploitation of the region.

Typically, Ramesses responded not simply by pumping Nubia of as much gold as he could. He acquired a reputation as an able diplomat and administrator in his dealings with Nubia. He also gave the country some compensation for the gold he removed by putting back into the landscape architectural riches – a whole string of temples, hewn from the rock of the escarpment in a style that had rarely been used in Egypt before his reign. Amongst the sandstone cliffs of Lower Nubia his workers created temples at Derr, Wadi es-Sebua, Gerf Hussein and Beit el Wali. The series culminated in the two temples on the west bank of the Nile at Abu Simbel.

For his greatest temples, Ramesses and his architects decided to adopt the method of rock-cut construction, tunnelling deep into the cliff to create the temple chambers, and carving the cliff face itself with superb facades. At the

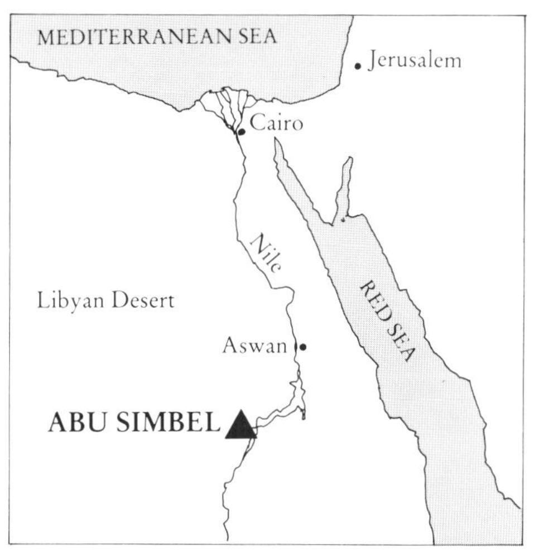

Great Temple, the facade is dominated by four colossal statues of the king himself. The smaller temple to the east also has colossal statues, this time four of the king and two of his queen, Nofretari. With the two principal members of the Egyptian royal family immortalized in Nubian stone in this way, the locals could not forget for one moment who their rulers were. Presumably Ramesses intended that this should be the result.

A sacred site

Why did Ramesses choose to build such a great temple in Nubia, so far away from the centre of his empire? There were probably several reasons: religious, economic, artistic, and political. First, it is probable that Abu Simbel was already a sacred site when the Egyptians arrived. Second, the fact that there was a fair expanse of fertile land nearby meant that the necessary large team of workers could be supported. Third, the great rock face must have been inviting to the pharaoh's stonecarvers; further south, the lie of the land did not lend itself to rock-cut architecture, and Ramesses had to build temples of masonry in the more traditional style. Fourth, the position of the site near the second cataract was adjacent to the traditional boundary of Egypt; by making his presence felt here, Ramesses was implying that his power was effective right up to the borders – it was like a challenge to the people of Upper Nubia to defy him if they dared.

The Great Temple

Ramesses II's Great Temple is one of the most striking surviving examples of Egyptian architecture. Its glory is its facade, with the four mighty statues of Ramesses, each of which is almost 20 metres (65 feet) tall. There is little doubt that the king was the most important person as far as the temple builders were concerned, but there were other figures on the facade. The three gods to whom the temple was dedicated – Ptah, Amun, and Re-Harakhty – feature prominently. Members of the king's family are lower down near the king's feet.

Several of the carvings on the facade would have reminded the Nubians of their position as conquered subjects of the pharaoh. For example, the pedestals on which the colossi are placed bear carvings of captive Asiatics and Africans. The thrones on which the statues of Ramesses are seated have carvings representing the union of Upper and Lower Egypt, confirming the power of the pharaoh that is suggested by the great size of the statues themselves.

Faience head from furniture inlay

But the facade is not simply a political statement. The statues are identified by inscriptions that show them to be religious objects. In particular, Ramesses is linked with the sun-gods of Egypt, and his four statues are described as 'The sun of the rulers', 'The ruler of the two lands', 'The beloved one of the god Amun' and 'The beloved one of the sun-god Atum'. Egyptians would have recognized not only the figures of the gods and the significance of Ramesses' titles, but also the row of baboons along the top of the temple frontage, sitting in a posture usually associated with sun worship.

Inside, the link between worship of the Egyptian gods and the power of the pharaoh is also stressed. The first chamber is a hall containing eight massive pillars. Each one bears an image of Ramesses, this time standing, but still wearing the double crown of Upper and Lower Egypt and holding the crook and flail, traditional insignia of kingship. The wall reliefs show a mixture of the worldly and the godly, with accounts of the king's battles vying for space with inscriptions concerning religious rituals. But even the battle reliefs have a religious context. Ramesses is shown achieving his famous victory over the Hittites single-handed; he does this with the aid of the sun-god Amun, and as a representative of the sun-god on earth. Beyond the large hall is a smaller chamber, and here, as in the sanctuary that is yet deeper inside the temple, the wall decorations all have religious subjects. But the statues in the sanctuary again remind one of the close link of secular and sacred in Egypt.

The gods of the temple

Two of the gods of the Great Temple, Amun and Re-Harakhty, were sun-gods; the third, Ptah, was a creation deity and god of craftsmen; the fourth was the god-king Ramesses himself. The gods were linked by their close association with the pharaoh.

We have already met Amun, the king of the gods, at his temple at Karnak. Amun, always closely linked with the pharaoh, was the deity reputedly invoked by Ramesses II during the battle of Qadesh; he was supposed to have given the king the strength of 10,000 men, allowing him to defeat his enemies single-handed. Amun also had a close relationship with Nubia, mainly as a result of a campaign of temple-building specifically designed to foster Egypt's presence in the southern province. The Great Temple was one in a line of temples to Amun, a line that included the temple at Amada (between the first and second cataracts) built by Tuthmosis III and another temple at Gebel Barkal (in the area of the fourth cataract) built by King Horemheb.

Re-Harakhty was another of the Egyptian sun-gods. His name indicates a combination of deities, the sun-god Re and the god Horus. In fact Harakhty means 'Horus of the horizon', illustrating the idea of the god, like the sun, rising in the east at dawn. This deity's association with the king is shown on inscriptions that equate the pharaoh with Harakhty. Ptah, the creator-god, is not a sun deity, but has his own importance. His link with Ramesses is shown by the statues the king had erected in the temple of Ptah at Memphis.

It was in the sanctuary that the ritual offerings to these gods would be made. The priest would prepare himself in one of the small unadorned rooms that lead off the main hall, before processing towards the inner sanctuary and making his offerings in the usual Egyptian manner. But there was one crucial difference at Abu Simbel. Being a rock-cut temple it had no windows to let in the light, so the interior was normally very dark and mysterious.

But at certain times of the year,

because of the way the temple was oriented, the light of the rising sun would stream through the entrance doorway and shine right through the main and inner halls to the sanctuary itself. The drama of this moment, illuminating the coloured wall reliefs so that they could be seen properly, and flooding the sanctuary of the sun-god and the four cult statues with light from the sun itself, is even more dramatic than sunrise at midsummer at Stonehenge.

The builders of Abu Simbel

An inscription on one of the internal doors in the Great Temple dates to the first year of Ramesses' reign. It is therefore likely that work on the temple was already well underway when Ramesses came to the throne, and likely that the monument was planned by Seti I. This is further indicated by the fact that there are so many reminders of the younger pharaoh. Egyptian kings were good at claiming the imagery of earlier pharaohs and calling it their own, and Ramesses II is known to have done this at other sites, claiming the credit for work carried out in earlier reigns. In this case it is more likely that the basic excavation was done in Seti's reign, while the decoration and the carving of the facade were carried out in Ramesses' time.

Whichever pharaoh commissioned the temple, the actual work was carried out by slaves, prisoners of war from the Egyptian campaigns in Nubia. This was common practice in this part of the Egyptian Empire and elsewhere. As well as an inscription at Abu Simbel telling how captives were used in this way, similar inscriptions have been found relating to Ramesses' use of Libyan captives at Wadi es-Sebua, and to his donation of prisoners to the temple at Buhen. It is difficult to see vast stone-moving projects succeeding in remote parts of the kingdom, such as the one that must have been undertaken at Abu Simbel, without some form of slave labour.

The great rescue

The story of Abu Simbel does not end in the Egyptian New Kingdom. The twentieth century AD has added its own remarkable chapter. In the 1960s it was realised that the construction of the Aswan High Dam would push up the level of the Nile so that many of the Nubian temples would be flooded. An international rescue effort was launched and many different schemes were proposed to save the temples. Attention was naturally focused on the Great Temple at Abu Simbel as the most important monument under threat.

Among the suggested rescue plans were the raising of the temples on hydraulic jacks; the construction of a massive concrete raft under the temples, causing them to float upwards as the water level rose; and a scheme involving cutting up the stones of the temples and moving them piecemeal to a higher site. It was this proposal that was finally agreed on in 1963.

Special techniques were developed for the cutting up of the facade. Although large mechanical saws were used to cut most of the depth of the blocks, specially designed handsaws were employed to cut the stone nearest the visible surface of the carving. This meant that the smallest possible damage was done to the surfaces of the colossal statues and the other details of the facade. Another special technique had to be developed to lift the stones, since no lifting equipment was permitted to touch the delicate surfaces of the sandstone. The solution here was to drill holes into the hidden surfaces of the stone and insert steel bolts which could then be attached to the cranes for lifting.

The temples were repositioned on the same cliff from which they had originally been carved, but further up, away from the dangers of high water. They were oriented in the same way, so that the effect of the sun entering the temple would be preserved. When the stones had been relocated in their new home, a concrete dome was built over the temple to take the weight of an artificial earth mound that finally covered the whole construction, imitating the original effect of an underground temple. The whole story of the removal of the Great Temple and its smaller neighbour at Abu Simbel is one full of drama and incident, to which whole books have been devoted. Fortunately it is also a success story, ensuring the beginning of another chapter in the history of these temples' survival.

A plan and cross-section of the temple show how the chambers penetrate into the rock. The line drawing of the facade illustrates the temple's state of repair today.

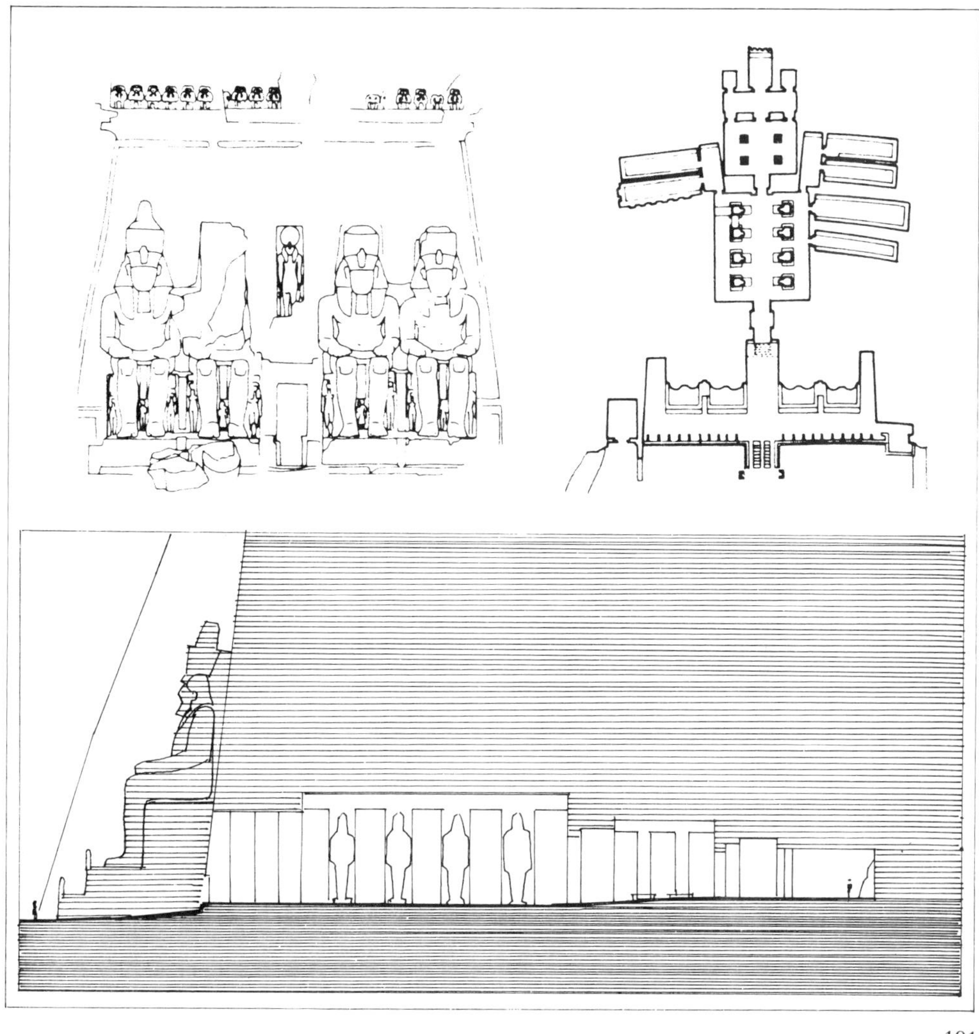

ALEXANDRIA

City of Alexander the Great and the Ptolemies, seat of learning, and sight of the famous lighthouse

The career of Alexander the Great was one of the most extraordinary in the ancient world. By the age of twenty-five, this brilliant general from Macedonia had conquered Greece, Persia, and Syria. Once it had become clear that Alexander was the enemy of the Persians, Egypt also fell to his might. So for the first time; the kingdom on the Nile found itself part of a vast empire that was not centred on the Egyptian corner of northern Africa. With Egypt on the edge of an empire rather than its focus, Alexander looked for a new capital that gave him easy access to the Mediterranean and the rest of his possessions. And so he came to settle on a town called Rhakotis.

Rhakotis was a relatively unimportant Egyptian town. Being on the coast, it must have gained some wealth from local trade, but Alexander planned much greater things for the town. The main feature that attracted him to Rhakotis was the excellent natural harbour. The town was situated halfway along a spur that jutted out from the mainland at the western end of the Nile Delta. To the south, the waters of Lake Mariout provided a sheltered haven for ships. But boats could also moor to the north. Here there was a long island, which was to become the site of the famous lighthouse. One of the major projects of the builders of the new city was to create a barrier linking the island with the spur, which created harbours on either side. The port could thus hardly have been better served for Alexander's ships.

Evidence from ancient coins and mosaics gives us some idea of the overall shape of the lighthouse, its multi-tiered structure, and the number of windows. We are less sure about the interior. As well as stairs or ramps there would certainly have been a fire at the top. Some accounts mention elaborate mirror arrangements to direct the light.

So the ancient Egyptian port of Rhakotis became the city of Alexandria. The Macedonian emperor commissioned his architect Dinocrates to build a city in the Greek style on the site – to base it on a traditional gridiron plan, to create the harbour, and to adorn it in the classical style. Unlike the great Greek cities like Athens and Sparta that no doubt influenced its planning, Alexandria was a city built from scratch and designed as a whole. It had a visual unity that few other classical cities could match. But although the building work was started quickly, Alexander was to see little of the city that bore his name. The necessities of conquest took him far across his empire, and it was only when he died that his body returned.

The emperor died young, at the age of thirty-seven. His successor was his half-brother, Philip Arrhidaeus, who chose one Ptolemy, son of Lagus, one of Alexander's most successful military commanders, to be governor of Egypt. Meanwhile the central power of the empire was weakened when Philip was assassinated in 317 BC; his successor Alexander IV met the same fate seven years later. The result of these events was that Ptolemy's power in Egypt increased until it was virtually an independent state. Ptolemy finally declared himself king of Egypt in 305 BC and took the title 'Soter', meaning 'saviour'. The dynasty that Ptolemy founded was to last until the time of its most famous daughter, Cleopatra, on whose death in 30 BC Egypt was taken over by the Romans.

In the meantime, Ptolemy's family was to have a lasting effect on the history of Alexandria, the city from which they ruled. If the grand conception of the city was Alexander's, many of the actual buildings were created under the patronage of the Ptolemies. The first three Ptolemies, Ptolemy I Soter (305–282 BC), Ptolemy II Philadelphus (282–246 BC), and Ptolemy III Euergetes (246–221 BC), were the kings whose building work left a strong imprint on the fabric of Alexandria. In particular the most famous building, the lighthouse, was constructed in the reign of Ptolemy II (although it may well have been part of Alexander's original plans for the city), while the city's most prestigious institution, the library and the university that surrounded it, was founded by Ptolemy I. Their family turned out to be successful at adapting themselves to the cosmopolitan culture of the area and also endowed the city with a palace complex so large that it almost comprised a city in its own right, with temples and other public buildings. It was as much their city as the city of Alexander.

A beacon and a watchtower

The lighthouse, or *pharos* as it was known, was the most remarkable building in Alexandria – it was one of the Seven Wonders of the World. Tall and white, it dominated one of the best sites in the city and became the

Adorned with temples and other public buildings, Alexandria at the time of the Ptolemies was a typical Hellenistic city, its architecture influenced by that of many other Mediterranean ports. But the lighthouse was a unique building, constructed in a style quite unlike anything that had gone before. No wonder that it became the symbol of the city.

Alexandria, the city and lighthouse 270 BC

symbol of Alexandria to all who travelled there. In building the pharos, Ptolemy II was meeting two needs felt by the city. First, the alluvial coast of Egypt was difficult to navigate for shipping approaching from the Mediterranean. Reefs of limestone also line the shore, making the approach doubly treacherous, and rocks like the Bull's Horn at the harbour entrance were notorious with sea captains. A beacon marking the position of the city, and guiding the ships along the safest route, was therefore vital. The city also needed defending – in spite of the difficult coastline, attack from the sea was always a possibility. A tower from which a lookout could be kept, combined with a light to alert shipping to the position of the coast, was the obvious solution.

What was less obvious was that Ptolemy's architect would come up with a building of such magnificence in response to this need. But the architect, a contemporary of the mathematician Euclid, brought the great learning of the city of Alexandria to bear on the project. First and foremost the pharos was huge – its four storeys reached at least 122 metres (400 feet), possibly even 152 metres (500 feet). Second, although our knowledge of the mechanical working of the lighthouse is limited, it incorporated some of the most advanced developments in engineering and design for its time.

The lighthouse stood on the island of Pharos, from which it takes its name, to the northwest of the main city. The island was a community in its own right, housed in a small walled town, and no doubt many of the residents worked as mechanics, labourers

or lookouts in the great tower. At one end of the island stood the lighthouse, a gleaming white stone structure built either of limestone or marble. At its base was a platform surrounded by a wall to protect it from the sea. This was where drinking water was stored.

The lowest storey of the lighthouse itself was square. Quite plain, it housed the rooms in which the maintenance staff and lighthouse-keepers were stationed. Lookouts could also be placed at the many windows. This part of the pharos also contained a ramp that gave access to the upper levels. This was probably a spiral – indeed it could have been a double spiral, with one ramp for people going up, another for those going down. In addition there may have been a simple but sturdy elevator at the centre of the spirals. This could have been used for transporting fuel up to the light quickly and efficiently.

The second storey was octagonal, and narrower than the storey below it. It probably contained only the access ramps and elevator, as did the small circular third storey above it. Above these two levels was the light itself. Its flames would have given a bright signal by night: mirrors were probably used to focus the light and direct it out to sea. During the daytime, smoke from the fire would have billowed out to provide the required signal. The mirrors provide one of the mysteries of the pharos: early accounts mentioned glass and 'transparent stone'. But it is more likely that the Alexandrians used a large polished metal reflector as polished metal was the usual material for mirrors in the ancient world.

At the most northeastern point of its island, the pharos stood guard over the eastern harbour of Alexandria. This was no accident, since the royal fleet was anchored here. Although its style was Hellenistic – the late Greek mode that Alexander brought to Egypt – the solid, monumental appearance of the lighthouse also recalled the appearance of some of the great Egyptian temples. Like many things in Alexandria, the pharos was cosmopolitan in its origins. Curiously, we do not know for certain the name of the architect responsible for this dual effect. It used to be thought that the pharos was the work of Sostratus, who is mentioned in a dedication reported by the writers Strabo and Lucian. But it is now thought that Sostratus was more likely to have been a wealthy courtier who paid for the lighthouse, so the name of the designer remains a mystery.

A seat of learning

The great library of Alexandria is famous because it was destroyed. It used to be thought that Caesar burned down the library during his struggle to take the city. But it is now thought that fires in the harbour destroyed only books that were being sent to the library, and that the main collection remained intact until the Christians burned the library down in AD 391.

Whoever dealt the final blow, they were wiping out an unrivalled tradition of learning. It was not simply a collection of books. The library formed the heart of a complex called the *museion*. A museion was literally a shrine where the muses could be worshipped, and such mouseia were common in ancient Greece. But by the time of the Ptolemies, the idea of a museion was much broader – the word suggested a cultural and intellectual complex where the muses could be worshipped by means of scholarly activity. The museion at Alexandria was founded by Ptolemy I, who wanted an institution based on the museion at Athens. He brought the philosopher Demetrius Phalerus to Alexandria to start the museion, which grew larger than its Athenian model. It consisted of the library itself, laboratories and observatories, together with a zoo, and facilities for scholars such as a dining room. There were probably also lecture halls. The activities of the museion were thus very varied. Both literary and scientific work was embraced, and the scholars almost certainly gave lectures as well as undertaking research. The museion filled the niche in Alexandrian society that a university fills today.

But the museion was not simply a university with a different name. It retained its status as a religious centre, and was presided over by a priest appointed by the king. With this royal patronage and with a body of scholars second to none, the museion flourished in the third century BC. Philosophers came from far and wide and for a while Alexandria was the intellectual centre of the world. But after this first great century, there was a transfer of intellectual leadership to native Alexandrians – to the exclusion of others from farther afield. Not surprisingly, the overall standard of scholarship declined, although the museion was still an important centre of learning within Egypt itself.

The library

Not unnaturally, the growing assembly of scholars in Alexandria needed a source of books. The famous library that fulfilled this need was not begun until the reign of Ptolemy II, well after the museion was founded. Like the museion, it enjoyed royal patronage, and the post of librarian was a royal appointment. We do not know a great deal about how the library was organized. We do not know, for example, whether it had its own accommodation for readers or whether it was simply a book store, with stacks of scrolls that were taken to readers in the museion itself.

But we can guess that it was well organized. There certainly seems to have been a methodical procedure for cataloguing new books – full details of the person who had brought the book to the library and where they had come from were recorded together with the sort of information (author, title, and so on) that one would expect in a modern library catalogue. There would also have been an office for scribes responsible for making copies of the books as they came in – this was essential in a culture in which printing was unknown. The scribes of Alexandria set high standards in the legibility of their work and the quality of their presentation.

Such high standards of organization and presentation were vital in such a large library. And large it was. The most reliable sources talk about almost half a million scrolls, but the majority of scrolls contained more than one work. They seem to have been divided between two buildings – a large library in the palace, where most of the books were kept and a smaller one, perhaps in the museion, which had about one tenth of the total holdings. Perhaps we can see here the origins of the modern librarian's habit of keeping many books in a private store or 'stack', while leaving only those most often consulted on open shelves. Or it may be that the smaller library contained a master set of material, with duplicates kept in store in the palace.

What sort of books did the library contain? Certainly, the librarians aimed at collecting as many works in Greek – in all subjects, from natural science to imaginative literature – as they could: these formed the core of Alexandrian culture. But, in keeping with the city's setting, works of Egyptian literature (in translation) were also collected, together with texts from Persia and the Bible lands.

Greek sculpture of the time of Alexander

The world of affairs

Alexandria was not simply a great seat of learning. Its founder had chosen the site because of its accessibility to shipping, and the city remained an important port, a business centre, and the home of kings. The harbour was perhaps the most magnificent feature of the city apart from the pharos. Whereas today the island on which the pharos stood is joined to the mainland by a substantial isthmus that has built up over the centuries, at the time of the Ptolemies it was connected only by an artificial causeway. Known as the *heptastadion* (it was seven stades long), it had several uses. It allowed people to pass easily from the main city to the island of Pharos; it enabled a supply of fresh water to be piped to the island; by dividing the harbour into two it reduced the effects of some of the treacherous currents that made this stretch of water difficult to navigate; and, by having two arches in the centre, ships could still pass through from one harbour to the other if necessary.

Of the two harbours created by the heptasadion, the eastern or Great Harbour was the most important. Some of the buildings of the royal palaces, which were situated on the promontory of Silsileh at the eastern end of the harbour, adjoined the quays. It was therefore natural that this should be the mooring place for the royal ships. But the Great Harbour was divided up by numerous jetties into different quays, and as well as the royal area, there were many places where other ships could dock. The waters were deep right up to the edge, so the largest ships of the time could come alongside and be unloaded with ease.

The royal palaces themselves were superb. We know little in detail about how they were built, but the records that do survive show that the offices of government were inside the palace precincts, so that the whole would have made a very large complex. Perhaps the closest parallel would be the Ottoman palace of Topkapi in Istanbul, where military headquarters, audience halls, offices, libraries, kitchens, and private apartments jostle together – again on an excellent site overlooking the sea. But the style would be classical rather than Islamic, and the overall effect would have been more spacious – apparently a large park was included in the grounds, and there would have been many broad courtyards.

What was life like in this Hellenized Egyptian city? In the beginning, the Egyptians were pushed to one side. All the responsible jobs went to the foreign colleagues and relatives of the Ptolemies and the only Egyptians who retained anything like their former status were the priests. Although the Greek community brought their own gods with them, the Egyptians continued to revere their own deities. And they even had some influence on the Greeks, who identified their god Dionysus with the Egyptian Osiris. There is no evidence that this was a real coming together of the two peoples, though. It was more a case of the enquiring minds of the Greeks coming into contact with a culture that was new to them and trying make it their own.

The Egyptians recognized the Ptolemies as their rightful rulers. In a way, they had no choice in the matter, but the Ptolemies wisely made it easier for them to stomach by claiming the title of pharaoh. But the different elements in Alexandrian society did not come very close – the Greeks kept to themselves and kept the powerful jobs; the Egyptians, to begin with at least, obeyed their masters; there was also a substantial Jewish population that made up a separate element.

Gradually the discontent of the Egyptians started to come to the surface. There was a revolt during the reign of Ptolemy III, and his successors had to deal with similar unrest. This led to greater power as the Egyptians began to move once more into positions of influence, and to a corresponding decline in the influence of the Greeks. By the time the Romans took over Alexandria and Egypt an enfeebled monarchy and a disorganized administration torn between Greek and Egyptian interests meant that the country was not difficult to dominate. The golden age of Alexandria was short-lived: for most of its history it has looked back on the brief blaze of glory at its beginning.

LEPTIS MAGNA

North African port, rebuilt by the Romans in civic splendour 46 BC–AD 211

One of the most successful parts of the Roman Empire was northern Africa. The Romans planted the fields of their African province with grain, they built roads and they constructed cities. By the first century BC the area we now know as Algeria was enjoying a boom, supplying grain far and wide.

The remains that the Romans left behind them reflect this prosperity. Cities such as Timgad had all the trappings of Roman towns – public buildings, amphitheatres, temples, and baths. In the fertile zone made up of the plains and valleys of Algeria one can see how the wealth provided by agriculture could bring about this luxury in the towns. But further to the east, in modern Libya, lies another city, just as magnificent, but surrounded by the arid Sahara. This town, Leptis Magna, was like a miniature Rome on the edge of the desert. In a matter of just over a century, a magnificent city was constructed, a city that was added to in later years and embellished with triumphal arches and monumental sculptures of superb quality. But why did the Romans choose to build here – in the far east of their remote southern province, on a road to nowhere but the desert?

Roman legionaries admire the temple in the forum. With its high podium and tall granite columns this building dominated the forum, which was one of the parts of the city rebuilt by the emperor Septimus Severus. The local people would have been constantly aware of the success of their fellow-citizen Severus, even though he probably never returned to his home town to see the buildings he had commissioned.

The beginnings

The story of Leptis Magna goes back a long way before the Romans. As early as the seventh century BC it had been a trading post of the Phoenicians. A trading people who hailed from the eastern shore of the Mediterranean, the Phoenicians travelled widely. Their most important city in northern Africa was Carthage, the site of which gave them a good base in the central southern Mediterranean from which to sail on their trading missions. But they needed another north African base nearer home, and Leptis suggested itself because it had a water supply and an inlet – the River Lebda – where ships could dock.

Leptis served the Phoenicians well, although it did not rival the importance of Carthage. It eventually became capital of one of three Carthaginian colonies, known as the 'Tripolis'. This new-found status established Leptis as a city of some importance. It had its own legal system and would certainly have had a harbour and storage facilities for the goods that the Phoenicians were buying and selling. But so extensive was the Roman reconstruction of the city that we know little about what it looked like in its early days.

The great advance for Rome in north Africa came in 146 BC, when they conquered Carthage. The repercussions for Leptis were major, but they did not come immediately. It was not until 46 BC that Julius Caesar brought the city into the empire, after decades of peaceful trade between Rome and the surviving Tripolis. A period of prosperity and rapid change was about to begin.

Romanizing the city

Leptis probably already had many of the features of a Roman city when it became part of the empire in 46 BC. There would have been administrative and public buildings built around a central forum, and, as we have seen, a harbour would have been essential. But the early years of Roman rule saw massive rebuilding programmes, which led to the city being given a new addition to its name – it became Leptis Magna ('Leptis the Great'), to distinguish it from another, smaller Leptis on the coast to the south of Carthage.

A truly Roman forum seems to have been the first requirement. A central paved area where citizens could meet, talk and walk, it was surrounded by temples and the basilica, the hall where the city's administration was carried out and the courts were held. The temples were imposing structures, built on high platforms, fronted by pillared porticos and approached via flights of steps.

From the forum, which was situated in the northeastern part of the city, quite near the sea, the main street of Leptis ran southwest. Smaller streets came off the main street at right-angles, to form the typical Roman grid-plan of the city. The main street contained important public buildings, including a spacious market, a building known as the *chalcidicum* (which may have been another market), the theatre, and further temples. All of

By the end of the reign of Severus, Leptis Magna was a truly classical city. Some buildings, like the marketplace (the rectangular courtyard containing two octagonal pavilions) had been rebuilt in the classical style quite early in the Roman period. Structures such as the temple and the basilica facing it across the forum were rebuilt in Severus' time. The harbour was also renovated and new warehouses were provided, but it was never to attract as much shipping as the local citizens hoped.

these were built between *c.*9 BC and AD 12, in the period when Leptis was establishing its identity as a truly Roman city.

The market is a good example of the buildings added at this time. Built in *c.*9–8 BC, it consisted of a long rectangular courtyard with arcading. In the middle were two elegant octagonal buildings, known as *pavilions*, which were also surrounded by pillars. The ruins today – and the mechanical line drawings that archaeologists have drawn to give an impression of what the market would have looked like new – give an impression of a severely classical building. There was little decoration apart from the corinthian capitals of the columns. But picture the market in use – thronging with traders and their customers – and a different image comes to mind. Between the columns stood the stalls. These consisted of marble tables that stood on supports carved with gryphons and dolphins.

There were also stalls around the octagonal pavilions – two on each side with a gap between the two central pillars to allow access to the area behind the stalls. The variety of produce, together with the fact that architraves above the columns were probably originally covered with painted plaster decoration, would have made the market a colourful centre to a cosmopolitan city. Roman, Punic, and native Libyan would have mingled together. This mixture of peoples is demonstrated by the stone in the market that was set up as a standard of measurement of length – it has the units of all three cultures engraved upon it.

The next stage of building was during the reign of the emperor Hadrian (AD 117–138). One of the most impressive monuments from this period was the Hadrianic Baths. It was here

that marble was used at Leptis for the first time. With their hot and cold rooms, open-air swimming pool, changing rooms and latrines, the baths were like so many others throughout the empire. A place for men to meet and talk business as well as to relax and bathe, they signal the fact that Leptis was truly a part of the empire where Roman habits and lifestyles were catching on.

The social life of Leptis Magna

But one should not imagine a city of transplanted Romans making life comfortable for themselves in northern Africa. Many – perhaps most – of the people of Leptis had their racial origins among the Phoenicians who came directly from the middle east or from Carthage to settle here. Even so, their society was arranged along Roman lines. There were the Roman social strata – slaves, workers, the urban middle classes, and a small, wealthy upper class of landowners. And there were the typical Roman pursuits – the social life of the baths and forum, chariot races at the circus, and gladiatorial combat in the amphitheatre.

And yet the Phoenicians left strong influences, if we look a little below the surface. For example, the gods who were worshipped at Leptis had Roman names, but they were really Phoenician deities. Even many of the citizens had middle eastern names. Sometimes they added Roman names to the Phoenician originals to produce bizarre hybrids. One prominent citizen, for example, was called Boncar Clodius; another was named Annobal Rufus Tabahpi, although he romanized his last name so that he became known as Annobal Rufus Tapapi.

The early benefactors

The family of Annobal Rufus was one of the most influential in Leptis Magna in the early period of Roman occupation. Annobal Rufus himself built the covered market and later, in AD 1–2, he sponsored the building of the theatre, on which his name is inscribed in both Latin and Punic, the language of Carthage. In AD 42 another member of the Tapapi family linked the theatre and the market by building a portico and a temple. Later still, in c.AD 62, a third Tapapi embellished the harbour with another portico. These men were among the first loyal citizens to make improvements to their city in this way.

The local emperor

The flowering of Leptis Magna came during the rule of Emperor Septimus Severus. Born in Leptis, Severus came from a family which contained several officers of the imperial government. His grandfather had been a prefect and his uncle was governor of the province of Africa. In spite of their success, the family kept their strong African connections; indeed, some members of his family stayed on at Leptis and never even learned Latin.

Severus, on the other hand, travelled widely. He had employment with his uncle the consul of Africa, then with the emperor Marcus Aurelius in Rome. Next he had a brief spell in Athens, then ruled the province of Upper Pannonia (in Austro–Hungary) before finally being proclaimed emperor in AD 193. Trained as a soldier, Severus pursued vigorous military campaigns when established as emperor. He defended the eastern frontiers of the empire and the trade routes that linked Rome with Asia. Nearer to home he campaigned in Egypt and Nubia, before going on his longest journey, to Britain, in AD 211. This journey was his last. Severus died at York the same year, about as far from his birthplace as he could get while staying within imperial territory. In fact there is no evidence to suggest that Severus ever returned to Leptis once he had been made emperor. But if he did not go there, he did not forget his home town, for it was during his reign that Leptis was endowed with its most ambitious monuments and its greatest buildings.

The buildings of Severus

The emperor's building projects took several different forms. Some, on the surface at least, were purely functional. Perhaps the most important of these was the extensive harbour development that was fitting to a town which had started life as a trading port. Many of the other buildings were more for show than anything else. A very good example was the monumental road, with columns and shops, that connected the old forum area with the new sector of the city. A new forum and basilica completed the impression of a city with rich and prosperous connections.

Ship from the harbour

The Severan arch

One of the most showy of Severus' buildings was a large triumphal arch standing at the junction of the city's two main roads. Built on a square plan, it was effectively four arches in one presenting a finely-carved arch, with enormous corinthian columns on either side, from whichever direction you approached it. The Severan arch was built from a core of limestone, but was faced with marble. This stone facing was carved with scenes glorifying the emperor. There are friezes showing the emperor with Empress Julia Domna and their sons; the killing of a sacrificial bull; the siege of a city and its capture by the emperor; groups of city magistrates and imperial soldiers; and scenes showing the emperor with various tutelary gods.

The Severan arch is one of the great works of Roman sculpture – the figures are carved with a fluent realism. One way in which this was achieved was a technique using a 'running drill'. This involved drilling a series of holes and breaking the spaces between them to produce a line. In the right hands this was a method that was both precise and expressive. And it allowed the sculptors to cover a large area of stone and to carve deeply – some of the incisions on the surviving fragments go 25 centimetres (10 inches) into the stone and they would have been even deeper before the surfaces wore away with age.

Many fragments of the arch have survived, but strangely no inscription has been found. This is odd because the Romans – great writers and carvers of inscriptions that they were – would certainly have left an explanation in stone of the reason why the arch was built and the events it commemorates. The arch is therefore something of a mystery. Some authorities think it celebrates the return of the emperor to his home city, but there is no written evidence for this. It is more likely that it was built by the relatives of Severus to mark a trium-

Fragment of sculpture from an archway

phal occasion in Rome. Or it could have been built in anticipation of a visit to Leptis that never occurred – perhaps something that was planned after Severus' visit to the northern reaches of the empire.

The forum

The most outstanding of the other buildings from Severus' time were around the new forum that was built south of the original forum. It was dominated by a temple and the basilica. The temple was especially noticeable, not simply because of its many pillars of pink Egyptian granite, but because it stood on a tall podium about 5.8 metres (19 feet) high and was reached by a broad flight of twenty-seven steps. Once at the top of the steps, the visitor could appreciate another surprising feature of the temple. The square panels that make up the bases of the columns were richly carved with scenes from the Gigantomachia. These were classical myths connected with the giants, in particular their battles with the gods, who defeated them with the aid of the hero Herakles. The giants themselves were extraordinary figures – large, muscular men from the knees up, but with bizarre serpent-like legs.

No doubt the people of Leptis shared some of the wonder of their less sophisticated ancestors for these fantastic warriors who rose up out of the earth and, when defeated, were thought to have been buried beneath the world's volcanoes. But the Romans probably had another motive for depicting the triumph of the gods over the giants on the greatest temple in the city. Representing the subjugation of barbarians by the Roman authorities, the scenes also would have acted as a warning about rebellion against the empire.

Many of these column bases, and other blocks of carved stone in the city, are signed with the names of their masons. It is one of the mysteries of Leptis that many of these names are not Roman, Punic, or Libyan as one might expect, but Greek. We do not know the story of these Greek workers. They may have worked the stone in their native land – the fact that much of the carved marble was imported from Greece supports this theory, although the workers may have travelled to Leptis with their raw material. But measurements taken from columns and other fragments on the site have shown the sort of slight differences that suggest 'prefabricated' units made overseas and assembled at Leptis.

The Roman port

Leptis had always been a port. A sheltered natural harbour at the mouth of the River Lebda made it as ideal for this function in the time of Severus as it had during the Carthaginian period. It was no doubt due to the influence of Severus that the harbour area was refurbished. Warehouses were set up along the two bars that curve into the Mediterranean from the mouth of the river. A lighthouse was built on the outermost tip of the eastern bar.

No doubt these excellent facilities were well used – both by passing ships on their way east and west along the coast of northern Africa and by ships that came specifically to Leptis to supply the city with everything the empire had to offer. They would return with the luxury goods that Africa supplied to Rome – precious metals and gems, ivory, ebony, slaves, and animals.

While Leptis was supported by the emperor and his family, this trade worked well. But after the Severan period there seems to have been a decline. No doubt the Romans found easier ways of getting the goods they had obtained via Leptis and continued with their trade with Africa by going further east. Here they had access not only to luxury goods but to a more basic resource – grain. It was always a weakness of Leptis that, although it had some agricultural land nearby (olives were an important crop), it was too near the desert to produce very much food or to create much of a market for any goods produced in the city. So, without Severus' patronage, the city fell on hard times and the ambitious harbour complex languished unused.

The fate of Leptis Magna

During the fourth century AD Leptis was a much quieter place than it had been. Buildings on the edges of the city were abandoned as the population declined. An attempt to redefine the city was made when a new wall was put up. No doubt this also offered some protection against the approaching desert sands. In AD 455, North Africa started to suffer from invasions by Germanic peoples. They were not interested in restoring order to the troubled town and simply pulled down the walls.

There was a brief return to order when the walls were rebuilt under the Byzantine emperor Justinian. But the Byzantine walls only enclosed a tiny area of the city – the region around the harbour. From AD 533 to 643, when the Arabs invaded, a small community hung on next to the harbour, which was rapidly silting up. The Arabs found little of value when they arrived, and soon left the once-great city to the encroaching sands.

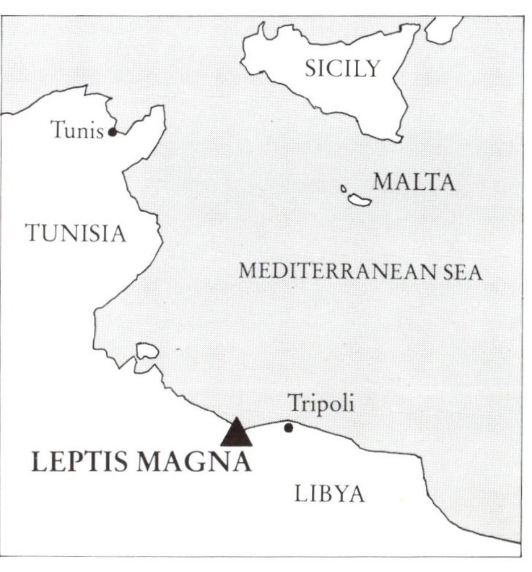

GREAT ZIMBABWE

African stone enclosures AD 1200–1450, at the centre of a network of agriculture and trade

About 240 kilometres (150 miles) north of the Limpopo River, in the country we now know as Zimbabwe, lie some of the most extraordinary ruins in the African continent. These stone ruins were once also called Zimbabwe, a name that derives from words of the local Shona language – either 'dzimba daz babwe' (houses of stone), or 'dzimba woye' (venerated houses, in other words the houses of the ruler or chief). They are now known as Great Zimbabwe, to distinguish them from the name of the country in which they lie. In fact there are numerous stone ruins on the high plateau, some 900–1,200 metres (3,000–4,000 feet) above sea level, between the Zambezi and Limpopo Rivers. Great Zimbabwe is simply the largest and most archaeologically important.

The buildings that have survived at Great Zimbabwe are round or oval stone enclosures that originally contained dwellings made of daga – a clay soil used to bind together fine gravel and finished on the surface with a smoothly applied layer of clay to give a hard, attractive finish. The people of Great Zimbabwe were highly accomplished in the craft of daga building. Their huts were circular, between 3–6 metres (10–20 feet) in diameter, and had walls 30–45 centimetres (12–18 inches) thick. The floors were finished in the same way as the outer walls, and there were doors in strong timber frames. But the daga construction was not solid enough to support the heavy roofs of timber and thatch that were favoured at Great Zimbabwe, so these had to be held up by rows of wooden posts that surrounded the outer wall. Inside, the huts had either one or two rooms according to size, and most contained daga platforms probably used for sleeping.

Traders travelling inland from the ports of eastern Africa may well have stopped at Great Zimbabwe, leaving beads, ironwork, and cowrie shells. The enclosure would also have been a centre for the local exchange of goods, with agricultural produce coming in from the surrounding countryside and craft items going in the opposite direction.

The largest of the stone enclosures is known today as the Elliptical Building. Its walls describe an oval 100 metres (300 feet) across at the broadest point, and the masonry is of a very high standard, built with blocks of uniform size and decorated along the top with a zigzag pattern. Inside there was room for several buildings of daga as well as daga platforms (which may have contained religious statues), smaller stone enclosures (that probably also contained daga huts), and a mysterious conical tower built of solid masonry.

One of the most baffling riddles concerning the Elliptical Building is its double wall. The superbly built outer wall encloses a less well constructed inner one that seems to have formed the original boundary of the building. Why do these two walls exist side by side? One theory has it that the ruler ordered the new wall to be built, but did not allow the original wall to be demolished until the new one was completed. This would therefore ensure that the site remained well defended throughout the operation. But it is hard to understand why the inner wall was not completely demolished when the new defences were complete.

Perhaps a clue lies in the purpose of the walls. The situation of Great Zimbabwe, exposed on the high plateau, suggests to some authorities that the main purpose of the buildings was not so much to defend their occupants as to indicate their status. If this is the case, double walls might have been even better status symbols than single ramparts.

All the walls were built without mortar. They were started at one end and built to the full height. The wall was then extended out along the ground. The lower courses of the wall itself could thus be used to give the masons access to the upper courses eliminating the need for scaffolding. There were no windows in the walls, and the wall curved gently so that corners were not needed. The result was a strong but simple form of construction that has lasted well.

The size of the Elliptical Building and the other ruins that surround it, together with the quality of the surviving work, has made Great Zimbabwe one of the most misunderstood of archaeological monuments. For such was the prejudice of the archaeologists who first investigated the site at the end of the last century that they could not believe that the indigenous people of the area could have been capable of creating anything so sophisticated. They found it especially unlikely that the local people would have built in stone, a material they saw as unusual in Africa, in spite of the many stone ruins in the area around Great Zimbabwe.

The community of Great Zimbabwe AD 1300

The stone ruins that have survived at Great Zimbabwe today would have been the centre of a community living in houses made of more perishable materials – clay and thatch. This community would have supplied the workforce and the skills in stoneworking needed to build the walls, and the necessary administration that kept the community going.

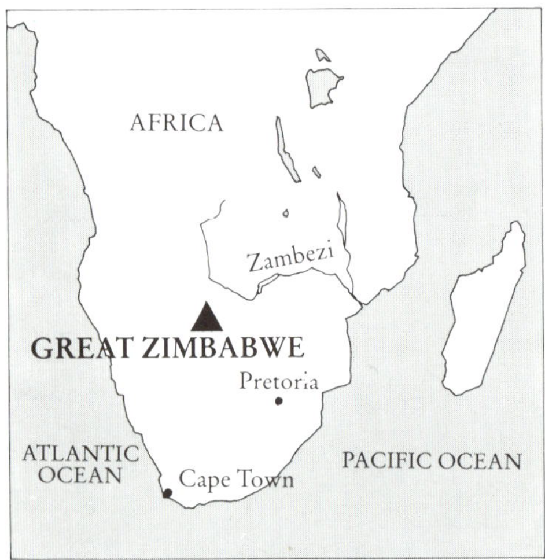

Hints of a trade in gold gave some Europeans the excuse to speculate that they had found the mythical site of King Solomon's mines, a theory that resulted in an unseemly scramble for hidden treasure, and the removal of much useful archaeological evidence as a result. A rival theory brought the Arabs of northern Africa to Great Zimbabwe and attributed the building work to them.

Sadly, such theories tell us more about the prejudices of nineteenth-century archaeologists than they do about the history of Great Zimbabwe. More recent investigators have looked at the site more dispassionately, and have found nothing to suggest that the walls were not built and planned by local people. Against the argument that stoneworking was unusual in this part of the world between the thirteenth and fifteenth centuries AD when Great Zimbabwe was built, is that one can trace the way in which the local masons learned their craft. The earliest walls are built rather unevenly, with different shaped blocks in meandering courses. But the later stonework is superb – with blocks of uniform shape and size laid in straight, even courses. In this light, it hardly looks as if a race of master-masons appeared out of nowhere to teach the natives how to build in stone.

What is more, stone walls were not

reserved solely for the elite. True enough, the ruler of the area probably lived in the great Elliptical Building. But there were many surrounding stone enclosures for other people, many of them almost as large, though not quite so well built, as the Elliptical Building itself. Such a settlement pattern does not look like the work of a foreign invader.

The people of Great Zimbabwe

So who built and lived at Great Zimbabwe? By the fourth century AD, the area had been settled by subsistence farmers. They grew grain, raised some livestock, and lived in huts made of daga, probably not unlike those that were to be built at Great Zimbabwe centuries later. They could also make iron, and early Iron Age objects from this period have been found beneath some of the ruins at Great Zimbabwe.

In the ninth or tenth century there was a change. A new people, who relied more on cattle breeding (and for whom cattle probably had some religious significance) appeared in the area. They were a successful people, settling new lands and building new villages, starting to mine gold, and beginning to build in stone. They must also have been traders, since many glass beads from outside the immediate area have been discovered on their sites and in their graves. These people, or people who developed in a similar way, must have founded Great Zimbabwe. Their agriculture gave them sustenance, their production of gold gave them the wherewithal to trade, and their newfound skill in stoneworking gave them the ability to produce rather more permanent settlements than their forerunners had managed. The foundations for a long period of prosperity had been laid.

The extent of the stone buildings can give us an idea of how many people there were. Estimates are bound to be tentative, but with knowledge of roughly how many huts there were in each enclosure and how many people modern Shona people accommodate in each hut, Peter Garlake, the foremost authority on Great Zimbabwe, has come up with a figure of between 100 and 200 adults living in the ruins. There would have been a much larger population outside the walls, and Garlake has estimated the total population at somewhere between 1,000 and 2,500 adults. Such a population could have undertaken the work of building the enclosures as well as providing artisans and labourers in the craft workshops and in the fields.

As well as this core population, there were the other stone enclosures in the surrounding countryside, which were probably under the control of the ruler in the Elliptical Building at Great Zimbabwe. These 'provincial courts' (as Garlake calls them) extended the scope of Great Zimbabwe's influence, but even so the number of people involved was quite small – probably no more than 750 people in the outlying ruins, and rather more living in daga homes outside.

Each of the provincial courts had lands that stretched from the watershed down to the low veldt. This meant that the farming people could move around according to seasonal conditions. In the rainy season the high plateau near the watershed would be best. There would be plenty of water for grazing the cattle and no danger from the tsetse fly, which would make the veldt uninhabitable at this time of the year. But in the dry season, after the departure of the tsetse fly, they would go down to the veldt to graze their stock. This life on the move corresponds to the settlement patterns of the outlying regions.

The power of the Shona

Yet these small communities had power and wealth. Much of this came from trade. Imported items such as bowls from Persia and dishes from China have been uncovered amongst the ruins. These have not appeared in great numbers, leading to the suggestion that they may have been occasional gifts or purchases from merchants passing through who were trading in different commodities. Objects discovered in larger numbers include ironwork, brass wire, glass beads, and cowrie shells. The beads, in particular, are similar to those found on the east coast of Africa, and it may be that Great Zimbabwe was a stopping-off place for merchants travelling inland from the eastern ports.

Much has been made of another source of the wealth of the Shona people – gold. It is true that there was gold in the hills to the north of the town. But it is unlikely that there were ever the great storehouses of treasure the early explorers hoped to find, or that the proponents of the 'King Solomon's Mines' theory were convinced were lurking somewhere beneath the ruins.

It seems unlikely that the original inhabitants of the town – or the people with whom they traded – valued gold very highly anyway. Of the objects found most are bracelets and anklets made of gold wire. The fact that very similar jewellery has also been discovered made of copper and bronze, and that there is little difference in quality between pieces made of the different metals, suggests that gold was not held in higher esteem than these other metals.

Carved soapstone bird

The craftworkers

It may be that the skill in making items of iron was as important to the people of Great Zimbabwe as those made of metals thought more precious today. There is a great deal of evidence that ironworking was a flourishing craft in the town. The iron products are impressive in their quantity. Arrowheads, spearheads, knife blades, axeheads, and hoes have all been uncovered. Archaeologists have also discovered many of the ironworkers' tools – tongs for picking up lumps of red-hot metal and hammers for beating it into shape, as well as tools used in wire-making.

The Shona were particularly adept at beaten metalwork, and they used an unusual technique of hammering an object inwards from either edge. This produced spearheads with a pronounced ridge along the centre where the two sets of hammer-blows met. There was an advantage to this in that it gave the object extra strength. Interestingly enough, Shona metalworkers of more recent times used a similar technique.

Other crafts practised by the people of Great Zimbabwe included pottery. They produced rather basic pots made by coiling long 'sausages' of clay in circles – they did not have the potter's wheel. There pots were also limited in size. It is unlikely that they had any success in trading them and so were probably intended for domestic use only. A craft which might have brought them more success in trading was spinning and weaving. Hundreds of discs with holes at their centres have been found – probably the whorls used to weight wooden spindles. The Shona are known to have grown cotton since the beginning of the sixteenth century – they may well have been harvesting it before this time during the Great Zimbabwe period.

Sacred symbols

Some of the objects found at Great Zimbabwe are a great deal more mysterious than tools and spindle whorls. Amongst these are carvings of birds, made in grey-green soapstone. About 35 centimetres (14 inches) high, these appear to have been mounted on columns 1 metre (3 feet) tall. Although the birds are well carved it is impossible to distinguish their species – these carvings are more stylized than realistic.

Early explorers also found columns that were not topped with bird statues. Some of these were placed on the tops of the enclosure's outer walls, others were arranged in groups on daga platforms. These columns and statues, clearly not useful in any practical sense, were almost certainly religious objects. The grouped columns on platforms especially suggest that these places were sacred areas. One suggestion is that the columns were memorials to the dead. Ancestors have long played an important part in Shona religion, and some central African peoples still use similar-shaped objects to appease the spirits of their dead. So it is not too fanciful to imagine people coming to these 'altars' to give offerings of food to their ancestors.

Another clue to these symbols would be the most mysterious structure in Great Zimbabwe, the great conical tower. This is a solid stone circular construction built near the outer wall in the southeastern corner of the Elliptical Building. It is 5.4 metres (18 feet) in diameter at the base and rises to a height of 9 metres (30 feet). It was obviously the focal point of the whole compound and, fronted by a large stepped platform, it must have served some ceremonial purpose. Its shape is reminiscent of the daga bins used until the last century by local people to store their grain.

It has therefore been plausibly suggested that the tower could be a symbolic grain bin, beneath which the ruler of Great Zimbabwe would proudly stand to receive tribute in the form of grain from outlying territories. If the ancestor-theory of the local religion is also true, we can imagine the ruler accepting the tribute on behalf of his forebears as well as himself. This ceremony may have been combined with some form of fertility ritual. The shape of the tower would remind the participants of the fully stocked grain bins that they would have at the end of the next harvest.

Such an interpretation is persuasive, and it reminds us that, even though the Shona benefitted from wealth derived from trade, agriculture would still have played a vital role in the economy of this rural community. What is more, control of this essential resource – the soil's fertility – gave the inhabitants of the Elliptical Building great power over their subjects.

The decline of a community

Great Zimbabwe was a highly successful community. By exploiting the potential of the countryside for agriculture, the geographical position that allowed trade, and the local stone that lent itself so well to building, the people of Great Zimbabwe adapted well to their environment. At no time was this more true than during the period when the stone buildings were made and occupied – the thirteenth to the fifteenth centuries AD.

So why were the bastions of the Elliptical Building and the surrounding enclosures abandoned by their inhabitants? European archaeologists, who tended to overestimate the wealth of the trade in gold, used to put the blame on the coming of Portuguese traders who took over control over the east coast of Africa. In terms of time this is not far out. Great Zimbabwe seems to have gone into decline and stopped trading during the sixteenth century. But Portuguese traders wanted as much as any others to exploit the route inland to the gold fields on which Great Zimbabwe stood, and the town would have been in a good position to trade with the newcomers or at least to control their trade across the continent – the arrival of the Europeans ought not to have wiped out the local people.

A more likely cause of the decline, according to more contemporary thought, is agricultural failure. This could have taken one of many forms – exhaustion of the land as a result of overcultivation; cattle disease; or a series of droughts. Whatever the cause, the result was famine and a drastic reduction in the population of the area. This may have been enough to open the gate to the people of the middle Zambezi area, who seem to have taken over the trade with the coast and increased in wealth as the fortunes of Great Zimbabwe declined.

PUEBLO BONITO
CHICHEN ITZA
TENOCHTITLAN
COPAN
MACHU PICCHU
EASTER ISLAND

NEW WORLD

It is one of the clichés about America that it is a continent without a history. Until recently this has been substantially true, to the extent that the records of the peoples of America have been very sparse – at least those dating from before the arrival of the Europeans. This fact has tended to make people forget that America has a long and rich prehistory. It is thought that the first people arrived in North America by way of a land bridge from Siberia some time between 40,000 and 25,000 years ago. Gradually these people moved south and east, hunting animals such as the woolly mammoth and the giant buffalo, and gathering plant food. By 10,000 years ago the people had moved across the whole continent.

Round 300 BC the people of Mexico had begun to cultivate the crops that were to provide a rich source of food in the area for millenia to come – corns, beans, chilies, squash, and avocados. Without crops like these, both nourishing and suitable to the climate and the terrain, the extraordinary succession of civilizations that were to come and go in Central America would not have been able to flourish.

The first of these cultures was the Olmec (*c.*1200 BC–AD 400). These people lived in an area around San Lorenzo, a region consisting of a mixture of mountains and plains, with little building stone. They therefore built in clay, and their clay pyramids were the forerunners of similar stone structures made by later Central American peoples. The Olmec were also superb sculptors.

Two other important features of Central American civilization, the calendar and writing, also appeared with the Olmecs. But these emerged at the very end of the Olmec period, allowing them only limited use of these inventions. Similarly, the Olmecs did not develop the city quickly enough to become a fully fledged civilization.

The Olmecs were followed by the Maya, who shared a common group of languages and occupied an area including Guatemala, the Yucatan peninsula, and parts of El Salvador, Honduras, and Belize. The achievements of the Maya in hieroglyphic writing, sculpture, and architecture mark them as the first fully developed American civilization. The lowland Maya, in particular, have left a notable legacy. Maya architecture was dominated by great stone pyramids, their sculpture included carved stone stelae commemorating rulers and their deeds and marking the passage of time in terms of the Maya calendar.

The city of Copan, in western Honduras, has been selected to represent the Maya in this book. It could easily have been one of a number of other cities, such as Tikal or Palenque. But Copan, although it is at the eastern extreme of the Maya region, has many typical Maya features – pyramids, carved stelae, large public plazas – together with a unique beauty.

The Maya were followed by the Toltecs, a people who flourished between the tenth and twelfth centuries AD. Named after their capital city of Tollan or Tula, 55 kilometres (35 miles) north of Mexico City, they dominated the north-central and western areas of Mexico, and the northern part of the Yucatan peninsula. Represented here by their great city of Chichen Itza, the Toltecs were influenced by the Maya. Indeed they took over much Maya territory and it is not always that easy for the non-specialist to see where Maya work ends and Toltec begins. Although the two cultures were similar, the Toltec seems to have been more dominated by rituals involving human sacrifice.

The Toltecs were eventually followed by the last of the great Central American cultures, the Aztecs. They are more familiar to people brought up in the European tradition, since they were the people the Europeans encountered in Mexico. The story of their abrupt rise and fall is embodied here in Tenochtitlan, their capital on the site of modern Mexico City.

Machu Picchu represents the Inca culture in this book, the other famous American civilization that demands inclusion. With its more extensive remains of domestic buildings it tells us more about how people lived their daily lives than many another American site. It is also a unique testimony to mankind's ability to settle successfully in the most improbable place.

North America yields fewer obviously mysterious places. But its prehistoric sites, such as Pueblo Bonito, have unique fascination – as well as uncanny similarities with settlements from much earlier periods in other parts of the world. A comparison of the architecture of Pueblo Bonito with that of the much earlier Catal Hüyük in Turkey shows how people at different times and in different places often hit on similar very architectural solutions in their efforts to provide protection and shelter.

COPAN

Classic Maya city of about AD 725, rich in temples and carved stone stelae

In western Honduras, on a sixty-acre site in a valley near the border with Guatemala, lies the Maya city of Copan. It is neither the first nor the largest of the great Maya sites, but it is one with a special character. With its two great plazas and their stunningly carved pyramids, its numerous carved stelae, and its extraordinary hieroglyphic stairway bearing the largest known collection of Maya glyptic writing, it is a unique site but one that sums up many of the mysteries that surround the early Central American civilizations.

The first and most fundamental question that the visitor asks is: How did people of such sophistication get here in the first place? They came very early and developed very gradually. The first people, probably Indians migrating from the north, arrived in Mexico and the surrounding areas around 10,000 BC. They lived by hunting and followed their prey, and did not settle down until the development of agriculture, some time between 6500 and 1500 BC. As they learned to cultivate crops such as corn, avocados, beans, and tomatoes, they abandoned their nomadic life and, towards the end of this period, began to gather together in villages.

Increased skill in food production meant a rising population, larger villages, and more specialist workers – potters, weavers, traders, and priests. So by about 500 BC, villages on and around the Yucatan peninsula started to turn into towns, and started to build the striking pyramidal temples that were to become the hallmark of Maya civilization. This was the time of the Olmec culture, the first of the Mexican civilizations, which developed and flourished from 1200 to 100 BC. The Olmec, who inhabited the lowlands of the Gulf coast, had numbers and writing – in fact they were probably the people who invented these concepts in Central America. They also bequeathed to the Maya important religious symbolism – not just the idea of the pyramid-temple, but also some of the ways in which the gods were portrayed. The jaguar, for example, so central in Maya culture, was an Olmec symbol.

During the heyday of the Olmec, other centres in Mexico were starting to develop. In the Valley of Oaxaca, for example, the city of Monte Alban grew up, stimulated partly by contact with the Olmec, partly by the need of the local people to create their own independent urban base. Meanwhile, to the north, the city of Teotihuacan was expanding in a similar way. It went further to become the centre of its own empire and to herald the Classic period of Maya civilization, AD 300–900. Copan, in the form in which we see its ruins today, is a product of this Classic period, although recent work suggests that the city was founded by the Olmec much earlier.

At Copan, as at many Maya cities, the ball game was a crucial part of the ritual life. This player's headdress shows how lavish the costumes of the participants could be.

The Maya world

The Central American civilizations of this period had several common features that set them apart from other settlements in the New World. Their people could write, using a form of hieroglyphics that is still in the process of being deciphered, and carved these signs on stone stelae and wrote them on folded 'books' made of fig-bark paper or animal skins. They were advanced in their knowledge of astronomy and had an elaborate calendar system involving a repeating view of history that enabled them both to record the past and to predict the future at the same time. They played a strange quasi-religious ball game in courts set aside for this purpose. They had a complex religion with many gods and the familiar pyramidal temples. And they were preoccupied with sacrifice – both with the sort of self-sacrifice entailed in drawing blood from one's body and with the sacrifice of human life.

It was a sophisticated culture but it had surprising limitations. Metalworking was not mastered until quite late, and when it did develop it was for luxury and ceremonial items, not for tools. Perhaps this was less of a disadvantage than it seems since the Maya were superb stoneworkers and could produce razor-sharp stone-cutting tools. Another lack was wheeled transport. They had the wheel – wheeled toys have been found – but relied on human labour to carry heavy loads. And although they were highly successful arable farmers they nevertheless had little or no experience of domesticating animals.

The city in the southeast

Copan owes much of its considerable character to its position in the southeastern part of Maya territory. Geographically it belongs to the highland

The city of Copan AD 725

Although only a selected few could attend the ceremonies that took place on top of the pyramids, the open spaces in the city could accommodate a great number of people. They could look in awe at the tall pyramids and read their people's history in the carved stone stelae in the plazas.

zone of the Maya territory and we can imagine it in its clearing in the tropical forest, the local greenish stone reflecting some of the colours of the foliage. But culturally it belongs to the lower central areas, its pyramids and other monuments mirroring the style of the cities further north in the Yucatan peninsula.

At Copan many of the important religious buildings are given extra height by being set on a raised stone platform, which European explorers immediately dubbed the 'acropolis'. Amongst the temples on the acropolis is the most famous, the temple of the hieroglyphic stairway. In front of the acropolis is the other large ceremonial area of the city, the Great Plaza. Here there are more temples, together with more open space, punctuated with the carved stone stelae that are another of Copan's most celebrated features.

The local stone lends itself well to carving, and the sculptors of Copan built up impressive skills when using it. Their stelae (some as tall as 4 metres/13 feet), altars, and decorative carvings on temple doorways and facades, give us some of our most vivid pictures of the Maya gods – the young rain-god, and the maize-god with foliage from the corn plant in his headdress, for example. Their faces are vigorously carved, but the rest of their bodies seem to disappear in a riot of decoration. One of the impressive

things about these sculptures is their realism. Unlike many Maya carvings, they give the impression of real portraits – of a round-faced, slant-eyed people who were shorter and stouter than the people represented on sculptures in other Maya centres.

It is important to remember that what we see today is only the city's ceremonial centre – almost all the buildings are religious. The people would have lived in more basic houses – probably of wood – which surrounded the central precinct and have long since perished. And the indication is that the residential area was extensive. Archaeologists have estimated a population as large as 40,000 for the great Maya city of Tikal in the heart of the central Maya area. Copan would have been smaller, but still had many thousands of homes.

The scribes and their calendar

At least one traveller has found something of the atmosphere of a university town in Copan. The profusion of inscriptions and the high quality of the surviving art seem to suggest a place steeped in Maya lore and learning. This was no more than an impression until recently when one of the large buildings known as palaces on the site was found to be dedicated to the Monkey-man scribes. The Monkey-men were a pair of figures in the Maya mythology of the underworld who were the patrons of scribes, artists, and dancers.

The palace of the Monkey-man scribes may therefore have belonged to a high-ranking scribe and his family. The scribes were an important class in Maya society. They probably played the role of priests (there is no evidence for a separate priesthood during the Classic period), and they were responsible for working out the calendar – which gave Maya society its most important way of making sense of life and history.

The scribes of Copan were particularly influential in their work on the lunar calendar. In AD 682 they began a system of calculating this on the principle that a lunar month lasts 29.53020 days. Since today's astronomers reckon this figure to be 29.53059, the scribes of Copan were clearly capable of making very exact calculations. Their methods eventually spread to other Maya centres.

The role of the city

Maya civilization did not make up a unified empire like so many civilizations in the Old World. It was more like a loose collection of city states, although these states did not exist in a vacuum. Each of the main centres – such as Tikal, Copan, Uxmal, and Chichen Itza – had a territory surrounding it which embraced agricultural land and smaller urban centres. Typical of these is Quirigua, about 48 kilometres (30 miles) north of Copan, a site that is not remarkable except that, like Copan itself, it contains some remarkable stone carvings. But for the Maya it was important because it had a source of obsidian, that glass-like mineral that could be sharpened to make valuable tools. It gave the rulers of Copan great power to have obsidian mines within their territory and they did what they could to hang on to them.

Glyphs from a Maya calendar

On top of the pyramid

The Maya used their pyramids very differently from the ancient Egyptians. Whereas an Egyptian pyramid was built to contain a sarcophagus, Maya pyramids were meant to be ceremonial centres. Each one was topped by a temple that was approached by a long staircase. Probably only a small group of elite citizens (mainly the scribes who were also priests) would be allowed to climb to the top of the pyramid and perform the ceremonies.

But many others would watch in the plaza below, or crowd on to the stairs. From the top of the pyramids the 'priests' would burn incense and might even offer human sacrifices to the rain-god or the maize-god, in the hope of benefitting from weather that would give a good harvest and prosperity in the coming year. Although the ceremony itself, taking place on high, would seem rather remote, the people would watch spellbound, the angled lines of the pyramid leading their eyes to the action taking place on top of the pyramid.

If there was going to be a sacrifice, the ritual would be attended by four prominent elders. These four men appeared in various Maya ceremonies and were known as the *chacs*. Their presence was to honour the rain-god Chac Xib Chac. The chacs also had a practical role to play in the sacrifice. It was they who held down the victim – taking one limb apiece – so that any struggle would be minimized and decorum (if one can speak of decorum when describing such a grisly performance) would be maintained.

In place of a human sacrifice, animals might be killed as offerings. One authority, Michael D. Coe, believes that during the Classic period the sacrifice of dogs, squirrels, iguanas, and birds was far more widespread than human sacrifice. Another alternative to the sacrifice of life was mutilation. The Maya were impressed by any spilling of blood, small or large. They would mutilate themselves by drawing blood from the most sensitive parts of the body – lips, tongue, cheeks, ears, and penis. Stingrays and, later, sharp pointed metal needles would be used to make the necessary wound. The Maya had one of the most gruesome religions humankind has known – and it became even more gruesome in later periods.

On occasions when there was no sacrifice other forms of ceremony might take place on top of the pyramid. In one famous example, the *chilam*, a kind of soothsayer, might be present. He would reach a trance and make oracular statements which the scribes would then have to interpret.

The gods of the Maya

Who were the gods that inspired these extraordinary rituals? They were many and various. Most of them seem to have been the offspring of Itzamna and Ix Chel, the two senior deities. Their particular areas of concern show the aspects of life that were most important to the Maya. Itzamna was the god of writing and learning; Ix Chel was the goddess of childbirth, medicine, and weaving.

Other prominent deities had to do with the mercurial climate of Central America. The four chacs or rain-gods appeared frequently and, as we have seen, were represented in various Maya rituals. Ah Kinchil, the sun-god, was also prominent. Each social class had its own deity, and there were gods of agriculture, hunting, poetry, dancing, and a host of other activities. What was more, each god had a counterpart in the underworld (that of Ah Kinchil, for example, was the famous jaguar god), and many of the gods had counterparts of the opposite sex. The pantheon also grew as time went by. It was not until later, for example, that Kukulcan or Quetzalcoatl, the plumed serpent god of the ruling classes, became prominent. It is little wonder that it is difficult to see who is who in Maya carvings and inscriptions.

Quetzalcoatl

Rituals of life and death

As one would expect from a people obsessed by the order of the calendar and the seasons, the Maya lived according to a well regulated regime, guided by religion and custom from birth to death. In early life children underwent a ceremony of baptism, at which four of the elders of the city were present, together with a priest or scribe who would perform purification rituals with holy water and incense.

After this time, according to reports recorded after the Spanish conquest, boys would live apart from their families. They would paint themselves black (the colour of Maya warriors) and learn the skills they would need in adulthood – especially the skills of war. Girls would be brought up by their mothers, and the sexes would only reunite in marriage, after which time the men would abandon their black body paint for the more colourful decorations – including tattoos – for which the adult Maya men were famous.

An adult Maya would find himself or herself born into a fairly rigid social class system. At the top were the great nobles who owned land and were the leaders in politics and war. Their ranks probably also provided the more senior scribes. Lower down were free commoners, and lower still, slaves who worked for the nobles. Most of these bondsmen were probably prisoners of war.

Death brought the final rituals, and the final segregation. Most people were buried under their own homes with grave goods consisting of their belongings and with food put in their mouths. Nobles were allowed the privilege of mortuary temples above their sepulchres.

War and peace

Maya society was dominated by war. The division of the Maya lands into numerous city states made for frequent clashes over territory and resources, and the troops of one city would often make an unannounced raid on another town. This would be followed by a formal battle, in which the main body of spear-carrying foot soldiers, dart throwers and sling shooters marched together with their mascots and idols. After an initial assault, freeform combat would again establish itself when one side reached the city precincts of the opposition, although, amongst the chaos of pillage and destruction, the main objective would still be to capture the leaders of the enemy, who would usually be beheaded.

But fighting, bloodthirsty as it was, took up a small amount of the time for the average Maya adult. The day-to-day necessities of food production were far too pressing to be ignored for long. Fruitful agriculture played a vital part in the success of the Maya cities, especially those in the lowlands. The same crops that the forerunners of the Maya had cultivated continued to be grown – corn, pulses, squashes, chilies – the people cutting away the forest as their need for farmland increased. Tree felling must have been difficult without metal tools, and it may be that some form of ring-barking was used to kill the trees before they were pulled down.

At the time of the Spanish conquest, Maya families kept their own kitchen gardens, with vegetables and fruit trees, to provide a supplementary source of food. It may be that such gardens also existed in the Classic period, when Copan was at the height of its power. The Maya also hunted wild animals such as deer and wild pigs using darts fired by a type of spear-thrower called an *atlatl*, and also used snares and pitfall traps. Fishing provided another important source of food. A particularly ingenious technique was used to catch fish, involving the use of drugs (such as the leaves of the aptly-named fish-fuddle tree) in the water to knock out the fish.

A Classic city

Copan's period of glory coincided with the Classic period of the Maya civilization. This civilization's fall came about with the rise of the Toltec, an equally sophisticated but still more barbaric people whose stronghold was in the northern Yucatan, in the cities of Tula and Chichen Itza. From here, the Toltec captured much territory in the central Maya area, but they tended to ignore more southern cities like Copan. Yet Copan did not last. Perhaps because it lost its all-important hinterland, it gradually declined in prosperity towards the end of the Classic period, and at some point during the Post-classic era the people simply seem to have moved away.

But although southern cities like Copan lost their importance as ceremonial centres, the Maya themselves did not disappear. The ancestors of the present people of the Yucatan peninsula and of parts of Guatemala and Honduras, they continued to thrive in the lowlands and amongst the lush tropical forest that eventually reclaimed their architectural ruins.

CHICHEN ITZA

One of the greatest cities of the Toltec people dating from around AD 1000

Some of the places described in this book are mysterious because it is difficult to untangle the myths that surround them from the realities of what actually happened in their history, or what remains of their buildings. Babylon is such a place, steeped in myths that have become part of its history. In Central America the city of Chichen Itza offers a similar mix of history and myth, similarly difficult to disentangle.

Chichen Itza is a city in northeastern Yucatan. It has many of the features of a Classic Maya site – the extensive plazas, pyramidal temples, ball court, and stone carvings. But the site is more complex than many a Maya city. First of all, it is very large – the ball court, for example, is the biggest in all Central America. Second, it seems to have been built in two distinct periods. Third, the artistic style of the second period is very different from the first and from other Maya cities like Copan. The carvings show more warlike scenes, more processions of warriors, and more scenes of human sacrifice. It seems likely that this change in artistic motifs mirrored a change in the civilization that produced them. What brought about this change?

The coming of the Toltec

The evidence of the art at Chichen Itza suggests that there were close links between the city and Tula, the capital of the coming power in the Yucatan between AD 950 and 1150, the Toltec. The briefest of glances at both centres shows striking similarities. Friezes of soldiers, jaguars, and people wearing butterfly pectorals on their chests appear at both sites. Another common feature is a sculptural figure called the *chacmool*. This is a life-size human male lying on his back with knees bent and the head pointing towards the right; he supports the weight of his upper body on his elbows and holds a plate in his hands.

A procession is passing a reclining Chacmool, a figure typical of Chichen Itza. The figure holds a plate on which would be placed the hearts of the sacrificial victims.

If one looks at the architecture of the two cities, further similarities emerge. Special attention to the design of columns appears at both Tula and Chichen Itza – there are columns in the form of human figures and in the form of serpents – and some of the buildings are filled with columns. Racks of skulls point to a preoccupation with death and sacrifice even greater than that at earlier Maya centres. These similarities suggested to the early archaeologists who worked at Chichen that the Toltec brought their art from Tula and built their second city at Chichen Itza. But Chichen was already a thriving centre before the Toltec came to power, and there is evidence that some of the 'Toltec-style' art at Chichen was actually produced before that at Tula. So did the influence work the other way?

Nigel Davies, a prominent authority on the ruins, believes that the influence did not come directly from one city to the other. In the late tenth century AD some of the Toltecs travelled from their homeland north of what is now Mexico City, to Tabasco, the original homeland of the Itza people. From here they carried on, probably at the Itza's bidding, to Chichen. Here they created their singular style of art, which Davies has called 'a marriage of Toltec militarism with Maya genius', before some of them returned to Tula to recreate some of the magnificent buildings they created at Chichen. Both cities then prospered, probably under the rule of the Toltec generals, until their decline in the later twelfth century AD.

Such a chain of events at least partially explains the combination of architectural styles and building methods that exists at Chichen Itza. For example, there is one type of masonry with large, rather roughly-cut stones, another style in which the finish is much better. However, the first style of masonry seems to have been held together with a better quality mortar than the later (the heavy stones have fallen in large groups in some places and remain firmly cemented together). So it is not a simple question of better techniques being learned as time goes on, but rather of two different approaches to building.

The Davies theory of the arrival and dominance of the Toltec also helps to explain the reference in the *Book of the Jaguar Prophet*, which says that a ruler called Quetzalcoatl came to Chichen Itza to rule the city at some time between AD 968 and 987. In particular, it explains the proliferation of serpent images in the carvings of Chichen, for Quetzalcoatl was the plumed-serpent god of the Maya ruling classes. But there is still a confusion between myth and history, since the original Maya god of that name

Sacred buildings at Chichen Itza AD 1180

The pyramidal temple known as the Castillo and the peculiar round-towered Caracol dominate the centre of Chichen Itza. The Castillo contains the remains of earlier temples, and this reconstruction shows it in its grandest and most elaborate state.

was a peaceful deity, while the Quetzalcoatl who ruled at Chichen seems to have been a warrior. Presumably the monarch took the name of the god, but changed his cult to fit his militaristic values.

Toltec life...

Life for the people of Chichen Itza would have been similar to that in Mayan cities like Copan. There would have been a close reliance on agriculture, backed up with activities such as weaving, pottery, and the production of obsidian knives and other tools. Military service would have been required of adult men – and the length of service was probably longer, given the smaller size of the cities and the reputation of the Toltec for the arts of war.

But the distribution of people was probably slightly different. Fewer seem to have lived in the cities themselves, with more of the population consigned to small villages some distance away from the ceremonial centre. Here they would have lived in small, close-knit groups of adobe dwellings, with perhaps four or five related family groups sharing a patch of land. These workers and craftsmen led lives quite separate from the upper classes, who, as with the Maya, occupied the posts of military leaders and priests. Indeed it is likely that these two roles overlapped under the Toltec, so closely linked were war and religion at every level of their lives. The fact that the king was habitually

Ball Court
Platform of Venus
Temple of the Warriors
Temple of the Eagles
Castillo
The Thousand Columns
Market Place
Caracol
Cenote of Xtoloc
N
Monjas
Iglesia

called both a warrior and a high priest, for example, may mean that he actually played these roles, although in other civilizations these were mere courtesy titles.

...and death

One of the dominant areas at Chichen Itza is the plaza housing the ball court. This large arena was 128 metres (420 feet) long and about 60 metres (197 feet) wide. It was surrounded by walls that were 8 metres (26 feet) high, but buildings beyond, such as the viewing platform reserved for the nobles, and the terraces of the surrounding temples, gave a good view of the game.

In fact it was less a game than a sacred ritual. We know something about how it was played from accounts written at the time of the Spanish conquest of Mexico. There were two teams and a rubber ball. The object was to pass the ball through stone rings placed high on either side of the court. This must have been very difficult, particularly as you were not supposed to hit the ball with your hands, or to kick it with your feet – the ball was meant to be propelled by the players' knees, shoulders and arms. Given these bizarre rules, it is not surprising that scoring by passing the ball through the rings was unusual. Generally victory was awarded to the team that had made the fewest mistakes.

Many Maya reliefs that illustrate the game show the players dressed as gods. Perhaps the aim was to appease the gods represented by your team. At Chichen Itza (though not, it seems, at every site where there was a ball court) this appeasement took the most final form. The losing team lost their lives. Beheading was the usual fate of the losing players, and a relief at Chichen Itza shows a beheaded player with seven serpents appearing from his neck – representing, presumably, not just the streams of blood that issued from his body, but the presence of the serpent-god himself.

The gods and the sacrifices

Although Quetzalcoatl was in many ways a peaceful god, human sacrifice was clearly part of some of the myths to which he was linked. One story told how the sun was the fifth in a series of suns, the previous four having been destroyed one after the other by jaguars, fire, wind, and water. Quetzalcoatl was supposed to have made this fifth sun, and restored life to earth, by sacrificing himself and giving his heart and blood. Human sacrifice was an attempt to delay the eventual destruction of the fifth sun and the removal of life from earth once more. The peculiar chacmool figures played their part in these sacrifices, for the plates that they carried are thought to have been the places where the offerings of human hearts and blood were left for the god.

Skull relief from the ball court

The centre of the cult of Quetzalcoatl was the large pyramid in middle of the Toltec city, known today as the Castillo. The most impressive structure in Chichen Itza, it stands 24 metres (78 feet) high, and each of its four sides has a stairway to the temple at the top. This is a fairly simple square structure, with openings on each side. But the Castillo and its temple are not as simple as they seem. They reflect the Maya and Toltec preoccupation with the calendar, both in the history of their building and in their architectural features. At the end of each fifty-two-year cycle the Toltec rebuilt their temples, destroying the old buildings. At the Castillo, the old temple was entombed inside the new pyramid as excavation has shown, so what we see today is a temple within a temple.

Indeed the archaeologists who have excavated the inner temple report that it was just as spectacular as – if smaller than – the larger one that encases it. There was a stone throne in the form of a jaguar with eyes of jade and teeth of shell; there were also chacmool sculptures. Other features of the outer pyramid that reflect the calendar are the 365 steps that lead from the plaza to the temple and the pyramid's nine terraces, which relate to the nine regions of the Maya underworld. Masks of the sky-god embellish the exterior, but not all the carvings are religious in subject – there are reliefs depicting Toltec warriors on the jambs of the temple doors.

War dominates the other large temple in the centre of Chichen Itza, the Temple of the Warriors itself. A stepped platform that looks like an unfinished pyramid supports the temple, and the platform was surrounded by a low building with a roof held up by a forest of columns. These columns are what give the temple its name, for they are decorated with carvings of soldiers that are clearly Toltec. They wear butterfly-shaped breast plates, have bands of feathers on their heads, wear earrings and nose ornaments, and carry javelins and spears – they are typical Toltec warriors. Inside the temple on top of the platform are more warrior figures, but the religious theme is taken up with columns bearing a plumed serpent design at the temple entrance. So the building shows once more the blend of sacred and secular typical of Toltec culture.

The sacred well and the rain god

Yet another place that is connected with human sacrifice at Chichen Itza is the sacred well or *cenote*, reached by way of a causeway 275 metres (900 feet) in length that leads due north of the Castillo. The tradition is that people were thrown into the well in times of drought, to appease the rain-god Tlaloc. It was believed that the victims survived in some way, even though they were not seen again.

Later writers, keen to emphasize the gruesome tastes of the Toltec, have retold stories of the sacrifice of beautiful virgins thrown down the well. Archaeology revealed a different story. When the well was investigated, a total of forty-one skeletons were found, of which eight were adult females, thirteen were adult males and twenty were children. But more surprising than this, most of the bones date from times after the decline of the Toltec people. It seems that in the Toltec period, offerings were made to the rain-god, but that these consisted mainly of pieces of jade and discs of gold. These superb pieces of beaten metalwork showed images of Toltec warriors subduing their Maya victims. But they do not have any obvious connection with the well or with those who might be thrown down it – except that they were valuable items that would make a meaningful offering to the god of rain.

And the cult of the rain-god was certainly a strong one – as one would expect in a tropical area. Some 4 kilometres (2.5 miles) to the east of Chichen is a cave dedicated to the rain-god, in which dozens of incense burners were placed. A number of these burners, which were made of either pottery or stone, were in the form of Tlaloc's head. These vessels were placed in the centre of the cave, around a great pillar made when a stalactite and a stalagmite joined together. No doubt the humid atmosphere of the cave, and the steady dripping of moisture from ceiling to floor, made places like this likely homes of the god of rain – but there is little evidence that sacrifices of human life were part of his damp cult.

The mysterious 'snail'

One building in Chichen Itza which, although surrounded by mystery, is definitely not linked with death or sacrifice is the only circular building from Maya or Toltec times. It is called the *caracol*, or snail, and it stands about 122 metres (400 feet) high in the southern area of the city. It owes its popular name to the spiral staircase that took one from the ground to the room at the top – an unusual structure in the architecture of this time and place. The use to which the caracol was put is uncertain, it may have been an observatory from which scribes looked at the heavens and checked the calendar calculations of early Maya scholars. Like many tall buildings in the ancient world it no doubt also did service as a watchtower, allowing the sentinels to warn the people of approaching enemies.

The final enigma

The last of the many mysteries surrounding the great Toltec city is why it was abandoned. For this seems to have been its fate, in about AD 1224. Tula, the other major Toltec city, was destroyed in a fire in the late twelfth century, but no one knows for certain whether it was rebuilt before its next residents, the Aztecs, arrived to take it over. There are legends that the last Toltec ruler, Topiltzin, was expelled from Tula by invaders, and infiltration from outsiders who had no respect for the gods of this great ceremonial centre may have sealed the fate of Chichen, too.

But at Chichen there is no evidence for the violence and fire that dealt such a blow to Tula. It may be that the collapse of Tula brought about the decline Chichen. Clearly the fates of the two cities were closely linked, and Chichen is one of the few places at some distance from Tula where significant numbers of artefacts have been discovered that indicate trade and communication between the two. Certainly the Toltec, for all their warrior image, did not have anything like an extensive empire, so the outlying city of Chichen could have perished for lack of support from the capital. Perhaps the science of studying the inscriptions of the early Central American peoples – still very much in its youth – will provide more answers in the future. But for now it seems at least that Chichen Itza was more peaceful in its decline than at the height of its power.

A ball game at Chichen Itza; high officials look on as players try to get the ball through the ring

TENOCHTITLAN

Aztec capital of the fifteenth century AD, on the site of modern Mexico City

After the fall of the Toltec, and the abandonment of their great cities, such as Tula and Chichen Itza, a number of peoples tried to take the reins of power in Mexico. There were the people of Culhuacan, and semi-nomadic groups like the Chichimecs and Otomis. Then there were the Tepanecs and the Acoolhuas, both of whom tried to establish an empire with more than merely local power; their capitals were respectively at Azcapotzalco, on the shores of Lake Texcoco, and at Coatlichan.

The group who were to gain domination amongst this confusion of warring peoples were the Mexicas. They came from Aztlan, and it is from this place that their more familiar name derives – they were to be known as the Aztecs. They first come to our notice in the thirteenth century AD, as a wandering people who started to settle in Chapultepec, near the west bank of Lake Texcoco in about AD 1250. They were a savage people who claimed a dual ancestry – on the one hand from the rough-and-ready nomadic tribes of the south, on the other from the cruel but otherwise civilized Toltec people. It was a gruesome heritage, and so barbaric were the Aztecs that their neighbours expelled them from the area of Chapultepec in AD 1319. They were condemned to a wandering life once more.

It was as a result of this period of wandering that the great Aztec city of Tenochititlan, on the site of present-day Mexico City, came into being. The legend says that the Aztec god Huitzilopochtli told the people to travel until they came to a place where they could see a cactus on which an eagle sat eating a serpent; it would also be a place where fish would swim. The Aztecs are reputed to have wandered for some one hundred years before they came to such a site, where they began to build their city of Tenochtitlan, the name of which means 'the place of the cactus'.

Based on an Aztec codex, this illustration portrays the legend of the city's foundation, with the eagle landing on a cactus in a swamp. Below are scenes from the lives and legends of the Aztec people.

The city in the lagoon

It was an inauspicious site for a city. The marshy area on which Tenochtitlan stood was as unlikely a place for a dense concentration of buildings as Venice. And yet the harsh conditions brought benefits. The marshes were an excellent source of wildfowl – indeed such birds had fed people in the area as early as 15,000 years ago. The rich, silty soil in the surrounding area was fertile enough to support agriculture, as it had done for the Olmec people around 1000 BC.

But there was little obvious incentive to build a city. There were no building materials and the Aztecs had to trade with the surrounding people to get what they needed. From the start this brought them into contact with the Tepanec, their main rivals for power in the valley of Mexico. For a time, the Aztecs were under the Tepanec thumb. Their kings were nominated by their rivals and they had little independence. But eventually they shook off the yoke to become the undisputed leading power in Mexico.

The Aztec city began to develop around two centres, but by the beginning of the sixteenth century, when it reached its height, Tenochtitlan was a huge single metropolis. Although it grew gradually over several hundred years, it was a highly organized place. It was divided into four large sectors, which in turn were split into groups of houses called *calpulli*, which was the basic unit of Aztec society. Some of the calpulli were the homes of specialist craftworkers or traders, others were made up of families of workers who were lower down the social scale. But in their diversity they were united in several ways. Each had its own temple, each had the right to elect an elder to the government, and each had its own school. As the Aztecs' success in military conquest grew, these schools became especially important. It was here that future warriors could be trained and toughened for demanding military campaigns.

Most people lived in single-storey homes built round courtyards. To begin with, these were built of wood, but later, as the Aztecs increased in prosperity and building skill, they were made of adobe or stone. Since most of the houses were on reclaimed land, which at any time might subside back into the water, the houses had to have special foundations – long poles were sunk deep into the mud to support the walls above.

As in Venice, most of the main streets were canals, and these were crossed by numerous bridges carrying

Like a central American Venice, Tenochtitlan was a water-based city. It consisted of a network of canals dividing islands, sandbanks, and piles. At its heart was the sacred complex surrounding the Great Temple, which was tall enough to dominate the entire city.

smaller streets and alleys. To protect the occupants from flood or invasion, most of the windows of the houses looked in towards the courtyards rather than out to the streets or canals. In the courtyards themselves vegetables were grown and turkeys were raised – these were very functional homes designed to give their inhabitants as much as possible of what they needed to stay alive.

In every conceivable way, water dominated the huge city. It was not just that the main highways were for canoes rather than carts. Traffic to and

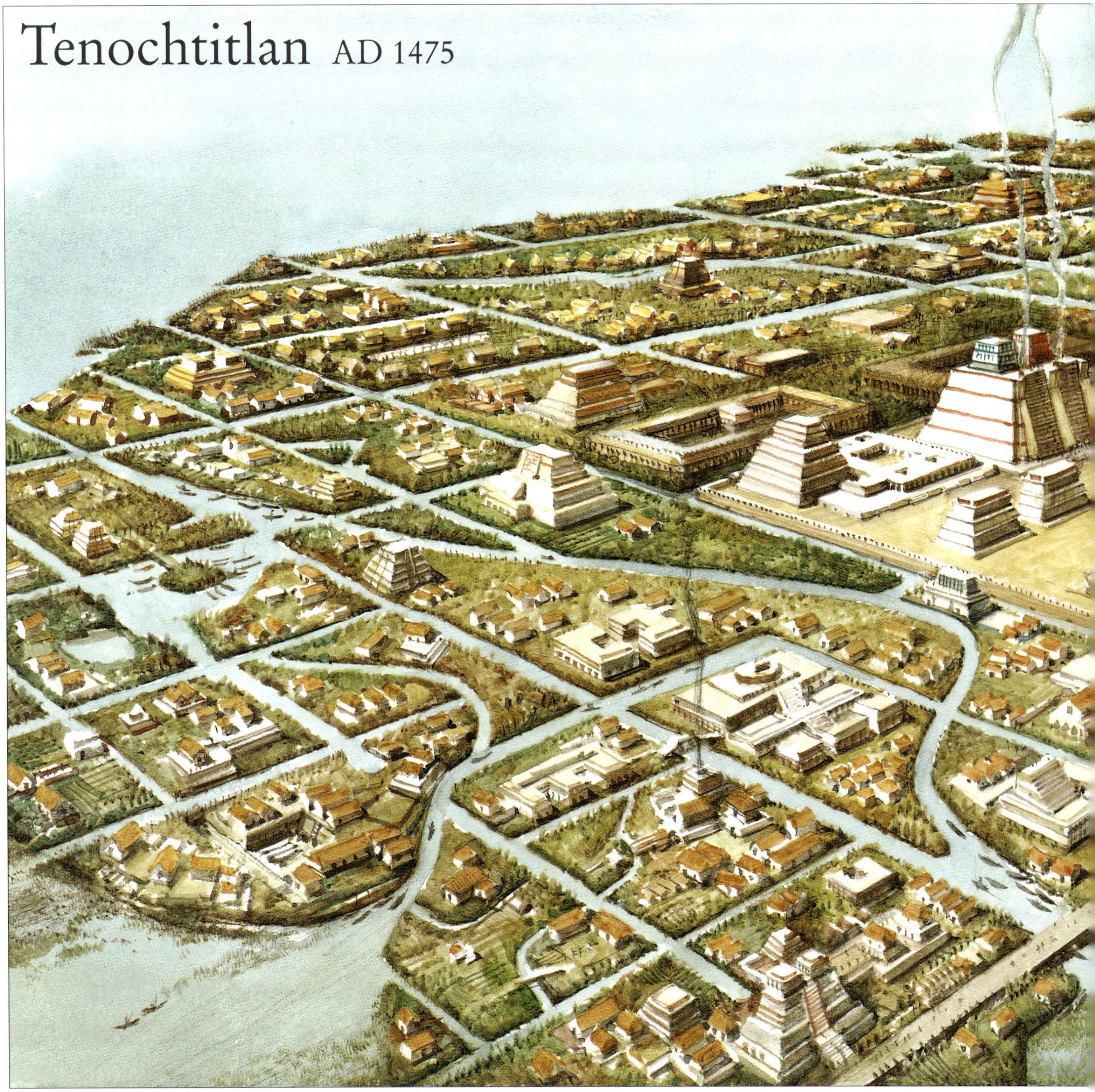

Tenochtitlan AD 1475

from the mainland used three broad causeways. The lagoon-setting of Tenochtitlan meant that water for drinking had to be piped in. This was done using two aqueducts, one of which had a double pipeline, so that one pipe could be used while the other was being cleaned or repaired. If this implies a concern for cleanliness, such a view is confirmed by the reports of the Spanish conquerors who arrived in 1519. The roads were cleaned regularly, and big barges were used to take away the rubbish.

On the outskirts of the city, water control was also important. Here a dyke cut off the freshwater marshlands in the west, which could be used for agriculture. Such an area – where farming could be carried out intensively – was essential for a city which, by the time of the Spanish conquest, must have had a population approaching 200,000. So the Aztecs became skilled in reclaiming land. One way they did this was to create platforms in the lagoon made of mud and water plants, retained by a surrounding basketwork barrier. The platforms – which amounted to small islands – were usually long and thin (about 100 x 20 metres/328 x 66 feet). Trees were planted around the edges of each of the islands, and their roots added to the effect of the basketwork barriers, helping to bind together the soil at the edges and stop the land from being washed away.

The soil in the drained and reclaimed land was rich and fertile, and crops were rotated on different strips of land so that there were always plants at different stages of development, to ensure a continuous food supply. Planting beans in rotation with the

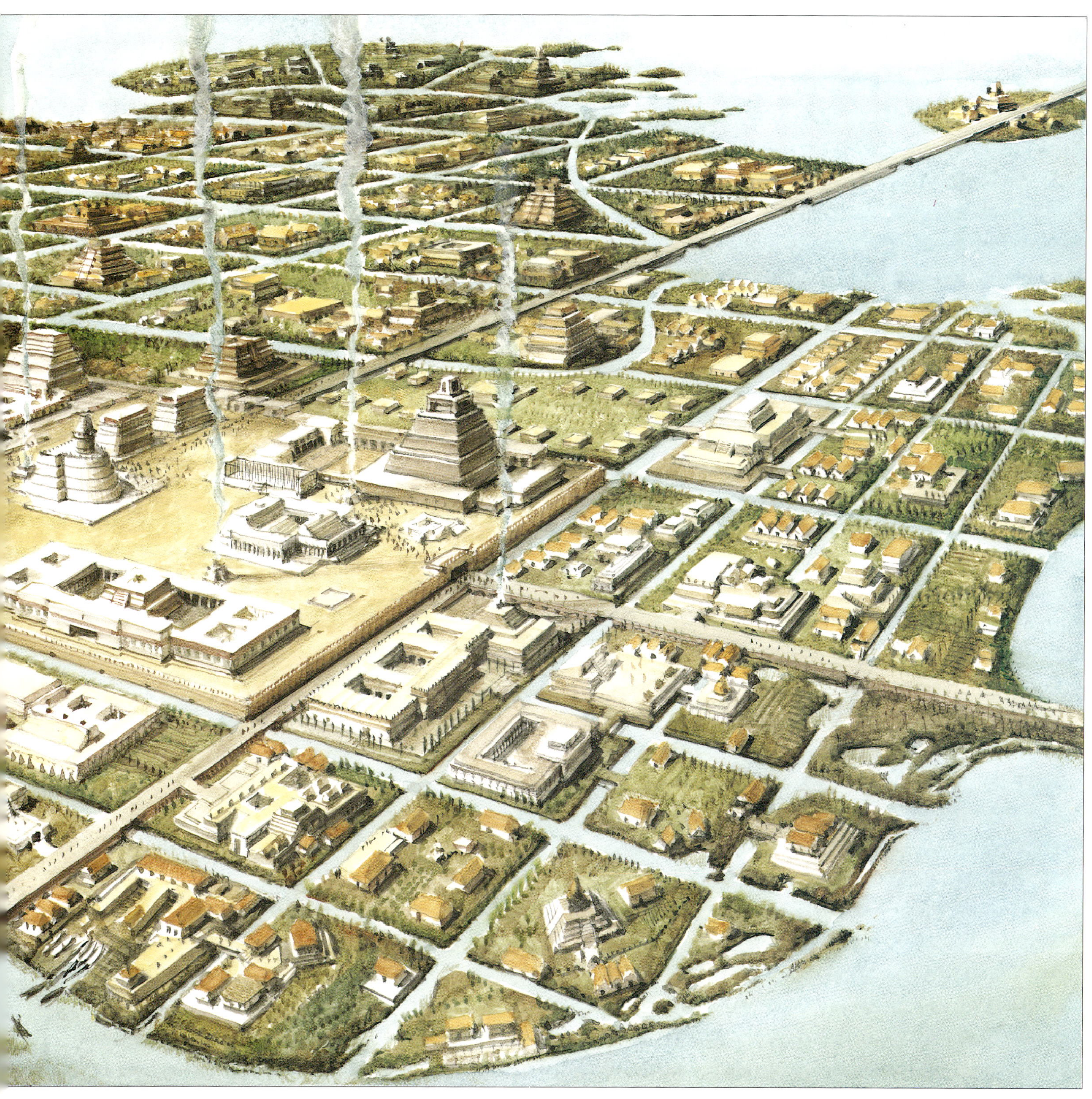

staple maize put back nitrogen into the soil, so that much of its fertility was preserved.

The sacred precinct

At the heart of the city, at the point where the roads from the three great causeways converged, was the area that contained the temples. The precinct was protected by a high wall, which was surmounted by carved serpent heads. Here there were sanctuaries to gods such as Quetzalcoatl, the plumed serpent god of the wind and the morning star; Tezcatlipoca, god of the night sky and of young warriors; and Ciuacoatl, the mother goddess. The sacred precinct also contained the city's ball court, where the ritual game played by the Maya and the Toltec was still enacted, and a skull rack, where hundreds of skulls of sacrificial victims were piled up.

But the most magnificent building in the sacred precinct was the great pyramid, topped by not one but two temples, one to Huitzilopochtli, god of war, conquest, and tribute and the Aztec sun-god, the other to Tlaloc, god of rain, life-giving water, and agriculture. The pyramid, 100 x 80 metres (328 x 262 feet) at its base and about 30 metres (10 feet) high, towered above the surrounding buildings and was a focal point at the centre of the city. Outstanding enough for its great size, the temple would also have stood out because of its bright colours. The central staircase had balustrades that were adorned with painted stone plumed serpents' heads. The temples themselves were brightly decorated. Huitzilopochtli's temple was painted with skulls picked out in white against a red background. The temple of Tlaloc was striped in white and blue. The priests who presided at these shrines, no doubt wearing gaudy costumes, would have made these buildings look more striking still.

Pot with mask of the rain god Tlaloc

It is obvious that this was a building of vital importance to the Aztecs. Its size, its central position in the city, and the fact that the gods of the temple controlled the two most important aspects of Aztec life – agriculture and warfare – show this to be the case. What is more, the people of Tenochtitlan confirmed this importance by continually rebuilding their temple. Excavations have shown that seven major reconstructions took place, together with various lesser restorations. There could hardly have been a time when building work was not in progress at the centre of the sacred precinct.

The thousands of offerings placed at the temple also testify to its importance. Over 7,000 objects have been discovered that were deliberately left at the temple as tribute to the gods. These gifts range from crocodiles to sculptures. The most common were statues of the god Xiuhtecuhtli, father of the Aztec gods. Masks, carved conch shells, corals, and carved serpents were also offered. Of the two gods of the temple there were many images of Tlaloc, but none of Huitzilopochtli – the god of warfare was probably presented with goods from the conquered territories rather than with images of himself.

Trade and tribute

A city of the size of Tenochtitlan must have had access to lavish riches in order both to sustain itself and to keep rebuilding its ceremonial centre in the way that it did. The large market in the city centre (where you could buy anything from clothes to obsidian, copper to ceramics, and where rich traders and small stallholders alike would congregate) shows that Tenochtitlan was an important trading centre.

The merchants were one of the most important classes of the Aztec state. They had great wealth, their own courts, and their own system of ranks and privileges. They also acted on behalf of the government – and not just in matters of trade. The most well-travelled and cosmopolitan class in the city, they were ideal spies and many were the Aztec merchants who returned to Tenochtitlan with information that shaped future military campaigns.

But the wealth of the Aztecs did not come only from trade. Tribute was brought to Tenochtitlan from all over Central America. Many of the most valuable items that have been unearthed in Mexico City – artefacts in jade and precious metals – come from these outlying areas, as did many of the fabrics worn by the priests and high officials. More mundane things – even supplies of food – were also obtained as tribute from neighbouring areas. Provided that this tribute was forthcoming, dependent states were left very much on their own. Native rulers were allowed to rule in their own land, and there was a minimum of Aztec occupation – just an official or two from central government making sure that the tribute was paid.

Some of the gifts seem excessive even for a city with a population as large as Tenochtitlan's. The Codex Mendoza, one of the major documents that gives us our knowledge of the Aztec state, lists 123,400 mantles of cotton, a cloth that only the upper classes were allowed to wear. Materials like this were probably traded on, to provide more usable wealth, an example of how trade and tribute were closely linked in many ancient civilizations.

Who were the beneficiaries of these lavish 'gifts'? Briefly and simply, the king and his government and the high priests. In the earlier cities of the Maya and Toltec, these would probably have been the same people – temple and palace precincts have a habit of merging into each other at Maya centres such as Teotihuacan. But at Tenochtitlan there is evidence that the priests and the rulers were two separate groups of people. The temple precinct wall separated the pyramids from the palaces, which were to the east of the temples and consisted of two-storied buildings grouped around courtyards, with lakes and gardens, domestic offices and administrative headquarters.

The king was an exalted figure who kept his distance from the people, who were not allowed to look him in the eye. Even the courtiers customarily cringed in his presence. He was surrounded, advised and assisted by an inner council of four men, two of whom were military commanders. This group was responsible for planning military campaigns and deciding on overall policy. There was also another, larger council (we do not know how many members it had – estimates range from twelve to

Carving of the goddess Coyolxauqui, the excavation of which led to the discovery of the Great Temple

twenty), which was presumably concerned more with the minutiae of government – it is not known exactly how it worked. Below these were ruling classes of judges (who were rigorously controlled and heavily punished if they showed any signs of corruption), officials and merchants, and, most important in a military empire, army commanders. Lower still were the artisans and ordinary workers.

Even the artisans had quite high status. They were important because they created the insignia by which the upper classes were recognized. The feather workers, for example, were highly skilled makers of dazzling headdresses and ceremonial shields. They had a status comparable to that of goldsmiths in other societies although amongst the Aztecs, goldsmiths – who also made a big contribution to the splendour of the rulers' personal appearance – were valued highly too.

A short-lived splendour

Tenochtitlan began its history by developing steadily, beginning as a collection of makeshift wooden buildings. By about AD 1415, it was a true city, but it was during the eighty or so years after this date that Tenochtitlan grew to become the vast 1,000 hectare metropolis that the Spanish conquerors reported. We can imagine their amazement when they arrived in 1519. The city was far bigger than anything they would have seen before. Seville, the largest Spanish city, had a population of only 15,000, a mere tenth of the most conservative estimate of the population of Tenochtitlan. The inhabitants of the Aztec city had an alien way of life and worshipped strange gods. And the very newness of so many of the buildings must have been a shock. Here was a civilization that had risen like a comet, rather than growing slowly like a medieval Spanish city.

Given that the two civilizations were so different, it is a wonder that the Aztec ruler Moctezuma and the Spanish leader Cortes came to any sort of understanding at all. But they did, and for a while the Spanish walked freely in Tenochtitlan. The crisis came when Cortes left the city and the Aztecs tried to expel his deputy, Alvardo. Cortes returned and compelled Moctezuma to put down the rebellion, but in doing this the Aztec leader lost credence with his own people. He faced a humiliating stoning and a miserable death. Meanwhile, Cortes was on the horns of a dilemma. On the one hand, many of his companions wanted to take the country by force so that they could settle down to exploit its resources and its people. On the other, the Spanish government wanted him to treat the local people fairly and Cortes himself had built up a relationship of mutual respect with the Aztec leaders.

Cortes withdrew, but only to return about six months later, swayed by the would-be exploiters in his party, and resolved to take the city by force. And it was then that the differences between the two cultures really started to show. Cortes fought in a way that was totally alien to the Aztecs. The people of ancient Mexico looked upon war as an elaborate ritual. Killing the enemy on the battlefield was not the major objective. Taking prisoners, who could then be ritually sacrificed was more important. Cortes, with his European methods of fighting, was thus able to defeat the Aztecs with a small, relatively weak force. Some of the nearby locals, such as the people of Tlaxcala, saw his potential strength and joined him. With this increased manpower, Cortes was able to cut off the water supply, quell resistance, and destroy the city.

PUEBLO BONITO

New Mexico home of the Anasazi people AD 1100–1200, an ancient town designed in the manner of an apartment block

Chaco Canyon contains the most important concentration of archaeological remains in the USA. Today it seems an unlikely spot for an American cradle of civilization, a dry strip of land about 20 kilometres (12 miles) long and a mile wide, stretching through the state of New Mexico about 160 kilometres (100 miles) northwest of Albuquerque. But 900 years ago it had a supply of water good enough to support a thriving agriculture. The canyon was home for about 10,000 people, most of whom lived in spectacular and complex stone-built towns called pueblos.

The largest of these was Pueblo Bonito, a complex that contained both dwellings and ceremonial centres, and that was both well defended and well designed for domestic life. It was a successful society, highly developed in some ways, primitive in others. For example, there was a complex social organization, with a matrilineal form of descent; the people developed a sophisticated irrigation system; they produced superb earthenware pots; and they created extraordinary buildings. On the other hand, they could not read or write and had only basic stone tools. In some ways their lives are very clear to us. In others, notably the way in which their culture declined, they remain enigmatic.

People first came to the area later to be known as New Mexico in *c.*7000 BC. The new arrivals were nomadic people, and it was only when crops like maize were introduced from Central America around AD 100 that they began to settle down, farm the land, and make the baskets for which they became famous. They lived in underground shelters and caves congregated near round ceremonial chambers, but after about AD 700 they began to build above ground and the period of the pueblos had arrived.

Rain was vital for the agriculture of the people of Pueblo Bonito, and the thunder was almost certainly regarded with supernatural awe. This inhabitant of the pueblo has paused at the top of one of the ladders to pay homage to the god on which his livelihood depends.

The first apartment blocks

It took the inhabitants of Chaco Canyon another 400 years to develop their architecture to the level of sophistication that produced Pueblo Bonito. This is a large semicircular structure with the long straight side facing towards the River Chaco in the middle of the canyon, the curved wall turned towards the cliffs at the edge. The dwellings rose quite high – as much as four floors above the ground – at the edges of the pueblo, creating high windowless walls that gave a good defence against enemies, particularly the nomadic peoples who still roamed in the area. Inside, the houses got lower nearer the centre of the complex, giving way to a central courtyard area.

Buildings of this complexity did not grow up in isolation. By the time of Pueblo Bonito, Chaco Canyon was criss-crossed with a network of roads, which linked to stone stairways on either side of the canyon. These roads therefore provided good communications within the canyon, as well as links, via the stairways, with the outside world. The fact that the thirteen major ruins in the canyon are linked by these roads suggests both an intricate social system and a well developed network for trade and the distribution of goods.

The homes that made up the bulk of the rooms in the pueblo consisted of good-sized chambers around 5 x 4 metres (16 x 13 feet). Windows looked out on to the courtyard and many of the upper levels were reached via ladders and through holes in the roofs. As in some early settlements in the Old World, the rooftops became a thoroughfare and also a place where people could sit and work. In the majority of the dwellings, thick walls with cores of stone or brick faced with sandstone made for rooms that were pleasantly cool in the desert heat. Some of the lower ones would have been rather dark and airless, however, and these were probably used for storage. At the end of the period when Pueblo Bonito was occupied, when the population declined and fewer of the rooms were needed for everyday use, a number of these lower rooms were turned into rubbish dumps. Heaps of debris were swept away into the corners of these rooms, providing modern archaeologists with a fascinating collection of source material that has told them much about the pots and tools used by the people of the pueblo.

Not all the rooms in Pueblo Bonito were built in the same way. There is a core of older rooms that seem to have been built before the rest were constructed. These occupy an arc in the middle of the great semicircle. They are distinguished by their cruder masonry, which consists of roughly-

A great D-shaped complex hard by th side of the canyon, Pueblo Bonito was made up of a mixture of rectangles (th homes and storerooms) and circles, the ceremonial rooms or kivas. The kivas were clearly visible from above becaus they were open to the sky – both to allow smoke to escape and to enable the men seated inside to contemplate the sky and to wait for the thunder clouds to form.

shaped sandstone blocks held together with generous amounts of mud. Handprints are visible on the mud fillings, showing that the early builders used the simplest of methods to even out the surface.

It is interesting that, when the pueblo was extended, these old houses were built into the new structure rather than being rebuilt in the new style. This, together with the fact that the tools and implements found in the older houses are themselves simpler and cruder, has led some archaeologists to a particular interpretation of

Pueblo Bonito AD 1100

the pueblo's history. They suggest that the original population were conquered by newcomers who built themselves new homes next to the old houses. The two populations then lived side-by-side, the original people clinging conservatively to their old ways. It certainly appears that the dwellers in the new houses were some sort of elite. But it does not seem necessary to attribute technological advances to the influence of an invading force; the new skills may have evolved at Pueblo Bonito amongst those who were already the leaders.

Everyday life

What was it like to live in these strange, prehistoric apartments? The rooms seem large, but a whole family would have filled them. They seem to have had a minimum of furniture. Excavators found only one piece of movable furniture – a stool made of pine wood – in the entire pueblo. Studies of more recent local peoples suggest that most of the inhabitants would have sat on the floor to take their meals. They probably also slept on the floor, on mats made of rushes or willow shoots, or on blankets. Corpses were also buried on rush or willow matting. Some of the rooms had stone benches built into the walls, and storage was also built-in. Many rooms had clothes racks – poles attached to the wall from which spare clothes and blankets could be hung. Some homes also had built-in shelves or cupboards hollowed out of the walls. Clutter was kept to a minimum. For storage on a larger scale there were the rooms on the pueblo's lower levels. Here a good supply of food would be kept, to help safeguard against the periodic droughts that the

area suffered. A reserve of food would also help if the pueblo came under attack from enemies.

Another apparent drawback was the dearth of windows. One would imagine that the dwellings were rather dark and airless. But the pueblo builders found ways around this problem. Nearly every room had a ventilator which kept air circulating and, as well as making the place more comfortable, presumably also helped the fire to burn. The interior walls were whitewashed to make the rooms seem lighter. Many of the dwellings were repeatedly given fresh coats of whitewash, no doubt to reduce the blackening effects of smoke from the fire.

If the people of Pueblo Bonito did what they could to make their homes more habitable than they might seem, the bulk of their life was in any case spent outdoors. The men provided food, working in their irrigated lands with a minimum of tools (digging sticks and the occasional simple hoe) and a maximum of physical effort. The food supply would be supplemented with meat brought in from the hunt – deer, elk, antelope, and mountain sheep being the most popular if we are to believe the testimony of the bones left on the pueblo rubbish heaps. Meanwhile, the women would work at spinning, weaving, and other crafts. Much of this work was probably done on the flat roofs of the dwellings.

The religious centre

There was one other type of room in Pueblo Bonito. A number of subterranean circular chambers, known as *kivas*, formed the centres of the community's religious life, as they had done for the earlier cliff-dwellers of the area. Each kiva had a stone bench built into the inner wall and a central hearth for the ceremonial fire. As well as a few large kivas, which were clearly the pueblo's main 'temples', there were also smaller circular chambers which probably served the members of particular families.

The people of the pueblo took a great deal of care over the construction of these kivas. Each had an effective ventilation system made up of an air intake feeding an underfloor duct which gave out to an air vent near the fireplace. This presumably helped the ceremonial fire to burn at the time when the kivas were roofed. For there is evidence that for at least part of

Cutting corn with a flint knife

their history the kivas had intricate roofs made of numerous overlapping pine logs, with just a central hole to allow smoke to escape.

The size and number of kivas at Pueblo Bonito suggests that religion was important to the inhabitants. What form did pueblo religion take? Although the people of Pueblo Bonito could not write, they have left us evidence in the shape of religious objects and the kivas themselves, which can help us to make informed guesses about their religion. There are also the religious customs of more recent pueblo-dwelling peoples which undoubtedly reflect those of their ancestors. The kivas themselves were most probably used for religious rituals. They were also used by gatherings of local men who went there to contemplate and, as Neil Judd, the archaeologist who excavated the site put it, to 'loaf around'.

Fragments of peeled willow found on the site suggest that the people of Pueblo Bonito made prayer sticks, an activity of modern pueblo people. These would be carved and adorned with feathers and could be offered to the gods in a variety of ways – by being buried in the ground, thrown into a river, or built into the wall or under the floor of a new dwelling. The bones of various species of birds have been unearthed in the rubbish heaps of the pueblo (the range extends from various species of falcon, through parrots and macaws, to turkey bones) and actual feathers of the macaw have also been found.

Archaeologists have uncovered other items that were probably used in religious rituals. Long sticks with curved ends and rolls of frayed cedar bark used as torches have been found in great numbers. Pipes also seem to have played an important part in pueblo ceremonies (if more recent practise is anything to go by, they would have been ritually smoked at the beginning and end of any ceremony). The pipes discovered on the site include many earthenware ones with striking geometrical designs like those on many more utilitarian pueblo pots.

Pipes, torches, and ceremonial fires suggest a religion bound up with fire and burning. The weather was also central to pueblo religion, and one can imagine the two elements coming together in thunder, which must have evoked a supernatural feeling for the pueblo's inhabitants. The coming of rain was vital to their agriculture and therefore to their very survival, and many offerings were probably made to the violent, inexplicable, but life-giving force of the thunder.

Because of the lack of written records, it is easy to simplify pueblo religion into a primitive weather cult. It was undoubtedly more sophisticated than this, although we will probably never know exactly what it entailed. The hoards of items hidden away as offerings are varied in the extreme. In one place, excavators would find a traditional collection of tools, pots, and beads – the sort of collection of treasured items offered in many cultures in which the original function of the objects is of little relevance to the offering. But in another place would be an offering of animal bones – of the black bear, dog, and puma – that are likely to have some symbolic significance. We know that bears, coming from the west, were associated with death by recent pueblo peoples. Perhaps there was the same significance at Pueblo Bonito, though there is no way of knowing for sure. Pueblo religion in the twelfth century AD remains something of an enigma.

The pueblo crafts

Less enigmatic are practical objects found at Pueblo Bonito, many of which give vivid insights into the everyday life of the people. Pottery was their most highly developed craft, and the geometric designs of their wares are still admired. Pueblo pottery developed gradually with the rest of the culture, so the most beautiful pots were produced when Pueblo Bonito was at the height of its success during the twelfth century AD. These pots carry striking black-on-white designs achieved by first applying a whitish glaze of liquid kaolin to the pots, after which they would be painted with a black paint. The paint could be made from iron oxide, or from a dye derived from the Rocky Mountain bee plant *Cleome serrulata*. The absence of kilns on the site does not necessarily mean that these pots were made elsewhere. Modern pueblo peoples usually make temporary kilns for firing pottery, and the inhabitants of Pueblo Bonito may well have done the same. Some members of society had large collections of these objects. One grave offering alone contained sixty-two food bowls, as well as various jugs and pitchers. Elsewhere on the site more of these vessels have been found, together with different-sized jars (including bulbous containers for water and portable 'canteens' with loops to take a carrying cord), ladles, and other earthenware utensils.

The pueblo people also made baskets. They inherited a tradition of basket-making from their ancestors who first settled in Chaco Canyon and, although in many ways their culture was different from these early 'settlers', baskets continued to be made and decorated. Weaving and sewing – giving such useful products as bags and blankets as well as clothing – was an allied craft that was carried out by the pueblo women. Organic remains of cloth from the town's heyday are very rare, but a few fragments of sandals have survived to show that footwear was also made of woven cloth.

Pot with typical geometrical design

Personal adornment

With their textiles and feather-tipped prayer sticks the people of Pueblo Bonito no doubt cut colourful figures, especially during ceremonial occasions. Their jewellery gave further opportunities for brightening up their personal appearance. Beads have been discovered in abundance at Pueblo Bonito. Two burials alone yielded about 15,000 turquoise beads – turquoise was a favourite colour. More recent people in the area have told how it symbolizes summer skies and the distant Pacific Ocean: it may have had similar connotations in the twelfth century.

Turquoise was a precious stone that had to be mined from solid rock some distance away. Materials like jet (of which finger rings were made) and copper (bells made of copper survive from Pueblo Bonito) were also scarce. So more easily available materials were also used for beads. Commonly occurring rocks such as shale were carved in this way. More surprisingly, shell seems to have been a popular and readily available material for beads. Presumably it was traded by travellers tempted on to Chaco Canyon's well developed road network by the likelihood of a large and easily accessible market.

Wherever the beads and other items of jewellery were made, they were the products of simple but painstaking craftsmanship. The objects are not intricately carved but they have some surprising features. The holes through the centres of many of the beads, for example, are so narrow that it is difficult to imagine how they were made. Members of Neil Judd's excavation team had to resort to a drill tipped with a cactus spine and a sand abrasive to produce comparable holes with objects that the workers of Pueblo Bonito could have found around them.

The brightly decorated impression would be completed, at least on important ceremonial occasions, by body paint. Like the modern Navaho, the pueblo inhabitants may have used red pigments to protect their skin from sunburn. Other colours, yellow and brown from iron oxides, green and blue from copper carbonate, would also have been available.

Why the people left the pueblo

After the twelfth century AD the population of Pueblo Bonito seems to have declined until the town was eventually abandoned. No one knows the reason for this. Attacks from marauding nomadic Indians may have contributed, but this seems unlikely since the pueblo was well defended and had been built specifically to keep off such attacks. The cause may lie closer to home. Control of the water supply was essential to the success of the pueblo. So the people stored water in rock-cut cisterns to meet their personal needs and distributed it in channels that ran across their fields to supply their crops. This type of irrigation led to better crops and, ultimately, a larger, healthier population.

But this control of the water supply could easily be upset, and ironically this became more likely to happen as the community became more successful. The larger town needed an increasing amount of wood. Many trees in the areas were undoubtedly felled during the lifetime of the pueblo – for roofing, ladder-making, and fuel. This made the canyon less able to stand the heavy run-off of water that would happen after storms. The resulting torrents would sweep away much of the topsoil and would also create a large channel in the middle of the canyon, along which the water would finally flow. The lack of topsoil and the difficulty of controlling the floodwaters rendered the land – once fertile – almost useless for agriculture. And the crops that sustained Pueblo Bonito's once-burgeoning population would fail, leading to famine, death, and decline.

MACHU PICCHU

Mountain-top town in Peru, once thought to be the lost city of the Incas

Some places have to wait many years for their fame. These are sites that are of relatively minor importance to the cultures or civilizations that produced them, but become well known when explorers and archaeologists turn their attention to them. Machu Picchu, the Inca town on a mountain ridge in the southwestern Andes about 100 kilometres (62 miles) north of the Inca capital Cuzco, is such a place.

For the Inca it was just another small town, home for about 1,000 people, and away from the main routes that passed through their great empire. Their territory stretched from the present border of Ecuador and Colombia to southern-central Chile; it also took up much of Bolivia, as well as the region of the Andes. A town of 1,000 people is a tiny element in such a large and complex empire. But today Machu Picchu is one of the most famous Inca settlements, a begetter of nineteenth-century myths that has provided us with much knowledge about the people who lived there and in similar towns. Its very minor nature, and its isolated position, have actually made it more valuable to us – because the Spanish conquerors passed it by, unwittingly contributing to its impressive state of preservation today. Above all, the town's superb setting, on terraced slopes next to sheer cliffs, has only added to its fame and helped to make it a superb advertisement for Inca culture.

A scene amongst the well-packed buildings of Machu Picchu shows the immaculate masonry and rock-cut features of the town. In the centre is the stone known as the Intihuatana, dedicated to the sun-god Inti. The stone was used as a sundial and may also have been used to create alignments with the sun's rays at the solstice.

Inca society

What sort of civilization built Machu Picchu? The geography of Peru tended to preserve a rural society. Communications in this mountainous area were not easy, and so many of the villages and towns kept mostly to themselves, subsisting by farming vegetables. As well as the foods that were also known to the great Mexican civilizations (maize, squash, chilli, pulses, and so on) ancient Peru produced the potato and coca, two crops that were unknown in Europe until the Spaniards brought them back from South America. The potato, in particular, was popular amongst the farmers of the highlands. The diet was mainly vegetarian, but animals such as llamas, alpacas and vicunas were raised for their wool, which was used to create the beautiful textiles for which Peru has long been famous.

This sort of agricultural community had existed before the Inca built up their empire in the fifth century AD. The Inca inherited the agricultural methods and also the form of social organization that went with them. Villages were made up of several families, who tended to claim descent from a common ancestor. The people lived in small houses often built of stone or brick. Their elders chose their own village chief, who was the nominal head. But land was held in common and cultivated using a system of crop rotation.

A network of villages like this, in a land where communication was not easy, needed pulling together in some way. In this, the Inca were helped a little by the fact that these small-town societies were quite rigidly structured. The architecture of towns like Machu Picchu demonstrates this. Centred on a large plaza, the town spreads outwards. In the middle are the temples, other public buildings, and the houses of the upper classes – the priests and priestesses and the leading local families. Houses belonging to less influential people lie beyond.

Such a layout reflects the power of the local lord. But the Inca did not rely totally upon these lords to run their own lands. They developed a system of travelling officials called *tucricucs*, who provided a way in which the royal family and elders at Cuzco could keep in touch with the provinces. They also held censuses and developed an unusual method of keeping records of the results. They used knotted strings called *quipus* to record numbers in a decimal system similar to the one that we use today.

The resulting statistics told them where they could find men for military service and for work on civil projects such as the building of roads (another vital element in the organization of the Inca Empire) and the construction of terraces for agriculture. The civil projects also included vast warehouses in the major cities, which could contain prodigious amounts of grain and other foodstuffs. Unlike many emperors, the Inca rulers controlled their resources not by regulating trade, but by physically gathering together the produce of the fields.

The superb setting of the town provided excellent defence and good stone for building. There was enough space for the houses to be arranged around quite a large central plaza. But the mountain environment was not ideal for the agriculture the people of Machu Picchu depended on, and so land around the town had to be terraced to give space for cultivation.

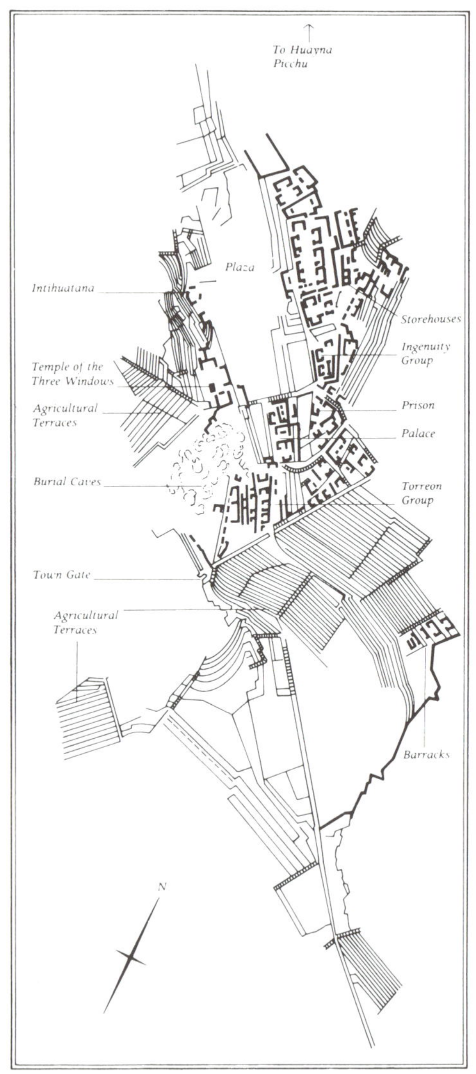

The town of Machu Picchu
AD 1500

Town and environment

In some ways Machu Picchu is hardly a typical Inca town. Its site on a narrow ridge of rock meant that traditional Inca architecture had to be adapted to meet its peculiar needs. Yet it can still tell us much about how the Inca built and lived. The simple stone houses mostly had only one storey and had simple cloth coverings over the doorways. Access to the upper floors of any taller buildings was probably by rope ladder. The houses would mostly have been thatched with ichu grass. The thatch was attached to the masonry by lashing it to a stone peg on the gable.

A number of houses may have had corbelled stone roofs, the upper part of the walls sloping to meet each other at a central ridge. Few of the houses were perfectly rectangular; they were shaped into irregular trapezoids to fit the available sites. But these irregular shapes were handled with great skill by the Inca builders – all the odd angles of Inca houses were intentional, and the Inca were quite capable of building square rooms when the occasion arose.

The stonework of the houses shows that their builders were accomplished masons. They did not use mortar so, to produce stable structures, the local white granite had to be cut very carefully with their simple stone tools. For the best quality surfaces, the stones were finished by polishing with sand and water. Then the edges were bevelled to make even more obvious the precision of the joints, and the blocks were fitted together. The result was buildings that not only looked good, but also, because of their mortarless construction, could withstand the earth tremors to which the region was prone without the walls cracking and falling down.

But more remarkable than the rather humble houses at Machu Picchu were the rock-cut features of the town. Stairs up and down the ridge, water channels, ponds, and fountains were all excavated directly from the rock, giving a unique impression of a settlement growing directly out of the land on which it was sited. Water was particularly important to the people of this mountain settlement. There were springs from which water could be fetched, but these were supplemented by an aqueduct and a series of rock-cut basins, many of which, though large, were cut out of single slabs of granite. Some of these containers had holes cut in one corner so that the water could flow through underground channels to further basins – evidence of a sophisticated water-supply system that must have reduced the need for Machu Picchu's women repeatedly to climb the city's stairways to carry water to their houses. The water containers are sometimes referred to as 'baths', but it is unlikely, in Peru's mountain climate, that they were used for outdoor bathing.

There were even rock-cut features inside some of the houses. Where a building has been erected over a large boulder, this was sometimes carved into something useful such as a quern for crushing corn, rather than laboriously removed. The group of buildings put together in this unusual way were referred to by Hiram Bingham, who rediscovered the town in 1912, as the 'ingenuity' group.

Furniture was minimal. Sometimes a stone bench was built into an inner wall. Utensils and other belongings were stored in wall niches or hung from pegs on the walls. The people slept on reed matting on the floor. But, like many early peoples, the Inca lived outside much more than we do today. Most of the domestic chores like weaving and cooking were done outside, in the central spaces between the groups of houses.

The manufacture of textiles was one activity that would have taken place here. Inca textiles were among the best ever made. The quality of their spinning was second to none: they used the wool of animals like the llama and alpaca to make yarn that was almost as fine as cotton. This they achieved with the simplest of spindles. They had a vast range of weaving techniques, which were again carried out using very basic equipment, but which produced fabrics of the highest quality. And they were skilled in the art of dyeing, using local plants and the red insect cochineal to produce different coloured yarns.

Cutting corn with stone mattocks

Most of our evidence for the quality of Inca fabrics comes from towns on the Peruvian coast, where the dry climate and deep burials have preserved examples of the ancient cloth. Matters are different in highland Machu Picchu where most of the burials had been disturbed before the city's discovery and excavation by Hiram Bingham; in any case it is unlikely that textiles would have been preserved in this colder, damper region. But so central were fine textiles to Inca culture that they must have been produced in the mountains as well as on the coast. In the town's heyday, the grey granite walls and stairs of Machu Picchu would have formed the backdrop for a blaze of colour and pattern as the people went about their daily business.

The Inca people were also great potters. Again, the most substantial evidence comes from the coastal regions, but Hiram Bingham found a quantity of pottery in the graves just outside Machu Picchu, and some of this is of impressive quality. As Bingham himself pointed out, it was natural in a mountain community for the body to crave extra heat and liquid, needs that were well supplied in the form of soup and beer. Consequently, many of the pots found at Machu Picchu are containers for these liquids – fire-blackened cooking pots and elegant jars with geometrical decorations.

An isolated city

Machu Picchu was a superb natural fortress. The town was surrounded on three sides by cliffs and mountains, and some of the cliffs were 457 metres (1,500 feet) tall. It was only accessible from the south, and here the inhabitants built a massive wall to protect the town. The city gate was at one end of the wall. Like many Inca doors, gates, and windows it is trapzoid in shape, tapering towards the top. Stone loops at the top and sides suggest that the original wooden door was secured by a wooden bar that was lashed tightly to the wall with rope when the city needed to be defended.

Lost in the mountains and stoutly defended, there was some danger that Machu Picchu would become isolated from the rest of the Inca Empire. The system of couriers that the Inca developed for message-carrying no doubt reached the town, but it is unlikely that it was a regular port of call for imperial messengers. Instead, the people probably used smoke signals from tall buildings at the summits of Machu Picchu and the neighbouring mountain, Huayna Picchu. The signal station at the topmost peak of Machu Picchu, built with great skill and nerve in the face of the danger of a 915 metres (3,000 feet) drop, would have made a superb look-out tower. In fact, it may have helped foster the town's isolation as much as its links with the empire, since one can imagine the arrival of unwelcome officials from Cuzco being detected long before they arrived, so that locals could take the evasive action they wanted, to avoid paying taxes or going to the capital for military service.

All around the city is evidence of the great building skills of the Inca. This is true even outside the city wall, to the south of the town, where great banks of agricultural terraces were built into the hillside. The slope is quite steep here, with the 5-metre (15-foot) walls only separated from each other by about 3.5 metres (10 feet) of land. Each strip had to be carefully prepared for cultivation, with gravel and then topsoil being specially brought up the hill from more fertile areas to make the terraces viable for agriculture. These valuable strips of land are guarded by a group of barracks to the southwest, and the pick of the vegetables that were grown here probably went to the household of the town chief and his staff. The rest of the produce would feed the town, giving it the measure of self-sufficiency that it needed to survive in its isolated position. Men from the barracks would occasionally be called upon to join the army of the emperor himself, to swell the forces for the imperial military campaigns.

The religious centre

In the middle of Machu Picchu, to the east of the main block of residential buildings, lay the great central plaza. A large assembly space, this adjoined a separate sacred plaza that contained open-fronted stone temples and a substantial stone building known as the Priest's House. Potsherds below the temple windows suggest that offerings were made here. Nearby was one of the more mysterious structures, the so-called *intihuanta* temple. This name, which means 'the place to which the sun is tied', suggests that the temple was connected with ceremonies celebrating the sunrise at the June solstice, at the start of the ceremonial year of the Inca. It contains an altar with an unusual stone pillar, which may have been used to align with the sun at the solstice, although the exact details of the ceremony involved are not known. Most Inca shrines and temples were oriented towards either the east or the west, towards either sunrise or sunset.

Jar for storing maize beer

The Inca are famous for their sun worship. Although the sun-god, Inti, was not their chief deity (this distinction was reserved for Viracocha, the god of creation), Inti was their most popular god, a symbol of life and fertility, giving heat and light. The Inca priestesses, known as the Chosen Women, presided at the cults of all the gods (those of the Stars, Moon, Thunder, and Venus were all important). But the Chosen Women were most closely associated with sun worship.

Hiram Bingham, his imagination fired by the beauty of Machu Picchu, its superb setting, and perhaps its very mountaintop closeness to the sun, saw Machu Picchu as a religious capital built specifically for sun worship, and the last stronghold of the Inca. Modern archaeologists think differently. Machu Picchu is simply not big enough for a religious capital, and the temple at the administrative capital Cuzco was far bigger than anything at Machu Picchu. What is more, the mysterious Vilcabamba, the city for which Bingham was searching, finally turned up far away from Machu Picchu on the edge of the tropical rain forest of Amazonia. Nevertheless, sun worship there would certainly have been in the mountain city, and a great gold disc, probably with a human face and surrounded by golden rays, would have been held aloft in the temples of the sacred plaza.

No doubt another prominent god would have been Illapa, god of the weather and thunder. In more arid regions he would have been invoked to bring water for the crops. In this mountain community, trapped under the moist clouds, the priestess would have appealed to his mercy more often. And an agricultural community would in addition have worshipped the earth goddess Pacamama.

The enigmatic city

Machu Picchu brings us close to the lives of the Inca people. And yet it still holds many mysteries. It is not the great city of Vilcabamba that Hiram Bingham believed. We do not know what name its original inhabitants called it – Machu Picchu is simply the name of one of the nearby mountains.

Neither do we know what the fate of those inhabitants was. Machu Picchu does not feature in any of the records of the Spanish conquerors. It seems to have reached its heyday shortly before the conquest, but to have been abandoned before the Spaniards actually arrived – its total lifespan cannot have been more than the 134 years between AD 1438, the beginning of the Inca Empire, and the Spanish arrival in 1572. What caused its demise? Perhaps the people were victims of some sort of epidemic. It would have been a closed, isolated community and disease would be able to spread quickly. This certainly seems a more likely outcome than a violent end – there is no evidence of mass destruction or carnage. But we will never know for certain.

N

EASTER ISLAND

Home of the world's most enigmatic stone sculptures

It is one of the loneliest places in the world. Almost 4,000 kilometres (2,485 miles) from the nearest large landmass (the coasts of Peru and Chile) and nearly 2,000 kilometres (1,243 miles) from its nearest island neighbours, this tiny island is only about 25 kilometres (16 miles) long. One of the greatest mysteries surrounding it is where its first inhabitants came from and how they found the island at all. It seems a barren place, with hardly any trees, its land joining the craters of extinct volcanoes. And yet it would have been a welcome sanctuary to the first travellers who came there, some time before AD 400, after their long sea journey.

Easter Island would then have looked slightly more welcoming than it does today. Analyses of pollen remains show that there were once palm trees on the island, and the people were soon able to grow a number of crops, such as yam, banana, and sugar cane, which came, perhaps with the early settlers themselves, from Polynesian islands to the west.

When the first Europeans found Easter Island in the eighteenth century, they came upon the sad remains of the culture that had once flourished there. But even these were surprising. The gigantic stone heads, set up in rows on stone platforms near the coast, their faces turned inwards to the island and their heads surmounted by enormous stone topknots, must have been as awe-inspiring then as they are now.

The stone heads of Easter Island were probably levered into place on their platforms. A stone ramp would protect the statue on one side and provide a surface against which to push the levers. The topknot may have been lashed in place with ropes at this stage.

The fact that the native people spoke a virtually incomprehensible language meant that the first explorers gleaned little about their culture – and this lack of knowledge was only made worse because no one could stay for long on an island where food and water were so short in supply that there was scarcely enough for the natives. In the nineteenth century the majority of the island's population was taken away to Peru to become slaves, but most of them died. Shameful in itself, this episode is also regrettable in that another opportunity to learn from the traditions of the local people was lost. It is thus left to today's archaeologists to try to piece together the story of this island culture and to attempt to discover where the people came from, how and why they built their statues, how the statues were used, and how the people lived their lives.

The growth of a culture

No one knows for sure when the first settlers arrived on Easter Island. The earliest carbon-14 date established for the island is AD 400, so it was clearly inhabited by this time. For convenience, archaeologists have divided the prehistory of the island into three stages after this date. In the Early Period (AD 400–1100) the people built ceremonial terraces of superb, accurately cut masonry. These terraces were usually oriented towards the sunrise, suggesting that the people of this period were sun worshippers. Some statues were built during this period, but they were not the large sculptures for which the island is now famous. They were smaller figures, and they were made of a variety of different types of stone.

Stepped stone ceremonial platforms called *ahu* were built in the Middle Period (AD 1100–1680). In many cases these were converted from the earlier ceremonial terraces. It was on the ahu that the famous large statues were erected. These had long heads and long ears. They were carved from a uniform material – a yellow-grey tuff – and had topknots of red tuff. Most were between 3–6 metres (10–20 feet) tall, although one 10-metre (32-foot) statue was erected and an unfinished statue of 21 metres (68 feet) has been discovered.

During the Late Period (AD 1680–1868) the island culture suffered a decline and the population dropped. It was once thought that there was a distinct break between the first two periods with an invasion or at least the arrival of influential newcomers. It now seems that there was more continuity between these two periods and that the main break was between the end of the second period and the era of decline.

One of the fiercest controversies surrounding the island is the question of where the people came from in the first place. The first settlers could have come either from the other Polynesian islands to the west, or from South America to the east. Most archaeologists today favour the route from the west. There are cultural similarities between Easter Island and others in the Polynesian group: South America is more distant – both geographically and culturally.

The major proponent of the South American theory has been the Norwegian archaeologist Thor Heyerdahl. He emphasized the physical similarity between the long-headed Easter Island statues and some South American ethnic types. He also pointed out that the sweet potato, an important Easter Island crop, must have come originally from the Andean region. The main objection, in his view, was the difficulty of the journey. So he set out to prove that the journey could be done by sailing his raft of balsa logs, *Kon Tiki*, from Callao, on the coast of Peru, to Easter Island in 1947. The journey was a triumphant success. Heyerdahl showed without doubt that the journey could be made with the technology at the South Americans' disposal. But he did not prove that the journey actually took place. Subsequent archaeologists have been cautious about accepting a South American origin for Easter Island's population.

But it may well be that a few people arrived there from what is now Peru or Chile. Such a small expedition would explain the presence of the sweet potato on the island, the one plant that must have come from the east and that is very unlikely to have arrived there by natural distribution processes. The most recent computer studies have also raised an intriguing possibility. It was once thought most likely that the sweet potato was brought to the island by an odd drifting boat that had lost its way far out at sea. But analysis of currents has shown that it is well-nigh impossible for a boat to drift to Easter Island. We are therefore left with the possibility that some form of deliberate voyage to the island did take place – even if it was not the influential invasion force that Heyerdahl's *Kon Tiki* expedition seemed to suggest.

The statues

Whoever they were, the people of Easter Island erected some of the most justly famous megalithic sculptures in the world. How were these statues made, and what was their significance?

Fortunately, the islanders abandoned their statue-building in a way that gives us much insight into their working methods. They left behind, *in situ*, many half-finished statues in a number of quarries. The quarries are at Rano Raraku, an extinct volcano towards the eastern tip of the triangular island. The stoneworkers used tuff from both inside and outside the rim of the crater, and took their statues to a state of near-completion before removing them from the quarry. They would chip away the unwanted rock with their stone tools and carve the features of the front and sides of the head. Gradually, the huge head would emerge from the living rock, and the carver would work around to the back of the figure until only a narrow spinal ridge attached the statue to the rock of the quarry. Massive wooden posts were then set in the rim of the crater and strong ropes were tied to these. The ropes were then used to lower the almost-finished statue down the side of the volcano to a gathering point on the ground below. Here groups of statues would be collected together and the final touches made to their carving before their trip to the appointed ahu. Meanwhile, another extinct volcano supplied the red tuff needed for the statues' topknots. This stone came from Puna Pau, to the west of the island. A network of tracks connected the two quarries to the various ahu around the island.

The great mystery is how these heavy stones were transported from the quarries to the ahu. There were no wheeled vehicles on the island, and the most likely form of transport was some form of sled, which would be dragged along by a large group of islanders. A sled would have the added advantage of protecting the carved surface of the statue from damage on the ground. The next problem would be getting the statue vertical at the ahu. One authority, William Mulloy, suggests that a stone ramp was built in front of the ahu, against which the statue could be pushed up using levers. To avoid the problem of raising the topknot to the great height of the erected statue's head, it was probably lashed to the main statue with rope. Both ramp and rope would be removed when all the statues on the ahu were erected. All that remained was the decoration of the figures, including the insertion of coral whites and red tuff irises into the eyes, so that the statues could stare across their domain.

What was the significance of the statues? Captain James Cook, who visited the island in the seventeenth century, was told by the people that each of the statues had a name. These names often included the title 'ariki', meaning chief or king. More recent natives have told visitors that when a king died, a statue was erected and given his name. Ancestor worship is not uncommon on other islands in this part of the Pacific, so it is reasonable to assume that it was also practised on Easter Island.

Finds from the caves on the island – carvings of a reed boat and a woman with a fish

The islanders at home

Finds recorded on Easter Island reveal a people who fed themselves by fishing and basic agriculture. They made fish-hooks from stone and bone, ate from stone bowls, cut down trees or carved wood with stone adzes, and used knives of obsidian and basalt. No pottery has been discovered, a fact that makes a South American origin for the people very unlikely indeed, since the pottery of the Andean region was highly developed.

When the first explorers arrived at Easter Island, they were surprised how few houses they could see, compared with the large number of people who appeared, apparently out of nowhere, to welcome them. The main reason for this was that by the time of their culture's decline many of the islanders lived underground. The rest occupied simple huts made of a framework of wooden posts filled in with vegetable material and topped with thatched roofs.

But the islanders did not always live in buildings like these. There are also remains of stone houses – circular, elliptical, and boat-shaped – on the island. These houses received little attention from archaeologists until Thor Heyerdahl's important expedition to the island in 1955. Work done by Heyerdahl's team rectified this, and it is now thought that the stone houses date from the Middle Period. It is hardly surprising that people who were such masters of stonework should also build their homes at least partly from stone. In fact they had thick, low stone walls, just over a metre (3 feet) high. A tall roof of thatch gave the houses additional height, and they were entered through full-length doors for which part of the roof had to be cut away.

Another type of stone building found on the island is a short tower called a *tupa*. This is a structure with rather haphazard stonework and a corbelled roof. Some of the stone seems to have been reused from earlier houses, and this has led archaeologists to the view that the tupas belong to the Late Period. Their purpose is unknown. They are not likely to be houses, since they are in odd, exposed positions on the coast. Perhaps they were shelters for fishermen or, as natives improbably claimed, watchtowers – the view they give of the sea is hardly better than the view from the adjacent ground.

We do not know who ruled over the people, who lived in these houses, or how Easter Island society was organized in the period when the statues were built. Some archaeologists point to the territorial divisions that existed at the time of Cook's eighteenth-century voyage. The island was divided up into individual sectors, each presided over by a chief, and each with a length of coastline, its own ahu, and a portion of inland territory. With such an arrangement religion would be power, and the chief with the biggest ahu would be the most influential person on the island. It may be that these essentially Late Period divisions were also prevalent in the Middle Period. But other scholars, looking at the similarities between the statues in different parts of the island, and noting the fact that the stone for all the statues came from the same quarries, prefer a picture of unity under a single chieftain. This seems more likely since it is improbable that the owner of the quarry would let others use the valued source of stone to set up an ahu in competition.

A lifestyle in the balance

The way of life on Middle-Period Easter Island was precarious. As soon as the limited supply of timber was used up – for house roofs and for levers to manipulate and transport the statues – the figures could no longer be transported, and the ceremonial life of the island would come to an end. What is more, the production of such large-scale monuments as these would have depended on a strong, centralized authority. It was labour-intensive work, and the labour-force had to be controlled. For example, it has been calculated that the largest statue to be found in position on an Easter Island ahu would have taken thirty men a year to carve with the stone tools at the islanders' disposal. Ninety men would have needed five months to drag it from the quarry to the ahu and to erect it there. Of the 600 statues found on the island, 450 had been installed by the time work at the quarry came to a halt. It was an awesome task for a population of a few thousand.

A mere problem with the timber supply – or a simple food shortage – could bring this work to a stop. But the reality may have been even more harsh than this. Tradition has it that warfare was rife on the island from the seventeenth century on. The archaeological record, in the shape of numerous spearheads from this period, confirms the tradition. It is said that there were battles between two factions, the 'Long Ears' and the 'Short Ears', a series of conflicts that may have lasted decades. This not only stopped the statue building. Work on stone house-building also ceased and most people started to live in makeshift shelters or caves. The majority of the existing gigantic statues were torn down. With the end of the stability that produced them, their purpose seems to have been ignored, and many of the ahus were turned into burial grounds for those who died in the fighting. The time of peace and stability had passed, and its symbols toppled about the feet of the few sad survivors.

Other discoveries have thrown light on the later history of Easter Island. One intriguing nineteenth-century find was a series of wooden tablets containing writing in an unknown script referred to as *Rongo rongo*. No one has been able to decipher this writing satisfactorily, and the death of the islanders on the slave route to Peru ensured that the last writers and readers perished before the script was discovered by archaeologists. But the fact that all the evidence of the script seems to be from the Late Period suggests that it has little or nothing to do with the ancestor cult of the statues. And yet it does seem likely that the tablets have some ritual significance – the usual theory is that they formed a memory aid for chanting.

In what sort of religion would the tablets have been used? One candidate is the bird cult that seems to have been practised at Orongo, on the southwestern tip of the island. Orongo was a village of nearly fifty stone houses built at the beginning of the sixteenth century. A short distance from the coast at Orongo was a small island called Motu Nui. The rocks near the coast here have many carvings of bird-headed men, some carrying eggs. It was at Orongo, according to island tradition, that the chief members of prominent families would gather each year. Each would send a servant to swim to the island of Motu Nui, where they would wait for migratory Sooty Terns to arrive to lay their eggs. The master of the first servant to find an egg would be honoured for the rest of the year.

Like many of the other places described in this book, Easter Island poses many questions which are difficult to answer with any certainty. Its isolation, away from the paths of all but the most adventurous tourists, serves to heighten its mystery for modern westerners. And yet it is with the simplest of questions – how a particular people responded to their environment and their specific spiritual needs – that we have to confront Easter Island if we are to come anywhere near understanding its monuments. These are the basic questions that that we should ask of any place we wish to understand, whether it is near or far, mysterious or mundane.

GAZETTEER

Tarxien
Archaeology: In spite of the accidental discovery of the Hypogeum at Hal Saflieni by building workers in 1902, systematic excavation did not start until 1907 with the work of Themistocles Zammit. He surveyed and recorded the Hypogeum, and carried out important and meticulous excavations at Tarxien. Further advances in the study of Maltese prehistory had to wait until after World War Two, when a full survey and report on the numerous monuments was commissioned by the Royal University of Malta. Most of the finds from the Maltese sites are displayed in the National Museum at Valletta.
Access: Fortunately for the traveller, Malta is a small island about 25 kilometres (16 miles) in length, and the temples are easily accessible. Many of the ruins are now in the suburbs of Valletta, and can easily be reached from the centre of the city. There are also remains on Gozo, accessible from Malta by boat.

Skara Brae
Archaeology: Skara Brae was revealed to the world after a great storm in 1850 blew away some of the sand dunes on the shore of the Bay of Skaill. The partially uncovered ruins of the settlement were not systematically excavated until 1927, with the work of V. Gordon Childe. At this time it was only possible to date the well-preserved ruins by comparing finds with similar items in the south of England. Consequently the village was not accurately dated until the excavations of 1972 and 1973. The majority of the finds from the settlement are in the National Museum of Antiquities of Scotland, Edinburgh, although some items are displayed on the site.
Access: Skara Brae is on Orkney Mainland, the largest of the Orcadian islands. On the west coast it is an easy drive either from Kirkwall, which has an airport, or Stromness, the main ferry port.

Stonehenge
Archaeology: Our view of Stonehenge has changed with the times. James I's architect Inigo Jones thought it was built by the Romans, whilst eighteenth-century antiquary John Aubrey first voiced the theory that it was built and used by the Druids. The Victorians began the fashion for visiting the stone circles at the summer solstice, and marvelled that godless primitives could have produced such a structure. In our own age, theories of the scientific Stonehenge have gained fame, with studies of the monument's astronomy. As the science of archaeology has also grown in stature the work of authorities like R. J. C. Atkinson and Aubrey Burl has taught us more about Stonehenge than fashionable theories.
Access: On Salisbury Plain in southern England, Stonehenge is easily accessible by road from Salisbury itself. The authorities currently ensure that it is not accessible at the summer solstice.

Knossos
Archaeology: We owe much of our knowledge of Knossos to Sir Arthur Evans, who began digging there in 1900. His excavations were pioneering but controversial: his records were not as complete as those of a modern archaeologist and the reconstruction work done on the extensive palace remains is not to everyone's taste. After 1928, archaeological work was carried out by a team from the British School at Athens. More recently there have been intriguing investigations of the burials at Knossos, including the evidence of human sacrifices. Many finds from the palace and the other Minoan sites are displayed in the museum at Herakleion.
Access: Knossos is very easy to get to. It is just south of the Cretan capital Herakleion (Iraklion), which has an international airport and all major services.

Mycenae
Archaeology: It was the excavations of Heinrich Schliemann that brought Mycenae to the notice of archaeologists in modern times. The great treasure-hunter's sensational finds made headline news, but his work made the efforts of later archaeologists more difficult – Schliemann was too interested in finding gold and making comparisons with Homer to be a serious archaeologist in the scientific sense. Subsequent workers – notably Alan Wace and Georg Karo – have done much to redress this balance, contributing a great deal to our understanding of the sprawling ruins, especially the chamber tombs and shaft graves. From a different point of view, the work of the brilliant cryptographer Michael Ventris in deciphering Linear B has thrown much light on Mycenae.
Access: Close to the main western route from Corinth (Korinthos) to Nauplia (Nauplion), Mycenae is easily accessible by road. There is a bus service from Argos and also a local railway station.

Biskupin
Archaeology: Excavation began in 1933 under Jozef Kostrzewski and a team from the University of Poznan. The methods were a model of archaeological science, with painstaking record-keeping and annotation of finds. Sadly, much of this work was destroyed after the Nazi invasion during World War Two, and much damage was done to the site itself. But in 1947 the Polish archaeologists returned and resumed their methodical work. The result is that Biskupin, although not a well known site outside Poland, is extremely well documented and has a good museum and excellent accurately reconstructed buildings to show visitors what the original settlement was like.
Access: The nearest major town to Biskupin is Poznan, which is linked by both road and rail to Berlin and Warsaw. Biskupin is near the village of Rogowo, some 80 kilometres (50 miles) by road from Poznan.

Delphi
Archaeology: Reconstructing a place like Delphi is rather like doing an enormous three-dimensional jigsaw puzzle. Many of the stones of the sanctuary of Apollo are still on the site, but they are no longer in their intended positions. So the task of the archaeologists, from the very first teams of the French School of

Archaeology at Athens at the end of the last century to today's investigators, is to measure the stone blocks, plot their original positions, and reconstruct the buildings. Much of this work has been done, enabling the impressive ruins at Delphi to be imagined in their former glory. There is an excellent museum on the site, with a wealth of material including the famous statue of the charioteer.
Access: Delphi is on the main road from Thebes (Thirai) to Amtissa, about 130 kilometres (80 miles) northwest of Athens. It is easily accessible by road.

Epidauros
Archaeology: Epidauros was first excavated by Panayotis Kavvadias and a team from the Archaeological Society of Athens. Their digs lasted from 1881 until 1928, and Kavvadias' work forms the basis of all subsequent studies of the place. The German scholars Armin von Gerkan and Wolfgang Müller-Wiener are the only ones to have made an extensive study of the theatre. Accounts of the theatre also have to rely on the work of the many scholars who have examined and commented on the surviving theatrical texts, which were written not for Epidauros but for Athens. There is a museum on the site containing many sculptures and architectural fragments from the sanctuary of Asklepios. Other finds are in the National Archaeological Museum at Athens.
Access: Epidauros is just off the main eastern route from Corinth (Korinthos) to Nauplia (Nauplion). It can be reached from either of these two towns. The site is a few miles south of the modern village of Epidauros.

Rhodes
Archaeology: The Colossus of Rhodes is so long vanished that it has no archaeological history in the conventional sense – we do not even know exactly where it was. So our knowledge of this Wonder of the World relies on the accounts of ancient writers – Pliny, Strabo, and Philo of Byzantium.
Access: The city of Rhodes is at the northernmost tip of the island of the same name. It is separated from Turkey's southwestern coast by the Strait of Marmara. There is an airport (with flights to and from Athens and further afield), and boats connect the island with the Greek mainland.

Hagia Sophia
Archaeology: Justinian's great church still stands. The problem of reconstructing it is partly to restore is furnishings and wall decorations, especially the mosaics, and partly to remove from one's mind's eye the additions to the building since the fall of Constantinople, particularly the minarets and the inscriptions in the interior. Of the many architectural historians who have helped in this task, W. R. Lethaby and H. Swainson, who published a large study of the building in 1894, have been among the most influential. More recently Rowland Mainstone has published the most exhaustive account yet of Justinian's great church, its architecture, decoration, history, and liturgy.
Access: The church of Hagia Sophia is in the centre of the old city of Istanbul. The city has an international airport and good communications with the rest of Turkey.

Mistra
Archaeology: Few travellers visited Mistra after the collapse of the Byzantine Empire. Byzantine art remained unfashionable and the city decayed in isolation. The decay was arrested with the help of one man, a French scholar of the late nineteenth century, Gabriel Millet. Millet wrote books about the churches of Mistra, with special reference to their wall paintings. His enthusiasm was extremely infectious. Other scholars, as well as the Greek authorities themselves, began to take an increasing interest and gradually, during the first half of the twentieth century, buildings were restored and frescoes were meticulously and painstakingly cleaned. Later still, the well-known doyen of Byzantinists, Steven Runciman, wrote the history of Mistra.
Access: Mistra lies in the heart of the Peloponnese, a few miles west of the city of Sparta. Its proximity to this important centre makes it easy to reach by car. There are also buses that leave from Sparta.

Topkapi
Archaeology: In the modern state of Turkey, Topkapi is no longer a Sultan's palace – it has become a museum of the sultanate. This means that a visit to Topkapi is revealing – the treasures of the sultans with which it is filled are some of the most remarkable in the world. But it takes a creative leap to imagine the palace as it used to be. Sadly, scholarship has dwelt on the palace treasures – from miniatures to emeralds, porcelain to weaponry – at the expense of architectural history. Perhaps it is only in the cool courtyards and intimate rooms of the harem that one can recapture the atmosphere of the original palace.
Access: Topkapi lies near the middle of the old quarter of Istanbul, looking out towards the Bosporus. Istanbul is easily reached by air from all over the world and there are good communications with the rest of Turkey.

Catal Hüyük
Archaeology: We owe our knowledge of Catal Hüyük to the archaeologist James Mellaart, who began to dig there in 1961. Our debt to Mellaart is a double one: for finding the mound and deciding to dig there in the first place, and for his method of excavation. Instead of making a simple vertical trench through the mound, Mellaart excavated horizontally, taking a whole section of the city and gradually peeling back each layer. This has given invaluable information and has helped to preserve many shrines and their wall paintings.
Access: Catal Hüyük is about 50 kilometres (30 miles) south of Konya and is best reached by road from there. Konya is a large city with plenty of places to stay; it is accessible by road from Ankara. You leave Konya by the Karaman road (to the south of the city) and turn left after about 34 kilometres (21 miles) along the road towards Cumra.

Mohenjo-daro
Archaeology: Excavations began at Mohenjo-daro in 1922, a year after investigations at Harappa had for the first time revealed important remains of the Indus civilization. But the most influential work was done in the 1950s by Sir Mortimer Wheeler. Wheeler identified the granary, unearthed fortifications in the southeastern corner of the city, and made other discoveries that have shaped our understanding of the site. The surviving ruins are extensive. There is a small museum at Mohenjo-daro with a good collection of finds from the parts of the city that have been excavated. Further material is housed in the museums in Karachi and Lahore.
Access: You can reach Mohenjo-daro by train from either Lahore or Karachi, along the railway line built with the help of bricks plundered from the other major Indus city, Harappa. The site itself is some distance from the tiny station, so you have to take a tonga. The site can also be reached by bus from Larkhana.

Ur
Archaeology: The first and most famous scientific excavator of the ruins at Ur was the British archaeologist Sir Leonard Woolley. He it was who uncovered the fragile royal jewellery arranged on the heads of its wearers and even more perishable objects such as musical instruments. Woolley's finds were distributed equally between the British Museum, London, the Pennsylvania Museum, Philadelphia, and the Baghdad Museum. The visitor to Ur will find substantial ruins of the famous ziggurat together with acre upon acre of

ground containing remains of the foundations of houses and other buildings.
Access: The ruins of the city and ziggurat lie about 16 kilometres (10 mile) west of An-Nasiriyah, which is on the lower Euphrates river and about 2.5 kilometres (1.5 miles) from the local junction of the Iraqi Railway.

Boghazköy
Archaeology: The person who discovered Boghazköy for the west was a French artist and traveller called Charles Texier, who visited the place in 1834. But it was not until 1906 that the site was dug systematically by the German Hugo Winkler and the Turkish archaeologist Theodore Makridi. Their work revealed the importance of the site. Today there is a small museum at the modern village of Boghazköy. Many other Hittite items are in the museum at Ankara, and Istanbul's Museum of the Ancient Orient has one of the sphinxes from the sphinx gate. The ruins themselves consist of an evocative collection of walls and foundations in a stunning hillside setting.
Access: Boghazköy is best reached from the Turkish capital, Ankara, from where bus trips are arranged to the site.

Troy
Archaeology: No account of Troy can escape mention of the work of Heinrich Schliemann, who dug there during the 1870s. It is difficult to approve of Schliemann (he trenched his way through the mound that covered the ancient remains, destroying evidence in his unerring search for treasure and Homer), but it is also difficult not to admire his enthusiasm. And his work was important in revealing this important early settlement to the gaze of more sober archaeologists. His successors in the twentieth century, Wilhelm Dörpfeld and Carl Blegen have provided the framework that we needed to understand the complex remains of this multi-layered site. If as a result we are less certain about the Homeric connections, we can be more confident in our interpretation of the prehistory of the place. A small museum on the site gives further guidance.
Access: Troy is south of Canakkale in Turkey, and buses depart frequently from Canakkale to the ancient remains. Canakkale is well served by buses from Bursa, Istanbul, Izmir, and Edirne.

Khorsabad
Archaeology: Paul Emile Botta was the first person to excavate the site, under difficult conditions, in the mid-nineteenth century. In 1851 Botta's job was taken over by Victor Place, who made the first plans and reconstructions of Khorsabad, which are beautifully presented in his books on Assyria. Subsequent work was carried out during the years 1928–35 by the Oriental Institute of the University of Chicago. The American team revised Place's conclusions and also uncovered additional areas of the city, including temples and public buildings. For those unable to visit Khorsabad, there are fine displays of relevant material at the British Museum, London.
Access: Khorsabad lies to the northeast of the city of Mosul in northern Iraq, from where it can be reached by road. The other major Assyrian site, Nineveh, is nearby.

Babylon
Archaeology: The architect turned archaeologist Robert Koldewey directed the first excavations at Babylon between 1899 and 1917 on behalf of the Deutsche Orient-Gesellschaft. He made the first accurate plans of the city. More recently, the Department of Antiquities of Iraq has continued Koldewey's work, as well as carrying out carefull restorations of some of the buildings, such as the temple dedicated to the mother goddess Ninmah. Visitors can also see the magnificent Ishtar Gate, but other remains are minimal. For those who are unable to travel to Iraq, some of the best material from Babylon can be found in the museums of East Berlin, particularly the splendid Vorderasiatisches Museum.
Access: Babylon lies by the Euphrates river, near the modern town of Al-Hillah, about 88 kilometres (55 miles) south of the Iraqi capital, Baghdad.

Persepolis
Archaeology: Work at Persepolis began during the 1920s and 1930s under a team from the Oriental Institute of Chicago, and was continued in the 1940s by the Iranian Archaeological Service. More recently, the Service has done further work, and an Italian team has restored parts of the already well preserved structure of the palace. A museum on the site displays finds from Persepolis, including sculpture from Xerxes' audience hall, together with prehistoric objects from the surrounding area. Other finds are kept by the Archaeological Museum in Tehran, but for those unable to visit Iran, the best collections of relevant material are in the Louvre, Paris and the Metropolitan Museum of Art, New York.
Access: Persepolis is in the province of Fars, about 80 kilometres (50 miles) northeast of the city of Shiraz, near the main road from Shiraz to Isfahan. Travel in Iran has been difficult since the recent war with Iraq.

Petra
Archaeology: Petra was rediscovered for the west by John L Burckhardt, a young scholar and adventurer who disguised himself as a Moslem from India to gain admittance to the 'forbidden city'. Later visitors included Alois Musil, who carried out the first systematic research on Petra, and published in 1907. Sustained archaeology on the surviving rock-cut buildings and the rest of the site has been carried out more recently by the British School of Archaeology of Jerusalem, the Jordanian Department of Antiquities, and the University of Jordan. A visitors' centre gives information about the site and has displays of some of the artefacts found in the city.
Access: Bus services and tours depart from Amman, including one-day round trips to the city. Service taxis also travel the route from Amman to the nearest village to Petra, Wadi Musa.

Great Wall of China
Archaeology: Although much work has been done on the Great Wall in China, little of this has filtered through to the west. For many years after the Cultural Revolution, the First Emperor was not linked with the Great Wall at all. More recently, attention on the First Emperor has been focused on his tomb at Mount Li, with lengthy excavations and big exhibitions of the finds around the world. But the wall is being restored, and is in good condition near the main visiting points.
Access: The principal visiting point for the Great Wall is at Ba Da Ling, about 64 kilometres (40 miles) from Peking. This place is accessible by both train and road from the capital.

Yoshinogari
Archaeology: The recent excavations at this site have met an enthusiastic response in Japan and have been widely published there. But it is too early to come to any firm conclusions about the exact significance of the site.
Access: Yoshinogari is on Kyushu, near the modern city of Saga, from which it is easily accessible.

Ellora
Archaeology: The early years of archaeology in India were dominated by the Asiatic Society, founded at Calcutta in 1784. This society was originally begun for linguistic research, but, as a result of the study of inscriptions, members began to take an active interest in archaeology. In particular, the pioneer H. H. Wilson worked on inscriptions before turning attention to the temples of Ellora, which had first been described in English by Sir Charles Ware Malet in 1794. In spite of this activity,

Captain J. B. Seely, who travelled to the temples in the early nineteenth century, had to campaign in 1824 for the preservation of the monuments of Ellora, which had fallen into disrepair. It was thanks to his efforts that the temples have survived into this century in fair condition.
Access: Ellora is in the state of Maharastra in western India. There are daily flights from Bombay to Aurangabad and frequent buses between these two centres, but the rail journey is difficult. Ellora is 29 kilometres (18 miles) from Aurangabad, and there are local buses, guided coach tours, and taxis from there to the temples. There is also accommodation at Ellora for those who want to stay longer than a day.

Nara
Access: The buildings of ancient Nara are easily accessible from the modern city of the same name. Regular buses leave from Nara, which has good communications with the rest of Japan.

Angkor
Archaeology: News of the well-preserved ruins of Angkor began to spread to Europe in the middle of the nineteenth century. In 1860 Henri Mouhot saw Angkor for the first time. Mouhot was a naturalist who turned archaeologist when he stumbled on the Khmer city. He made the first accurate plans and drawings, and inspired many peoples' fascination for Angkor. The work of French archaeologists has long been important at Angkor, the most notable being George Coedès and others working under the auspices of the Ecole Française de l'Extreme Orient.
Access: In northwestern Kampuchea, Angkor is situated just to the north of the modern town of Siem Riep. Access is difficult for all but the most intrepid travellers, the only reliable way being to charter a plane to Siem Riep for the day. Roads are currently closed to foreigners and the distance from Phnom Pehn is considerable.

Peking
Archaeology: Westerners' first knowledge of the imperial city of Peking came with arrival of a group of Jesuits there in 1600. Subsequently, travellers, diplomats, and missionaries from Britain, the Netherlands, and Russia visited Peking and sent back reports to amazed compatriots at home. Today the Forbidden City still has an air of exoticism for those who have not been to China. In fact, much of the imperial city has been restored and many of its rooms and halls are used to display Chinese art treasures such as bronzes, paintings, and jade sculptures.
Access: The imperial city is in the middle of modern Peking. It is therefore easily reached by all who travel to China.

Taj Mahal
Access: The Taj Mahal is at Agra, in the state of Uttar Pradesh, about 175 kilometres (115 miles) south of Delhi. Delhi has a major airport and is linked to Agra by both road and railway.

Saqqara
Archaeology: French archaeologist Auguste Mariette was the first to excavate systematically at Saqqara. He did a great deal of work on the site, and although he did not live to complete it, he made many others interested in Saqqara. Britons C. M. Firth and J. E. Quibell excavated Zoser's step pyramid in the 1920s. Their work revealed the size and complexity of the mortuary buildings, from the pyramid itself to the surrounding precinct. They also investigated some of the other temples on this large site. As a result of the work of Firth, Quibell, and the many other archaeologists who have worked at Saqqara, a number of the mortuary buildings have been reconstructed in situ, so that visitors can get a good idea of what the place would have originally been like. Many of the tombs, with their paintings and wall reliefs were excavated by Walter Bryan Emery between 1936 and 1956. Numerous archaeologists are still working on this rich site.
Access: Adjacent to Memphis, which is 32 kilometres (20 miles) southwest of Cairo, Saqqara is easy to get to. There are regular international flights to the Egyptian capital.

Karnak
Archaeology: Unlike many Egyptian sites, which were completely buried in sand, Karnak, vast as it is, was never lost to view. Nevertheless, there was a very large clearing and excavating task to be done by the end of the last century, and this was begun by Georges Legrain in 1895. His work involved clearing away debris, restoring many of the columns to their standing positions, rebuilding the collapsed second pylon, and discovering many sculptures, stelae, and other items. French archaeologists Henri Chevrier and Pierre Lacau continued the work of Legrain, and numerous other archaeologists have continued to work on the vast and imposing ruins of this important site. Nearby Luxor has a small but well designed museum.
Access: Karnak is on the east bank of the Nile near the modern city of Luxor, itself 670 kilometres (400 miles) south of Cairo on the site of ancient Thebes. Cairo and Luxor are connected by regular flights and trains. Horse-drawn carriages can be hired from Luxor to the various nearby sites.

Abu Simbel
Archaeology: The temples of Abu Simbel were buried under the sand until they were rediscovered by the Swiss explorer Burckhardt in 1813. Many other travellers and archaeologists followed in his footsteps. The temples' fame reached new heights when the threat from inundation that would be caused by the Aswan Dam was revealed. The successful salvage operation and the rise in the water level of the new lake have meant that the temples are now in a similar relationship to the water to their original position. The temples' orientation towards the sunrise has also been maintained.
Access: Ramesses' massive temple stands by the Nile in Upper Egypt 1,230 kilometres (768 miles) south of Cairo. Excursion flights are available from the Egyptian capital or from Aswan, but these have to be booked well in advance.

Alexandria
Archaeology: Since the Pharos, the great library, and many of the other monuments of the time of Alexander and the Ptolemies have left no traces, archaeology at Alexandria has concentrated on parts of the city outside the scope of this book. The work of scholars who have tried to reconstruct the great Ptolemaic buildings has had to focus on the ancient writers who described the city. Fortunately Alexandria has always been an intensely literary place, so descriptions are easy to come by. The scholar who has put most energy into examining and assessing these sources is P. M. Fraser, whose massive book *Ptolemaic Alexandria* is one of the most exhaustive accounts written of any city. In Alexandria itself the Graeco-Roman Museum gives some idea of the city's classical glory.
Access: The city is on the Nile delta and is Egypt's principal port. It is 190 kilometres (110 miles) northwest of Cairo and there are regular train services between the two cities. There is also an air service.

Leptis Magna
Archaeology: Because Leptis was not invaded but was abandoned, and because, like Persepolis, the ruins were covered in sand, it was not difficult to excavate. Once the sand was removed, strikingly complete remains of many buildings were revealed. In some cases columns retained their full height and statues were in their original positions. This work of revelation was carried out

first by an Italian team under Pietro Romanelli; more recently the Libyan Department of Antiquities has undertaken the task. Many of the best finds are in the museum at Tripoli.
Access: Leptis Magna is near the town of Al Khums on the Libyan coast, about 100 kilometres (60 miles) east of the capital, Tripoli. A major road connects Tripoli and Al Khums.

Great Zimbabwe
Archaeology: The German geologist Carl Mauch was the first person from the north to visit Great Zimbabwe. After his visit in 1871 he proposed the 'King Solomon's mines' theory, which gained popularity among white settlers. So much was this the case that at the end of the century a company, Rhodesia Ancient Ruins Ltd., was formed with the express purpose of digging for treasure. The finds were disappointing from a financial point of view and the company ceased trading. Professional archaeologists of the early twentieth century, such as David Randall-MacIver and Gertrude Caton-Thompson, took a different view of the site. Both concluded that the ruins were built by local people and, far from being Biblical in date, were constructed in medieval times. That black people of comparatively recent times were capable of such a feat offended the white settlers of southern Africa but subsequent surveys confirmed this finding: Zimbabwe was morally 'returned' to the black people, giving them a meaningful name for their country.
Access: The ruins of Great Zimbabwe are several miles south of Masvingo. Masvingo is itself some 250 kilometres (160 miles) south of the capital Harare, to which it is connected by road.

Copan
Archaeology: The first person to publish a description of the ruins of Copan was Colonel Juan Galindo. His book of 1835 inspired other explorers to look at Maya sites, notably John Stephens and Frederick Catherwood, who bought the ruins, drew them and excavated there, and Percival Maudslay, who made the first accurate survey in the 1880s. It was Maudslay who discovered the hieroglyphic stairway, and many other important features of the site. He was also a good photographer, and his pictures have been invaluable to students of the site. Many American-sponsored digs occurred between 1935 and 1947, involving much restoration work. A museum was also established.
Access: Copan is in Honduras, near the border with Guatemala. It is accessible by chartering an aircraft from Guatemala City or Tegucigalpa. Alternatively, buses can be caught from San Pedro Sula to La Entrada, and from La Entrada to Copan.

Chichen Itza
Archaeology: The travellers and archaeologists John Stephens and Frederick Catherwood were the first to describe the ruins of Chichen Itza. Stephens and Catherwood did not excavate at Chichen. One of the first to do so was E. H. Thompson, who dredged the Cenote of Sacrifice, revealing the notorious human remains and many other items. But this was not a scientific excavation: rigorous work began in 1924 with a team working for the Carnegie Institution, Washington. This project, which went on for some seventeen years, set the style for Maya archaeology for decades to come. The site was studied exhaustively from nearly every point of view – from language to architecture, medicine to ecology. In addition, many of the buildings were faithfully restored.
Access: Chichen Itza lies on the Yucatan Peninsula, just west of Valladolid and about 110 kilometres (75 miles) east of the major town of Merida. It can be reached by bus from either Valladolid or Merida. There is also an airstrip nearby.

Tenochtitlan
Archaeology: Tenochtitlan lies beneath modern Mexico City. The site of the great Aztec temple was unknown until the discovery in 1978 of a large carved stone which was found to mark the place. Since then there have been further excavations, and the Mexican Institute of Archaeology has inaugurated the Great Temple Project. A large section of Mexico City was demolished to allow excavation of the Great Temple to take place on a full scale. As a result, the detailed history of the temple, with its many reconstructions, has at last been unravelled. Finds are displayed in the Museo de la Ciudad de Mexico.
Access: In the middle of Mexico City, the archaeological site is easy to get to.

Pueblo Bonito
Archaeology: The rediscoverer of Pueblo Bonito was Lieutenant James Simpson, an American army officer who was part of an expedition against the Navajo. His travel journal, published in 1852, contains a lengthy description of the impressive ruins of the settlement, a description that was to inspire visitors, and, towards the end of the century, professional archaeologists. The most important work on the site was undertaken by Neil M. Judd's teams from the 1930s to the 1950s. His conclusions, published by the Smithsonian Institution in Washington, are the standard guides for anyone interested in the culture of Pueblo Bonito.
Access: Pueblo Bonito is in northwestern New Mexico, about 160 kilometres (100 miles) northwest of Albuquerque. It is accessible by way of several different, but equally difficult, routes from Albuquerque.

Machu Picchu
Archaeology: Hiram Bingham and the Yale Peruvian expedition of 1911 were the first archaeologists to see Machu Picchu. Fired by the beauty of the site and intrigued by its buildings, Bingham suspected that he had found the semi-legendary city where the Incas had their origins. He returned to Machu Picchu the following year, backed by the National Geographic Magazine and Yale University, cleared the site and carried out an excavation that seemed to confirm his notion of the town's importance. Subsequent archaeologists located the lost Inca city of Vilcabamba elsewhere and showed Machu Picchu to have been of minor importance to the Inca Empire. But these conclusions have not detracted from the sheer beauty of the place – it remains important today.
Access: The town is in the southwest Andes, about 100 kilometres (62 miles) north of Cuzco. Access is by train and then bus from Cuzco, where the nearby accommodation can also be booked.

Easter Island
Archaeology: The explorer Captain James Cook was the first to inspire outsiders with an interest in Easter Island. Ever since, remote as it is, the island has been a place for explorers and adventurers. The most famous in this century is Thor Heyerdahl, who originally thought that the people of Easter Island might have come from South America, and set out on his balsawood raft Kon Tiki to prove that the journey could be made. He also carried out extensive excavations on the island. Recent researchers, however, while acknowledging the value of much of Heyerdahl's work, assert that there is no archaeological evidence for a major American settlement on Easter Island.
Access: Easter Island occupies an isolated position in the Pacific Ocean, west of the coast of Chile. There are flights to the island from Tahiti and Santiago.

BIBLIOGRAPHY

Tarxien
Evans, J. D. *Malta* (London, 1959)
Evans, J. D. *The Prehistoric Antiquities of the Maltese Islands* London, 1972)
Trump, D. H. *Malta: An Archaeological Guide* (London, 1972)
Trump, D. H. 'Megalithic Architecture in Malta', in *Antiquity and Man: Essays in Honour of Glyn Daniel* (London, 1981)

Skara Brae
Childe, V. Gordon and Clarke, D.V. *Skara Brae* (Edinburgh, 1988)
Ritchie, Anna. *Scotland* BC (Edinburgh, 1988)

Stonehenge
Atkinson, R. J. C. *Stonehenge* (rev. ed., Harmondsworth, 1979)
Burl, Aubrey. *The Stonehenge People* (London, 1987)
Chippindale, C. *Stonehenge Complete* (London, 1983)

Biskupin
Gardawski, Alexander. 'An Early Bronze Age Kraal at Biskupin', *Antiquity*, Vol XXXII, 1958, pp 121–3
Kostrewski, J. 'Biskupin: An Early Iron Age Village in Western Poland', *Antiquity*, Vol XII, 1938, pp 311–17

Knossos
Evans, Sir Arthur. *The Palace of Minos* (London, 1921–35)
Graham, J. W. *The Palaces of Crete* (Princeton, 1962)
Hood, Stuart. *The Minoans* (London, 1971)
Willetts, R. F. *Everyday Life in Ancient Crete* (London and New York, 1969)

Mycenae
Higgins, Reynold. *Minoan and Mycenaean Art* (London, 1967)
Hooker, J. T. *Mycenaean Greece* (London, 1977)
Taylor, Lord William. *The Mycenaeans* (London, 1964)

Delphi
Andronicos, Manolis. *Delphi* (Athens, 1985)
Coulton, J. L. *Greek Architects at Work* (London, 1977)

Epidauros
Tomlinson, R.A. *Epidauros* (London, 1983)

Rhodes
Clayton, Peter and Price, Martin. *The Seven Wonders of the Ancient World* (London, 1988)
Craik, Elizabeth M. *The Dorian Aegean* (London, 1980)

Hagia Sophia
Kinross, Lord. *Hagia Sophia* (London, 1973)
Lethaby, W. R. and Swainson, H. *The Church of Sancta Sophia, Constantinople* (London, 1894)
Mainstone, Rowland J. *Hagia Sophia* (London, 1988)

Mistra
Chatzidakis, Manolis. *Mystras: The Medieval City and Castle* (Athens, 1985)
Runciman, Steven. *Mistra: Byzantine Capital of the Peloponnese* (London, 1980)

Topkapi
Aksit, Ilhan. *Topkapi* (Istanbul, n.d.)
Liddell, Robert. *Byzantium and Istanbul* (London, 1956)

Catal Hüyük
Mellaart, J. *The Archaeology of Ancient Turkey* (London, 1978)
Mellaart, J. *Catal Hüyük: A Neolithic Town in Anatolia* (London, 1967)

Mohenjo-daro
Marshall, J. *Mohenjo-daro and the Indus Civilization* (London, 1931)
Raikes, R. L. 'The End of the Ancient Cities of the Indus', *American Anthropologist*, Vol 64, no 2, 1964
Wheeler, Sir Mortimer. *Civilizations of the Indus Valley and Beyond* (London, 1966)
Wheeler, Sir Mortimer. *The Indus Civilization* (rev. ed., Cambridge, 1968)

Ur
Kramer, S. N. *From the Tablets of Sumer* (Indian Hills, Colorado, 1956)
Kramer, S. N. *The Sumerians* (Chicago, 1973)
Lloyd, Seton. *The Archaeology of Mesopotamia* (London, 1978)
Woolley, Sir Leonard. *Ur 'of the Chaldees'* (rev. ed., P. R. S. Moorey, London, 1982)

Boghazköy
Bittel, Kurt. *Hattusha, Capital of the Hittites* (New York, 1970)
Gurney, O. R. *The Hittites* (rev. ed. Harmondsworth, 1980)
Hicks, J. *The Empire Builders* (Amsterdam, 1974)
Macqueen, J. G. *The Hittites and their Contemporaries in Asia Minor* (rev. ed., London, 1986)

Troy
Blegen, Carl. *Troy and the Trojans* (London, 1963)
Wood, Michael. *In Search of the Trojan War* (London, 1987)

Khorsabad
Olmstead, A. J. *History of Assyria* (New York, 1923)
Saggs, H. W. F. *Everyday Life in Babylonia and Assyria* (London, 1965)
Saggs, H. W. F. *The Might that was Assyria* (London, 1984)

Babylon
Koldewey, R. *The Excavations at Babylon* (London, 1914)
Oates, Joan. *Babylon* (rev. ed., London, 1986)

Saggs, H. W. F. *The Greatness that was Babylon* (London, 1962)

Persepolis

Arberry, A.J. (ed). *The Legacy of Persia* (rpt, Oxford, 1989)
Collins, Robert. *The Medes and Persians* (London, 1974)
Hicks, Jim. *The Persians* (London, 1979)
Matheson, Sylvia A. *Persia: An Archaeological Guide* (rev. ed., London, 1976)
Sami, Ali. *Persepolis* (Shiraz, 1955)

Petra

Browning, Iain. *Petra* (rev. ed., London, 1986)
Khoumi, Rami G. *Petra: A guide to the Capital of the Nabataeans* (London, 1986)
Kennedy, A. *Petra: Its History and Monuments* (London, 1925)
Murray, M. *Petra: The Rock City of Edom* (London, 1939)

Great Wall of China

Cotterell, A. *The First Emperor of China* (London, 1981)
Fryer, Jonathan. *The Great Wall of China* (London, 1975)
Hay, John. *Ancient China* (London, 1973)
Jin, Yu. *The Great Wall* (Beijing, 1986)
Needham, J. *Science and Civilization in China*, vols I–V (Cambridge, 1956–65)

Nara

Kidder, J. E. *Early Buddhist Japan* (London, 1972)
Noma, Seiroku. *The Arts of Japan: Ancient and Medieval* (Tokyo, New York, and San Fransisco, rpt 1982)
Paine Robert T., and Soper, Alexander. *The Art and Architecture of Japan* (Harmondsworth, rpt 1974)
Ooka, Minoru. *Temples of Nara and their Art* (New York and Tokyo, 1973)

Ellora

Le Bon, G. *The World of Ancient India* (Geneva, 1974)
Rowland, Benjamin. *The Art and Architecture of India: Buddhist, Hindu, Jain* (rpt, Harmondsworth, 1967)
Shearer, Alistair. *The Traveller's Key to Northern India* (London, 1987)
Watson, F. *A Concise History of India* (London, 1975)

Angkor

Cohen, J. *Angkor: Monuments of the God-Kings* (London, 1975)
Krasa, Miloslav. *The Temples of Angkor* (London, 1963)
MacDonald, M. *Angkor and the Khmers* (Oxford, 1987)
Mazzeo, Donatella and Antonini, Chiara Silvi. *Ancient Cambodia* (London, rpt, 1980)

Peking

Arlington L. C. and Lewisohn, W. *In Search of Old Peking* (London, 1967)
Bonavia, D. *Peking* (London, 1978)
MacFarquhar, R. *The Forbidden City* (London, 1972)
Soren, O. *The Imperial Palaces of Peking* (London, 1926)
Yutang, Lin. *Imperial Peking* (New York, 1961)

Taj Mahal

Carroll, David. *The Taj Mahal* (rpt New York, 1978)
Gascoigne, Bamber. *The Great Moghuls* (New York, 1971)

Saqqara

Edwards, I. E. S. *The Pyramids of Egypt* (Harmondsworth, rpt 1988)
Lauer, J.-P. *Saqqara: The Royal Cemetery of Memphis* (London, 1976)

Karnak

Breasted, James. *A History of Egypt* (London, 1950)
Kamil, Jill. *Luxor: A Guide to Ancient Thebes* (London, 1983)

Abu Simbel

Adams, W. Y. *Nubia: Corridor to Africa* (London, 1977)
Emery, Walter B. *Egypt in Nubia* (London, 1965)
Keating, Rex. *Nubian Rescue* (London, 1975)
Säve-Söderbergh, Torgny. *Temples and Tombs of Ancient Nubia* (Paris and London, 1987)
Trigger, Bruce. *Nubia under the Pharaohs* (London, 1976)

Alexandria

Bell, H. I. *Egypt from Alexander the Great to the Arab Conquest* (Oxford, 1948)
Fraser, P. M. *Ptolemaic Alexandria* (3 vols, Oxford, 1972)
Wallbank, F. W. *The Hellenistic World* (London, rpt, 1986)

Leptis Magna

Bandinelli et al., Ranuccio Bianchi. *The Buried City: Excavations at Laptis Magna* (London, 1966)
Perkins, J. B. Ward. 'The Art of the Severan Age in the Light of the Tripolitanian Discoveries', *Proceedings of the British Academy* XXXVII, 1951

Great Zimbabwe

Caton-Thompson, G. *The Zimbabwe Culture* (Oxford, 1931, rpt London, 1971)
Garlake, P. S. *Great Zimbabwe* (London, 1973)
Summers, R. *Zimbabwe: A Rhodesian Mystery* (Johannesburg, 1963)

Copan

Coe, Michael D. *The Maya* (London, rpt, 1987)
Gallenkamp, Charles. *Maya* (London, rpt, 1985)
Thompson, J. E. S. *Maya History and Religion* (Norman, rpt, 1972)

Chichen Itza

Davies, Nigel. *The Ancient Kingdoms of Mexico* (Harmondsworth, rpt, 1987)
Ivanoff, Pierre. *Maya* (London, 1973)
Ruppert, Karl. *Chichen Itza: Architectural Notes and Plans* (Washington DC, 1952)

Tenochtitlan

Broda, Johanna, Carrasco, David, and Matos, Eduardo. *Moctezuma, The Great Temple of Tenochtitlan* (Berkeley, Los Angeles, London, 1987)
Sabloff, J. *The Cities of Ancient Mexico* (London, 1989)

Pueblo Bonito

Judd, Neil M. *The Material Culture of Pueblo Bonito* (Washington, 1954)
Judd, Neil M. *The Architecture of Pueblo Bonito* (Washington, n.d..)
Willey, Gordon R. *An Introduction to North American Archaeology* (2 vols, Englewood Cliffs NJ, 1966)

Machu Picchu

Bingham, Hiram. *Lost City of the Incas* (London, 1951)

Easter Island

Bellwood, Peter. *Man's Conquest of the Pacific* (London, 1978)
Bellwood, Peter. *The Polynesians: Prehistory of an Island People* (London, 1978, rpt, 1987)

INDEX

References to illustrations are shown in italics.